International Conference on e-Learning 2016

Held at the Multi-Conference on Computer Science and Information Systems (MCCSIS 2016)

Madeira, Portugal
1 – 4 July 2016

Editors:

Miguel Baptista Nunes
Maggie McPherson
Piet Kommers
Pedro Isaias
Luis Rodrigues

ISBN: 978-1-5108-6525-9

Printed from e-media with permission by:

Curran Associates, Inc.
57 Morehouse Lane
Red Hook, NY 12571

Some format issues inherent in the e-media version may also appear in this print version.

Printed by Curran Associates, Inc. (2018)

For permission requests, please contact International Association for Development of the Information Society (IADIS) at the address below.

International Association for Development of the Information Society (IADIS)
Rua Sao Sebastiao Da Pedreira
No. 100, 30, 1050-209
Lisbon, Portugal

Phone: 351 21 3151373
Fax: 351 21 3151244

secretariat@iadis.org

Additional copies of this publication are available from:

Curran Associates, Inc.
57 Morehouse Lane
Red Hook, NY 12571 USA
Phone: 845-758-0400
Fax: 845-758-2633
Email: curran@proceedings.com
Web: www.proceedings.com

INTERNATIONAL CONFERENCE

E-LEARNING 2016

part of the

MULTI CONFERENCE ON COMPUTER SCIENCE AND

INFORMATION SYSTEMS 2016

PROCEEDINGS OF THE INTERNATIONAL CONFERENCE

E-LEARNING 2016

Madeira, Portugal
JULY 1 - 4, 2016

Organised by
IADIS
International Association for Development of the Information Society

Sponsored by

TURISMO DE PORTUGAL madeira islands

Official Carrier

TAP PORTUGAL
with arms wide open
A STAR ALLIANCE MEMBER

Volume Editors:
Miguel Baptista Nunes and Maggie McPherson

Computer Science and Information Systems Series Editors:
Piet Kommers and Pedro Isaías

Associate Editor: Luís Rodrigues

TABLE OF CONTENTS

FULL PAPERS

SHORT PAPERS

REFLECTION PAPERS

POSTER

FOREWORD

These proceedings contain the papers of the International Conference e-Learning 2016, which was organised by the International Association for Development of the Information Society, 1 - 3 July, 2016. This conference is part of the Multi Conference on Computer Science and Information Systems 2016, 1 - 4 July, which had a total of 606 submissions.

The e-Learning (EL) 2016 conference aims to address the main issues of concern within e-Learning. This conference covers both technical as well as the non-technical aspects of e-Learning.

The conference accepted submissions in the following seven main areas: Organisational Strategy and Management Issues; Technological Issues; e-Learning Curriculum Development Issues; Instructional Design Issues; e-Learning Delivery Issues; e-Learning Research Methods and Approaches; e-Skills and Information Literacy for Learning.

The above referred main submission areas are detailed:

Organisational Strategy and Management Issues
- Higher and Further Education
- Primary and Secondary Education
- Workplace Learning
- Vocational Training
- Home Schooling
- Distance Learning
- Blended Learning
- Change Management
- Educational Management
- Continuous Professional Development (CPD) for Educational and Training Staff
- Return on e-Learning Investments (ROI)

Technological Issues
- Learning Management Systems (LMS)
- Managed Learning Environments (MLEs)
- Virtual Learning Environments (VLEs)
- Computer-Mediated Communication (CMC) Tools
- Social Support Software
- Architecture of Educational Information Systems Infrastructure
- Security and Data Protection
- Learning Objects
- XML Schemas and the Semantic Web
- Web 2.0 Applications

e-Learning Curriculum Development Issues
- Philosophies and Epistemologies for e-Learning
- Learning Theories and Approaches for e-Learning
- e-Learning Models
- Conceptual Representations
- Pedagogical Models
- e-Learning Pedagogical Strategies
- e-Learning Tactics
- Developing e-Learning for Specific Subject Domains

Instructional Design Issues
- Designing e-Learning Settings
- Developing e-Learning Pilots and Prototypes
- Creating e-Learning Courses
  - Collaborative Learning
  - Problem-based Learning
  - Inquiry-based Learning
  - Blended Learning
  - Distance Learning
- Designing e-Learning Tasks
  - E-learning Activities
  - Online Groupwork
  - Experiential Learning
  - Simulations and Modelling
  - Gaming and Edutainment
  - Creativity and Design Activities
  - Exploratory Programming

e-Learning Delivery Issues
- e-Delivery in Different Contexts
  - Higher and Further Education
  - Primary and Secondary Schools
  - Workplace Learning
  - Vocational Training
  - Distance Learning
- Online Assessment
- Innovations in e-Assessment
- e-Moderating
- e-Tutoring
- e-Facilitating
- Leadership in e-Learning Delivery
- Networked Information and Communication Literacy Skills
- Participation and Motivation in e-Learning

e-Learning Research Methods and Approaches
- Action Research
- Design Research
- Course and Programme Evaluations
- Systematic Literature Reviews
- Historical Analysis
- Case Studies
- Meta-analysis of Case Studies
- Effectiveness and Impact Studies
- Evaluation of e-Learning Technologies
- Evaluation of Student and Tutor Satisfaction
- Learning and Cognitive Styles
- Ethical Issues in e-Learning

e-Skills and Information Literacy for Learning
- Teaching Information Literacy
- Electronic Library and Information Search Skills
- ICT Skills Education
  - in Schools and Colleges

- for Business, Industry and the Public Sector
  - in Adult, Community, Home and Prison Education
  - Informal Methods (Peer Groups, Family)
- Education for Computer-Mediated Communication Skills
  - Netiquette
  - Online Safety for Children and Vulnerable Users
  - Cybercrime Awareness and Personal Prevention
- Student Production of Online Media
  - Web Design
  - Digital Storytelling
  - Web 2.0 Tools
  - etc.
- Digital Media Studies

The e-Learning 2016 conference received 121 submissions from more than 30 countries. Each submission has been anonymously reviewed by an average of four independent reviewers, to ensure that accepted submissions were of a high standard. Consequently, only 17 full papers were approved which meant an acceptance rate of 14 %. A few more papers were accepted as short papers, reflection papers and posters. An extended version of the best papers will be selected for publishing as extended versions in the Interactive Technology and Smart Education (ITSE) journal (ISSN:1741-5659) and also in the IADIS International Journal on WWW/Internet (ISSN: 1645-7641). Other outlets may also receive extended versions of the best papers, including journals from Inderscience.

Besides the presentation of full papers, short papers, reflection papers, posters and a workshop, the conference also included one keynote presentation from an internationally distinguished researcher. We would therefore like to express our gratitude to Professor Tony Bates, Distinguished Visiting Professor, Chang School of Continuing Education, Ryerson University, Toronto, Canada, as the e-Learning 2016 keynote speaker.

A successful conference requires the effort of many individuals. We would like to thank the members of the Program Committee for their hard work in reviewing and selecting the papers that appear in this book. We are especially grateful to the authors who submitted their papers to this conference and to the presenters who provided the substance of the meeting. We wish to thank all members of our organizing committee.

Last but not the least, we hope that everybody will have a good time in Madeira, and we invite all participants for the next edition of this conference.

Miguel Baptista Nunes, School of Information Management, Sun Yat-Sen University, Guangzhou, China
Maggie McPherson, University of Leeds, United Kingdom
e-Learning 2016 Conference Program Co-Chairs

Piet Kommers, University of Twente, The Netherlands
Pedro Isaías, Universidade Aberta (Portuguese Open University), Portugal
MCCSIS 2016 General Conference Co-Chairs

Madeira, Portugal
July 2016

PROGRAM COMMITTEE

E-LEARNING CONFERENCE PROGRAM CO-CHAIRS

Miguel Baptista Nunes, School of Information Management, Sun Yat-Sen University, Guangzhou, China
Maggie McPherson, University of Leeds, United Kingdom

MCCSIS GENERAL CONFERENCE CO-CHAIRS

Piet Kommers, University of Twente, The Netherlands
Pedro Isaías, Universidade Aberta (Portuguese Open University), Portugal

E-LEARNING CONFERENCE COMMITTEE MEMBERS

Adamantios Koumpis, Universität Passau Fakultät für Informatik und Mathematik, Germany
Alex Voychenko, International Research and Training Center for ITS, Ukraine
Andreas Bollin, Klagenfurt University, Austria
Andreas Papasalouros, University of The Aegean, Greece
Annette Payne, Brunel University, UK
Antoanela Naaji, Vasile Goldis West University of Arad, Romania
Antonio Hervás-Jorge, Universidad Politécnica de Valencia, Spain
Antonio Navarro, Universidad Complutense de Madrid, Spain
Antonio Panaggio, Italian Ministry of Education, Italy
Apostolos Gkamas, University Ecclesiastical Academy of Vella of Ioan, Greece
Benedict du Boulay, University of Sussex, UK
Charalampos Karagiannidis, University of Thessaly, Greece
Christos Bouras, University of Patras, Greece
Claudia de Witt, Fernuniversität in Hagen, Germany
Claudia Steinberger, Klagenfurt University, Austria
David Guralnick, Kaleidoscope Learning, USA
Demetrios Sampson, Curtin University, Australia
Dessislava Vassileva, Sofia University "St. Kliment Ohridski", Bulgaria
Dimitra Pappa, National Center for Scientific Research – Demokritos, Greece
Dimitris Fotiadis, University of Ioannina, Greece
Dirk Ifenthaler, University of Mannheim, Germany
Egle Butkeviciene, Kaunas University of Technology, Lithuania
Eliza Stefanova, Sofia University, Bulgaria
Elvis Mazzoni, University of Bologna, Italy
Erick Araya, University Austral of Chile, Chile
Esteban Vázquez Cano , Spanish National University of Distance Education, Spain
Eugenia Kovatcheva, University of Library Studies and Information Technology, Bulgaria
Eva Jereb, University of Maribor, Slovenia
Francesca Pozzi, Instituto Tecnologie Didattiche – CNR, Italy
Fridolin Wild, The Open University, UK
Gabriela Grosseck, West University of Timisoara, Romania
Gary Wills, University of Southampton, UK
Geoffrey Lautenbach, University of Johannesburg, South Africa
George Palaigeorgiou, University of Western Macedonia, Greece
Giovanni Bonaiuti, University of Cagliari, Italy
Giuliana Dettori, ITD-CNR, Italy

KEYNOTE LECTURE

TWENTY-FIRST CENTURY SKILLS, TECHNOLOGY AND OPEN LEARNING: RE-DESIGNING TEACHING FOR THE DIGITAL AGE

Professor Tony Bates, Distinguished Visiting Professor, Chang School of Continuing Education, Ryerson University, Toronto, Canada

ABSTRACT

High-earning jobs require the development of a wide range of intellectual skills in students which go far beyond understanding content. New technological developments now allow for the redesign of teaching to support the development of such skills. This presentation provides guidelines and examples of how to do this.

WORKSHOP

MAKING SUSTAINABLE ONLINE LEARNING A REALITY INFORMED BY THE COMMUNITY OF INQUIRY FRAMEWORK

(A workshop exploring how the Community of Inquiry Framework has informed the transition of a face-to-face master's professional programme to the online environment. This workshop is specifically for those wishing to explore online learning, and are planning and/or reviewing their online offerings)

Dr. Susi Peacock[1] and Dr. Lindesay Irvine[2]
[1]*Centre for Academic Practice , Queen Margaret University, Scotland*
[2]*Department of Nursing, Queen Margaret University, Scotland*

ABSTRACT

Over the last two decades, continuing interest in online higher education has resulted in a rapid growth in its number of programmes and learners, leading some to assert that it has become the ". . . preferred or 'new normal' mode of study throughout the world" (Brown, 2015, p. 1). Online numbers worldwide are set to grow further, as institutions reach out to widening markets, whilst also responding to learner requirements for more flexible and accessible learning opportunities. There has, however, been an ambivalent response to these innovative developments with many, including employers, doubting the value and legitimacy of accredited online learning especially in view of its high attrition rates, and low levels of learner attainment and progression (Allen & Seaman, 2013; Columbaro & Monaghan, 2009). Negative learner responses to online learning such as fear, anxiety, alienation, guilt, and stress are also well-documented (Zembylas et al. 2008). The aim of our workshop is to address such issues. We introduce participants to the Community of Inquiry Framework (Garrison 2011, and 2013), broadening and deepening their notions of planning, maintaining and evaluating online learning endeavours, through experiencing an online community. We draw extensively upon our experiences of moving our programme online, discussing the challenges we have encountered and our solutions. Our target audience includes academics in any discipline, educational developers, learning technologists, and researchers.

KEYWORDS

Online learning; community of inquiry

1. INTRODUCTION TO THE WORKSHOP

In this interactive workshop, participants and facilitators build an online community. Moving between online and face-to-face activities, we explore together some of the challenges of designing and running an online programme.

We use as evidence our experiences of the development of an online professional programme that has been informed by the Community of Inquiry Framework. Participants will experience first-hand learning in an online community. Throughout this workshop, participants critique materials, templates and activities used by the team. Working individually and in groups, participants will explore how they can use these online resources to support them in moving online but without compromising the educational experience, so that learners can succeed and prosper.

By the end of the session, participants will have:

- an introduction and/or refresher of the Community of Inquiry framework
- experienced working and learning in an online community
- analysed barriers and enablers in relation to learner and facilitators' experiences of online learning
- debated and critiqued materials, and templates supporting :

- transitioning to online learning
  - tutoring online
  - group work online
- reflected on learning from the session, and addressed how will it change their practice

The participants leaving our workshop will have continuing access to these resources and our emergent online community.

2. OVERVIEW OF THE WORKSHOP

2.1 Session One – using the Community of Inquiry Framework to inform the Educational Experiences of Learners Online (120 minutes)

One of the most prominent models of online learning is the Community of Inquiry Framework which has at its heart educational experience (Garrison 2011). Participants experience a community online, working through an introduction to this Framework. This is followed by a face-to-face break out session in which participants explore their conceptualisations of learning online.

Secondly, we consider how learners, who are often ill-prepared for the transition from the more traditional, didactic face-to-face learning to student-centred online learning, can be supported. An online induction has been designing and trialled with our learners, based upon the Community of Inquiry Framework. As our participants work through our induction to online learning, we use breakout sessions to address some of the well-known issues accompanying online learning.

2.2 Session Two – The Role of the Tutor in Student-Centred, Community-Based, Collaborative, Online Learning (120 minutes)

Participants are required to explore their notions and understandings of tutoring online. We call upon our experiences (positive and negative) of the tutoring presence, debating how much tutoring presence online learners require, when, and what type of interventions. Our discussions call upon the conceptualisations of the online tutor in the Community of Inquiry Framework.

Collaborative learning is at the heart of a community of inquiry; however, many learners dislike group work, finding it a distraction at best especially when undertaking professional programmes. We raise awareness of the potential issues that learners may encounter in working in groups online and explore how such challenges may be addressed.

REFERENCES

Allen, E. and Seaman, J., 2013. *Changing course: ten years of tracking online education in the United States* [online]. Babson Survey Research Group [viewed 8 March 2016]. Available from: http://www.onlinelearningsurvey.com/reports/changingcourse.pdf

Brown, M., Hughes, H., Keppell, M., Hard, N. and Smith, L., 2015. Stories from Students in Their First Semester of Distance Learning. *The International Review of Research in Open and Distributed Learning.* vol. 16, no. 4.

Columbaro, L. and Monaghan, C., 2009. Employer perceptions of online degrees: a literature review. *Online Journal of Distance Learning Administration.* vol. 12, no. 1. [viewed 8 March 2016] Available from: http://www.westga.edu/~distance/ojdla/spring121/columbaro121.html.

Garrison, D.R., 2013. Theoretical foundations and epistemological insights of the community of inquiry. In: Z. Akyol and D.R. Garrison, eds. *Educational Communities of Inquiry: theoretical framework, research and practice.* Hershey: IGI Global., pp. 1-11.

Garrison, D.R., 2011. *E-learning in the 21st century: a framework for research and practice.* 2nd ed. New York: Routledge

Zembylas, M., Theodorou, M. and Pavlakis, A., 2008. The role of emotions in the experience of online learning: challenges and opportunities. *Educational Media International.* vol. 45, no. 2, pp. 107-117.

Full Papers

DETERMINING FACTORS OF STUDENTS' PERCEIVED USEFULNESS OF E-LEARNING IN HIGHER EDUCATION

Aleksander Aristovnik, Damijana Keržič, Nina Tomaževič and Lan Umek
University of Ljubljana, Faculty of Public Administration, Gosarjeva 5, SI-1000 Ljubljana, Slovenia

ABSTRACT

Blended learning is already a strongly established way of teaching in higher education. In support of face-to-face teaching, e-courses may vary in structure, assignments, prompt examinations, interaction between students and teachers etc. In the paper, we present an analysis of factors that influence the usefulness of e-courses as perceived by students. A survey was conducted among students of the public administration programme at the Faculty of Public Administration, University of Ljubljana. Students evaluated 13 different aspects of e-courses in which they were enrolled. These aspects were assessed on a 7-point opinion scale. Results obtained in the survey were connected with certain demographic data, such as gender, high school final grade, year of study, study programme etc. A multiple linear regression was used with perceived usefulness as the response (dependent) variable and the 12 other e-course aspects as predictors (independent) variables. Further, the same regression analysis was performed on different subgroups of students based on demographical data and analysed where the impacts differ from the results for the whole sample. The empirical results showed that the general impression regarding the e-courses, their consistency with the face-to-face teaching and the teacher's responsiveness had a significant influence on the students' perception of the usefulness. On the other hand, the structure of an e-course and the variety of different assignments did not have a significant impact on perceived usefulness. Further analysis based on demographic data revealed several interesting subgroups of students where the perception of usefulness was influenced by completely different aspects compared to the results for the whole sample. The results may help teachers with managing the content and structure of an e-course and, as assumed, improve the perceived usefulness of blended learning for different subgroups of students.

KEYWORDS

e-learning, blended learning, usefulness of e-course, questionnaire analysis, public administration education

1. INTRODUCTION

In the last two decades, the use of information and communications technology (ICT) in the education process has triggered many changes in teaching approaches and techniques. Teachers therefore have new possibilities to make the pedagogical process more interesting and interactive. They can offer different assignments and ways of communicating without limits (regarding the place and time of teaching and learning). In this way, they go along with the new generations of students that were 'born with smartphones' and are very familiar with the latest technologies. According to Jones et al. (2010) and Kubiatko (2013), today's young generation has a different way of thinking and functioning to previous generations.

E-learning involves the use of ICT to deliver teaching and learning and is becoming increasingly important in higher education (Penny, 2011). When talking about changes in higher education, the introduction of new ICT tools into the teaching and learning processes has to be successful in the eyes of all stakeholders – students, teachers and management of the higher education institution. Based on adequate measurements, statistical analyses of the consequences of implementing a learning management system (LMS) have to be performed regularly and improvements made in order to find out whether the results are acceptable or if any improvements are needed. When deciding on the introduction of an LMS and when measuring its effectiveness and usefulness, many factors have to be taken into account. Especially on the teachers' side, many doubts emerge when a new ICT is in question. Many aspects have to be considered, especially when deciding whether to completely replace face-to-face learning with e-learning in a selected LMS or to choose blended learning where the virtual classroom supplements lectures in traditional classrooms. The students' point of view is also important since they are the main users of the offered teaching technique and can cooperate in implementing and improving an e-course as a very important stakeholder in the e-learning process. Therefore, both teachers and students should be regularly asked to give their opinion on the work and their feelings in the virtual classroom.

In our study, we analysed only the students' point of view on the courses in which they were enrolled. We examined the results received from students of the two undergraduate programmes at the Faculty of Public Administration, University of Ljubljana where LMS Moodle is used for e-learning. The purpose of the paper is thus to present an analysis of the factors that influence the usefulness of an e-course as perceived by the students. The paper explains how the students evaluate the usefulness of e-courses at the faculty level and discusses the variances among the different subgroups of students.

The paper is structured as follows: after the introduction, a brief literature review on various aspects of blended learning and its usefulness through a presentation of previous work in the field is given. The third part includes a presentation of the empirical research. At the end, based on the examined data, interpretations, conclusions and suggestions are offered. They are accompanied by the paper's limitations and avenues for further research.

2. LITERATURE REVIEW

The impact of the Internet on education at all levels has captured both teachers' and students' attention in recent years (Elkaseh et al., 2016). In some countries, the use of ICT in schools at all levels of education has been strongly supported by the government through initiatives for primary schools through to higher education. They have encouraged the acquisition of laptop computers for students and teachers with favourable conditions and secured broadband connections in all public establishments (Carvalho et al., 2011).

With the ever present need to demonstrate value for money and maximise efficiency and effectiveness from training and development within an often restricted time and expenditure framework, measuring the impact of enhancing knowledge management by using technology is of constant interest and importance (Smedley, 2010). The assessment of whether the implementation of an e-course is successful or not should be given by both groups of users, teachers and students. Of course, the management of the educational institution also has to discover if the introduction of blended learning leads to better student results (higher grades, fewer admissions to exams), lower costs and the satisfaction of all stakeholders (Hall, 2006; Kohang and Durante, 2003; Upadhyaya and Mallik, 2013, Yukselturk & Bulut, 2007).

Although many universities across the world have incorporated Internet-based learning systems, the success of their implementation requires an extensive understanding of the end-user acceptance process (Al-Adwan et al., 2013). Saade et al. (2007) point out that "in general, like any information system, user acceptance and usage are important primary measures of system success". The user perspective is therefore crucial to examine in the implementation of an LMS and to evaluate its success (Hall, 2006). Živic-Butorac et al. (2001) claim that students' perception of e-learning is one of the most important steps in developing and implementing a successful e-learning environment. Hrastinski (2009) provides a review of the literature in the area of online learner participation, and claims that participation and learning are intricately interrelated and that, in order for learners to take full advantage, the participation experience needs to be satisfactory.

To understand the importance of the students' point of view, in our study we focused only on them. According to Francis and Raftery (2005), we examined the usefulness of blended learning, whereas there are two other modes of e-learning engagement (1. baseline course administration and learner support, and 2. a fully-fledged online course). Blended learning is a combination of traditional face-to-face teaching and an online course. This mixes the features of virtual and real environments to provide for the holistic production of information and enhance students' learning experience (Al-Adwan et al., 2013).

When talking about blended learning, the successful implementation of e-course, in which students and teachers cooperate in both a virtual and classical classroom, depends on many factors. Vonderwell and Zachariah (2005) claim that online learner participation is influenced by technology and interface characteristics, content area experience, student roles and instructional tasks, and information overload.

The open-source Moodle LMS can be found in many segments of education and higher education is no exception. Its popularity, except for the fact it is free, is mainly based on its flexibility, adaptability and the possibility of personalisation while, on the other side, the system contains many standard features which make the learning process easy to implement. As Liao et al. (2011) stated: "Moodle e-learning platform is easy to use and provides a good communication tool, discussion area, group space, workspace, and makes learning more interesting". When comparing some open-source LMSs, Kareal and Klema (2006) concluded that Moodle is one of the most adaptable systems and highlighted this feature as a significant element of an effective e-learning system. They also stressed that Moodle is the most user-friendly e-learning system among the systems under comparison. Carvalho et al. (2011) studied students' perceptions of Blackboard and Moodle at Portuguese universities and ascertained that all their findings "reveal a student preference towards Moodle". In their research, they also found that e-learning materials substituted the traditional courses.

The Faculty of Public Administration implemented blended learning via the Moodle LMS platform in the 2010/11 academic year. After three years of gradually introducing them, e-courses became mandatory for all undergraduate study courses (for more, see Umek et al., 2015). Until now, quite a few changes have been made and some additions introduced in virtual classrooms. Currently, each lecture is supported by e-content followed by a quiz to check understanding of the prepared content in the e-course. For the tutorial, two extensive classroom assignments are prepared during the semester and the teacher gives feedback on the correctness of the solutions.

In our study, we determined 12 factors which we assumed influence students' perceptions of the usefulness of the Moodle LMS. They are related to organisation of the e-course (goals, materials and assignments), the lecturers' activities (assessments, responses), the students' preferences regarding learning online or in the classroom, the general impression of the e-course and the degree of consistency with the lessons in the classroom. We believe that the study presented below contributes some important findings to both theory and practice in the field of blended learning.

3. EMPIRICAL RESEARCH

3.1 Methodology and Data

In our study, we analysed how different aspects of an e-course influence students' perception of the usefulness of blended learning. For this reason, we developed a questionnaire and asked students from the Faculty of Public Administration, University of Ljubljana to participate in the survey. We limited our survey to courses that were obligatory for undergraduate students. Blended learning is mandatory for these courses.

The questionnaire consisted of 13 statements (Table 1) describing the e-course and some other questions about the students (high school final grade, occupation with other activities outside of study etc.). The students expressed their opinion regarding the statements in Table 1 on a 7-point Likert scale from "totally disagree" (value 1) to "totally agree" (value 7). The statements were based on empirical findings from recent literature (Upadhyaya and Mallik, 2013, Živic-Butorac et al. (2001)). Since the primary focus of our study was to analyse factors which influence students' perceived usefulness, statement Q13 was chosen as the dependent variable.

Table 1. Statements from our survey with abbreviations Q1–Q13

Abb.	Statement about e-course
Q1	The virtual classroom of the course is organised transparently.
Q2	The goals (workload demands, grading) of this e-course were clearly stated at the start of the semester.
Q3	This e-course offers a variety of ways to assess my learning (quizzes, written work, forums, files, ...)
Q4	I receive the teacher's comment/feedback on an assignment in less than 7 days.
Q5	I prefer fewer lectures in the traditional way (face-to-face) and more learning material processed in the e-course.
Q6	More tutorials in the course could be carried out in the e-course instead of in the classroom.
Q7	My general impression of the e-course is good.
Q8	The study material and tasks of the e-course are presented in a clear and understandable way.
Q9	Finding certain activities in the e-course is simple.
Q10	The prepared learning material and tasks are consistent with the lectures in the classroom and supplement them.
Q11	The prepared material and assignments supplement the tutorial in the classroom.
Q12	The teacher gives me feedback/a response on my submissions (assignment, forum posts).
Q13	Learning materials and activities in the e-course helped me to effectively study this subject matter.

Source: Survey, 2015

The questionnaire was completed by 315 students, with each student evaluating 3 to 5 different e-courses. We received a total of 1,456 e-course evaluations. Due to missing values, we removed some records from our initial data set. The final sample for analysis is contained in 1,083 records, each representing a student evaluating one e-course. We then added certain demographical data (gender, year of study, study programme etc.) to our final data set. Our goal was to relate the students' perceived usefulness of blended learning (statement Q13) with the other variables from Table 1. We built a multiple linear regression model with variable Q13 as the response variable and the others (Q1–Q12) as predictors.

In the empirical results part which follows, we report the coefficients, unstandardized and standardized, and the corresponding p-values. We highlight and discuss variables showing a significant impact on the mean perceived usefulness of blended learning. For the level of significance, we chose $\alpha = 0.05$.

Our recent studies (Umek et al., 2015) have already shown the heterogeneity of students at the Faculty of Public Administration. Regression analysis on the whole sample could therefore hide interesting patterns in our data set. For this reason, we repeated the analysis on different subgroups of students based on their demographic characteristics. For convenience, in the subgroup analysis we report just the predictor variables with a significant impact and do not report the p-values. Due to the high number of tested hypotheses, we used a Bonferroni correction to control the familywise error rate.

3.2 Empirical Results

The multiple linear regression showed that variables Q1–Q12 have a significant impact on students' mean perceived usefulness ($F_{12,1070} = 106.065$, $p < 0.001$). The model explained 54.3% of the variance in students' perceived usefulness, while the standard error of the estimate was 1.039. Table 2 shows coefficients (unstandardized and standardized), t-statistics and the corresponding p-values for all predictor variables Q1–Q12. Predictors with a significant impact on the mean value of Q13 (usefulness) are shown in bold.

Table 2. Parameters of the linear regression model with the perceived usefulness of blended learning as the response variable

	Unstandardized Coefficients		**Standardized Coefficient**		
Variable	**B**	**Std. Error**	**Beta**	**t**	**Sig.**
intercept	−0.541	0.185		−20.922	0.004
Q1	−0.002	0.043	−0.002	−0.047	0.963
Q2	−0.024	0.039	−0.021	−0.605	0.545
Q3	0.037	0.035	0.032	10.062	0.288
Q4	−0.093	0.026	−0.095	−30.554	**0.000**
Q5	0.123	0.024	0.168	50.096	**0.000**
Q6	−0.015	0.024	−0.021	−0.623	0.534
Q7	0.252	0.042	0.222	60.033	**0.000**
Q8	0.151	0.040	0.131	30.814	**0.000**
Q9	0.010	0.018	0.012	0.548	0.584
Q10	0.252	0.042	0.215	60.018	**0.000**
Q11	0.210	0.041	0.181	50.155	**0.000**
Q12	0.180	0.030	0.164	60.035	**0.000**

The strongest impact on perceived usefulness was found for variable Q7 (good general impression of the e-course) which has the largest standardized regression coefficient of 0.222. This means that an increase in the general impression of an e-course by 1 standard deviation on average increases the perceived usefulness by 0.222 of a standard deviation.

The other predictors with a very similar (yet somewhat weaker) impact on response Q13 are Q10 and Q11 (e-course supplements face-to-face learning well), Q7 (general impression of the e-course), Q5 (preference for e-learning over face-to-face learning), Q12 (teacher's response), Q8 (understandability of the study material) and Q4 (teacher's prompt feedback). The impact of all mentioned predictors (with the exception of Q4) is positive, i.e. an increase in them on average increases students' perceived usefulness.

On the other hand, the impacts of the other predictors are not significant. These predictors are Q1 (transparent structures of the e-course), Q2 (workload demands clear in advance), Q3 (a variety of activities), Q6 (e-courses instead of a face-to-face tutorial) and Q9 (simplicity of finding relevant activities).

The empirical study of the whole sample showed that a good general impression of the e-course and supplementing traditional face-to-face learning with e-learning increase students' perceived usefulness of e-course. It means that an e-course which offers additional topics to face-to-face learning and makes a good general impression on the students is more likely to be perceived as useful by students.

As already mentioned, our previous study (Umek et al., 2015) revealed that the student population at the Faculty of Public Administration is very heterogeneous. We showed that the introduction of the Moodle LMS in recent years has had different impacts on various subgroups of students. Therefore, we expected that the perceived usefulness of blended learning could also be influenced by different factors among various subgroups of students. We applied the same linear regression model (response variable Q13, predictors Q1–Q12) to 15 subgroups of students based on their demographic characteristics. These subgroups were established based on their gender, high school final grade (four groups: from sufficient (final grade 2 out of 5) to excellent), year of study (three groups, one for each year), study programme (two groups: university, professional), region (the nine regions of Slovenia from where students come) and their occupation with other regular activities besides study per week (six groups based on the amount of student work, sports training etc.). Our preliminary study suggested analysing just two 'regions' (students from the Ljubljana region where the faculty is located, and all other regions). Due to transparency, we reported just two subgroups of students based on their other activities (no other activities, more than 6 hours of extracurricular activities per day).

Table 3 shows the results of the linear regression on the 15 analysed subgroups, where each row presents the results for a particular subgroup. The first two values are the size of the subgroup (n) and its coefficient of determination (R^2) of the related linear model, followed by the impacts of predictors Q1–Q12, indicating factors with a significant impact on the mean perceived usefulness. Instead of reporting the p-values, we divided the impacts into four categories, from non-significant with an empty cell to highly significant with ***). The table allows us to see how the analysed subgroups differ (which factors are important for usefulness in which subgroup).

Table 3. Linear models on different subgroups of students. We report their sizes (n), coefficients of determination (R^2) and indicate predictors Q1– Q12 with a significant impact on the mean of Q13

	Subgroup	n	R^2	Q1	Q2	Q3	Q4	Q5	Q6	Q7	Q8	Q9	Q10	Q11	Q12
	whole sample	1083	0.543				*	***		***	*		***	***	***
Gender	male	284	0.514							*					*
	female	799	0.560				*	**		**	*		***	**	***
High school final grade	sufficient	442	0.530				*	***		*	*		*		**
	good	318	0.568										***		*
	very good	205	0.570												
	excellent	113	0.724							*				***	
Year of study	1st	698	0.527					*		***	*		*	***	**
	2nd	161	0.556							*					
	3rd	224	0.598										**		***
Programme	university	436	0.564				*			*			*		***
	professional	647	0.549					**		***	*		***	**	
Region	outside Ljubljana	473	0.600										**	*	
	Ljubljana	610	0.525					**		***	*		**	**	***
Other activities	no activities	71	0.522					**	**						
	more than 6 hours per day	289	0.601					*		**					*

Legend:

empty cell	Bonferroni adjusted α > 0.05
*	0.01 < α <= 0.05
**	0.001 < α <= 0.01
***	α <= 0.001

Table 3 shows that the interpretation of the results is the same for the whole sample and for female students. The predictors with a significant impact on perceived usefulness are the same. On the contrary, only two aspects are important for the male university students: the general impression of the e-course and the teacher's responsiveness. The analysis showed differences among students based on their high school grades; students with the best high school grades find the usefulness of blended learning in supplementing the tutorials. In contrast, students with lower high school grades see the usefulness in the replacement of face-to-face learning.

The factors influencing perceived usefulness also change when comparing the year of study. In higher years of study, the teacher's feedback and supplementing the tutorials have an influence on perceived usefulness. On the other side, the general impression of the e-course does not play a significant role any more. Table 3 also shows that in the first year of study many aspects are significant whereas later only a few of them remain important.

Table 3 shows differences between the two study programmes, the amount of other activities outside of study and the region of Slovenia where students come from. Students who live away from the university campus (region: outside Ljubljana) find the usefulness of blended learning in supplementing traditional learning, both tutorials and lectures. For this subgroup, only two aspects have a significant impact.

Although our sample is very mixed, some characteristics of all analysed subgroups are the same. We found no significant impact on perceived usefulness for predictors Q1 (transparent structures of the e-course), Q2 (workload demands clear in advance), Q3 (a variety of activities) and Q9 (simplicity of finding relevant activities).

To clarify our study, we presented the results from Table 3 in the form of a network (Figure 1). The network consists of two sets of nodes which represent the analysed subgroups (black dots) and statements from the questionnaire (independent variables, grey dots). Two nodes are connected if a variable has a significant impact on perceived usefulness of the analysed subgroup. Note that some of the analysed subgroups and statements are not shown in the network since they do not reflect any significant findings. Our network was plotted using the Pajek software (Batagelj & Mrvar) with a Fruchterman-Reingold (Fructerman & Reingold, 1991) drawing algorithm.

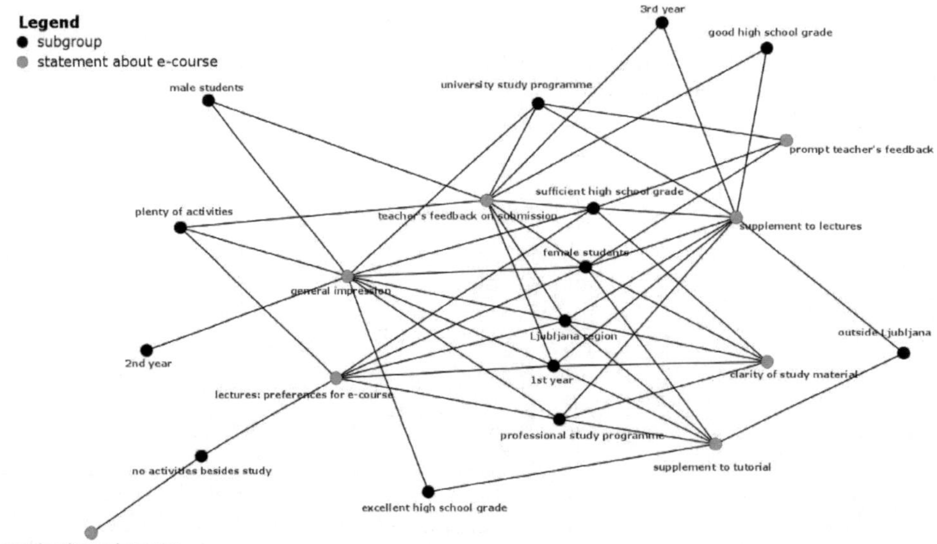

Figure 1. Network of variables and subgroups. A subgroup (black dot) and a variable (grey dot) are connected if we found a significant impact of the variable on the perceived usefulness of blended learning in a subgroup of students

We can clearly see in the network in Figure 1 which vertices have many connections. If a grey node is connected to several subgroups it means that the variable has a significant influence on perceived usefulness for different subgroups of students. We can deduce such statements from Figure 1: general impression, teacher's feedback, clarity of study materials etc. On the contrary, the nodes with less connections are specific to fewer subgroups. Some statements from the questionnaire are missing, which means we did not find any subgroup where they play an important role regarding perceived usefulness.

Similar conclusions can be drawn for the black dots. If a subgroup is connected with several variables it means there are several factors which influence the students' perceived usefulness. Examples of such subgroups are female students, students from the Ljubljana region, students with a sufficient high school grade etc. In contrast, for students in the second year of study just the general impression plays a significant role. There are some other subgroups with only two influencing factors, such as male students, students with excellent high school grades etc. Since various subgroups are connected to different variables, Figure 1 clearly shows the heterogeneity of the population we analysed.

4. CONCLUSION

The main goal of the paper was to present an analysis of the factors that influence the usefulness of an e-course as perceived by students. We examined results received from students of two undergraduate programmes at the Faculty of Public Administration, University of Ljubljana where LMS Moodle is used for e-learning. In this respect, the paper's key contribution is explaining how the students evaluate the usefulness of e-courses at the faculty level and the discussion of the variances among the different subgroups of students.

In order to confirm theoretical expectations, we empirically analysed the influence of 12 aspects of an e-course. Four of them (structures of e-course, workload demands being clear in advance, a variety of activities and simplicity of finding relevant activities) had no significant impact on perceived usefulness – on either the whole sample or on each subgroup analysed. Our empirical results also showed that the general impression regarding the e-course, their consistency with face-to-face learning and the responsiveness of teachers had a significant positive influence on the students' perceived usefulness. More detailed analysis revealed interesting subgroups of students where the relationship between perceived usefulness and the other analysed aspects differs. We discovered that the general impression plays an important role in determining a higher level of perceived usefulness in the majority of subgroups we examined. For male students, besides the teacher's responsiveness, the general impression was the only significant aspect in relation to perceived usefulness. However, we discovered that the general impression loses its impact in higher years of study when the other aspects become important (teacher's feedback, supplement to face-to-face learning).

Interestingly, the factor "transparent organization of the virtual course" was non-significant in all subgroups we analysed. On the contrary, the intuitively similar "general impression" factor played an important role in almost all subgroups. The results therefore reflect the fact that "transparent organization" and "general impression" measure two different aspects – the e-classroom can be transparent but its general impression may still be poor. Such courses probably only provide basic information in basic colours and fonts without any additional pictures, links to multimedia sources etc. In contrast, some students may prefer a less organized structure with lots of colours in the title, funny pictures etc. Accordingly, these findings may provide useful guidelines for the structure and design development of e-courses in the future e-learning system at the Faculty of Public Administration.

However, as we focussed on the perceived usefulness of blended learning from the students' perspective, our study obviously neglects the teachers' perspective. To overcome this limitation, we plan to develop a new survey. We will ask teachers about their views on blended learning (amount of work needed for an e-course, communication with students, preferences (e-courses vs. face-to-face courses) etc.). In the next step, we will aggregate the current results to the level of an e-course and link them with the results emerging form the new questionnaire. Moreover, our recent study showed a significant increase in students' performance in the period after the Moodle LMS was introduced. Therefore, in our future research we plan to use data on students' performance and link the results with our current study. This extended study would indicate which aspects of e-courses are linked to better student performances.

ACKNOWLEDGEMENT

This research was supported by a grant from the Faculty of Public Administration (University of Ljubljana) as part of internal research and development projects.

REFERENCES

Al-Adwan, A. et al., 2013. Exploring students' acceptance of e-learning using Technology Acceptance Model in Jordanian universities. *International Journal of Education and Development using Information and Communication Technology*, Vol. 9, No. 2, pp. 4–18

Carvalho, A. et al., 2011. Students' perceptions of Blackboard and Moodle in a Portuguese university. *British Journal of Educational Technology*, Vol. 42, No. 5, pp. 824–841.

Elkaseh, A. M. et al., 2016. Perceived Ease of Use and Perceived Usefulness of Social Media for e-Learning in Libyan Higher Education: A Structural Equation Modeling Analysis. *International Journal of Information and Education Technology*, Vol. 6, No. 3, pp. 192–199.

Francis, R. and Raftery, J., 2005. Blended learning landscapes. *Brookes eJournal of Learning and Teaching*, Vol. 1, No. 3, pp. 1–5.

Hall, C., 2006. Lighting a fire or filling a pail? Users' perceptions of a virtual learning environment. Survey Report, University of Swansea. Retrieved 10 March 2016, from http://learninglab.swan.ac.uk/Downloads/User_Survey_Report%201.1.pdf

Hrastinski, S., 2008. What is online learner participation? A literature review. *Computers & Education*, Vol. 51, pp. 1755–1765.

Jones, C. et al., 2010. Net generation or Digital Natives: Is there a distinct new generation entering university? *Computers & Education*, Vol. 54, No. 3, pp. 722–732.

Kareal, F. and Klema, J. 2006. Adaptivity in e-learning. *Current Developments in Technology-Assisted Education*, pp. 260–264. Retrieved 5 April 2015, from http://karlovi.cz/filip/adaptivity_in_e-learning.pdf

Koohang, A. and Durante, A., 2003. Learners' Perceptions toward the Web-based Distance Learning Activities/Assignments Portion of an Undergraduate Hybrid Instructional Model. *Journal of Information Technology Education*, Vol. 2, pp. 105–113.

Kubiatko, M., 2013. The Comparison of Different Age Groups on the Attitudes toward and the Use of ICT. *Educational Sciences: Theory & Practice*, Vol. 13, No. 2, pp. 1263–1272.

Liao, C.-W. et al., 2011. Perspectives of university students on cooperative learning by Moodle. *International Journal of Digital Content Technology and its Applications*, Vol. 5, No. 6, pp. 190–197. http://www.aicit.org/jdcta/ppl/22_%20JDCTA_June-26.pdf

Penny, K. I., 2011. Factors that Influence Student E-learning Participation in a UK Higher Education Institution. *Interdisciplinary Journal of E-Learning and Learning Objects*, Vol. 7, pp. 81–95.

Saade, R. et al., 2007. Viability of the 'Technology Acceptance Model' in Multimedia Learning Environments: A Comparative Study. *Interdisciplinary Journal of Knowledge and Learning Objects*, Vol. 3, No. 1, pp. 175–184.

Smedley, J. K., 2010. Modelling the impact of Knowledge Management Using Technology. *OR Insight*, Vol. 23, No. 4, pp. 233-250.

Umek, L. et al., 2015. Analysis of Selected Aspects of Students' Performance and Satisfaction in a Moodle-Based E-Learning System Environment. *Eurasia Journal of Mathematics, Science and Technology Education*, Vol. 11, No. 6, pp. 1495–1505. doi: 10.12973/eurasia.2015.1408a

Upadhyaya, K. T. and Mallik, D., 2013. E-Learning as a socio-technical system: An insight into factors influencing its effectiveness. *Business Perspectives and Research*, Vol. 2, No. 1, pp. 1–12.

Vonderwell, S. and Zachariah, S., 2005. Factors that influence participation in online learning. *Journal of Research and Technology in Education*, Vol. 38, No. 2, pp. 213–230.

Yukselturk, E. and Bulut, S., 2007. Predictors for student success in an online course. *Educational Technology & Society*, Vol. 10, No. 2, pp. 71–83.

Žuvic-Butorac et al., 2001. Blended E-Learning in Higher Education: Research on Students' Perspective. *Issues in Information Science and Information Technology*, Vol. 8, pp. 409–429.

EVALCOMIX®: A WEB-BASED PROGRAMME TO SUPPORT COLLABORATION IN ASSESSMENT

Dr. María Soledad Ibarra-Sáiz[1] and Dr. Gregorio Rodríguez-Gómez[2]
[1]*Professor of Educational Assessment and Evaluation, Director of EVALfor Research Group, University of Cadiz, Spain*
[2]*Professor of Educational Research Methods, Member of EVALfor Research Group, University of Cadiz, Spain*

ABSTRACT

For many years assessment strategies and practices have emphasized on the one hand the importance of integrating assessment and learning and, secondly, the need to develop technological tools that facilitate this relationship and integration. In this paper, firstly we describe the EvalCOMIX® web service and then we present the opinions of university tutors and students that have used this web service in their courses. We conclude that EvalCOMIX® is actually more than a just a web-based programme for assessment. Through its use, on the one hand, it can encourage student participation in the assessment process, by selecting or defining criteria, building tools and processes used in self-assessment and peer assessment. In addition, students receive valuable and relevant information about their performance and progress, so that improvements can be incorporated both in their learning process and the results they achieve.

KEYWORDS

Assessment, e-Assessment, Assessment as Learning, Empowerment, Participative Assessments.

1. INTRODUCTION

For many years assessment strategies and practices have emphasized on the one hand the importance of integrating assessment and learning and, secondly, the need to develop technological tools that facilitate this relationship and integration.

To support the integration of learning and assessment the development of the EvalCOMIX® tool began in 2010. It has subsequently transformed into a web-based programme that both enables and facilitates the implementation of the concept of assessment as learning and empowerment.

In this chapter, firstly we describe this web programme and then we present the opinions of university tutors and students that have used the EvalCOMIX® programme in their courses.

2. FROM ASSESSMENT OF LEARNING TO ASSESSMENT AS LEARNING AND EMPOWERMENT

Traditionally the assessment of learning has been characterized by maintaining a separation between teaching and learning (Falchikov, 2005, p. 82) and employing a narrow range of systems which do not always reflect the objectives of the curriculum and often fail to specify the marking criteria, therefore giving little or no power to students, missing the opportunity to make them responsible for their own learning process and, among other things, causing adverse feelings and lasting negative consequences.

Faced with this situation, common in most educational contexts, many authors with innovative approaches to their practices and contributions are now proposing alternative scenarios that increasingly place the focus of assessment on students' progress and learning rather than on just providing a final grade.

In relation to this we would highlight the contributions of; Carless (2007) on learning-oriented assessment; Rodríguez-Gómez and Ibarra-Sáiz (2011) who expand this concept whilst emphasising the possibilities and importance of electronic forms of assessment; Taras (2010), who stresses the role of self-assessment; Nicol, Thomson & Breslin (2014) who focus on the value of peer assessment; the concept of sustainable assessment as expressed by Boud (2000); Boud & Molloy (2013) who concentrate on feedback to students or Price, Rust, O'Donovan, Handley & Bryant (2012) with their contributions regarding the need for both tutors and students to receive training in assessment processes.

The authors of this article are currently focused on the development and application of the concept of assessment as learning and empowerment (Rodríguez-Gómez and Ibarra-Sáiz, 2015; Ibarra-Sáiz and Rodríguez-Gómez, 2016) characterized by three main challenges: achieving the participation of students in the assessment process, incorporating self-assessment, peer assessment and shared assessment; feedforward, understood as strategies that provide proactive information on students' progress and results so that they can participate in their improvement; and high quality tasks, ie, challenging tasks that are motivational and related to daily life. The implementation of these three challenges allows university students to self-regulate their learning process and provides empowerment within their personal, professional and working environments.

3. THE NEED FOR AUTOMATION IN ASSESSMENT PROCESSES

Currently, within the contexts experienced by the authors, the process of teaching and learning takes place in classrooms with large numbers of students, despite what recent legislative changes intended to achieve. Furthermore, it covers both knowledge and skills and does not take place only within the classroom but in some cases is developed entirely outside them. These are factors that also imply a change in the conditions and characteristics of the relevant assessment. Within universities, the non-contact nature of some or all subject areas is a fact that requires the use of campus-based or virtual platforms and therefore appropriate and valuable tools are needed to undertake assessment through these platforms and which incorporate the latest thinking on assessment practice.

Assessing skills and knowledge involves using different strategies and undertaking assessment at different times with different objectives and criteria. This calls for an effort that has produced and is producing some unease and insecurity among university tutors, who face a demanding environment and who often do not have the most convincing answers. In this situation technology should facilitate the assessment process. It should support assessment, encouraging the staging of the progress that is taking place through the assessment process.

According to the concept of assessment as learning and empowerment, these technological tools must be integrated within high quality tasks, encourage the participation of students in their own assessment process and provide useful and relevant information on their progress so they can take appropriate decisions in order to improve their work and performance. It is with the express intention of connecting and consolidation these various propositions that the EVALfor Research Group has been developing the by EvalCOMIX® web-based programme which we refer to in the following sections.

4. HOW DOES EvalCOMIX® WORK?

EvalCOMIX® is a web-based programme (http://evalcomix.uca.es) that supports the creation and implementation of assessment tools (rubrics, grading scales, mixed instruments etc.) and their use in assessment process both by tutors and students. Consecuently, it demands their active participation in the assessment process.

Below we present how this programme works once installed on a virtual campus platform and we focus on answering the following questions: how can effective assessment instruments be designed?, how should the roles of assessors be assigned to tutors and students?, how can the weighted scores of the assessments provided by EvalCOMIX® be interpreted?, how can the results of the assessments be analysed?

4.1 Designing Assessment Instruments

Decisions on issues such as the design of assessment instruments, specifying the criteria or the selection of participatory assessment methods are all included within the programme (Rodríguez-Gómez and Ibarra-Sáiz, 2016). In this section we discuss how to design assessment tools using the EvalCOMIX® programme.

To design appropriate assessment tools it is first necessary to access the Tool Management section. From that screen New Instrument is selected. A list of the possible tools that can be built with EvalCOMIX® (Figure 1) is then displayed.

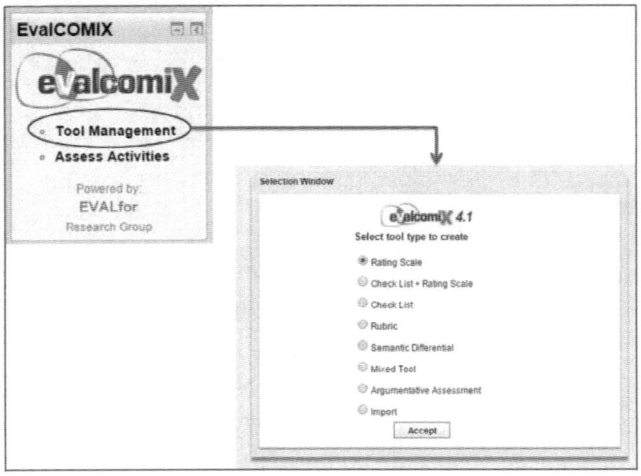

Figure 1. Options and assessment tools provided by EvalCOMIX®

EvalCOMIX® guides the process of construction of each instrument by offering options about which decisions must be taken (Figure 2). Before building the tools it is preferable to plan and determine the weighting that each aspect will have within the overall assessment. By default, EvalCOMIX® assigns a pro-rata weighting, but the percentages of all of the elements assessed (dimensions and attributes) can be changed as required. Once a new instrument has been created, it is automatically added to the full list of instruments available for tutors.

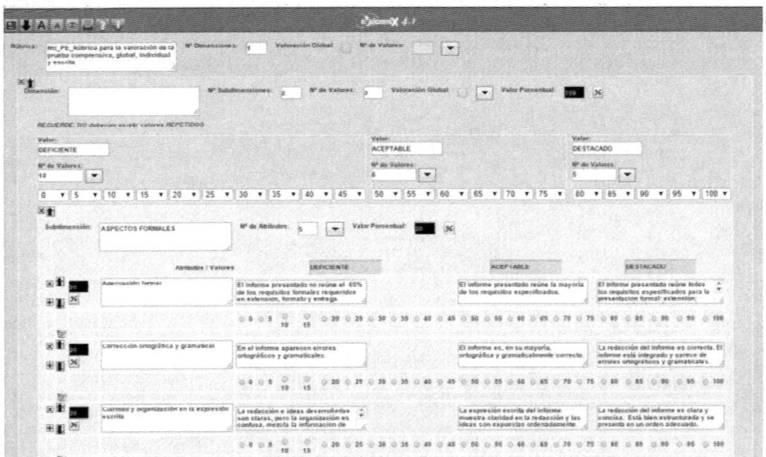

Figure 2. Screen for the construction of a rubric

4.2 Assigning the Roles of Assessor

One advantage of EvalCOMIX® is that the role of assessor can be undertaken by both the tutors and the students, through self-assessment, peer review, using all or some of the three modes of assessment. To do this each assessor is assigned the assessment tool they will use (Figure 3). The instrument can be the same or different for each of the assessors. Peer review can be anonymous or public. Furthermore, this type of assessment can be carried out by groups or by individual students.

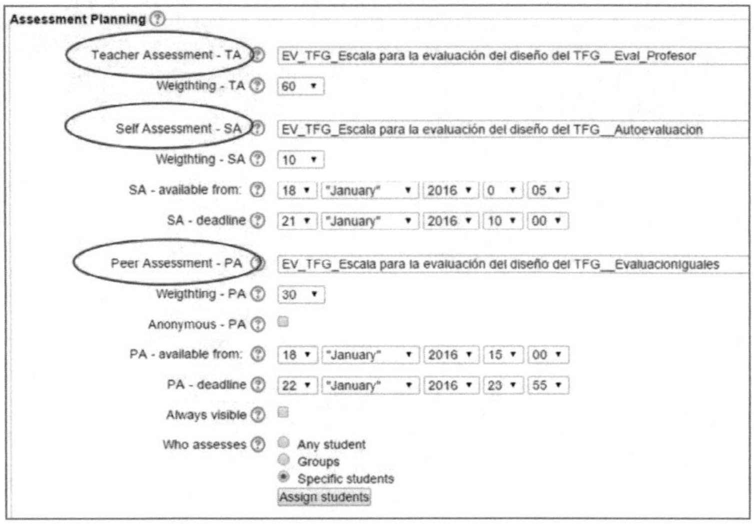

Figure 3. Assigning roles in assessment and weighting

4.3 Considerations on the Issue of Weighting

The weighting of the grades using EvalCOMIX® is achieved by two means. Firstly, for the elements of assessment in which the weighting of the instrument used in each type of assessment is specified (Figure 4) and, secondly, for the assessment tools where the weighting is provided for each component and, within them, to each of the separate elements, scored between a minimum score of 0 and máximum of 100. The following figure shows an excerpt from a rubric in which the weighting of the two elements that are assessed (format and content) are specified as well as the specific elements that are being assessed.

RU_PE_Rúbrica para la valoración de la prueba comprensiva, global, individual y escrita

100%		DEFICIENTE	ACEPTABLE	DESTACADO
30%	**ASPECTOS FORMALES**			
20%	Adecuación formal	El informe presentado no reúne el 60% de los requisitos formales requeridos en extensión, formato y entrega.	El informe presentado reúne la mayoría de los requisitos especificados.	El informe presentado reúne todos los requisitos especificados para la presentación formal: extensión, identificación, título, índice, desarrollo del informe, referencias bibliográficas, interlineado, márgenes, alineación, paginación; entrega en fecha e identificación correcta del archivo.
		0 5 10 15 20 25 30 35 40 45	50 55 60 65 70 75	80 85 90 95 100
20%	Corrección ortográfica y gramatical	En el informe aparecen errores ortográficos y gramaticales.	El informe es, en su mayoría, ortográfica y gramaticalmente correcto.	La redacción del informe es correcta. El informe está integrado y carece de errores ortográficos y gramaticales.
		0 5 10 15 20 25 30 35 40 45	50 55 60 65 70 75	80 85 90 95 100
20%	Claridad y organización en la expresión escrita	La redacción e ideas desarrolladas son claras, pero la organización es confusa, mezcla la información de los diferentes bloques.	La expresión escrita del informe muestra claridad en la redacción y las ideas son expuestas ordenadamente.	La redacción del informe es clara y concisa. Está bien estructurada y se presenta en un orden adecuado.
		0 5 10 15 20 25 30 35 40 45	50 55 60 65 70 75	80 85 90 95 100
20%	Precisión terminológica	En el informe no se utiliza un lenguaje apropiado, bien por ser repetitivo o por no ser técnico, o el vocabulario no es el mas apropiado al tema.	El lenguaje y el vocabulario empleado son apropiados.	El lenguaje utilizado es técnico y denota conocimiento del tema. En cuanto al vocabulario es empleado con rigor dominando términos y expresiones.
		0 5 10 15 20 25 30 35 40 45	50 55 60 65 70 75	80 85 90 95 100
20%	Pertinencia de la bibliografía	El informe carece de bibliografía o ésta no es pertinente. Algunas de las referencias bibliográficas no se ajustan a la normativa APA.	Las referencias bibliográficas se citan de acuerdo a la normativa APA. Se incluyen referencias del material aportado en clase relevantes para el problema.	Las referencias bibliográficas se ajustan a la normativa APA. La bibliografía es pertinente y relevante para la solución del problema y, además, se incluyen referencias de ampliación.
		0 5 10 15 20 25 30 35 40 45	50 55 60 65 70 75	80 85 90 95 100
70%	**ASPECTOS DE CONTENIDO**			
10%	Análisis e integracion de los contenidos.	Los contenidos destacados carecen de un análisis sistemático o presentan integración.	Se establece un análisis sistemático de los materiales trabajados en clase, pero no se demuestra una correcta integración de contenidos.	Los contenidos del informe analizan e integran sistemáticamente los contenidos y perspectivas de los diferentes materiales trabajados en la asignatura.
		0 5 10 15 20 25 30 35 40 45	50 55 60 65 70 75	80 85 90 95 100
10%	Coherencia y síntesis del informe	La redacción no es concisa se alarga innecesariamente o la información desarrollada denota escasa lógica en alguno de los apartados del informe.	La información presentada en el informe mantiene un hilo conductor, pero no se profundiza, o muestra escasa coherencia o profundidad en las inferencias de cada apartado o elementos.	El discurso es sintético y se establecen inferencias coherentes entre el nº de personas a contratar y su tiempo de dedicación, perfil académico y profesional y funciones o actividades a desempeñar.
		0 5 10 15 20 25 30 35 40 45	50 55 60 65 70 75	80 85 90 95 100

Figure 4. Example of weighting for each component and element in a rubric created using EvalCOMIX®

4.4 Analysis of Results

Once the assessment process is complete (construction of instruments and assessment by the tutors and students) EvalCOMIX® (Figure 5) enables both tutors and students to see all the assessments that have been completed and who has completed them following the appropriate assessment procedures. Tutors can also get an overview of the gradings in simple diagrams, where the maximum, minimum and median scores are shown. Assessment results can be analysed by student group, class and assessment methods used.

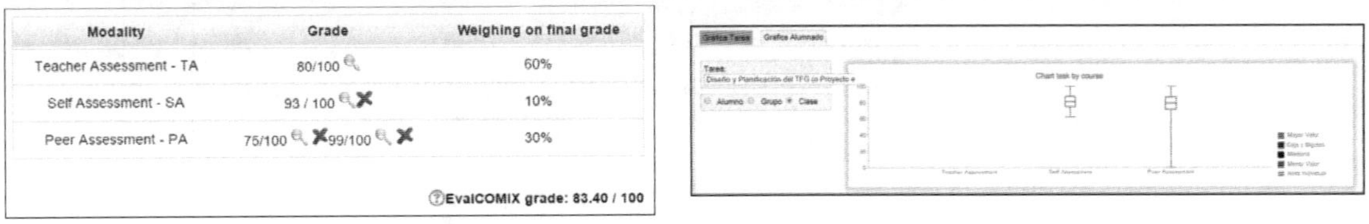

Figure 5. Grades achieved by assessment method and weighting and representation using box and whisker plots of scores on self-assessment and peer assessment of a class

5. WHAT DO USERS SAY ABOUT EVALCOMIX®?

Two of the main features of the EvalCOMIX® programme are that both tutors and students can use it (in groups and individually) and that it provides information on the results achieved for all of the elements assessed. This aligns with the concept of assessment as learning and empowerment as it facilitates the participation of students in their own assessment process and provides useful and timely information to students on their performance.

Specifically designed questionnaires were employed to obtain the opinion of tutors and students about a variety of issues after they had used EvalCOMIX® in their academic programmes, and the results are presented in the following sections.

5.1 The tutors' Views

During the academic year 2014/2015 a total of 65 tutors from Latin American universities completed a questionnaire regarding their opinions after employing the EvalCOMIX® programme. Table 1 shows the distribution of these tutors by gender, their university and subject area.

Table 1. Distribution of the sample of tutors by Gender, University and Subject area

	n	%
Gender		
Male	18	33.85
Female	43	66.15
University		
PUCESI (Ecuador)	31	47.69
UCR (Costa Rica)	27	41.54
UNA (Nicaragua)	7	10.77
Subject area		
Arts and Humanities	10	15.38
Science	12	18.46
Health Sciences	10	15.38
Social Sciences	21	32.31
Engineering and Architecture	12	18.46

In Figure 6 we see how, for most tutors, the EvalCOMIX® programme provides a simple process for the construction of assessment instruments which can be easily modified and shared with others in a way that encourages a collaborative approach to the design and creation of assessment instruments.

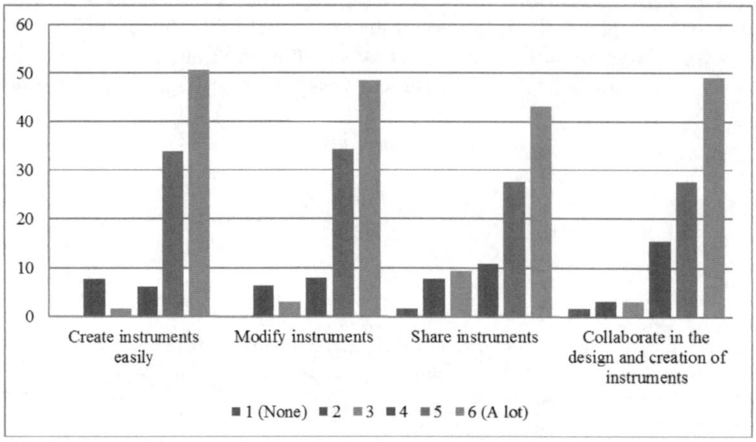

Figure 6. Tutors' opinions on the construction of instruments using the EvalCOMIX® programme

When tutors were asked about the usefulness and benefits of EvalCOMIX® (Figure 7), their opinion was in the main positive. They considered it to be a programme that simplifies the assessment process for tutors, is applicable to any subject area, improves the competence level of tutors in dealing with assessment, encourages innovation within the university and they believe it should be more widely used in all universities. Overall, 87.69% of tutors expressed a high degree of satisfaction with EvalCOMIX®.

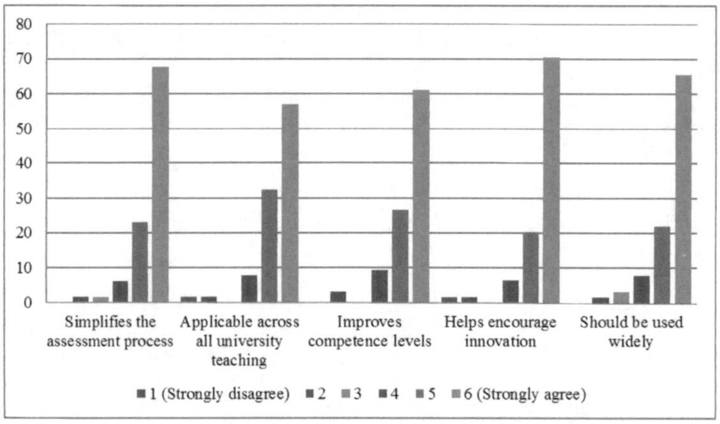

Figure 7. Tutors' opinions on the usefulness and benefits of the EvalCOMIX® programme

5.2 The students' Views

The students surveyed were undergraduates taking degrees in Business Administration and Management (BAM) and Finance and Accounting (F&A) who during the academic years 2012-13 (73 students) and 2013-14 (92 students) used EvalCOMIX® within their courses. Their opinions produce interesting results (Rodríguez-Gómez and Ibarra-Sáiz, 2016). The results obtained by asking students of BAM and F&A on using the EvalCOMIX® programme, on self-assessment and peer assessment are presented in Figure 8.

It shows that students show a higher degree of agreement to the issue that EvalCOMIX® was "useful to provide prior knowledge of the criteria and assessment tools, as well as the elements being assessed" (M = 4.65, SD = 1.09). They also consider using EvalCOMIX® as "simple and easy" (M = 4.61; SD = 1.10); "useful because the information that was provided enables subsequent tasks or activities to be improved"

(M = 4.50, SD = 1.14); "motivational because the feedback from tutor assessment, self-assessment, and peer assessment was available simultaneously and rapidly" (M = 4.49, SD = 1.17) and, finally, it proved to be a "friendly and intuitive environment" (M = 4.24; SD = 1.19).

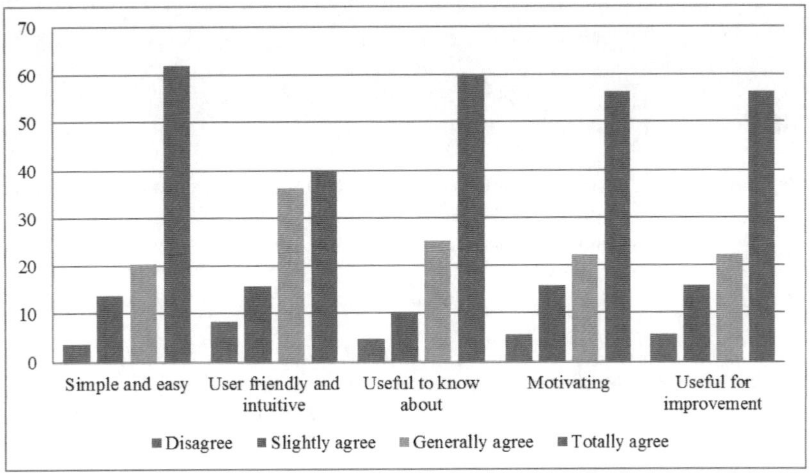

Figure 8. The opinions of students on using the EvalCOMIX® programme for self-assessment and peer assessment

6. CONCLUSION

In the previous section we have presented the very positive results on the opinions of tutors and students regarding the use of EvalCOMIX® in the assessment process.

These positive opinions focus on the one hand on the programme's characteristics, such as its simplicity and user friendly environment. The tutors further indicate that is applicable to all subject areas and it encourages collaboration in creating instruments and modifying them to adapt to different situations. The opinions of users also indicated that EvalCOMIX® promotes transparency in assessment, specifying the assessment criteria and making the instruments public prior to their implementation. Furthermore the feedback from students was particularly positive about how motivating it was and how they felt involved as a result of the speed with which they received feedback on their performance and progress. In terms of the concept of assessment as learning and empowerment it is important to emphasize the value of the information provided by the self-assessment, peer assessment and tutor evaluation via EvalCOMIX® which enables them to improve their subsequent work.

We conclude that EvalCOMIX® is actually more than a just a web-based programme for assessment. Through its use, on the one hand, it can encourage student participation in the assessment process, by selecting or defining criteria, building tools and processes used in self-assessment and peer assessment. In addition, students receive valuable and relevant information about their performance and progress, so that improvements can be incorporated both in their learning process and the results they achieve.

EvalCOMIX® is a web programme that promotes learning and assessment in a fully integrated way but, to achieve this it is vital we fully understand the concept of assessment. We will only be able to fully exploit the potential of EvalCOMIX® if we are able to; introduce innovations in assessment; ensure all assessment is fully transparent, proposing and agreeing in advance the activities and elements that will be assessed and the criteria that will be applied and agreeing in advance the products and actions to be evaluated; enable the full participation of students in the evaluation process; provide both tutors and students with feedforward on student performances; and fully integrate the use of of high quality tasks within assessment.

ACKNOWLEDGMENTS

This chapter was made possible by the DevalS Project [Ref.EDU2012-31804] funded by Spanish Ministry of Economy and Competitiveness and the DevalSimWeb Project [Ref. ALFA III (2011)-10] funded by ALFA Programme of European Commission.

REFERENCES

Boud, D., 2000. Sustainable Assessment: Rethinking assessment for the learning society. *Studies in Continuing Education*, *22*(2), 151–167. doi:10.1080/713695728.

Boud, D. and Molloy, E., 2013. Rethinking models of feedback for learning: the challenge of design. *Assessment & Evaluation in Higher Education*, *38*(6), 698–712. doi:10.1080/02602938.2012.691462.

Carless, D., 2007. Learning-oriented assessment: Conceptual basis and practical implications. *Innovations in Education and Teaching International, 44*(1), 57–66.

Falchikov, N., 2005. *Improving assessment through student involvement. Practical solutions for aiding learning in higher education and further education*. London: RoutledgeFalmer.

Ibarra-Sáiz, M.S. and Rodríguez-Gómez, G., 2014. Modalidades participativas de evaluación: Un análisis de la percepción del profesorado y de los estudiantes universitarios. *Revista de Investigación Educativa, 32(2),* 339-362. http://dx.doi.org/10.6018/rie.32.2.172941.

Ibarra-Sáiz, M.S. and Rodríguez-Gómez, G., 2016. *Guía Innovar en evaluación en la Educación Superior*. Producción: EVALfor - Grupo de Investigación. España:Cádiz. ISBN: 978-84-608-4483-9

Nicol, D., Thomson, A. and Breslin, C., 2014. Rethinking Feedback in Higher Education: A Peer Review Perspective. *Assessment & Evaluation in Higher Education, 39*(1), 102–122. doi:10.1080/02602938.2013.795518.

Price, M., Rust, C., O'Donovan, B., Handley, K. and Bryant, R., 2012. *Assessment Literacy. The Foundation for Improving Student Learning*. Oxford: Oxford Brookes University.

Rodríguez-Gómez, G. and Ibarra-Saiz, M.S., Eds., 2011. *e-Evaluación orientada al e-Aprendizaje estratégico en Educación Superior.* Madrid: Narcea. ISBN 978-84-277-1803-6.

Rodríguez-Gómez, G. and Ibarra-Sáiz, M.S., 2015. Assessment as Learning and Empowerment: Towards Sustainable Learning in Higher Education. In M. Peris-Ortiz & J. M. Merigó Lindahl (Eds.), *Sustainable Learning in Higher Education. Developing Competencies for the Global Marketplace* (pp. 1–20). Springer International Publishing. doi:10.1007/978-3-319-10804-9_1.

Rodríguez-Gómez, G. and Ibarra-Sáiz, M.S., 2016. Towards Sustainable Assessment: ICT as a Facilitator of Self- and Peer Assessment. In M. Peris-Ortiz, J. Alonso-Gómez, F. Vélez-Torres & C. Rueda-Armengot (Eds.), *Education Tools for Entrepreneurship.* (pp. 55–71). Springer International Publishing. doi: 10.1007/978-3-319-24657-4_5. Available at: http://link.springer.com/chapter/10.1007/978-3-319-24657-4_5

Rodríguez-Gómez, G. and Ibarra-Sáiz, M.S., 2016. *Guía Diseñar procedimientos de evaluación en la Educación Superior*. Producción: EVALfor - Grupo de Investigación. España:Cádiz. ISBN: 978-84-608-4484-6.

Taras, M., 2010. Student self-assessment: processes and consequences. *Teaching in Higher Education, 15*(2), 199–209. doi:10.1080/13562511003620027.

A HOLISTIC APPROACH TO SCORING IN COMPLEX MOBILE LEARNING SCENARIOS

Marcel Gebbe, Matthias Teine and Marc Beutner
Chair of Business and Human Resource Education II, University of Paderborn, Germany

ABSTRACT

Interactive dialogues are key elements for designing authentic and motivating learning situations, and in combination with learning analysis they provide educators and users with the opportunity to track information related to professional competences, but mind-sets as well. This paper offers exemplary insights into the project NetEnquiry that is concerned with the development of an m-learning app which provides learners with complex learning scenarios. In these scenarios, we combine different approaches to scoring and assessment. A specialty of the assessment is that it adapts to scenario settings given by the lecturer, and runs mainly in stealth mode. These settings consider formal correctness, social and communicative skills, but also norms that influence whether a given answer is correct, or not.

KEYWORDS

Scoring, dialogues, decision-making, assessment, formative learning analysis

1. INTRODUCTION

Assessment in e-learning in general, and digital game-based learning in particular reached a point where its opportunities are far beyond what would be possible with traditional testing formats. Particularly the user-interactivity and the adaptability of complex, authentic learning environments to the individual learners are the key to both high quality formal and summative assessment (cf. Scalise, K. 2006, p. 4). To realize such benefits, it is necessary to design task- and interaction-formats that allow us to gather meaningful evidence about the learners' performance, based on an effective scoring and score reporting (cf. Scalise, K. 2006, p. 4). Hence, underlying competences (see Roth, H. 1971; Reetz, L. 1984) can be observed and scored by focusing on the learners' visible performance in action (see Sloane, P. / Dilger, B. 2005, p. 7). Therefore, it is inevitable to create an evidence model that defines the connection in-between (see Shute, V. J. et al. 2009, pp. 309). The data and information gathered via such a stealth assessment can ultimately improve learning (cf. Shute, V. J. 2009). Tracked information about the learners' actions, his movements, events, made decisions, etc. can be used to design personalized debriefing sessions where the learners get detailed feedback, and where implemented solutions can be reflected based on sample or expert solutions (see Loreto, I. D. et al. 2013, pp. 169, Raposo, F. et al. 2013, p. 37, Reinmann-Rothmeier, G. 2005, p. 217). This does not only provide the learners with valuable information regarding how to improve, but it also allows the teachers to become the student's learning process facilitator, rather than the learners' opponent (see Shute, V. J. et al. 2009, pp. 298, Sykes, J. 2006, p. 4).

In the research and development project NetEnquiry, funded by the German 'Federal Ministry of Education and Research' (project ID 01PF10008) we are building a mobile learning app framework that allows to offer complex, role based and cooperative learning scenarios, including a holistic scoring system. Thus, the app is observing several learner processes to score and assess learning and offer a base for individual and team oriented reflection on the learning processes. For example, we use interactive, adaptive dialogues to observe the learners' competences and mind-sets. Following, we want to offer several insights into the scoring system and some challenges behind it.

2. THE NETENQUIRY APPROACH

NetEnquiry is a research and development project that aims to conceptualize, develop, implement, and evaluate both an m-learning tool (iOS app) and its web-based version that provide learning scenarios for the banking and finance sector. The Chair II for Business and Human Resource Education of the University Paderborn leads the project, and collaborates with representative organizations from all parts of the German universal banking system, to safeguard that their needs are met. This means that private sector commercial banks, saving banks, and industrial and agricultural credit co-operations are involved particularly into the creation process of the learning scenarios. Overall, NetEnquiry provides three complex learning scenarios:

1) Specific complex credits and handling of complicated clients,
2) Investment banking and consultancy concerning securities, and
3) Documentation of counselling and talks with clients in the field of investment.

The scenarios are usable for initial or further vocational education and training, and we conceptualized the app for the use in blended-learning scenarios. Thus, NetEnquiry can be used integrated into the everyday work-routine, in enterprise settings, or in formal educational settings in vocational schools as well. However, the learning scenarios focus on authentic situations from the world of work, and the learners have to cope with tasks that typically occur in reality (simulated practice). The learning situations and the task base on real processes which we observed by shadowing employees of the co-operating banks, analyzing internal process data (e. g. handbooks, field of activity-descriptions, organigrams, tools) and problem centered discussions.

The learners form teams of three each of them with a different role (e.g. loan consultant, loan manager, and head of department). For example, the loan consultant is the person that has direct contact to the clients; therefore, he is responsible for providing the team members with the needed information to solve the learning scenario successfully. Due to this, providing wrong information or missing out to provide information lead to wrong decisions of the whole team at succeeding stages of the learning process. The role of the loan manager is to provide feedback on loan applications, particularly in difficult cases, and he has specific instruments to review such applications. The information provided by the loan consultant influence this decision directly. However, the head of the department knows about strategic decisions, new strategies, and he has the competence to make decisions on a level of higher importance. Therefore, if the head does not provide all strategic information, or when he decides in a wrong way, this effects directly the work of all team members.

The quintessence is that the learners are required to co-operate, to support each other, and to communicate effectively because all decision-making and problem-solving processes are interdependent. Otherwise, they cannot solve the given problems successfully. Moreover, the result and the provided solutions for the learning scenario depend on the individual competences of each of the team members, and the solutions can only be as good as the weakest part of the team. Thereby, on the one hand, we address collaborative learning, and the development of social and communication skills. On the other hand, this offers multiperspectivity, and fosters the learners' understanding for the complex interdependences of their real-life actions.

Within the app, the learners have three different kinds of tools that help them to deal with the scenarios: *orientations tools*, *workplace tools*, and *learning support tools*. Depending on the role, the scenario, and the progress the learners can access only those tools that really are necessary to solve the scenario successfully:

- The orientation tools aim to help the learners getting involved into the scenario (e.g. a role-specific introduction video, a description of the own profile, etc.).
- The workplace tools help the learners to cope with the business challenges of the scenario (e.g. a telephone mailbox, an email tool, a loan calculator, etc.).
- The learning support tools help the learners to manage their learning processes (e.g. an interactive calendar, a mind-mapping tool, a tool to take notes, a photo documentation tool etc.).

However, particularly the loan consultant has to deal with clients, and therefore we had to design a complex dialogue system. Generally spoken, dialogues can be observing vs. interactive or sequential vs. interlinked and based on a parallel network-structure. To create authenticity and realism, dialogues need to depict interaction with real people and conditions of (operational) reality, such like information overload or the lack of information, as well as emotional reactions of the dialogue partner (e. g. clients). Interactivity then means that the learners are involved actively, they make decisions by clicking on given answer-options, and thus they change the way the dialogue goes. This is particularly the case with dialogues based on a "interlinked parallel network structure [which] is a decision tree in which each branch leads to a different outcome" (Beutner, M./ Pechuel, R. 2014, p. 175). Moreover, the opportunity of the learners to actively influence how the story of the learning scenario goes, and their variability based on the already made decisions are main drivers of the learners' motivation (see Westphal, A. 2009, p. 134). In NetEnquiry we use interactive and interlinked dialogues in which the client´s responses are provided by short videos. So, the structure of the dialogue is individualized.

Following, we will describe how the interdependence within the roles, the use of the three different kinds of tools, and the dialogue structure found their way into designing an assessment and scoring system.

3. ASSESSMENT AND SCORING IN NETENQUIRY

In NetEnquiry, we paid a lot of attention to the design of the assessment- and scoring-mechanism to support motivational aspects and feedback based reflection. The main principle behind the assessment is to judge the player´s actions based on their estimated real-life effectiveness (cf. Abt, C. C. 1970, p. 51, 58), and we use scores to provide the learners with a numerical measure of their performance (cf. Sykes, J. 2006, p. 4). This shows that we pursue different aims with our assessment and scoring system, and therefore we combined different scoring- and data collection-approaches as we will show now (cf. for similar approaches e.g. Raposo, F. et al. 2013).

As different teams are playing the scenarios at the time, there is an individual scoring, and a team scoring. Since a number of activities of the players affect the scoring opportunities of the other players; we decided that the team scoring is more important than the individual scoring. This decision had a strong influence on the actual design of the scoring system. Individual scores are related to individual learning tasks, tests, and assessments. Team scores are related to their decision-making, their working processes, their information transfer resp. communication, and the quality of their overall solution of the learning scenario. Moreover, as we will show during this article, the scoring provides an estimation related to the following three aspects (cf. Prensky, M. 2007, p. 121):

1) Did the learners stay within, or did they broke the rules of the scenario?
2) How close did the learners come to the ideal solution of the scenario?
3) How did the learners do, compared to their competitors?

A special focus was also on the scoring and assessment of decision-making processes within the learning scenarios, which is a topic difficult to grasp. In discussions with our partners from the banking sector it became clear that effective economic processes and methods of 'business handbooks' do not always match with the real life circumstances, especially in those cases where situational human competence is needed. For example, strategic habits and moral-ethical norms can lead to a decision that diverges from idealistic economic processes. Moreover, two or more conflicting economic goals can come into case within one situation. Hence, decision making in such situations needs to be trained, scored and assessed transparently for both learners and coaches. This will lead to a basis for discussion and reflection on learning and teaching processes (see Reinmann-Rothmeier, G. 2005 o. 141). Of course, trivial scoring systems and assessment methods alone won´t fit this challenging task. Following we will show how we addressed the different outlined challenges.

3.1 Activity and Quality-Based Quantitative Scoring

Contest and competition is what drives us when playing, as it is about winning or losing against others (cf. Rieber, L. P. 1996, p. 44.). Therefore, learners need information about how they are currently performing compared to the others, and scores provide us with an easy way to quantify the performance of learners. Thus, scores are a way to provide feedback and to let the learners know if they are progressing towards their goal (cf. Becker, K. 2007, p. 29), and thereby they enhance the learners' engagement (cf. Sykes, J. 2006, p. 4). The value of the score assigned to the learners depends on the quality of the performance (see Juul, J. 2005, p. 36), and can be visualized e.g. by using high-score tables (see Prensky, M. 2007, p. 121).

Within the NetEnquiry project, however, we use high-score tables as well. As we provide high-score tables for both an individual score and a team score, the learners can always see how they are performing compared to other learners, and other teams. In the projects' approach, we provide the learners with an absolute, and a relative score. Thereby, the current best absolute score is the benchmark for the relative score, which is an easy to interpret indicator for the learners then to see how they are doing. Within the app, the learners can always see their score, and they can see the data either in a tabular form, or as a bar chart. Anyway, following we want to describe how the learners can get score points, and how scoring takes place on an individual, and team level.

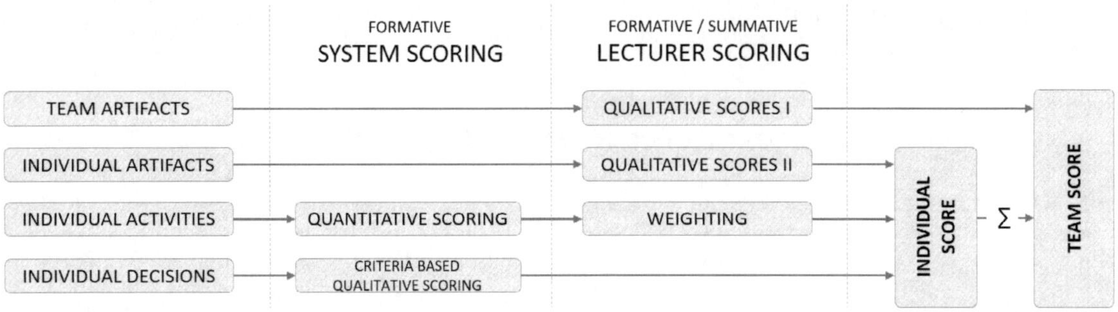

Figure 1. Overview about the NetEnquiry scoring system

The above standing Figure 1 provides you with a comprehensive overview about the NetEnquiry scoring system, which we will describe more in detail now.

3.1.1 Scoring of the Tools

In each of the different scenarios, all three players get individual scores for making use of the different orientation, work, and learning support tools. Moreover, the learners get team scores particularly for the use of work-related tools such like for making use of the mailing systems, the client information system, or the loan management system.

Orientation Tools: We decided to score the learners' use of the orientation tools to reward them for dealing with the app actively, even if these tasks are rather insignificant for the work process itself and not match winning. Anyway, they are important for the learner to understand the own role within the process and to be able to work in the right direction. Due to the nature of the orientation tools, the learners can receive a score here only once. For example, the learners receive 2 points when they fill in their own players' profile, or when they read the description of the others player profiles. These role-related scores are also summed up to a team score. As all teams consist of three learners, it would be possible to receive 6 points as a team by filling in all player profiles.

Workplace and Learning Support Tools: In contrast to the orientation tools, the workplace and learning support tools are designed to be used multiple times during the problem-solving process. The scores here assigned to each of the learners, not the team as a whole – they are role-related. However, partially the score bases on the quantity of use of the tools, but the learners have to reach different threshold to get higher scores. E.g., a learner will get a score of 1 for writing 5 work related emails to his team members, for writing 2 emails to his lecturer, or for writing 1 email to a client. Therefore, 15 mails written to team members result in a score of 3. Based on the importance of the different tools for the learning process, and the purpose of their use, weight varies.

Unfortunately, this quantity based approach leads to a serious problem, because the quantity of use does not say anything about the quality. Therefore, we decided to give the lecturer the opportunity to rate the quality of some quantitative oriented scores, where the quality becomes highly important and the system is not able to evaluate the quality on its own. This weighting of selected quantitative scores can be done formative or summative. Regarding the communication via email and the so-called quick notes tool (in-team communication), where arguments should be shared, we included such a quality evaluation opportunity. A lecturer can do so by assigning a weight from 0-times - which means bad quality of communication, to 3-times - which means excellent quality of communication (cf. Figure 1). The trainer determines the weight by using a slider, and the default value is 1-times. Thus, the final score for the communication is the product of the weight x original score. Moreover, some of the process-oriented tools are explicitly documenting the learners' decision-making processes and their results. Here, NetEnquiry uses not only quantitative but two kinds of qualitative data as well:

a) choosing an alternative through selection, or

b) by entering data (numbers, words, arguments).

Depending on the kind of data, the system is able to automatically score and evaluate the data put into the tools, by comparing it with the complex scenario settings, or to ask the lecturer to bring in his expertise (criteria based qualitative scoring, cf. Figure 1). Unfortunately, we do not have a semantic analytic system for complex texts at the moment. However, the scenarios can include conflicting solutions, where e.g. the strategic and moral-ethical norms come into case (see 3.2 for details).

Right now we would like to showcase an example regarding the so-called 'KDF-Tool' (Kapitaldienstfähigkeit, financial capacity to pay a monthly rate), which is offered next to a loan management system, a customer management system and a collateral tool. The KDF tool is available in a loan scenario and an investment scenario. It is useful to calculate the debt service coverage, and the income available for regular investments on a monthly base. However, for each information put into the KDF-tool via the different drop-down menus, the learners will receive a score of 2, regardless whether the solution was right, or not. This shall engage them, to move on, as they see progress. As the quality of decisions matters most, the system will check the quality of the solution, and the learners will receive a score higher than 2 (up to 6, depending on the importance) when they put into the correct solution.

As explained above, the right solutions depend on processes, rules, norms etc. of the actual institution (e.g. bank). For an adequate score, each institution or lecturer is able to pre-define what is the 'right' decision regarding the institutional norms. Thereby, they define, e.g., if the credit manager has only little or ample scope to agree on a credit when the financial capacity of the clients is low, but the purpose of the credit could be to pay for hospital-costs (ethical-moral dilemma). Moreover, we have variables that can be set within the scenario (e.g. income, spendings, residual debt, kind and amount of collaterals, instalment, external shocks (devaluation), expected chance of survival (cause of disease), etc.). Thereby, the rules for the scenario are set, and the app evaluates if the learners broke the rules, e.g. by not using their scope, or if they stayed within the rules. This information is particularly useful for reflection- and debriefing-sessions.

3.1.2 Scoring of Tasks and Tests

Within the different scenarios, the learners have to solve learning tasks and testing tasks. Learning tasks need to be solved by all learners together, and they are not automatically evaluated but by the lecturer. The learners receive a score only for completing the task. The test tasks are evaluated by the system automatically, and the team will receive 1 score point, independent from the quality of the solution. For a correctly dissolved task, the team will get 3 score points. Testing tasks are classical instruments like multiple choice and an optional addition for lecturers, but obviously not the core aims of the NetEnquiry-system.

3.1.3 Lecturer Scoring

In addition to the scores that are assigned automatically by the NetEnquiry app, the trainer has the opportunity to assign scores for

(1) the communication with the trainer,

(2) the quality of the mind-maps created by the learners,

(3) the quality of the solutions of the learning tasks,

(4) the quality of the whiteboard-use in the team, and

(5) for the quality of work in face-to-face situations, as the tool has a strong focus on blended-learning.

In these cases, the trainer has to provide scores between 0 and ten for each aspect. This offers the opportunity to combine the quantitative scores of the system for the online phases with scores for activities in face-to-face situations. Moreover, the teacher can score weights for the automatic scoring of communication by the system which is multiplied with the system scores, so that intensive and high quality communication gets more scores than only small talk of senseless communication.

3.2 Dialogue Related Scoring

A key element of the NetEnquiry learning scenarios are video-based, interactive dialogues with NPC-clients. Within the dialogues the customer consultant implements decisions that affect the whole problem-solving process, by choosing an answer-alternative. That also means, that the dialogue system always offers multiple alternatives to answer (see Beutner / Pechuel 2014). As the content of the alternatives is designed within the dialogue writing process, there is an opportunity to offer answers that vary in direction and quality.

Direction means, that learners can structure the topic and the path of the ongoing dialogue. For example, they can decide to lead the dialogue into a small talk, ask for information or give information. Of cause, leading the dialogue in the right direction is an indicator for quality as well. In some cases, it is not clever to provide the learners with information beforehand (e.g. conditions), but to let them request the information through the dialogues. Hence, we clustered and structured dialogues, which makes it possible to use them for scoring. By offering clusters at special moments within the process, we can check if the learners are able to structure the learning process in the right way, and to score this decision.

Quality in contrast, refers to the way of articulation, the formal correctness of answers, and the strategic quality. The latter point describes decisions between different formally correct alternatives. However, as we have several variables in scenario settings, the correct strategic decision can vary, too. For example, it could be economically right to give the customer a loan, but depending on the scenario settings, it could be better to offer a bullet loan rather than an annuity loan. Moreover, norms can be the guidance value for the 'correctness' of decisions in the dialogue. This can be massively important, as the whole scenario result can be right or wrong, only caused by a single norm. In the loan scenario, the lecturer not only has to set economic variables of the case, but also strategic norms that influence the 'correctness' of moral-ethical decision making. For example, the lecturer has to answer the following question within the scenario settings: "Could it be right to give a loan, while the single economic decision would be wrong (e. g. high risk taking)?" For the scoring process a 'yes' means, that economically wrong decisions are not scored negative by default, because the learner in a role of the loan consultant decided correct from an ethical-moral point of view – he used his scope. Thus, decisions can drift from clearly black or white into a 'grey area'. And as described at the beginning of this paper, these are learning goals that matter and should find their way into the reflection process.

But how do we score the quality of decision making and what is about quantitative scores within the dialogue system? We do not offer scores for simple action, but for quality. As reference system for quality, we use three sources: a) expertise of sales professionals, b) data based on economic scenario-settings, and c) data based on lecturer settings (variables) regarding moral-ethical and strategic aspects.

- *Expertise based scores:* To know what is right or wrong, we observed sales training courses and documented how to structure customer dialogues, how to articulate questions, and how to offer information in a customer and sales oriented way. Through the writing process, we were able to bring that information into the dialogue as answer-alternatives for learners. As only certain parts of the texts were variable (e.g. the income), we could easily give individual scores for choosing a certain statement. In contrast to the other scoring system described for the other tools, we decided to give negative, neutral and positive scores. The scores vary from minus 4 (massively wrong) to plus 4 (difficult, highest quality answers and statements).
- *Setting based scores:* The flexibility of the scenario through variables (e.g. income of the client which is pre-defined by the lecturer) is relevant for the dialogue scores. As described above, some statements were filled with variables. Thereby, in some cases, answers switch from formal correct into wrong caused by the interdependency of variables. In consequence, scores have to switch from positive to negative, depending on scenario settings. For example, with the income-spending-ratio the correctness of the statement "Your monthly debt service is positive." can change. Therefore, we identified those answers that vary in correctness, depending on scenario settings. We combined those statements with our logical-mathematical algorithms and defined dependent scores. Moreover, these scores are independent from institutional settings. The amount of scores also varies between plus and minus four.
- *Normative Scores:* As written above, moral-ethical and strategic aspects can massively influence the correctness of the learners' solution. So, next to the economic driven answers, we also identified statements that can drift into the 'grey area' of decision making. Here, logical-mathematical algorithms are not sufficient. Hence, we had to define the circumstances under which a 'switch' into the 'grey area' of decision-making is given. Moreover, we had to check, if the institutional norms allow bringing in aspects next to economic ones into case. If this is confirmed, you can earn scores for economically wrong decisions, because they meet the institutional 'corridor of decision making'. Here also, scores vary between minus and plus four.

As the dialogue system is partly open in result and offers several cross-dialogue pathways (to switch to another topic), we had another challenge to be handled. In some cases, learners can make decisions that lead to opportunities to restart dialogue-paths that they already took. This also means that learners can receive and ask for information twice, or more often. This is not only problematic from a didactical point of view, but it would also have consequences in real life, if a loan officer asks for the same information repeatedly. Therefore, we had to safeguard that the learners always have enough formally correct alternatives to give the dialogue another direction without making a fault. If the learner anyway decides to ask the client a second time, this will lead to a negative score of one. This should be the normal and intended way for the learner.

4. CONCLUSION

As Hattie found out, "the biggest effects on student learning occur when teachers become learners of their own teaching, and when students become their own teachers. When students become their own teachers they exhibit the self-regulatory attributes that seem most desirable for learners (self-monitoring, self-evaluation, self-assessment, self-teaching). Thus, it is visible teaching and learning by teachers and students that makes the difference." (Hattie, J. 2008, p. 22) A visible scoring in this case offers the opportunity for both, teachers and learners, to reflect their own teaching and learning. Moreover, we can recently observe astonishing advances in the field of scoring and assessment in e-learning in general, and serious games and digital game-based learning in particular. This makes it possible to not focus on the evaluation of profession-related competences or closed question formats only (e.g. Hansen, O. B. et al. 2013, Vandewynchel, J. et al. 2013, Loh, C. S. et al. 2014); but rather to successfully evaluate a holistic competence development, with the ability of decision making in dynamic, complex environments as one of them. Moreover, we can foster the learners' ability to reflect on several subjects as well as on moral-ethical norms of institutions and societies, as institutionalized compliance strategies, organizational cultures, and economic changes in the world show. This complexity of the scoring system, and the interdependences in-between the different scoring layers can be visualized as follows (see Figure 2).

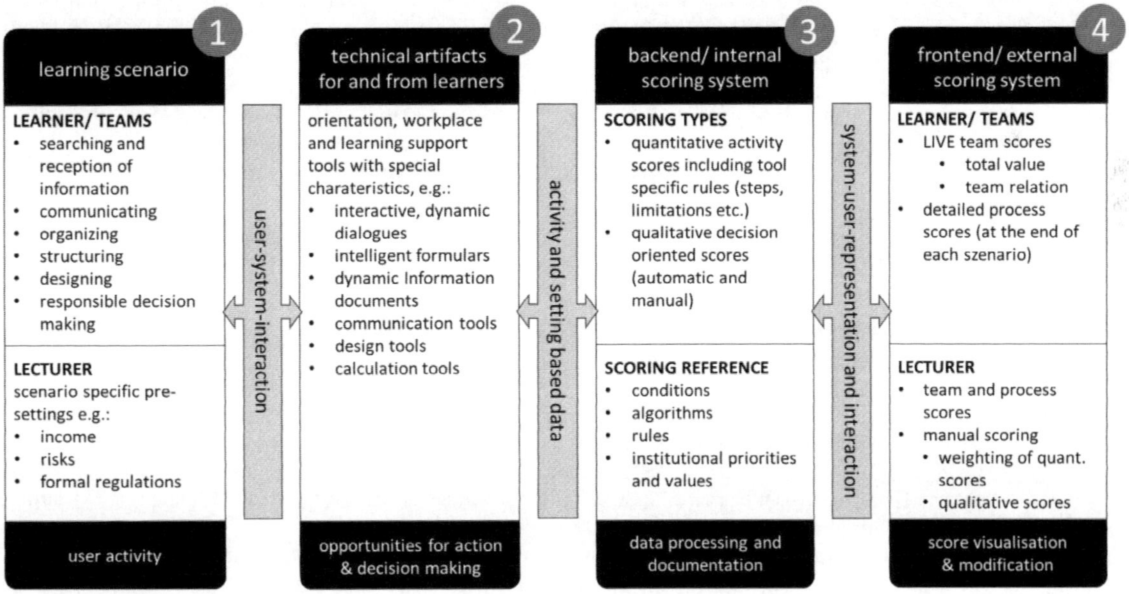

Figure 2. The systems' different layers and their interaction

In this paper, we presented a complex and variable assessment- and scoring system as a part of variable, complex, and partly open learning scenarios. It combines several scoring mechanisms like activity tracking, weighting of quantitative scores, lecturer scores for quality-driven elements, automatic quality scores for economic and strategic decisions as well as a dialogue oriented scoring system with automatic, qualitative oriented scores. Thereby, we addressed motivational goals, offered live feedback, and supported the learners' reflection on the quality of decision-making. Furthermore, the data helps the lecturer to identify the learners' strengths, and weaknesses, and to provide highly individualized feedback in reflection sessions. A specialty of the system is, that it adapts itself, based on the lecturer´s input.

Anyway, the NetEnquiry system provides data that can massively enhance the learning process by providing a valuable data basis for reflection, which is, referring to Hattie, the golden way to learn. Nevertheless, there are also shortcomings. Referring to Chung (2014) cluster-analyses could enrich our assessment system. The basic idea is to let experts play the different scenarios, which would provide us with the ideal path through the dialogues (best practice). Then, the learners' solutions can be compared with the best practices. Of course, this needs to be done with several experts. Moreover, different institutions have different organizational cultures that influence values, mind-sets, and norms, which will affect the ideal solution. This, however, needs to be considered when the same learning scenario shall be used in different organizations. We would propose to not only create one cluster-analysis per learning scenario, but to make an analysis per dialogue. The dialogues can furthermore be divided into different logical parts like, e.g. welcoming clients, asking for and recording private data, using cross-selling opportunities, etc. The paths of the learners, and thereby their decisions, can then be compared with the ideal paths, which are the results of the cluster analyses. Correlations will then give detailed information, and at the same time, the lecturer can point out and address the weaknesses of the learners more precisely for reflection sessions. However, one of the reasons why we did not make use of this approach are the costs, and the availability of enough experts that would be necessary to create a valid and reliable set of ideal pathways

Another shortcoming of the system is that we are scoring communication and social skills, but within the overall score we do not distinguish any longer. There is no opportunity for the learner to see where they got their scores from, and therefore their reflection processes cannot be as detailed as desired. However, here we have been in the trade-off of keeping the competition system clear, or providing the learners with as much data about his learning as possible. Of course, when the focus is on distance learning only, and when there are no opportunities to have reflection-sessions with the lecturers, the decision should be to provide the learner with an appropriate amount of data about his progress, and performance.

Moreover, we are thinking about clustering the scores by source to monitor, which kind of learning activities in a specific scenario leads to a small or big amount of the scores achieved. Ongoing, we are able to shift the scores given per action source. This would enables us to weight activities in relation to their relevance and learning goals within a specific scenario. However, even if the advantages in the field of assessment are astonishing, research and practice needs to come to a point where this data can be used to automatically adapt learning scenarios to the learners' needs and skills, maybe based on psychophysiological data and detected player-emotions (cf. Breuer, J. 2010, Sykes, J. 2006). Once, such approaches and measures will be taken for granted, digitalization really outscores traditional learning environments.

REFERENCES

Abt, C. C., 1970. Ernste Spiele. Lernen durch gespielte Wirklichkeit.

Becker, K. 2007. Pedagogy in Commercial Video Games. In Games and simulations in online learning. Research and development frameworks. Information Science Pub, Hershey, PA. Pp. 21-47.

Beutner, M. 2010. Authentizität als Forderung und Prinzip. Überlegungen zur dramaturgischen PLOT-Gestaltung in Lernsituationen. In: Kölner Zeitschrift für Wirtschaft und Pädagogik. Vol. 25, No. 49, Köln 2010, Pp. 123-146.

Beutner, M./ Pechuel, R. 2014. Didactical Use of Dialogues in Modern Authentic E-Learning Scenarios – Creating Dialogues in a Dialogue-Driven Learning Approach. In Proceedings of E-Learn: World Conference on E-Learning in Corporate, Government, Healthcare, and Higher Education. Pp. 171-177.

Breuer, J. 2010. Spielend lernen? Eine Bestandaufnahme zum (Digital) Game-Based Learning.

Chung, G. K. W. K. 2014. Guidelines for the Design and Implementation of Game Telemetry for Serious Games Analytics. In Serious Games Analytics, Advances in Game Based Learning. Pp. 59-79.

Hansen, O. B. et al. 2013. Emotion Recognition for Mobile Devices with a Potential Use in Serious Games for Autism Spectrum Disorder. In Serious Games Development and Applications. Springer, Heidelberg, Germany. Pp. 1-14.

Hattie 2008, Visible Learning. A Synthesis of Over 800 Meta-Analysis Relating to Achievement.

Juul, J. 2005. Half-real. Video games between real rules and fictional worlds.

Loh, C. S. et al. 2014. Serious Games Analytics: Theoretical Framework. In Serious Games Analytics, Advances in Game Based Learning. Pp. 3-29.

Loreto, I. D. et al. 2013. Supporting Crisis Training with a Mobile Game System. In Serious Games Development and Applications. Springer, Heidelberg, Germany. Pp. 165-177.

Prensky, M. 2007. Digital Game-Based Learning.

Raposo, F. et al. 2013. SimClinic – An Auxiliary Tool for Evaluation on Clinical Case Settings. In Serious Games Development and Applications. Springer, Heidelberg, Germany. Pp. 37-50.

Reetz, L. 1984. Wirtschaftsdidaktik: Eine Einführung in Theorie und Praxis wirtschaftsberuflicher Curriculumentwicklung und Unterrichtsgestaltung. Bad Heilbrunn, Germany.

Reinmann-Rothmeier, G. 2005. Blended Learning in der Lehrerbildung.Grundlagen für die Konzeption innovativer Lernumgebungen.

Rieber, L. P. (1996). Seriously Considering Play. Designing Interactive Learning Environments Based on the Blending of Microworlds, Simulations, and Games. In Educational Technology Research and Development. Vol. 44, No. 2, pp. 43-58.

Roth, H. 1971. Pädagogische Anthropologie. Bd. II. Entwicklung und Erziehung. Grundlagen einer Entwicklungspädagogik. Hannover, Germany.

Scalise, K. & Gifford, B., 2006. Computer-Based Assessment in E-Learning: A Framework for Constructing "Intermediate Constraint" Questions and Tasks for Technology Platforms. In The Journal of Technology, Learning, And Assessment, Vol. 6, No. 5.

Shute, V. J. et al., 2009. Medling the Power of Serious Games and Embeedded Assessment to Monitor and Foster Learning. Flow and Grow. In The Social Science of Serious Games: Theories and Applications. Pp. 295-321.

Sloane, P. F. E./ Dilger, B. 2005.: The Competence Clash. Dilemmata bei der Übertragung des 'Konzepts der nationalen Bildungsstandards' auf die berufliche Bildung. In: Tramm, T. / Brand, W. (Eds.): Prüfungen und Standards in der beruflichen Bildung: bwp@ ed. 8 (32 p.). Online: http://www.bwpat.de/ausgabe8/sloane_dilger_bwpat8.pdf.

Sykes, J. 2006. Affective Gaming: Advancing the Argument for Game-Based Learning. In Affective and emotional aspects of human computer interaction. Game-based and innovative learning approaches. IOS Press, Washington, USA. Pp. 3-7.

Vandewynchel, J. et al. 2013. Training Adapted to Alzheimer Patients for Reducing Daily Acitivity Errors. In Serious Games Development and Applications. Springer, Heidelberg, Germany. Pp. 28-36.

Westphal, A., 2009. Die Einbettung von Lerninhalten in Serious Games. In Herzog, M. A./ Sieck, J. (Eds.): Kultur und Informatik: Serious Games. Pp. 115-142.

CONTENT DEVELOPMENT FOR 72,000 LEARNERS: AN ONLINE LEARNING ENVIRONMENT FOR GENERAL PRACTITIONERS A CASE STUDY

Dr Dirk Pilat, FRCGP, PgDipGp (Otago), BSc (Open)
Medical Director for E-Learning
Royal College of General Practitioners
London, UK, NW1 2FB

ABSTRACT

Increasing workload due to reduced numbers of general practitioners, a population boom and an aging population has increased the need for accessible distance learning for the UK's primary care doctors. The Royal College of General Practitioners is now in its eighth year of delivering high quality e-learning to 72,000 registered users via its Online Learning Environment. In this case study we present the background around the RCGP's decision to deliver distributed continuous professional development and the workflows that enable its online learning team to produce high quality clinical continuous professional development courses for primary care.

KEYWORDS

Continuous professional development, E-Learning, General Practice, Andragogy, RCGP

1. INTRODUCTION

Patients and the wider public rightly expect the highest degree of professionalism from their physicians, but in an age in which all professions, including medicine, have seen their statue diminished, the demand for doctors who not only fulfill the traditional values of healers and sources of comfort, but also operate on the base of the latest scientific expertise is higher than ever (Cruess & Cruess, 2000). The complexity of modern medicine makes this demand ever more difficult to fulfill for the practising doctor who has to balance his work day between patient contact, administrative tasks and continuous professional development (CPD). As no newly qualified doctor's education will be sufficient to accompany him safely along the lifelong journey through medical practice, CPD is vital for patient safety (Tulinius & Holge-Hazelton, 2010). This involves responding to educational needs that arise during patient contact and continuously being up to date on the ever shifting evidence base around diagnostic and therapeutic methods. This is particularly difficult for general practitioners (GPs), who are expected to know something about everything at a time when knowledge is changing ever more quickly: while in the 1950s the doubling time for medical knowledge was approximately 50 years, this has now increased to ca 3.5 years in 2010 and is estimated to be just 73 days by 2020. This means that GPs who started practicing in 2010 by now have seen overall medical knowledge double since their graduation (Densen, 2011). At a time when overall government spending for primary care in the UK has been declining since 2005 – hitting its lowest point in 2014 – it is unsurprisingly difficult for GPs to find the time for CPD just when the UK is bucking a European trend, delivering an uncharacteristic baby boom with an increase in population of 5 million since 2001. Add to that an increased demand for primary care due to an ageing patient load with an ever increasing range of comorbidities, we have a perfect storm (Pilat, 2015). Traditionally, GPs would undertake their CPD at conferences, seminars or participating in problem based small group learning or reading professional printed journals but there just doesn't seem time for such activities. Over the last 15 years the national transition to computer-based practice management systems has effectively placed a PC on every GP's desk, presenting an opportunity for CPD to take place online (MacWalter, et al., 2016). Fortunately, GP's learning styles are very much in line with Knowle's six principles of Andragogy, as they are results oriented, self-directed, use their experience as clinicians to connect their learning, are relevancy oriented, inherently practical and highly motivated (VanNieuwenborg, et al., 2016). This makes on-line CPD such a favourable proposition, as the clinician can respond quickly to a perceived educational need that arose during a consultation without having to wait for a seminar or conference to come around. The immediacy of internet based learning is therefor one of the secrets to its success over the last 15 years and its broad uptake (MacWalter, et al., 2016). Effective and appropriate use of CPD by GPs in the United Kingdom is being assessed on a yearly base within a formative appraisal meeting between the individual GP and an appraiser - a specially trained GP from the same geographical area as the appraise - as part of an annual educational review process. The appraisal process covers six main elements: CPD, quality improvement activity, significant event analyses, feedback from colleagues, feedback from patients and review of complaints and compliments. After 5 yearly appraisal meetings in which all educational needs have been demonstrated to be met, the appraiser can then recommend that the appraise is revalidated by the regulator for the next five years (NHS Revalidation Support Team, 2014). As e-learning as a delivery method of CPD in general practice is not only popular but also both effective and highly regarded by learners (Robson, 2009) (Sandars & Walsh, 2006), the Royal College of General Practitioners (RCGP) in the United Kingdom started to produce e-learning in 2008 to provide high-quality CPD within a distant learning setting for both its members and other health professionals and now has 72,000 registered users. The RCGP is a network of more than 52,000 GPs and the voice of the profession on education, training, research and standards. It is the professional membership body and guardian of standards for family doctors in the UK, working to promote excellence in primary healthcare. The next two chapters aims to introduce the RCGPs online learning environment (OLE) and its two main branches of content delivery.

2. THE RCGP'S ONLINE LEARNING ENVIRONMENT

2.1 Essential Knowledge Updates

The concept of the Essential Knowledge Updates (EKU) programme arose from the need to provide general practitioners in the United Kingdom with a quick and accessible way of updating their knowledge on new and changing information relevant to the GP specialty and encourage effective application of the knowledge in clinical practice to enhance their skills and therefor patients' experience and care. Staffed by two part-time general practitioners and two full time administrators, the EKU team has a pool of 12 freelance authors who all work as doctors in primary care. Fully funded by membership fees and free for all of the RCGP's members, it enables GPs to meet previously identified and unrealised learning needs and enabling them to easily document their learning and application in their personal portfolio for appraisal and revalidation purposes. Written for GPs by GPs and led by dedicated EKU fellow, each Update highlights and delivers the most important new and changing information in primary care via a series of online modules and undergoes a 5 step quality assurance work flow. The topics for each individual update are chosen from a literature search by one of the RCGPs information scientist and is reduced by the lead GP for the programme from ca 300 papers and guidelines covering the last six months to about fifty, only choosing papers that are applicable for front-line general practice. These are then being voted on relevance and importance in anonymity by an editorial board of 10 academic GPs and further whittled down to ca 30. After the authors have delivered their drafts and have been edited by the EKU lead, they are being reviewed by the editorial panel before being handed back to the clinical lead for further edits. The final quality assurance (QA) round is then held by the medical director for e-learning, before being released. This multi-tiered QA process -while time-consuming-has so far prevented significant errors creeping into the content and guarantees a wide variety of views and opinions around the Updates, delivering broader content. Each Update consists of eight major items (each representing circa twenty minutes of learning) and twenty short briefings, with one update providing ca 3 hours of learning that can easily be broken up and done in various sessions. The major modules consist of self-test multiple choice questions (MCQs), text, scenarios, reflective questions, Articulate animations and practice based exercises. At the end of each major item there are suggestions for practice audits and a range of links to the module's topic. The briefings summarise new and changing knowledge in a more compact form and signpost the reader to more detailed sources. Feedback from learners is being encouraged via a five-star rating system and a free-text comment field, present throughout all of the modules. All updates are being accompanied by a podcast in which the most important aspects of the modules are discussed with the authors and by an Essential Knowledge Challenge (EKC) which encourages users to consolidate the information. This is being put together by the same group of GPs responsible for a component of the licensing exam and includes question formats as heterogeneous as Single Best Answer, Extended Matching Questions, Clinical Photograph and Statistical Graph interpretation as well as clinical algorithm flow charts (Hilton, et al., 2012). After 2 years each update is being reviewed to make sure that the clinical guidance is still up to date and -if necessary- archived or updated. Now in its 8th year, the EKU team is currently producing its 18th edition and has seen a steady growth of users over the years. As all of the RCGPs' e-learning products are being delivered via Moodle 2.7 with themes and modules having been applied uniformly across the site, it is possible to run the site with just one instructional designer and one senior web developer.

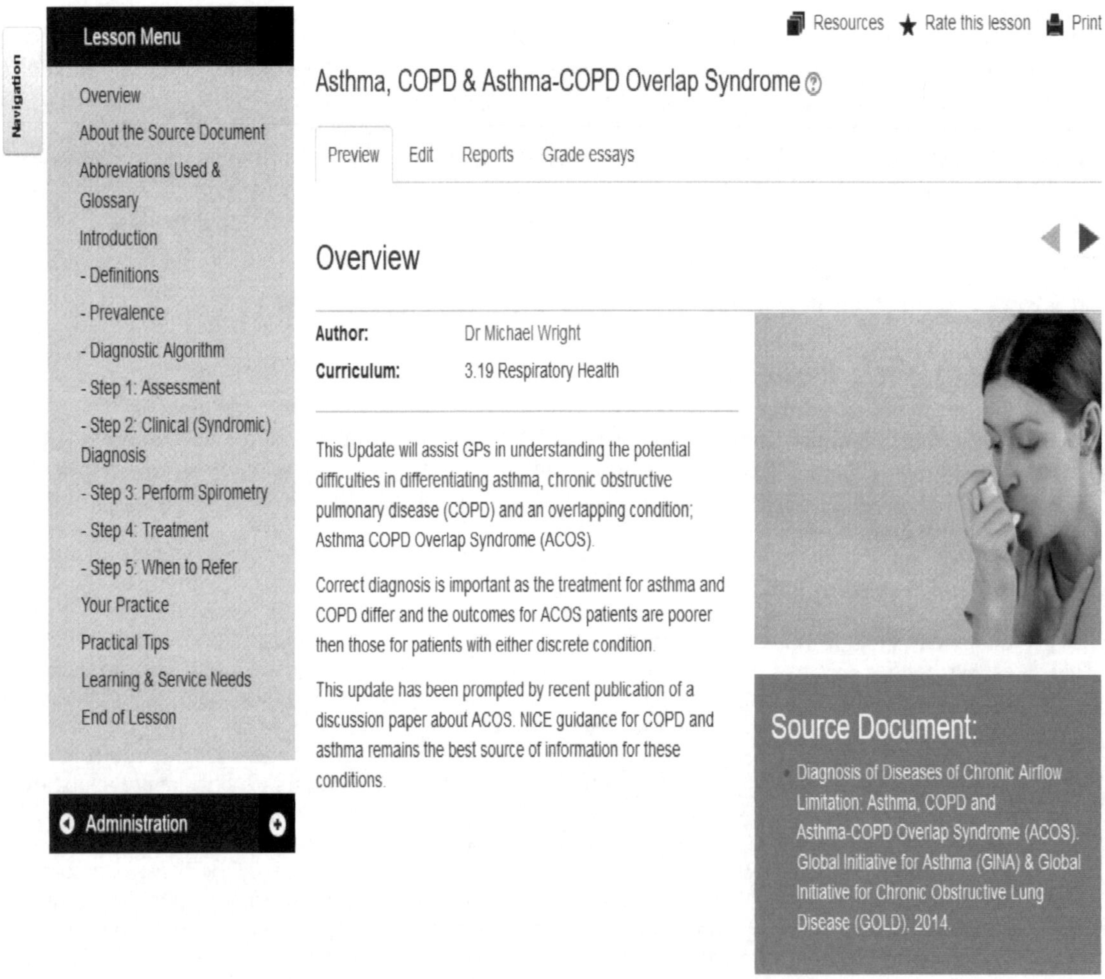

Figure 1. Example Essential Knowledge Update

2.2 Courses and Certifications

After the introduction of the Essential Knowledge Updates in 2009, it became clear that there is scope for more in-depth courses to cover the full spectrum of the GP-curriculum. These would attempt to introduce the learner to pathophysiology, epidemiology, diagnostics and treatment around the most common presentations in general practice as well as broader clinical areas. Mapped against ten RCGP's ten curriculum domains (Riley & Haynes, 2007) – each describing an aspect of general practice, forming a useful framework for learning the fundamentals of primary care – they function as both stand-alone courses for primary care physicians to use as CPD, and reference courses to 'dip in' when needed.

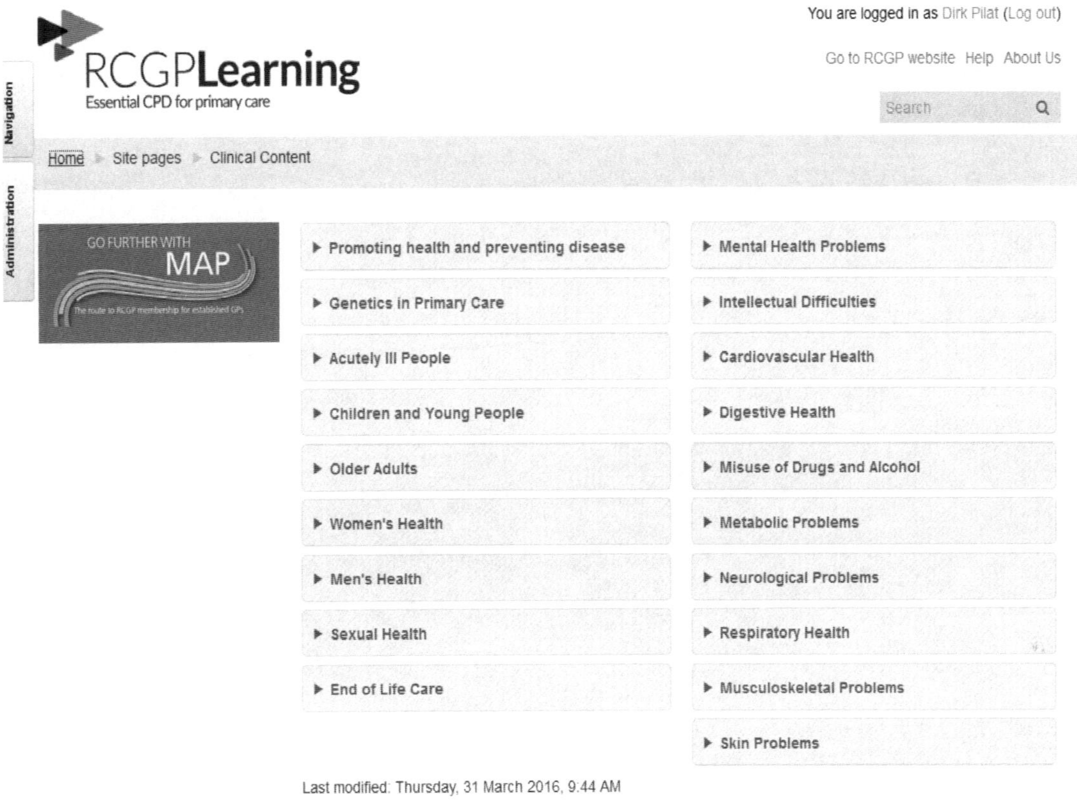

Figure 2. Clinical menu of courses and certifications

In comparison to the Essential Knowledge Updates, courses and blended learning are fully third party funded, hence production of new material usually arises from discussions with public health bodies such as NHS England or Public Health England, charities or pharmaceutical companies. Due to the third party funding, the RCGP is able to make the courses available for members and non-members alike and can often respond to clinical needs that arise in response to a national discussion around particular pertinent health issues such as Dementia, Hyperlipidaemia or health problems being discussed in the popular media, causing health uncertainties in vast ranges of the population, such as coeliac disease. A staff of four administrators works in close cooperation with five part time e-learning fellows and the medical director for e-learning who are all practising general practitioners. Production of a course usually follows a six step quality assurance workflow, starting with a scoping meeting of a peer review group (often a teleconference), in which interested general practitioners, specialists, the funders of the course, a GP author and a GP editor decide on the content and produce a scoping document. After the scoping document is being signed off by the peer review group, a GP author – in cooperation with an experienced editor – produces a first draft which is forwarded to the peer review group for the first round of comments. After incorporation of comments and suggestions, the course will be built on the OLE's Moodle platform, after which it will undergo a second round of peer reviews, mainly focused on the instructional design. The course will then again be adapted to incorporate the comments of the peer review group, before it will be quality assured by the medical director for e-learning and launched. Just like for EKU, this multilayered review-process ensures not only the content being appropriate for a broad primary care based audience, but also removes factual mistakes. With the learning objectives clearly defined at the beginning of each course, a finished module usually incorporates reflective questions, case-studies, a pre-and post-test and will provide the learner with a certificate for his revalidation portfolio once the post-test has been passed. Each module is being reviewed and updated every two years by a clinician with a special clinical interest the module is covering to make sure the content remains valid and up to date. There are now 79 courses online with 22 further in current production.

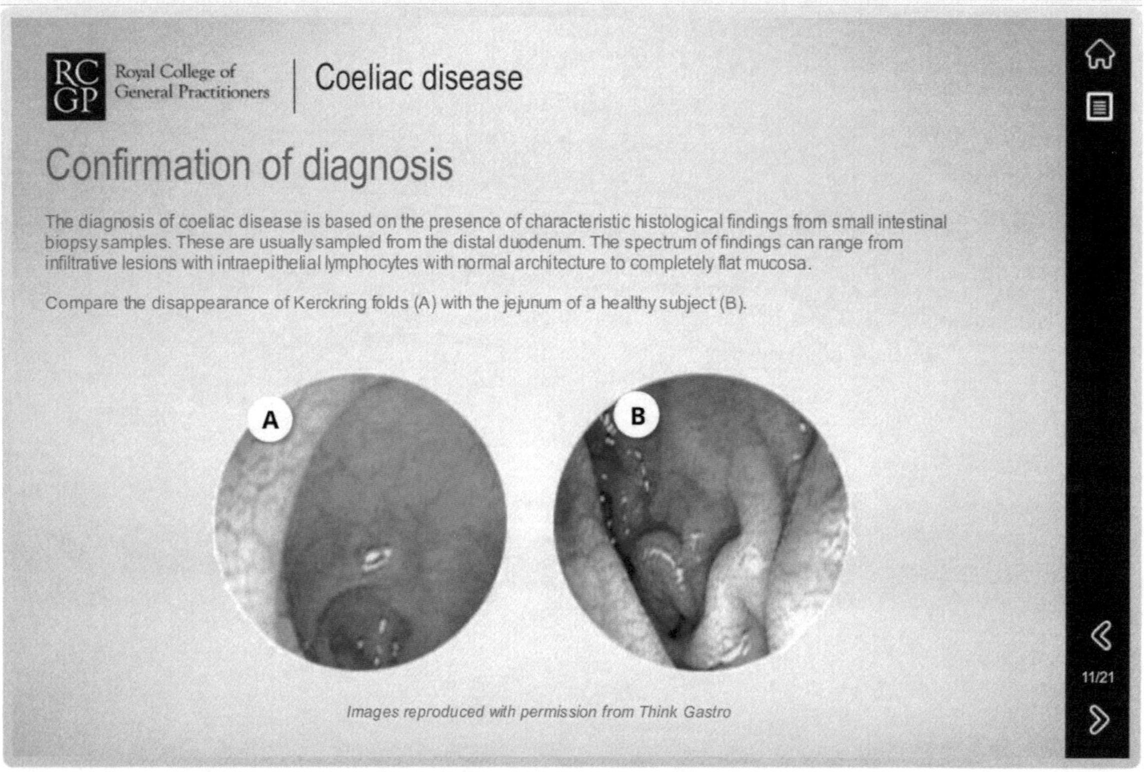

Figure 3. Example page from OLE course

2.3 Usage

Since its inception, the RCGP's OLE has been growing consistently, with unique users growing year on year from 9213 in 2009 to 30,938 in 2015 and it now has 72,000 registered users. Two qualitative evaluations of EKU and the OLE concluded that both compare favorably to other health related e-learning providers in terms of content and interactivity, with both topics and type of e-learning being unique to the market (Hilton, et al., 2012) (Cavill, 2015). A survey based evaluation of one the courses on improving prescribing in primary care in 2015 showed learners overwhelmingly agreeing that the use of the OLE not only increased their knowledge on prescribing, but also improved their skills at prescribing safely (Knox, et al., 2015). Both branches of the OLE are being used for both CPD and even in pre-specialty education (Hilton, et al., 2012).

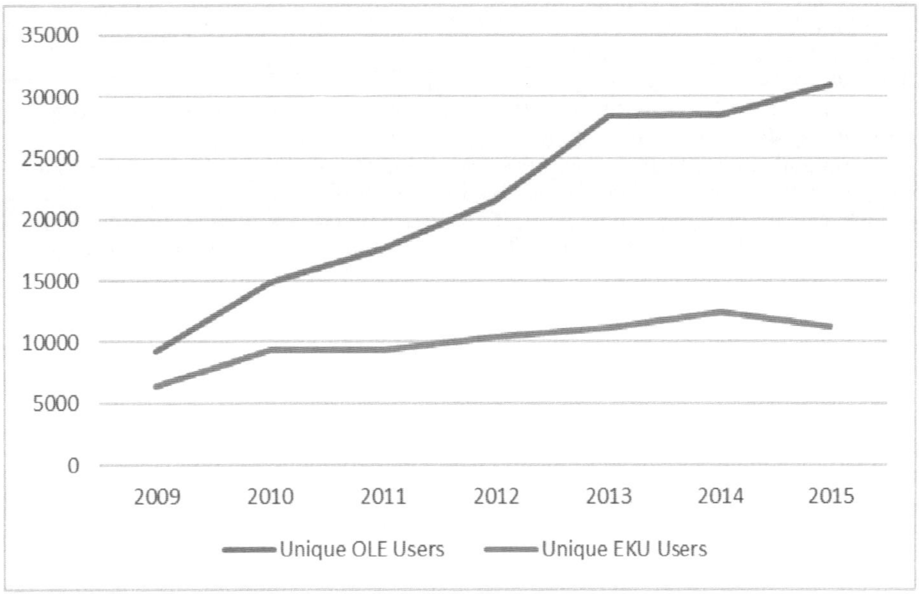

Figure 4. Year on year growth of RCGP online CPD

3. CONCLUSION

The RCGP's OLE demonstrates clearly that a small, mixed team of committed clinicians and admin staff can consistently produce high quality, highly rated CPD in a very competitive environment, thanks to clear and unambiguous workflows. This means that 72,000 registered health care professionals can not only fulfill their regulatory duties and stay up to date but also continuously improve patient care in highly challenging environment for general practice.

ACKNOWLEDGEMENT

Many thanks to Professor Sean Hilton and Annemary O'Dwyer for their suggestions.

REFERENCES

Cavill, M., 2015. *RCGP Online Learning Environment Research Project Report,* London: RCGP.

Cruess, S. R. & Cruess, R. L., 2000. Professionalism: a contract between medicine and society. *Canadian Medical Association Journal,* 162(5), pp. 668-669.

Densen, P., 2011. Challenges and Opportunities Facing Medical Education. *Transactions of the American Clinical and Climatological Association,* Issue 122, pp. 48-58.

Hilton, S., Pilat, D., Turnbull, C. & Milosevic, D., 2012. *Report on the Essential Knowledge Update Programme,* London: Royal College of General Practitioners.

Knox, R. et al., 2015. *Evaluation of an on-line learning moduleto improve prescribing in primary care,* Nottingham: University of Nottingham.

MacWalter, G., McKay, J. & Bowie, P., 2016. Utilisation of internet resources for continuing professional development: a cross-sectional survey of general practitioners in Scotland. *BMC Medical Education,* 16(24).

NHS Revalidation Support Team, 2014. *Medical Appraisal Guide,* London: NHS.

Pilat, D., 2015. Access and the great socioeconomic divide. In: R. CHarlton, ed. *Compassion, Continuity and Caring in the NHS.* London: RCGP, pp. 15-20.

Riley, B. & Haynes, J., 2007. Introducing the GP curriculum. *GP*, 21 September, p. 33.

Robson, J., 2009. Web-based learning strategies in combination with published guidelines to change practice of primary care professionals. *British Journal of General Practice,* 59(559), pp. 104-109.

Sandars, J. & Walsh, K., 2006. e-learning for general practitioners: lessons from the recent literature. In: J. Sandar, ed. *e-Learning for GP-Educators.* Milton Keynes: Radcliffe Publishing, pp. 8-13.

Tulinius, C. & Holge-Hazelton, B., 2010. Continuing professional development for general practitioners: supporting the development of professionalism. *Medical Education,* Issue 44, pp. 412-420.

VanNieuwenborg, L., Goossens, M., De Lepeleire, J. & Schoenmakers, B., 2016. Continuing medical education for general practitioners: a practice format. *Postgraduate Medical Journal,* Volume 0, pp. 1-6.

FIRST STAGES OF ADULT STUDENTS' RELATIONSHIP TO SCIENTIFIC KNOWING AND RESEARCH IN THE OPEN UNIVERSITY`S WEB-BASED METHODOLOGY COURSE

Leena Isosomppi and Minna Maunula
University of Jyvaskyla, Kokkola University Consortium Chydenius, P.O. Box 567, FI-67701 Kokkola, Finland

ABSTRACT

The adult students who participate in the web-based studies of the open university have in many ways heterogeneous starting points for studying and learning, for example, the educational backgrounds, the acquired work experience, the general academic skills and the objectives of the future can vary considerably. The adult students striving from the different starting points pursue their own individual objectives and the set educational dimensions of the academic education.

In the academic adult education, individuality and the adult student's autonomy are emphasized and at the same time, diverse knowledge, skills and understanding are sought after. One key objective of the higher education is the development of the scientific thinking and refining of personal epistemology and the readiness for their complementary reflection. The personal relationship of an adult student to the scientific knowledge and, at the same time, the academic identity are based dialogically and process-like in the dynamic and complex interaction field of cognitive, emotional and social factors. The adult student's genuine and profound learning experience touches personal epistemology and is strongly connected to the individual's meta-cognitive and cognitive processes. Furthermore, the feelings which are related to the adult student's study and the social life field are involved in the process.

In our article we examine the open university's adult students' personal relationship to science and to scientific knowledge which is structured gradually and in a process-like fashion. The examination adheres to the situation at the beginning of the open university e-learning course in qualitative methodology and on the students' own reflection. We focus the examination on those adult students who did not have earlier experience of carrying out research or of the methodology of qualitative research when the course in qualitative methodology began. The research material consists of the learning diaries the students (N= 41) kept during the course, the diaries which were also a part of the course work. From the material, five different personal, academic science relationships crystallize through a material based content analysis: outsider, superficial, timid, critical realist and user of the expert knowledge. Finally we present e-pedagogical conclusions as a summary of how the adults' learning process can be supported when aiming for the thinking which integrates personal everyday knowledge and scientific knowledge and how the commitment to the development of one's own thinking can be reinforced.

KEYWORDS

Adult learners, web-based learning, open university, personal epistemology, relationship to science.

1. THE CONSTRUCTION OF THE ADULT STUDENT'S PERSONAL RELATIONSHIP TO SCIENCE

The research field of scientific thinking and epistemology is wide and scattered both theoretically and methodologically (Buehl & Alexander 2001; Hofer 2004; Khine 2008). However, the different trends have been united by their strong tradition of theory which connects them to cognitive and developmental psychology. The empirical studies concerning personal epistemology have often applied to the university students (for example, Brownlee et al. 2009; Fulmer 2014; Richer & Schmid 2010; Spray et al. 2013) or teachers (Felbrich et al. 2008; Borg 2009), whereas the special starting points relating to epistemology and to the personal relationship to science of the adult students or particularly of the open university students have apart from some exceptions (Kasworm 2003; Kasworm 2008; Kallio 2011; King & Kitchener 2004) received little attention. The researchers of academic adult education are calling for better attention to be paid than before to the the adults' life fields (work, studying, family etc.) and adult students' earlier knowledge and experience (Malinen 2000) in the research concerning the epistemic beliefs and academic study. (Kasworm 2003; 2008.)

From the point of view of learning, the epistemic reduction of personal relationship to science which concerns scientific knowledge merely to the cognitive examination ignores emotional and social dimensions of learning which are essential from the point of view of an adult's learning experience. As the criticism of the purely cognitive basic starting point the opinions have emerged with education philosophical and sociological orientation, and in these the theoretical and methodological changes are proposed or required for the research of the epistemic beliefs and epistemology. The research tradition which stems from psychology has been criticized for the objectifying theories and models with similarities to personality theories and at the same time the writers who have orientated philosophically have tried to extend this research in the direction which takes into consideration the holistic conception of man and the contextual nature of thought. (Niessen et al. 2008.)

These additions concerning the starting points and processes of learning open new opportunities also for the examination of the personal *science relationship* of an adult university student. Then the dimension of learning which is related to scientific thinking and epistemology can be examined - not only as a cognitive development continuum or as a belief dimensions - but above all as a *personal relationship to scientific knowledge and knowing which is constructed individually and in process-like fashion in the adult student's life*. This kind of hermeneutic approach which aims for understanding binds the cognitive dimension to be a part of the adult's life field and relationship to science.

The beginning of the academic studies or of the study module is a stage which is central from the point of view of building the science relationship. At the orientation stage the adult student evaluates the possible meaningfulness of the future study process and one's personal commitment to the contents to be studied. The students reflect upon and evaluate their starting points, the demands of the study module and the support available. In an open university, the student's personal situation in life, possibly the new demands of e-learning and the physical detachment from the place of study and from the studying community restrict this commitment. These factors together with the earlier studying experiences and with the own capability beliefs have an effect on the personal significance network concerning the studies and the life field taking shape. An adult student also builds the personal relationship to science in this life field in the interaction with the teacher and possibly with other students. In our study we focus on examining the beginning stage of the web-based study module which is important from the point of view of the studies and the construction of the relationship to science.

2. WEB-BASED METHODOLOGY COURSE OF THE OPEN UNIVERSITY AS THE CONTEXT OF BUILDING THE RELATIONSHIP TO SCIENCE

Equal and individual supervision and treatment of students are connected to the basic values of the open university education which is a context of this study. In the starting points of the open university studies the clear restrictions and conditions are also realized, to which attention must be paid in the organization of the education and in the teaching of contents. The education is web-based and the assignments are applied in which case an adult student's earlier knowledge, practical experiences and new knowledge can bind themselves seamlessly and authentically (Malinen 2000) to each other. The pedagogical objective is to make profound learning possible and to help adult students to realize the stages of their own learning process – especially concerning personal epistemology.

In the article the novice students of the open university and their personal relationships to science are examined at the first stage of the methodology course. The methodology course of qualitative study (5 credits) in question was a compulsory part of the pedagogical candidate study module. The methodology courses are a central part of academic education in many ways. Students should at this stage at the latest become conscious of the processes of scientific knowledge, realize the demands of science and at the same time they should adopt the concrete stages of the study process and acquire the skills for carrying out a small-scale study. The contents and skills that have been adopted at the earlier stages of studies are set as the subject of the conscious examination and at the same time the students have to think about their own relationship to scientificity and to scientific knowledge.

3. METHODOLOGY

3.1 Research Task

The purpose of the study was to clarify how the novice students of the open university position themselves in relation to scientific knowledge and to research at the beginning of the web-based methodology course.

Term novice students refers in this study to the students at the first stage of the pedagogical studies of the open university who according to their own learning diary, do not have earlier experience or have only a little theoretical knowledge of writing a scientific thesis of research practices.

3.2 Learning Diaries as Research Material

The study module of qualitative methodology was implemented as a whole as web-based. The teaching consisted of recorded lectures, live and recorded supervision, the learning diary and online examination. The learning diaries written by the students during the study module were used as the research material. The learning diary consisted of five parts of assignments which progressed according to the qualitative research process. Furthermore, the students were given instructions to record their own thoughts in the form of a diary in connection to the contents of the study module. The literature and the lectures of the study module were to be utilized in the learning diary so that the student's own reflection of the contents was at its centre.

The initial instructions were to examine one's own relationship to scientific information and to carrying out research. With this, an attempt was made to get the students to think about the research orientation just through their own everyday conceptions and their concrete relationship. The examination of this dimension opens meta-cognitive processes and enables the "thinking aloud" -reflection from personal understanding and academic perspective on the central contents. From the learning diaries of all the students of the study module (N=63) we chose the more exact examination such as adult students' learning diaries, who in their diaries told about their very limited experience and knowledge of writing a scientific theses (N=41). In the learning diary both the thoughts on scientific contents of the study module as well as the personal considerations concerning learning and relationship to science are combined. The learning diary text served both as the assignment of the study module to be assessed and as a tool for the student's self-assessment.

3.3 Analysis

The method of analysis of the material is a inductive content analysis. In the content analysis the researcher triangulation was utilized. The dialogical analysis and the discussions of the two researcher-teachers who had taught the study module in question diversified and strengthened the hermeneutic understanding and interpretation process of the subject in carrying out the content analysis. The material was interpreted from the point of view of study questions by classifying the significant contents, in other words, the personal positioning of the scientificity and connections of contents.

4. RESULTS

4.1 The Adult Student's Personal Positioning to Scientific Knowledge and to Research

The first task in the learning diary brought out the students' own positioning in relation to scientificity and to scientific knowledge. In the analysis process five different positionings and relationships of importance in relation to science and scientificity of the adult students' were formed: outsider, superficial, timid, critical realist and user of the expert knowledge, these are examined in more detail in the following subsections.

4.1.1 Relating to Science as an Outsider

The adult students who regard themselves as outsiders to the science (N: 7) and to making science position themselves far from the science. Science and scientific operation, especially the qualitative study raised critical thoughts also in these students. The students didn't have a personal relationship to science and to scientific operation or the relationship was very brittle. On the other hand, a small number of the students told that they had carried out a small-scale "research" by themselves in their earlier vocational studies, however, it wasn't the case of the actual research in an academic sense.

The students relating as outsiders to science and scientificity knew how to use the basic terminology which is related to the research processes but they mainly presented opinions. The language used was ordinary, shaped as recall or wonder. The students thought about the research operation on the basis of their own criteria and by simplifying. The adult students who had defined themselves as outsiders were aware of their own attitudes, which is positive from the point of view of the progress of the learning process. Critical attitude and relating as an outsider did not form into a negative or down-playing attitude but instead into a challenging personal starting point in regards to the learning process.

Some of the students who defined themselves as outsiders in relation to science did not present a personal relationship to science at all in their learning diaries but they described general significances in connection to scientificity.

"It is important to do research. It usually gives reliable information about a matter because there are certain criteria on how research has to be carried out. The research studies are usually controlled by a body. Research provides such information that otherwise would not necessarily be obtained."

As their objective for the study module the students determined the analysis of the basic stages of the research process and becoming acquainted with carrying out a research study. At times an image was created of passing the studies and of the instrumental value of the contents to be studied based on the students' thoughts. The contentual significance of learning from the point of view of broadening one's own understanding was not conveyed.

4.1.2 Relating Superficially to Science

A superficial attitude to research activities and to scientific knowledge also prevailed (N: 3). These students defined research activity as close operation for themselves, as easy to approach and to execute. According to them, nowadays there is so much research available that every one can find an interesting research for themselves or can create such research. In an academic sense these students did not have experience of the scientific research process, but their experiences were based on the dissertations in vocational studies. The stages of the process of the scientific operation and the central concepts were tentatively and selectively structured for the students having a superficial relationship to science.

"Scientific research is, in my opinion, a matter which is based on some information that has already been researched earlier. Furthermore, there is the person's own interest in the matter which they want to clarify, for example, with questionnaires, interviews, observations etc. The researcher finds out about the matters that other people have researched earlier. The purpose of the study in my opinion is to prove the right and wrong of something, and to prove something to be true".

Research was defined as human operation which is a part of the ordinary everyday life. The students relating superficially to science determined science useful because it would give useful hints for everyday life and would save time. However, according to the students who related to science superficially, all research information was not thought to be good for everybody because "ignorance is bliss".

The students' attitude was mainly emotional excitement and partly professional reinforcement. The critical attitude to the processes of making science was minor or non-existent. Also the critical examination of one's own knowledge relating to research was minor, and one's own positioning to science and to carrying out research was light, even arrogant. The language used was in places over-complex and unclear which for its part portrayes the superficial level of understanding of the contents. At the first stage of the studies the reflection on one's own knowledge and new learning was minor.

4.1.3 Relating Timidly to Science

Some of the students related timidly to scientificity and the work in the field of science (N: 5). They stated repeatedly how research was difficult and distant and the concepts difficult to understand. They presented strong simplifications of what research is and what it is not. Research was organized in their perceptions to be a bunch of rules and instructions to be followed.

"The feeling was at first a little uncertain. The book was extremely difficult to read, in my opinion, containing many difficult words and concepts. Sometimes it seemed that even quite simple matters had been written in a seriously difficult to understand form. I had to "translate Finnish language" into Finnish for myself."

The adult students who related timidly to the science had "bumped" into the research results in connection with their studies or in the Internet. Some were wondering, how elements relating to research could be connected in everyday work and can a person with academic education be competent enough in their work without the knowledge and skills relating to research. In addition to timid, the general positioning to science and the processes relating to research was both respectful and sceptical. Earlier, the attitude had still been more strictly doubtful towards science and the orientation to research had even raised irritation. On the other hand, research and the researchers also inspired respect.

According to these adult students, there was a need for scientific knowledge in a developing society but they did not justify this in more detail. Their relationship to the scientific processes was complicated and unclear, and with the limited understanding, the emotional reaction was pronouncedly fearful. The more exact analysis of the research orientation was not achieved in the learning diary because the examination fluctuated in attempting to define general research regulation and in contemplation of their own emotional and inadequate knowledge.

"This subject seems chaotic, difficult to determine and vague. I can't get a hold on anything. I looked at the assignments and even don't even know what I don't know. I cannot ask when I don't know what I don't know."

The students who related timidly to the processes of science told their own objectives to be low at the beginning of the study module, the objective was to pass the course.

4.1.4 Relating Critically to Science

Critical realists (N: 21) position themselves realistically in relation to scientific information and processes of carrying out scientific work. They were aware of having the command of the basics but they still had a great deal to learn. The concepts which are related to research were used with caution and uncertainty and they wanted to learn them better. Students realistically realized their own knowledge and skill levels.

It was the critical realist's central objective to learn more of the research process, to understand its significance and to know how to use the relevant concepts. The knowledge of research methods was also evaluated as an instrumental value: one would proceed in the studies though learning the research methods, for example, one could prepare and gain the concrete skills for the Bachelor's thesis. At the same time, the students told about everyday challenges of time management and that everything would not be be learned during the study module anyway. The science relationship of these students had earlier been terrified, critical and skeptical, but studying the subject with the other students and the positive feedback had made their attitudes towards their own knowledge and skills more trusting.

"I am already eagerly expecting my own Bachelor's thesis where I am able for the first time to research a matter that interests me. However, I have noticed that the scientific research is an exact job, many different matters must be taken into consideration. I expect that I will learn the characteristics of the qualitative study and the basic principles of the progress of the research process. My learning motivation is at its top because the study module prepares me for carrying out my own study. I hope that when this course ends, I will have such knowledge and skills that I would know how to conduct a qualitative study by myself.."

The critical realist's attitude to scientific knowledge was partly critical and relative, partly also emotional and was based on early images. Research was not defined as difficult but challenging and interesting. The choices which are part of the research process were evaluated through their own starting points, not from the point of view of the phenomenon to be examined. The considerations on scientificity processed research choices suitable for oneself, an individual way to operate as well as the familiar concrete stages of carrying out research. The language used was simplified and based partly on opinions. In considering the own relationship to science the emotional approach and the features of the scientific process were present simultaneously and alternately. Students' own objectives with respect to the contents of the study module were presented with care.

4.1.5 Utilizing Scientific Knowledge as Experts

Some of the adult students of the study module (N: 5) told that they were using the information produced by the experts in their work or they were participating in the development projects relating to research even though they were not conducting actual research as their work. They had practical everyday understanding of the progress of the research process: interviews, acquisition of the project funding and the stages of development projects. The everyday experience and scientificity were seen as strengthening each other and their relationship as dialogic.

"I had years of fruitful educational cooperation with my researcher colleague. We obtained the explanation for many practical phenomena which I had perceived already for years without, however, knowing why this happens. It has been interesting to see in these research projects how the practical everyday knowledge transforms into research knowledge which is scientifically proven. It has also gone differently at times and the everyday knowledge was overturned to be the wrong belief, which has also been a significant matter from the point of view of the learning."

" I have worked for my whole adult life with different project funding for my whole adulthood and have participated in different development projects. Only afterwards as have I learned more about the research methods I have been able to name clear stages and methods in the processes."

The users of the expert knowledge expected that their understanding relating to research would continue increasing further. They described significant learning experiences which they had acquired during the study module, even though the research elements of the work context had already existed for years. According to the students' experience the studies and the work together had made the forming of a deeper understanding possible: the research elements they had met in practice received a name and a meaning in the methodology studies and, on the other hand, the contents to be studied were meaningful from the start and they could be practically perceived. The research orientation was familiar to them and part of the everyday development work. These adult students positioned themselves as a part of scientific practices and processes. They trusted their own skills realistically and wanted to be involved in research operation.

4.2 As Novice on the Fringes of the Academic Community

The adults novice students' position on the fringes of the academic community of practice and their relationship to academic knowledge and practices that are constructed during the studies of the open university can be understood and conceptualized from the starting points of the situated learning theory (Lave & Wenger 1991). The results that have been described above show that for the student's who position themselves as the users of the scientific knowledge, the expert identity makes it possible already for some of the adult students to have a deeper involvement than others in the practices and policies of the academic community. The students who were critical users of the expert knowledge and who described their relationship to science realistically showed stronger meta-consciousness in regard to their own relationship to science and their thinking than the other students. The transition to the circle of academic education in the open university for the first time can in turn create pressure and negative feelings for some of the adult students in regard to academic identity, own situation in life and connecting it with the studies (Askham 2008; O'Donnel & Tobbel 2007). However, the majority of the adult students positioned themselves realistically and critically to science and its knowledge practices. This positioning was based on their confidence in their own learning and their belief on the gradual construction of the personal relationship to science which will take place in the future.

In the open university, sharing the culture of the academic scientificity and the web-based participation in the independent distance learning are problematical from the starting points of adults' different everyday contexts. The experience of the personal involvement in the processes of the science is, however, one of the central objectives of studies. It is important to support the finding of connections between scientific knowledge and knowledge practices and of one's own personal life circle in web-based academic adult education (Isosomppi & Maunula 2014; Maunula & Isosomppi 2015.)

5. CONCLUSIONS

The different science relationships and positionings which have been organized in the analysis process of learning diaries are important information for planning the teaching and for the wholeness of pedagogical solutions. Adult students benefit from the versatile support in web-based studies (also Ke & Xie 2009; Ke 2010). By paying attention to the different starting points and needs, cognitive and social support as well as adaptive tools can be offered.

Participation in online interaction should be encouraged and supported. The construction of a personal relationship to science requires socio-cultural knowledge about web-based academic community and its practices and language (Eraut 2004; Tynjälä 2008). Teacher presence in an online course in this sense is important in the construction of the web-based learning community (Garrison & Cleveland-Innes 2005). Participation in the web-based learning community would be particularly important for the students who feel like outsiders or are timid in relation to science. At its best, the interaction supports the adoption of reflective thinking and makes it possible to deal with the feelings and thoughts raised by the studies in a socially safe atmosphere.

The balance between structuredness and interactivity in online course design needs to be considered. An online course design model should involve online interaction but simultaneously support adult students studying in both online and offline learning settings (Ke & Xie 2009). The interaction is often minor in the web-based academic adult education, as it was also in the methodology course which is the context of this study. One can indeed ponder to what extent minor interaction, and the learning diary which has encouraged personal reflection, direct the students to write their own considerations making them visible in the learning diary. Do the discussions of traditional lectures transfer to the learning diaries and does the quiet reflection make it also possible for the more uncertain students to venture into the written presentation of their thoughts? Different e-pedagogical solutions have clear strengths and weaknesses.

However, it is important to offer different ways to encourage adult students for the meta-cognitive processes and for the active construction of personal relationship to science. The different web-based cognitive tools and adaptive learning systems could be an advantage in this (Jonassen 2014; Tsai 2004; Tseng et al. 2008). The reflection on personally and individually developing knowledge and skills is central in order for the profound learning and the attachment of the learned content to the authentic contexts to take place (also Ke & Xie 2009). In the near future just the adaptive web-based tools could help to recognise the levels of knowledge and skills, the strengths and weaknesses even more strongly and offer individually meaningful inputs.

In order for the personal relationship to scientific knowledge to deepen, the profound personal considerations must genuinely be given room for and there needs to be a meaningful context during the web-based course. This is made possible when the adult students are provided opportunities to connect and to actively utilize the knowledge capital they have already acquired as well as their own meta-cognitive processes and contents to be studied (Hofer 2004; Malinen 2000). The individual participation and meaningfulness can be carried out by emphasizing the content reference of the material to be studied. The subjectivity of the material to be studied, the meaningfulness of the tasks and the applicability of the contents to be learned are the central e-pedagogical principles in this process. E-pedagogical solutions direct the students to operate online and in addition to this, the freedom and the wholeness of the learning process need to be remembered: learning takes place on several levels regardless of time and place. The construction of the personal relationship to science is not limited to the web-based environment or to the study module about the subject.

REFERENCES

Askham, P., 2008. Context and Identity: Exploring Adult Learners' Experience of Higher Education. *In Journal of Further and Higher Education,* Vol. 32, No 1, pp. 85-97.

Borg, S., 2009. English Language Teachers' Conceptions of Research. *In Applied Linguistics,* Vol. 30, No. 3, pp. 358-388.

Browlee, J. et al, 2009. The First Year University Experience: Using Personal Epistemology to Understanding Effective Learning and Teaching in Higher Education. *In High Educ,* Vol. 58, pp. 599-618.

Buehl, M. M. & Alexander, P. A., 2001. Beliefs About Academic Knowledge. *In Educational Psychology Review,* Vol 13, No. 4, pp. 385-416.

Eraut, M., 2004. Informal Learning in the Workplace. *In Studies in Continuing Education,* Vol. 26 No. 2, pp. 247-273.

Felbrich, A. et al, 2008. Epistemological Beliefs Concerning the Nature of Mathematics among Teacher Educators and Teacher Education Students in Mathematics. *In ZDM,* Vol. 40, No. 5, pp. 763-776.

Fulmer, G. W., 2014. Undergraduates' Attitudes toward Science and Their Epistemological Beliefs: Positive Effects of Certainty and Authority Beliefs. *In J Sci Educ Technol,* Vol. 23, pp. 198-206.

Garrison, D., R. and Cleveland-Innes, M., 2005. Facilitating Cognitive Presence in Online Learning Interacting Is Not Enough. *In American Journal of Distance Education,* Vol. 19, No. 3, pp. 133-148.

Hofer, B., 2004. Introduction: Paradigmatic Approaches to Personal Epistemology. *In Educational Psychologist*, Vol. 39, No. 1, pp. 1-3.

Isosomppi, L. and Maunula, M., 2014. Adult Students in Web-based Thesis Seminars: Insights and Challenges for Supervision. *Proceedings of MAC-ETeL 2014.* Prague, Czech Republic, pp. 1-8.

Jonassen, D., 2014. Using Cognitive Tools to Represent Problems. *In Journal of Research on Technology in Education*, Vol. 35, No. 3, pp. 362-381.

Kallio, E., 2011. Integrative Thinking in the Key: An Evaluation of Current Research into the Development of Adult Thinking. *In Theory & Psychology*, Vol. 21, pp. 785-801.

Kasworm, C. E., 2003. Adult Meaning Making in the Undergraduate Classroom. *In Adult education Quarterly* , Vol. 53, No. 2, pp. 81-98.

Kasworm, C. E., 2008. Emotional Challenges of Adult Learners in Higher Education. *In New Directions for Adult and Continuing Education* 120. Vol. 2008, No. 120, pp. 27-34. (Online) Available from: http://interscience.wiley.com

Ke, F. & Xie, K., 2009. Toward Deep Learning for Adult Students in Online Courses. *In Internet and Higher Education*. Vol. 12, pp. 136-145.

Ke, F., 2010. Examining Online Teaching, Cognitive, and Social Presence for Adult Students. *In Computers & Education.* Vol 55, pp. 808-820.

Khine, M. S. (Ed.), 2008. *Knowing, knowledge and beliefs: Epistemological Studies across Diverse Cultures*. Springer, Dordrecht, Netherlands.

King, P. M. & Kitchener, S. K., 2004. Reflective Judgment: Theory and Research on the Development of Epistemic Assumptions Through Adulthood. *In Educational Psychologist*, Vol. 39, No. 1, pp. 5-18.

Lave, J. and Wenger, E., 1991. *Situated Learning: Legitimate Peripheral Participation.* Cambridge University Press, Cambridge, UK.

Malinen, A., 2000. *Towards the Essence of Adult Experiential Learning: A Reading of the Theories of Knowles, Kolb, Mezirow, Revans and Schön*. Ph.D. thesis, University of Jyväskylä, Finland.

Maunula, M. and Isosomppi, L., 2015. Developing Web-Based Academic Adult Education: Learning Experiences as Starting Points for Planning and for Continuous Development. *In The International Journal of Interdisciplinary Educational Studies*, Vol. 10, No. 2, pp. 27-37.

Niessen, T. et al., 2008. Contemporary Epistemological Research in Education. Reconciliation and Reconceptualization of the Field. *In Theory & Psychology*, Vol. 18, No. 1, pp. 27-45.

O'Donnel, V. L. & Tobbell, J., 2007. The Transition of Adult Students to Higher Education: Legitimate Peripheral Participation in a Community of Practice? *In Adult Education Quarterly*, Vol. 57, No. 4, pp. 312-328.

Richter, T. and Schmid, S., 2010. Epistemological Beliefs and Epistemic Strategies in Self-Regulated Learning. *In Metacognition Learning*, Vol. 5, pp. 47-65.

Spray, E. et al., 2013. Personal Epistemological and Metacognitive Awareness in First Year Preservice Education Students. *In Australian Journal of Educational & Developmental Psychology,* Vol. 13, pp. 44-57.

Tsai, C.-C., 2004. Beyond Cognitive and Metacognitive Tools: The Use of The Internet as an 'Epistemological Tool' for Instruction. *In British Journal of Educational Technology,* Vol. 35, No. 5, pp. 525-536.

Tseng, J.C.R. et al., 2008. Development of an Adaptive Learning System with Two Sources of Personalization Information. *In Computers and Education*, Vol. 51, No. 2, pp. 776-786.

Tynjälä, P., 2009. Connectivity and Transformation in Work-Related Learning - Theoretical Foundations. In M.-L. Stenström & P. Tynjälä (eds.*), Towards Integration of Work and Learning. Strategies for Connectivity and Transformation*, pp. 11-37. Springer, Dordrecht, Netherlands.

A QUANTITATIVE ANALYSIS OF THE ROLE OF SOCIAL NETWORKS IN EDUCATIONAL CONTEXTS

Azam Shokri and Georgios Dafoulas
Computer Science Department, School of Science & Technology
Middlesex University

ABSTRACT

Recent advances in Information Technology (IT) and the advent of Web 2.0 created the path for education to ascertain its potential from this phenomenon. The role of e-learning has transformed completely as Web 2.0 technologies enabled the creation of learning content that is no longer based on textbooks and learning guides, but on manageable, modular learning components. The emergence of Education 2.0 enabled technology enhanced teaching and learning necessitating new pedagogical approaches while e-learning has evolved into an instrumental pedagogy of collaboration and sharing of resources through affordances of social media. Educational social networks were created as supportive mechanisms for special interest groups. Traditional teaching methods have been replaced with technology-enhanced media that enable ubiquitous learning. Social networks as educational tools have enabled individual and group learning through social engagement and social distribution of knowledge. Studies have demonstrated the role of social media as a complementary educational tool. Many studies have reported that a larger proportion of students spend more time engaging in social online activities than in classroom. However, there is a lack of quantitative study on how social networks such as Facebook can be influential on students' progress and achievement. This paper investigates how a quantitative overview of Facebook's influence on students' progress can be incorporated in a proposed e-moderation model of teaching and learning through Facebook. The proposed e-moderation model (Salmon, 2003) provides an emphasis on the theoretical perspectives that support socially situated learning environment of social networks such as Facebook.

KEYWORDS

e-learning, social learning networks, education 2.0, social media, Facebook, e-moderation model.

1. INTRODUCTION

The popularity of social media and their seemingly instant access to users have had unparalleled influences on different service industries. Academics have benefited from the favourable qualities of social networks in almost all education sectors. Students and instructors have adapted to unique capabilities and complementary affordances of social networks in their studies. Despite the popularity of Facebook as the favourable social network at university or colleges, there is a lack of quantifiable study on its role on student's performance. This is understandable as it is difficult to quantify the impact of a social network in teaching effectiveness, learning progress, or assessment results. There are several factors affecting such activities and it is difficult to prove that any significant changes can be attributed solely on the introduction of social networks in educational settings. Over the past few years, the authors have attempted several pilots with students in a Further Education Institution (FEI) and a Higher Education Institution (HEI) in order to investigate the impact of using social media in specific learning activities as well as the overall effect of introducing a social learning network in the classroom.

Generally, the literature suggests that Social Network Sites (SNSs) are mainly used in education as tools supporting existing social relationships and enabling the maintenance of social capital (Ellison et al, 2011), but their value as a learning environment is still questioned. However, regardless of scholars' views on the topic, Facebook has remained one of the most popular social networks amongst students, teachers and lecturers due to its availability and unique features over the last decade. This networking tool needs much more exploration not only as a LMS, but as a platform for delivery of educational purposes. Its use in education is still short of full investigation due to its privacy limitations. This paper reports on the findings of a study implementing Facebook as the complementary platform during a pilot involving several FEi and HEI undergraduate students.

For this study, the authors have focused on a well-established e-moderation model (Salmon, 2003). The e-moderation model consists of five stages describing the learning journey of a learner, achieving certain learning stages by following a constructivist approach. The model was based on the principle that learners will proceed through the stages with specific expected participation and interaction along with a given amount of interactivity through the experience. The study presented in this paper introduced the Facebook environment created for both FEI and HEI students in order to establish the transition from one stage to the next through the use of the Facebook features. The five stages of the e-moderation model within the context of the Facebook SNS are as follows:

- Access and motivation
- Online socialisation
- Information exchange
- Knowledge construction
- Development

The authors made a key assumption for the purposes of this study, which was that teaching and learning activities supported through Facebook features could be incorporated using the e-moderation model as proposed by Gilly Salmon (2003).

2. LITERATURE REVIEW

The role of SNSs in education has increasingly become the centre of a lot of work in the field (Boyd and Ellison, 2007; Hew, 2011; Junco, 2012). Facebook has been arguably one of the most successful social networks, used across several age groups (Grosseck, Bran, & Tiru, 2011; Roblyer, McDaniel, Webb, Herman, & Witty, 2010). Facebook offers integrated features that facilitate social interaction among users, and these features can be used effectively for the support of various learning activities. Facebook users with common interests can gather and share their goals in small, focused groups. Facebook pages enable the use of incorporated characteristics disseminating social interaction, and foundations of social knowledge construction. Social networks and their built in features have encouraged educational research interest in to the potential applications and the benefits of integrating Facebook in learning activities (Kabilan, Ahmad, & Abidin, 2010; Mazman & Usluel, 2010). The authors have published previously their findings on the role of social media in e-learning enhancement (Shokri and Dafoulas, 2014), the use of social networks in e-education (Dafoulas and Shokri, 2014a), delivering e-learning through social networks (Dafoulas and Shokri, 2014b), and integrating Web 2.0 technologies in learning (Dafoulas and Shokri, 2014c),

The social characteristics of Facebook seem to be ideal for facilitating learners in constructing knowledge through social interaction. Social knowledge construction encourages frequent social interaction and allows peer learning. By incorporating educational activities that facilitate knowledge construction, such as discussion, collaborative learning or project-based learning, students are encouraged to share, discuss and produce diverse concepts during the process of social interaction (Hou & Wu, 2011). Web 2.0 technologies have the potential to initiate the creation of on-line learning communities that can be particularly helpful across communities spread over different geographical regions (Mason and Rennie, 2007). These communities can also enhance engaged learning where participants gather their own knowledge through investigation and search for information on the Internet (Kamel Boulos and Wheeler, 2007). This paper discusses how the authors' efforts are currently shifting towards investigating whether it is possible to quantify the impact of Web 2.0 technologies to learning enhancement.

Social media create value for the online communities as a driver to enrich educational opportunity and enhance the quality of web-based learning. Social media can be used for the transition from content-focused e-learning towards social learning, where individuals have interaction on the Internet and can use multiple sources of data and information for their learning. The key difference between e-learning and social learning is that the latter supports multiple communication channels, leading to several sources of learning content, including the learners themselves. Social media enables the learning to happen unrestricted by physical locations and in all kinds of creative ways such as social interaction and online collaborations (Bingham and Conner, 2010). There are a number of studies that investigated the impacts of social media on e-learning. For example, it is argued that the future of e-learning will be a shift to knowledge networking and knowledge management (Chatti et al., 2007).

By taking advantage of structural and interactive features, social media provide a virtual environment that allows users to interact with each other, create, share, and exchange information and knowledge (Dickey and William, 2010, Aula, 2010, Kaplan and Haenlein, 2010). Social media users learn from each other by sharing their information, knowledge, and various experiences via such social media tools as twitter, blogs, YouTube, and Facebook. They also receive social support by participating in online activities and interacting with other members. For example, individuals share their knowledge in virtual communities, which is helpful for them to learn from each other and solve problems at both education and work (Hsu et al., 2007).

The traditional limitations of e-learning programs that mainly focused mainly on content delivery and less on frequent student interactions may be overcome by encouraging learners to share personal and professional interests and aspirations usually excluded from e-learning settings. According to Duffy (2011), SNSs offer a set of affordances for the creation of collaborative activities that occur online, mostly because many students are already using them for socialization and communication purposes and they would be willing to use these sites in learning as well; moreover, SNSs are free of charge and come without the restrictions usually found in many institutional Learning Management Systems (LMSs).

According to Greenhow (2011), SNS might be re-envisioned as support for student learning outcomes at least from two perspectives: first, they can provide peer/alumni support to manage the ups and downs of high school or college life, or help with school-related tasks; second, SNS can stimulate social and civic benefits, online and offline. This positive attitude is confirmed by other surveys (Fewkes & McCabe, 2012), the results of which showed that, in opposition to the claim that students do not use Facebook to support the learning agenda of the classroom, there are many in-depth examples of students who are using it for educational purposes. This paper focuses on the role of Facebook as a supporting tool for in-class educational activities as well as educational support in self-study between learning sessions.

A further research study (Mazman & Usluel, 2010) determined that the factors influencing Facebook users' adoption processes in an educational context rely on a positive relationship with usefulness, ease of use, social influence, facilitating conditions and community identity, and that among these variables the usefulness dimension is the most important determinant in Facebook adoption. In other words, learners must be persuaded for the impact the technology has on their learning. This has been one of the major challenges in this study, as apart from the obvious incentives through assessment and feedback, students were provided with guidance of how Facebook features would support their communication with peers and understanding of the topics covered in class.

Students' familiarity with Facebook and the ease at which its features can be applied to establish meaningful interactions, are the reasons for its popularity in particular amongst students. The new millenniums of learners depend on the new means of self-expression that exceed traditional communication technology tools. The new forms of literacy and students new digital needs demand innovative teaching practices without classroom constraints and traditional learning methods. Facebook offers ubiquity and mobility settings that flourishes student's engagement in academic content without strict boundaries of traditional teaching and learning. Features of Facebook that enrich and support interaction and discussion accelerate learner's participation, enabling classroom discussion and information exchange. A study highlighted the efficacy of Facebook as an informal learning tool, in which an optional Facebook activity was used to expose students to issues not covered in the core content of a formal course (Cain & Policastri, 2011). Two further studies found that Facebook has the potential to engage students in meaningful academic conversations depending on the timing as well as the topics of discussion (LaRue, 2012; Lim & Ismail, 2010). A Facebook application relating to learning about environmental issues allowed users to develop environmental behaviour through participation and peer role modelling (Robelia, Greenhow, & Burton, 2011). The use of Facebook for peer assessment and cooperative learning turned out to have a positive influence on the development of English writing skills and knowledge (Shih, 2011). Comparing statistics on the use of Facebook and Blackboard, for instance, in a study, found that students were more likely to post and be exposed to posts on Facebook than on traditional LMS (DiVall & Kirwin, 2012). All these studies seem to work towards quantifying the impact of Facebook on learning activities and overall learning enhancement.

The impact of any SNS is based on its social infusion of their technical capabilities within the population it serves. As Selwyn (2007a) stated, SNS capabilities and interactions are improving learning activities within a highly social environment. Recent studies have also found the adoption of Social Network Sites at all levels of education, as an example with higher education state: University students are very open to the possibility of using Facebook and similar technologies to support classroom work, (Roblyer et al 2010). In the following pages we will discuss our observations on the impact of Facebook in a number of learning activities and our early attempts to quantify how it affects student performance.

3. PILOT STUDIES

This research is based on a series of pilot studies with FEI and HEI students. Both pilot studies spread across two-three years and involved a range of modules. The aim of the study was to incorporate Facebook in the curriculum by enhancing learning activities through specific features. In particular the scope was to introduce Facebook as the means to communicate between group members, deliver content, provide collaboration across teams and evaluation feedback from peers, and instructors.

3.1 Pilot Methods

The first pilot series was conducted with the participation of both FEI students studying an advanced level diploma course and HEI undergraduate students. Both pilot series were involving students with IT or computing programmes, with sufficient skills in the relevant technologies. The study involved four groups of IT students during two pilot studies lasted between one to six weeks. Each seminar group consisted of 20 students with approximately 80 students taking part in the FEI pilots in three IT related modules including 4GL Programming, HCI, and advanced level Spreadsheet Design. Data was gathered in class through online activities designed and delivered through Facebook over the period of five weeks in the second semester. Each group completed module related activities with the combination of teaching concepts, exercises and formative assessment of their learning. Facebook pages were designed and created to correspond to the module delivery with focus on enabling learners understanding of topics, providing learning summaries and obtaining learners' opinions on the online task at hand. These pages were designed to reinforce the in-class delivery of topics and main emphasis was on consolidating and embedding focal learning material necessary for content delivery in the SNS as well as supporting assessment. Each weekly activity was delivered according to the schemes of work that had been planned for the teaching of the module. Weekly activities started with the tutor's instruction to handling the exercises, clear introduction to the topic being delivered and also the type of activity at hand. At the end of each activity learners were asked to complete a poll indicating their preference based on the scores given for the completed tasks. Results of the activities were assessed based on the comments and replies provided by the learners. Each individual learner was given scores based on the accuracy of the answers and efforts made in completing the exercises.

The first and second pilot study with HEI students involved more than 80 students from a first year undergraduate module in Business Information Systems. Participants' responses were collected through each individual's completion of the online survey and questionnaire submitted through the university Virtual Learning Environment (VLE). The questionnaire was designed to capture responses of participants' study of the social network representing other educational establishments namely Facebook pages of 10-12 other universities. Each participating group developed their own Facebook page and provided peer-evaluation to other student groups by completing a template with sections relating to strategy, operation, development, testing, evaluation and deployment of SNS. Participants' responses were focused on how each participating group in the study would integrate use of Web 2.0 in their Facebook page. The peer-evaluation section consisted of three parts focusing on goal-based evaluation, goal-free evaluation and criteria based evaluation. In the goal based evaluation section participants were asked to identify three specific and measurable goals for evaluating their Facebook pages in terms of user learning effectiveness. In the goal free evaluation section participants created a Likert scale poll based on the user learning operations. The criteria based evaluation asked participants to identify specific criteria you can use to measure and assess the effectiveness of the Facebook page in terms of: (i) Performance (focusing on the Facebook features available to the users) (ii) Functionality (focusing on the functions users can perform on the page), (iii) Usability (focusing on the page's look, feel and ease of use) and (iv) Sociability (focusing on creating and sustaining interactive user groups).

3.2 Data Collection

For the FEI students, the first weekly activity consisted of checking learners' prior knowledge and familiarization with the theoretical concepts followed by practical exercises to complete a Spreadsheet model. "Use of spreadsheet models in business" was the topic that learners had the opportunity to reflect on their prior knowledge and exchange their ideas through comment feature of Facebook. Each learner was able to read and comment on other learner's comments and also respond to other's questions or ideas. The completion of the practical exercise was an opportunity for the group to comment on how to use the formula and built in functions in the scenario design. Students were able to comment on the functions and formulas they could use and exchange of ideas were flowing between all members of this group. The second weekly FB activity was designed to explore students' understanding of their own stages of the software development lifecycle (SDLC). Students were poked to participate in an activity around a SDLC diagram that was uploaded, including questions that should be answered, invited comments, uploads of images, videos and documents. This activity attracted learners more, probably due to its visual and graphical representation of the SDLC concepts. Learners were able to respond better to each stage and recognise the stages and then identify the stage they were working on. Students were poked to share their ideas by uploading of images, photos and videos. The third weekly Facebook activity was designed to recap the use of different advanced functions and formulae by way of presenting the learners with the videos of the most useful features of the software. Students were poked to watch online video tutorials through Facebook activity and practice using the feature they have watched on their own practical assignment. The videos were aimed at different levels of learners from basic to more advanced features of the software. This activity was designed to recap student's basic understanding and skills of how to use functions and formulas to complement the design of their spreadsheet model. Learners were poked to share their views and the topics they have learnt through comments and photos. The fourth weekly Facebook activity was designed to enable students to relate the learnt classroom concepts to the design and implementation of their model. Learners were poked to comment on an incomplete design of a model and share their ideas on how to improve the model through the use of comments and images of their own design. Students were asked to upload their own design and comment on the storyboard of each worksheet and workbooks created individually as well as identifying the use of the functions on each worksheet design that enabled the creation of the model. Students were poked to share and view other individual's uploads of images and comments. The final week of Facebook activities was designed to recap and summarise the learning and practical concepts of the module. Leaners were poked to share and comment what they have learnt and summarise the concepts and also comment on each other's views and understanding of the topics.

On the other hand, HEI students participated in a Facebook activity that required the development of Facebook-based SNS in groups and then the evaluation of the created pages individually. The development report and the evaluation surveys consisted of sections on strategy, operations, deployment plan, testing, and evaluation. In the strategy sections participants studied the social network pages to provide their understanding of the goals and objectives of other universities with directions on enhancement of user learning. In the operation section of the questionnaire, participants studied other university Facebook pages and ranked these pages according to the learning opportunities offered to the online users. In the development plan section participants were asked to record the features of other universities Facebook pages focusing on certain features of Facebook. In the testing section of the questionnaire participants were asked to respond to a testing log with three parts: describe the testing feature, reflect on the feature and test the feature. In the evaluation section of the questionnaire participants were asked to complete questions on evaluation of the 10 university Facebook pages. The evaluation plan of the questionnaire consisted of three parts. Goal based evaluation to provide rating on other university Facebook pages of user learning operations. Goal free evaluation section of the evaluation log required participants response to 10 key questions in relation to the 10 university Facebook pages. The last part of the evaluation log consisted of participant's response to four key questions in relation to the 10 'university' Facebook pages. The deployment plan of the questionnaire gathered data through their response to identify 5 common ways that the 10 university Facebook pages utilise the Facebook features.

3.3 Observations

The FEI pilot study provided some interesting findings from early observations. It appears that most learners particularly those with specific cognitive deficiencies experience higher level of difficulties during an activity that would require their efficient processing skills. The Facebook learning activities should be created with an adequate level of intuition and challenge for the average learner but also with delicate attention to the learning cues to provide those leaners with mild cognitive difficulties to absorb the cues and process the instructions with more time frames for completion.

The second weekly activity emphasised the benefit and importance of using graphical images and diagrams when delivering learning activities. Most participants were drawn to the presentation feature of this activity and the use of colours and a diagram seemed to absorb student's attention even when the groups started to browse the page to become familiar with its content.

The third weekly activity needed the use of earphones by learners. It became clear that many learners expected the content of the tutorials to represent the exact topic that they were trying to learn by attempting the activity. This means that use of long trailers at the start of the tutorials to even relate to the subject should be avoided. Many learners found it frustrating to watch a video in anticipation of learning about the exact features of the software. Video tutorial lengths should be kept to the minimum requirement with clear content list and introduction of the topics.

The fourth week activity enabled students to take charge of their own learning and reflect on their own work. Learners were required to suggest improvements on an incomplete design and implementation of the spreadsheet model. Students compared their own project with the given prototype and reflected on what they had learnt and made suggestions by posting photos, diagram and text. Many found this very useful and the activity generated a flow of comments and feedbacks.

The final week of the activities meant that students were summarising their understanding of the topics by posting sentences, text, images, photos, videos, etc. Many chose to post text comments and show qualitative expression of what they had learnt. This activity should have been more carefully questioned in groupings of comments or directing the learners just to use the certain type of post. The question should have asked for the exact nature of the reply expected rather than a general summary.

4. QUANTIFYING STUDENT PERFORMANCE

In an effort to provide some quantifiable means for assessing student performance when using the Facebook SNS the authors attempted some statistical analysis of usage data in association to student performance in specific activities as well as their responses to the templates used for peer evaluation and group activities. This section describes work in progress that aims to provide a set of guidelines for using appropriate statistical methods in quantifying the impact of SNS in learning enhancement.

<u>Regression analysis</u>

Initial analysis was based on using two variables, namely total marks (referring to grades provided for in-class learning activities) and activity points (referring to grades provided for Facebook activities), use of descriptive statistics was used as in the following table. Data related to the participants' online activity scores that represented their participation with Facebook activities and also data related to the module scores in the classroom were used in the regression analysis. The linear regression factor of 0.526 indicated a positive correlation between students' efforts on completing Facebook activities and students' classroom based activities and achievement in the same modules. This was somehow expected as better students were more active on Facebook as well.

Table 1. Summary regression analysis

Model Summary

Model	R	R Square	Adjusted R Square	Std. Error of the Estimate	Change Statistics				
					R Square Change	F Change	df1	df2	Sig. F Change
1	.725[a]	.526	.498	5.428	.526	18.830	1	17	.000

a. Predictors: (Constant), Points from activity

The summary regression analysis corresponds with the linear regression graph that indicates the value of R squared to be 0.526 which is a positive and acceptable result indicating the correlation between the two variables of students total marks and Facebook activity scores. The result is positive although not very strong, it can be concluded that many other factors (necessitating further study) contribute to the strength of the R squared value.

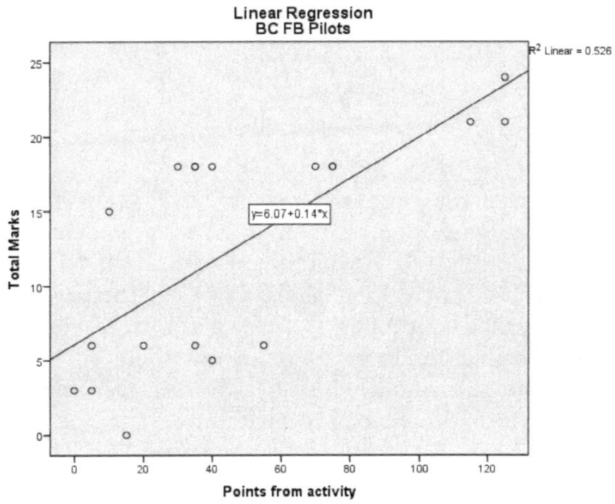

Figure 1. Regression graph

<u>Matrix Scattered Boxplot</u>

The same data set from the evaluation questionnaire was used for analysing responses from 40 HEI learners, using the matrix scattered plot to compare each evaluation question and identify its relation to other attributes of group Facebook pages. The matrix scattered plot reveals patters of similarity for reading posts and liking posts, writing comments and joining events. Other patterns were identified with Facebook pages followed and photos and videos watched. There was not a positive relation between number of days waited in relation to any other question or attribute of Facebook pages. In other words the delay in responding to Facebook comments did not affect any other features of the group pages. As in following graph, using boxplot to represent the data in the goal free evaluation of 40 individuals, it was revealed that "questions asked" had no relation to other factors on Facebook pages, representing the lowest scores on the group's pages collected. Similarly "Polls voted for" scored low and did not show a relation or effect from other Facebook features. There were similarities between "photos viewed" and "posts liked" and some relation also between these two variables existed with "posts read" on Facebook pages. It seems that there is an association between the number of photos viewed and the number of likes from the same users. This tends to be a pattern with more active Facebook users in both groups. "Comments wrote" and "videos watched" also were on the lower scale of values compared with "reading and liking posts" and "viewing photos". "Joining events" was not a very strong factor in all the Facebook groups and all participants' data revealed a minimum score. There generally was not strong consistency in how the group pages were rated, however there existed a strong link between "viewing photos" and "liking the posts/ photos" and then " reading the posts." In other words our study cannot provide conclusive evidence for association between Facebook features apart from the three mentioned above. It appears that patterns of Facebook use for educational purposes would emerge only for the number of photos viewed and liked leading to further reads.

The authors will direct future work towards this finding, trying to proof specific patterns between these three activities, as it could lead into a strategy for guiding student attention towards selected content and triggering reading of certain posts on Facebook pages or SNS in general.

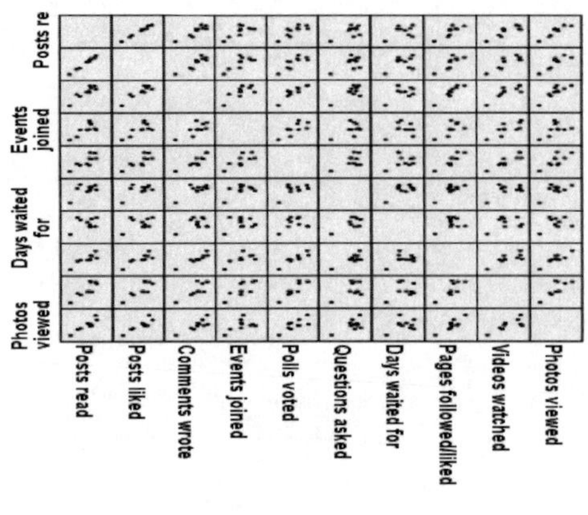

Figure 2. Matrix Scattered Boxplot

Bivariate (Pearson) Correlation (HEI factors)

Finally, analysing the survey responses from the goal free evaluation focused on how participants rated performance in Facebook group activities. Each survey question was identified as a variable, and Pearson Correlation factors were generated across all variables. As sown in the table, all variables (factors) have a positive Pearson Correlation of more than 0.9 indicating that all participants scored high in their goal free evaluation survey and also each factor is in a positive correlation with other factors. The findings here are consistent with the data analysis and findings of participants' online behaviour during completion of Facebook activities in the pilot studies conducted at the FE College. While there was a generally strong correlation between all variables (factors), one or two factors were more in correlation with each other. For example strong correlation existed between (there was some correlation between number of posts read and number of posts liked):

- Number of posts liked and number of events joined
- Number of pages followed and number of comments written
- Number of questions asked and number of events joined
- Number of videos watched and number of polls voted for

Descriptive Statistics

	Mean	Std. Deviation	N
VAR00001 Grp 1	108.90	108.588	10
VAR00002 Grp 2	8.80	6.529	10
VAR00003 Grp 3	102.50	106.544	10
VAR00004 Grp 4	75.00	73.077	10
VAR00005 Grp 5	53.80	41.368	10
VAR00006 Grp 6	80.90	73.944	10
VAR00007 Grp 7	87.40	76.164	10
VAR00008 Grp 8	86.60	81.019	10
VAR00009 Grp 9	76.80	77.737	10
VAR00010 Grp 10	46.70	32.701	10

Individual Survey data - Goal Free Evaluation

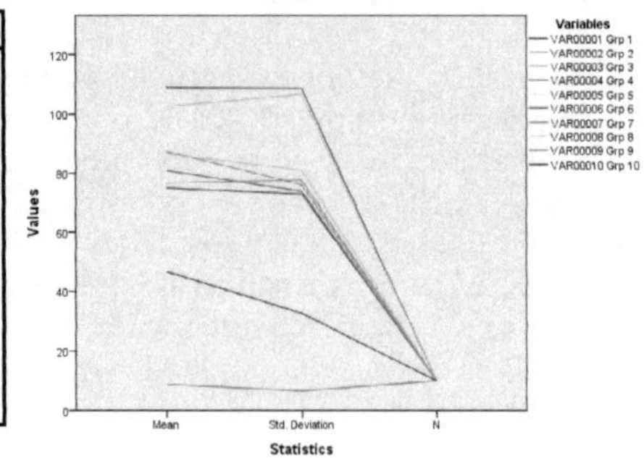

Figure 3. Descriptive statistics

The five dimensions of the e-moderation model serve as a reference point for the above analysis. The dimensions that are primarily supported by our findings include (i) access and motivation (through the contribution to Facebook pages), (ii) online socialization (through direct interaction between participants), and (iii) information exchange (through discussions between students and instructors). Further work is required to provide a direct association of SNS interactions and the remaining two dimensions, namely (i) knowledge construction and (ii) development. The study had access to both FEI and HEI students in the same discipline. The scope of including both was to investigate whether different patterns would emerge. The research hypothesis did not differentiate towards the two cohorts, as this was not the scope of the research. The emphasis of this paper was on the FEI student results.

5. CONCLUSION

The integration of Salmon's e-moderation model with the authors' investigation in Facebook activities and the role of SNS in education yielded some general positive outcomes. A broader acceptance of Facebook as a formal learning media necessitates configuration of the social learning environments and experimented controls over the required outcomes of each learning session. Further studies on full integration of Facebook as a formal learning environment will need to focus on evaluation of learning styles according to the subject area and examination of social boundaries and ties within which the deliverables are aimed at. The result of statistical analysis revealed that students' grades were positively influenced with the complementary use of Facebook on their courses of study. Using Facebook alongside delivery of courses expanded user participation as more students joined university events and asked questions when they enjoyed reading and liked a post.

REFERENCES

Aula, P. (2010), "Social media, reputation risk and ambient publicity management", Strategy & Leadership, Vol. 38 No. 6, pp. 43-49.

Boyd, D. M., & Ellison, N. B. (2007). Social network sites: Definition, history, and scholarship. Journal of Computer-Mediated Communication, 13(1):210–230.

Bingham, T. and Conner, M. (2010), The New Social Learning: A Guide to Transforming Organizations through Social Media, Berrett-Koehler Store, San Francisco, CA.

Cain, J., & Policastri, A. (2011). Using Facebook as an informal learning environment. American Journal of Pharmaceutical Education, 75(10), 1–8.

Chatti, M.A., Jarke, M. and Frosch-Wilke, D. (2007), "The future of e-learning: a shift to knowledge networking and social software", International Journal of Knowledge and Learning, Vol. 3 Nos 4/5, pp. 404-420.

Dafoulas, George and Shokri, Azam (2014a) An investigation in social network use for e-education: the case of Facebook. In: International Conference on eBusiness, eCommerce, eManagement, eLearning and eGovernance 2014.

Dafoulas, George and Shokri, Azam (2014b) Delivery of e-learning through social learning networks. In: 8th International Conference on e-Learning 2014.

Dafoulas, George and Shokri, Azam (2014c) Integrating web 2.0 technologies in higher education learning. In: 6th International Conference on Education and New Learning Technologies (EDULEARN 2014).

DiVall, M. V., & Kirwin, J. L. (2012). Using Facebook to facilitate course-related discussion between students and faculty members. American Journal of Pharmaceutical Education, 76(2), 1–5.

Dickey, I. and William, F. (2010), "The evolution (revolution) of social media and social networking as a necessary topic in the marketing curriculum: a case for integrating social media into marketing classes", Society for Marketing Advances Proceedings, pp. 140-143.

Duffy, P. (2011). Facebook or Faceblock: Cautionary tales exploring the rise of social networking within tertiary education. In M. J. W. Lee & C. McLoughlin (Eds.), Web 2.0-base e-learning: Applying social informatics for tertiary teaching (pp. 284–300). Hershey, PA: IGI Global.

Ellison, N. B., Steinfield, C., & Lampe, C. (2011). Connection strategies: Social capital implications of Facebookenabled communication practices. New Media & Society, 13(6), 873–892.

Fewkes, A. M., & McCabe, M. (2012). Facebook: Learning tool or distraction? Journal of Digital Learning in Teacher Education, 28(3), 92–98.

Greenhow, C. (2011). Online social networks and learning. On the Horizon, 19(1), 4–12.
Grosseck, G., Bran, R., & Tiru, L. (2011). Dear teacher, what should I write on my wall? A
case study on academic uses of Facebook. Procedia – Social and Behavioral Sciences,
15, 1425–1430.
Hew, K. F. (2011). Students' and teachers' use of Facebook. Computers in Human Behavior, 27, 662–676.
Hou, H.-T., & Wu, S.-Y. (2011). Analyzing the social knowledge construction behavioral
patterns of an online synchronous collaborative discussion instructional activity using an
instant messaging tool: A case study. Computers & Education, 57, 1459–1468.
Hsu, M.-H., Ju, T.L., Yen, C.-H. and Chang, C.-M. (2007), "Knowledge sharing behavior in virtual communities: the relationship between trust, self-efficacy, and outcome expectations", International Journal of Human-Computer Studies, Vol. 65 No. 2, pp. 153-169.
Junco, R. (2012). The relationship between frequency of Facebook use, participation in Facebook activities, and student engagement. Computers & Education, 58, 162–171.
Kabilan, M. K., Ahmad, N., & Abidin, M. J. Z. (2010). Facebook: An online environment
for learning of english in institutions of higher education? Internet and Higher Education,
13, 179–187.
Kamel Boulos, M.N. and Wheeler, S. (2007), "The emerging Web 2.0 social software: an enabling suite of sociable technologies in health and health care education", Health Information & Libraries Journal, Vol. 24 No. 1, pp. 2-23
Kaplan, A.M. and Haenlein, M. (2010), "Users of the world, unite! The challenges and opportunities of social media", Business Horizons, Vol. 53 No. 1, pp. 59-68.
LaRue, E. M. (2012). Using Facebook as course management software: A case study. Teaching and Learning in Nursing, 7(17), 17–22.
Mason, R. and Rennie, F. (2007), "Using Web 2.0 for learning in the community", The Internet and Higher Education, Vol. 10 No. 3, pp. 196-203.
Mazman, S. G., & Usluel, Y. K. (2010). Modeling educational usage of Facebook. Computers & Education, 55, 444–453.
Roblyer, MD, McDaniel M., Webb, M.,Herman J., Witty (2010) "Findings on Facebook in Higher Education: A comparison of college faculty and student uses and perceptions of social networking sites," The Internet and Higher Education, vol. 13, Jun. 2010, pp. 134-140.
Salmon, G. (2003). E-moderating: the key to teaching and learning online. London: Kogan Page
Selwyn, N. (2007a). Screw blackboard. Do it on F acebook! An investigation of students' educational use of F acebook.
Shih, R.-C. (2011). Can Web 2.0 technology assist college students in learning English writing? Integrating Facebook and peer assessment with blended learning. Australasian Journal of Educational Technology, 27, 829– 845.
Shokri, Azam and Dafoulas, George (2015) Guidelines for determining an effective role for social media in e-learning enhancement. In: 8th annual International Conference of Education, Research and Innovation. (Accepted/In press)

CARE MANAGEMENT: ON LINE-BASED APPROACHES TO NURSE EDUCATION IN ULTRASOUND IMAGING

Elena Taina Avramescu[1], Mitrache Marius[1] and Adrian Camen[2]
[1]*University of Craiova , A.I. Cuza, nr.13, Craiova, Romania*
[2]*University of Medicine and Pharmacy Craiova, Str. Petru Rareş nr. 2, Craiova, Romania*

ABSTRACT

Over the last two decades nurses have to face the need to be high qualified professionals with always updated competencies and practical skills. Learning on the Internet by the "e learning" method, fundamentally changed the way by which nurses can get information and be involved in educational activities designed to ensure their continuous medical education. The goal of our work was to provide e-education for ultrasound nurses by the use of a Learning Management Systems delivered through the Internet, within the framework e-EDUMED project. The project developed a virtual health educational center providing on-line education and training materials by 2 interactive training modules in ultrasound adressed to medical doctors and nurses and one module for patient education.

The e-learning platform hosts asynchronous online courses - educational materials in a traditional style of presentation, PPT and course notes (text and images), questions and quizzes associated with each section, multimedia lessons. Synchronous online courses are implemented in the virtual class e- EDUMED allowing a tutor via the Internet to bring together a group of students in real time. The teacher can present materials (case studies, moving images, ultrasound examinations) and can receive information and feedback from students. The nurse training module is included in the e-learning platform and the learning pathway has been realized through an innovative methodological model combining both theoretical and practical aspects, in order to enhance the learning skills based on the study of real cases. Content is structured in the best way to build gradual competences.

Another innovative approach in the development of our module is the importance of having a nurse as part of the ultrasound health team - a nurse whose presence conveys for the patient's psychosocial and physical needs. The usual patient reaction to ilness is anxiety. Ultrasound can intensify anxiety by augmenting a feeling of alienation, creating a deficit of knowledge and/or invading personal space. In this way the module also promotes the belief that the nurse s role in ultrasound has one proeminent goal-positive patients relations. The conclusion drawn at the end of the project was that 3D images and virtual classrooms can support medical and nursing professionals in training without having the presumption to be exhaustive, but propaedeutic to practice.

KEYWORDS

Nursing online education, problem based education, ultrasound medical education

1. INTRODUCTION

Medical sector is a particular field in which quality of contents and type of methodology need to respect specific requirements and high level standards. Swanwick (2008) suggests that in the late years postgraduate medical education is moving into a new era driven by the three interlinked trends of professionalisation, increasing accountability and the pursuit of excellence (9) . In this context E-learning can offer an alternative method of education (7).

Precisely for the acute need to be permanent "in touch" with the findings and important issues in medicine, the new technology facilitated learning online methods started to gain ground in recent years in medical education, at international level and in the process of obtaining credentials for the medical profession, also influencing the methods used now in the process of learning. Despite the great interest of medical specialists for this type of training, computer assisted education is sporadically included in medical training. A systematic literature review conducted to assess the impacts of e-learning in nursing education has emphasized that e-Learning or Internet-based learning, has reaped many positive benefits as an efficient and effective educational tool, but still remains comparatively low in usage compared to other tools (4). Another recent review on 35 evaluative studies of online interventions in medical education showed that e-learning methodology is mainly used to transfer theoretical topics (3). In his study, Feng et al also (2013) concluded that E-learning is a useful adjunct to traditional learning for medical and nursing students (6). Another study conducted by Kokol et al (2006) proved that e-Learning can have many benefits and that it can enhance learning experience in nursing education, if it is provided in a correct manner, but there are still a lot of things to be done in order to increase the experiences and attitudes towards e-learning and clinical skills training (8). Also we must underline that although there has been much research on e-learning in the educational context, far less has been written about e-learning in the workplace (5)

These findings are taking place in the framework of the Recommendation of the EU Parliament and of the Council of the Establishment of ECVET that showed there is a serious need of complementarity between vocational training and higher education (10,11). More, the EU Comission Comunicate on Rethinking Education issued in 2012 undelines that increasing transversal and basic skills alone is not sufficient for growth and competitiveness and VET must be able to react to the demand for advanced vocational skills (12). With the development of Multimedia and networking as well as their extensive application in educational field, the learning environment extends beyond the classroom and establishing an E-learning culture is seen as essential to the future of vocational and higher education and the facilitation of life long learning (1,2).

In the light of these previous researches and findings, we started from the idea that the scope of nurse practice must be expanded beyond the core competencies to incorporate additional skills and procedures that improve care for patients and their families and we proposed to provide information and education for nurses by the use of a Learning Management Systems delivered through the Internet, within the framework of e-EDUMED project.

2. E-EDUMED PROJECT

e-EDUMED which stands for e-Learning Educational Centre in Medicine was a two year European project started in January 2011 funded by the Lifelong Learning Programme (Leonardo da Vinci, Transfer of Innovation sub-programme) aiming to cope with the learning needs of medical professionals improving and updating their skills, knowledge and abilities towards a competitive European Medical Brand in ultrasound (US). The project developed a virtual health educational center , providing on-line education and training materials by 2 interactive training modules in ultrasound adressed to medical doctors and nurse education and one online module for patient education.

3. STUDY PROGRAM CONTENT

Medical professionals spend a lot of time in training, refreshment courses, job shadowing and discussions with peers. They daily exploit all main sources of information and deepen any topic relevant for their profession. In this context the challenge of E-Edumed project was to offer an innovative course for medical professionals, a flexible, attractive and focused e-learning training pathway.

The e-EDUMED project started with a research carried in all participant countries aiming to analyse the training needs in medicine and state of art of medical e-learning outlined three characteristics of Medical Professionals in terms of skills and abilities:

- To know: have updated theoretical knowledge;
- To do: have technical or manual skills;
- To be: have communication and relations' skills.

The study program was designed according to the research findings, aiming to provide students with an advanced level of theoretical and scientific knowledge, relevant to the enhancing of practice or management in culturally diverse populations, both nationally and globally. It describes nursing care issues and techniques as they apply to the ultrasound settings, providing informations on:

- Patient preparation before US Examination
- The role of nurse during special US examinations and for special categories of patients
- Patient education after US examination.

The syllabus includes the same topics as the ultrasound module addressed to medical doctors and patients, but from the point of view of the nurse.

4. ON-LINE ENVIRONMENT

For the delivery of the online courses and to host the PBL repositories, an interactive e-learning platform was set up from the beginning of the project. The main goal of the e-learning platform and its applications was to give students the possibility to download course materials, take tests or sustain final examinations and communicate with all involved parties. For this reason the learning platform has been designed to provide accurate, interactive models for student and instructor use and multimedia learning by offering a Managed Learning Environment (MLE), which provides a single point of access for both staff and students with a various range of e-tools and applications including a Virtual Learning Environment (VLE- curriculum, delivery, assessment, tutor support, communication, feedback, quality management) as well as access to related references, organisations, scientific events and research area. Beside the structure and functionalities of the Virtual Centre, the course is empowered by a very effective methodology namely "Problem Based" Learning (PBL) implemented into the PBL environment, the "Virtual Classrooms".

Claroline was the open source E-Learning platform that we implemented because its relevant added values. It is free, it is built in modules that is it is more flexible, customizable and, finally, it has a huge community of developers and users that means new enhanced releases and debugs and offered us suitable modules for our goals: Teaching Units (training modules), Documents, Forums, and Chats.

In developing the platform and other materials we kept in mind that we address to Medical Professionals interested in refreshing key concepts and acquire knowledge on specific case studies, sharing experiences between other professionals. For this reason the platform offers an attractive ICT environment, high level functionalities and innovative PBL methodology helping the target group to benefit from a very flexible learning system, high level didactic material as well as interactive videos and Virtual classroom to discuss with peers, refresh competencies and exchange best practices/daily work-experience through virtual classroom (figure 1).

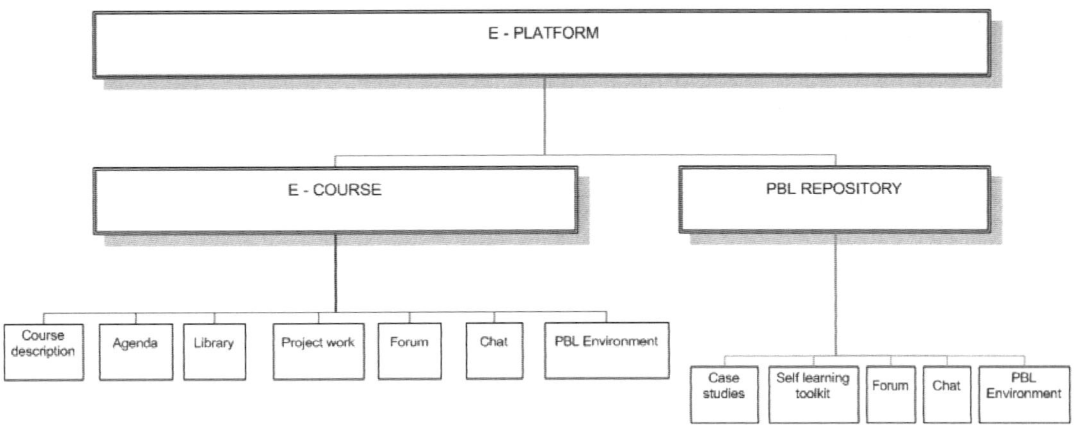

Figure 1. e-Learning platform diagram

The platform hosts asynchronous online courses - educational materials in a traditional style of presentation, PPT and course notes (text and images), questions and tests associated with each section, multimedia lessons that include sections with commented video images. Also the platform includes synchronous online courses - courses implemented in the virtual class E-Edumed allowing a tutor via the Internet to bring together a group of students in real time.

After entering the e-learning platform, the student can access materials and exercises for the courses available. According to individual profiles, each student has a different learning path through a sequence of materials and exercises, which are presented in different forms (visual, text, game-based). The learning path is defined by student type and learning style, and it is dynamically adapted if the student type or learning style changes.

In order to increase the impact of knowledge E-Edumed learning pathway is available in English and national language for Bulgarian, Hungarian and Romanian medical professionals.

5. NURSE TRAINING PACKAGE

This package was delivered for nurses and consisted of interactive nurse courses included into e-EDUMED e-learning platform. The package was divided into subsequent 3 modules and is available in EN, RO, BG, HU. For this modules we provided the curriculum/syllabus, schedule of courses and educational materials (WWW-based). All the materials are free to download. The total of developed materials was as shown in table 1.

Table 1. Nurse training package content

Text- pg	Multimedia lessons	PPT- s slides	Multimedia lessons	Virtual classes	Quizzes	Size
126	6	335	4	10	80	50 MB

The nurse ultrasound module entitled "NEW SKILLS FOR NEW CHALLENGES- THE ROLE OF NURSE IN ULTRASONOGRAPHY" includes texts and PPT presentations, addressed to the nurse and its roles in ultrasound: completing the report with aspect, dimensions and particularities of the investigated organ ,on the recommendation of the investigator, to know what kind of probe has to activate for this US evaluation, to place the patient in the proper position for examination, to prepare the patient prior to the investigation and to offer explanation to the patient after examination.

The proposed educational module is a continous medical education approach by internet, interactive on-line education by consultancy with acreditated programme tutors, assuring a secured final evaluation, as well as by the informational support offered, with links and specific portals.

6. THE LEARNING PATHWAY

The Learning pathway has been realized through an innovative methodological model combining both theoretical and practical aspects, in order to enhance the learning skills based on the study of real cases thanks to the Problem Based Learning (PBL) approach implemented into a virtual environment (virtual classrooms). The methodological approach is based on modular three-level architecture (presentation level, intermediate level, data level). The student can choose the level and/or type of training (competence in echography, nurse, LL training). In this way E-Edumed pedagogical model meets the medical professionals learning needs through the synergy of a virtual Problem-based Learning approach, a peer training methodology, and a self-direct learning approach, to promote the attainment of practical skills relating to ultrasound.

The virtual environment has a simple but effective structure and functionalities in order to allow the user to have suddenly clearer the core aims, the didactic and IT tutors and the key online tools. In particular, the learning pathway is introduced by a General presentation of the course with a description, targets, topics' list, help desk contacts, staff involved and learning tools. An agenda allows teachers or tutors to stress important course deadlines or events. A library allows teachers or tutors to add and store documents or links useful for the medical professional like Lecture notes to deepen the audio lesson contents, Reports, videos or Guidelines.

The virtual centre is also provided of a Forum which allows a classical asynchronous communication among professionals to share feedbacks and remarks; while a chat is at disposal for a synchronous communication tool. Access to virtual classrooms and to record virtual classrooms is also provided.

Once the trainee introduces his/her data, the first page of the course will open, with language options (RO, EN,BG, HU). The trainee can choose the option that he/she prefers and read the course description, consult the agenda or announcements for course schedule or events. Also he/she can use the platform facilities- forums, chat (figure 2).

For accesing the course materials there are 2 modalities:

- *Learning path* for a review of the educational material, videolessons and self assesment quizes
- *Document* for text (lecture notes).

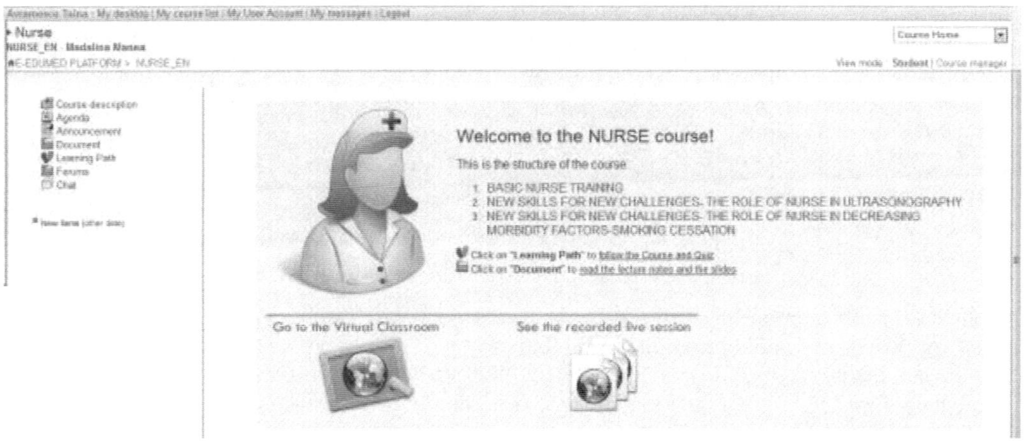

Figure 2. The learning pathway for the nurse module

The texts are stuctured as chapters of a book and follow the same order of contents. Each text beggins with the course objectives, prerequisites and gained competencies and ends with a selected bibliography. Power point presentations are included in a classical manner (figure 3) or in the form of multimedia lessons.

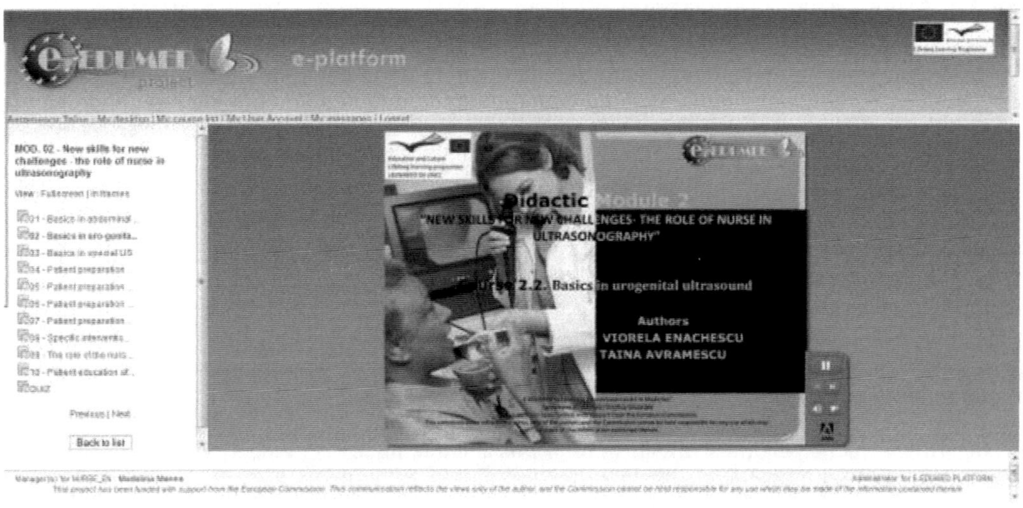

Figure 3. Classical Powerpoint presentation in the nurse ultrasound module

As concerns the key element of didactics, multimedia and dynamic lessons are provided with text, images and animations synchronized together with experts' audio contribution. The student has the total control of the audio lesson flow by clicking on the stop/go button, the forward button, the backward button, and with an index for jumping from one slide to another (figure 4).

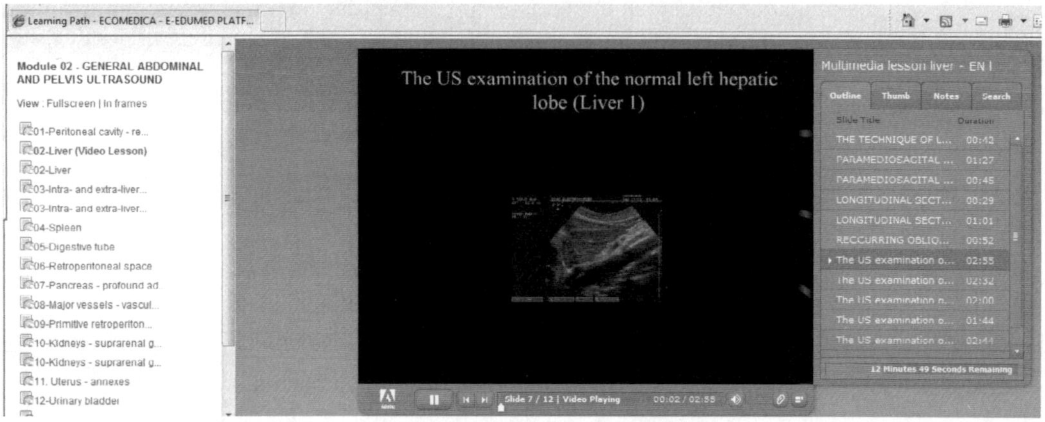

Figure 4. Print screen of a video included into multimedia lesson

Students are able to publish their work thanks to a Project work Qualitative assessment and Teachers give feedback on their works and assess students directly on-line. Quizzes are also valuable tool for the student to assess himself about a course module. The student ought to answer to different kinds of questions receiving an immediate feedback. Once a quiz session has been completed, the student will see the total score carried out and if he has passed the quiz.

Each module have a list of available learning objects SCORM compliant, ensuring the total reusability and tracking of student activities.

Pilot testing of the prototype of the platform was carried on in order to check the prototype fitness for the purpose, and the suitability of knowledge provided, user interface, language level, graphic approach and interaction level. Both trainers and trainees were involved.

Quality criteria of software characteristic were applied as follows: Functionality, Reliability, Usability, Efficiency Maintainability, and Portability.

Pilot testing by the users- test group- as training packages (after integration of the didactic material into the e-learning platform) was also carried, at the beginning of the training sessions. Tutorials evaluated the degree of successful usage and integration the system by the lecturers by the use of on line questionnaires.

87% of participants had witnessed a high level of satisfaction regarding the online environment and quality of didactic material.

7. CONCLUSION

The aim of this paper was to present the results of the LDV TOI project e-EDUMED, which resulted in an on-line educational platform in ultrasound imaging which is globally focused, flexible, innovative, diverse, contemporary and ICT-based (both in content and implementation) and focuses on meeting the needs of medical professionals.

An innovative aspect of the project is a virtual environment for clinical practice, which host trainees in an active learning environment by giving them problems and training them to identify what they need to learn to solve those problems. The e-modules provides students with extensive learning materials and the PBL environment. The main advantage is that the beneficiaries of the course, being professionals with different work experience, are able to choose their path according to their specific learning needs as well as medical field. Ultrasound is in fact a technique used in plenty of situations and medical contexts and therefore a user should have the possibility to quit some topics, deepening others and so on.

Another advantage is that content is structured in the best way to build gradual competences, by the use of:

- Internet resources
- Group discussions and ultrasound case analyses
- Quizzes & examinations
- Ultrasound laboratory live (virtual classrooms) & video demonstrations (multimedia lessons) Students' study trainings based on Power Point presentations and texts
- Students' self study trainings based on the references provided.

Based on students evaluation of the program, the interest shown for e-learning for all categories investigated in the target group was great. All partcipants were satisfied with both content and implementation of the training modules.

Analysing the field survey results and the documentary research, the general conclusions is that the use of ultrasound online platforms for medical education can be useful in the following conditions

a. To achieve competence in ultrasound. Considering the modality of examination that leads to obtain competence in ultrasound, online education can have a real value for theoretical module (teaching and assessment) by providing recent and systematized, specific information, in a didactic approach, a real opportunity for online evaluation of theoretical knowledge and possibility of simulation of examination. The e-platform also can be valuable in preparing for practical test examinations and video examination, but also to support video on line examinations. Other advantages consist in the possibility of accessing material at any time and from any location, the sharing of information between students on the forum, opportunity of brainstorming, access to trainer s opinion and Second Opinion.

b. In continuous professional training and obtaining CME credits e-learning is a reliable and superior alternative to classic courses that require accommodation, time, etc.

Our paper demonstrates that e- learning education in ultrasound and development of interactive learning platforms with an integrated imaging database remains a perfect option for continuing professional development and formal education by the possibilities offered in review and updating knowledge, sharing information and brainstorming. 3D images and virtual classrooms can support medical and nursing professionals in training without having the presumption to be exhaustive, but propaedeutic to practice.

ACKNOWLEDGEMENT

e-EDUMED (e-Learning Educational Center in Medicine) is a two year European funded project 2010-1-RO1-LEO05-07378 /contract LLP/LdV/TOI/RO/2010/006). The project has been funded with support from the European Commission. This publication reflects the views only of the author, and the Commission cannot be held responsible for any use which may be made of the information contained therein. Further details and contact information for the e-EDUMED project can be found on the project web page at http://www.e-edumed.ro.

REFERENCES

1. Aixia, D. & Wang, D., 2012. Factors influencing learner attitudes toward e-learning and development of e-learning environment based on the integrated e-learning platform. *In International Journal of e-Business, e-management and e-learning,* Vol.1, No.3, pp.264-268.
2. Button, D.A. et al, 2013. E-learning & information communication technology (ICT) in nursing education: A review of the literature, *In Nurse Education Today*, Vol. 34, No.10, pp.1311–1323.
3. Chumley-Jones HS, et al, 2002. Web-based learning: sound educational method or hype? A review of the evaluation literature. *In Acad Med.*, Vol.77 , No. 10 suppl, pp.S86-S93
4. Dalhem W. A., Saleh N., 2014, The impact of eLearning on nurses' professional knowledge and practice in HMC. *In Canadian Journal of Nursing Information,* Vol. 9, No 3 & 4
5. David, O., et al., 2012. The impact of e-learning in workplace: focus on organizations and healthcare environments. *In International Arab Journal of e-Technology.* Vol.2, No.4, pp.203-209.

6. Feng J.Y. et al, 2013. Systematic review of effectiveness of situated e-learning on medical and nursing education, *In Worldviews Evid Based Nurs*, Vol. 10, No.3, pp. 174-178
7. Lahti H. et al, 2014. Impact of e-learning on nurses' and student nurses knowledge, skills, and satisfaction: a systematic review and meta-analysis, *In International Journal of Nursing Studies*, Vol. 51, No. 1, pp. 136-49.
8. Kokol P. et al., 2006. e-Learning in Nursing Education – Challenges and Opportunities Series, Studies in Health Technology and Informatics - Proceedings of International Congress on Nursing Informatics, Monreal, Canada, pp. 387–390.
9. Swanwick, T., 2008. See one, do one, then what? Faculty development in postgraduate medical education. *In Postgraduate Medical Journal,* Vol.84, No. 993, pp. 339-343.
10. Council Resolution on modernising universities for Europe's competitiveness in a global knowledge economy 2832nd COMPETITIVENESS (Internal market, Industry and Research) Council meeting Brussels, 22 - 23 November 2007
11. Embedding E-Learning in Further Education The EU Health Policy Forum, Strategic Priorities Including Specific Priorities for 2009-2010, February 2009 Brussels
12. C 064/06 2013. Council Conclusions on investing in education and training — a response to 'Rethinking Education: Investing in skills for better socio-economic outcomes' and the '2013 Annual Growth Survey', Official Journal of the European Union, Volume 56, pg.5-9

CAN E-LEARNING CHANGE WORK PRACTICES?

Signe Schack Noesgaard
The KATA Foundation, Alsion 2, 6400 Sønderborg & It and Learning Design Lab, Department of Learning and Philosophy, Aalborg University, A.C. Meyers Vænge 15, 2450 Copenhagen S.

ABSTRACT

Stand-alone e-learning is unlikely to change work practices. This claim contrasts with a comprehensive body of research arguing that e-learning is at least as effective as face-to-face instruction in improving work performance. Such a comparison is, however, problematic. On the one hand, it relies on the premise that face-to-face instruction is effective in changing work behaviors. This article argues that instruction—whether e-learning, face-to-face, or a blend of both — cannot stand alone. Individualized on-the-job scaffolding of employees is needed for meaningful learning transfer and sustainable behavior change to occur. On the other hand, e-learning can be as important as face-to-face instruction in preparing the ground for advancing work practices, when e-learning is designed in acknowledgement of its strength and limitations. In outlining the above arguments, this article contributes a four-step model of intervention-based change. The model lists the key motivational drivers of employee persistence and commitment to change. The article illustrates e-learning as an assimilative learning catalyst and offers an overview of the scaffolding needed for advancing workplace practices. Ultimately, the article acknowledges organizational cost concerns regarding individualized scaffolding and discusses how a redefinition of e-learning can cost-effectively scaffold employees to sustainable change.

KEYWORDS

Professional Development, E-learning, Persistence, Motivation, Scaffolding, Sustainable Change

1. INTRODUCTION

The only constant is change. This statement has its roots in Heraclitus' ancient Greek philosophy. It does, however, also describe a premise of work that many employees experience today: a new business strategy, a new manager, a new It system, new standards, and new procedures. Change is exciting and change is stressful. When external or internal pressure deems organizational change necessary, employees need situated support to reduce potential anxiety and to navigate new paths to individual and organizational performance. If only we could accomplish this by sending our employees on a course.

The objective of professional development (PD) is to advance workplace practices. Professional development interventions (PDIs) are often formalized courses that are comparable with those of higher education; however, another layer of complexity is added to PD as the objective is reached *after* the PDI has been completed. Hence, the end objective is not to learn certain concepts, which can be applied and assessed in a test; it is after those tests that the real learning challenges lie.

E-learning for PD has become increasingly popular within organizations (Ho & Jones 2015). The prevailing e-learning intervention delivers a self-paced instructional learning path with programmed and/or recorded content that often includes learner–material interactions with programmed feedback and multiple-choice tests. Stand-alone means that there are no additional activities or processes added to the e-learning course; it is self-contained. The popularity of using this form of e-learning for workplace learning is related to an underlying assumption that e-learning is as effective as face-to-face interventions. A comprehensive body of research supports this assumption (fx. Maloney et al. 2011; Jackson & Lichtenstein 2011). As a consequence, the aim of e-learning becomes the digitalization of face-to-face training and the development of e-learning *instead* of face-to-face training. Formalized instruction may, however, not have been the answer in the first place—at least, not the complete answer. Hence, in PD, the comparison between e-learning and face-to-face instruction diffuses important discussions on the change needed, the possibility of change occurring, and whether instruction is the right means to achieve the objectives.

In light of the above concern, the purpose of this paper is to present a model for broadening the understanding of intervention-based change to individual employee behavior and to show how e-learning can contribute in the process. Specifically, the paper is structured around the following research questions:

(i) What drives intervention-based change to work practices? (Section 2)

(ii) What is needed to ensure change to work practices? (Section 3)

(iii) Which roles can e-learning play in the change process? (Section 4)

2. WHAT DRIVES INTERVENTION-BASED CHANGE TO WORK PRACTICES?

The purpose of the model below is to 1) synthesize recent findings in social-psychological and educational research into an intervention-based change process with key motivational drivers for employee commitment to change and consequently 2) highlight the complexity in changing work behaviors through PDIs.

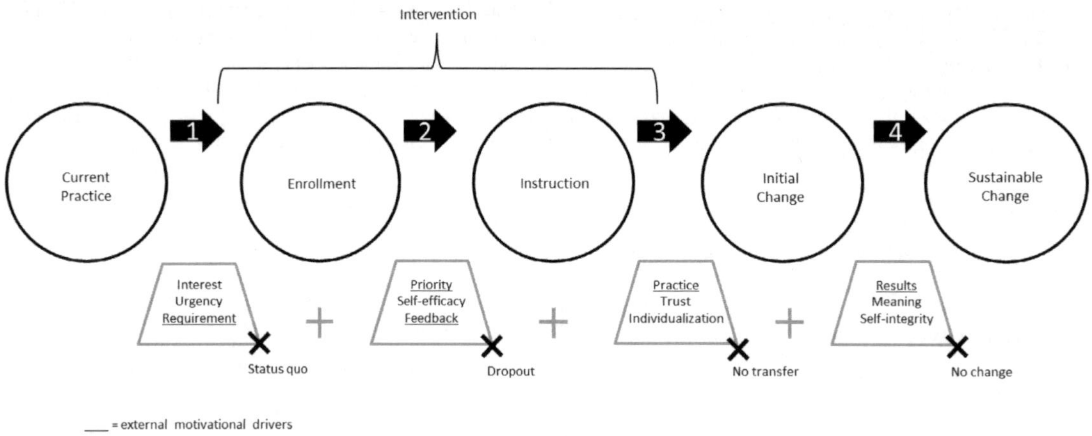

Figure 1. The four-step change process

The five circles in the above model (Figure 1) are components of the intervention-based change process. The arrows illustrate the critical steps in the process, while the trapeziums list the key motivational drivers that are critical to proceed to the next step. The X in each trapezium indicates the likely consequence of missing motivational drivers. Previous drivers should be added to each new list of drivers. As an example, an employee loses interest (step 1 driver) in the topic during the course (step 2) and drops out. Another employee experiencing the hardship of building new work habits (step 4) may terminate her efforts due to organizational changes at work, which no longer make the change a priority (step 2 driver). The intervention includes the enrolment in (circle 2), engagement with, and completion of formalized instruction (circle 3).

The drivers can be roughly divided into internal motivational drivers, fx interest and urgency, and external motivational drivers, fx priority and feedback (Halawa et al. 2014; Lee & Choi 2011). The external factors are underlined in the model. There is, however, a strong interrelatedness between external and internal drivers, and it can be challenging to decide whether a drop in commitment is caused by a drop in internal or external motivational drivers (Halawa et al. 2014).

The model is a simplification and generalization of extremely complex and heterogeneous human motivations, learning, and action; in many instances, the intervention and changes in work behaviors would be interwoven and the process possibly more circular or spiral-shaped than linear. The simplification aside, the model illustrates how changing work practice is a challenging and vulnerable process that requires more than formalized instruction. Each step will be explained below before returning to this argument.

2.1 Step 1: Motivation to Enroll

The first step in the model occurs when the employee decides to enroll in the PDI. The internal motivational drivers are the employee's **interest** in the content and sense of **urgency** to become competent in the field to sustain or increase work performance. As mentioned, the drivers uphold their importance throughout the change process. Thus, the employee's interest in the material must also be present during the intervention (step 2) because *"lack of interest can cause students to dedicate less time to the course, leading them to skip pieces of content, disengage from assessments, or simply proceed through the content at a slow pace"* (Halawa et al. 2014, p.2).

A key external motivational driver ensuring enrollment and persistence is the **requirement** from a manager or workplace to participate in the PDI. The use of compliance and mandatory PD varies greatly from industry to industry; most employees do, however, experience participation in mandatory PD during organizational changes (Miller et al. 2014). A requirement to enroll, complete, and change practice will have a positive impact on persistence throughout the change process, especially when the alternative has negative consequences for the employee's job tasks or employment. Employee engagement and general performance may, however, suffer along the way.

2.2 Step 2: Motivation to Engage and Complete

The second step is where the employee engages in and completes the intervention. In addition to previous drivers, persistence requires that the participation take **priority** over other job tasks. A temporary decrease in workload can also allow for engagement in PDIs. Once the workload increases, however, the PDI may be down-prioritized, resulting in dropout. Participants in PD are primarily working adults with many responsibilities and distractions (Kaiden 2002). Hence, even when PDI initially takes priority over other tasks, priorities easily change. The low exit barriers for e-learning means that the decision to leave can easily be provoked by any number of factors in the employee's life (Halawa et al. 2014).

Focusing on internal drivers, ability is an apparent predictor of persistence; low-performing participants tend to disengage more frequently than high-performing ones (Hoskins & Van Hooff 2005). However, the effects of ability on dropout are mediated by the employee's self-perceived **self-efficacy**—the degree to which the employee believes that she can achieve a particular goal. Self-reported self-efficacy has predictive value for persistence and performance (Zimmerman 2000). Though self-efficacy is widely accepted as a key driver of persistence, the timing of high self-efficacy in the change process could be important; high self-efficacy on PDI objectives *prior* to the intervention may undermine a sense of urgency to change, because the employee believes that she is already capable of and possibly already doing what is taught in the PDI. Hence, the employee must find the content sufficiently challenging to be worth the time investment, but not so challenging that content incomprehensibility and volume impede self-efficacy and knowledge gain. Individuals' self-efficacy is formed by their own interpretations of their performance and by social cues (Bandura 1982). Thus, **feedback** can be an important enhancer of self-efficacy. Effective task-related feedback generally contributes to performance improvement. To be effective, *"feedback needs to be clear, purposeful, meaningful, and compatible with (...) prior knowledge (...) It also needs to prompt active information processing on the part of learners, have low task complexity, relate to specific and clear goals, and provide little threat to the person at the self level"* (Hattie & Timperley 2007, p.104). Hence, effective feedback continues to be vital throughout the change process.

2.3 Step 3: Motivation to Transfer and Initiate Change

In step three, the motivated employee initiates changes to his work. For more than a century, researchers within the field of learning transfer have discussed this process: how knowledge and skills learned in one instructional context can be applied in another context, such as the workplace. There is, however, little agreement among researchers about the nature of learning transfer, the possibilities of its occurrence, and the mental or social mechanisms that may underlie the concept (Lobato 2006). That said, several researchers agree that employees should **practice** new skills both during and after the intervention and, thus, be able to immediately act on the new learning (Wahlgren & Aarkrog 2012). The employee must be motivated to practice, which requires actionable PDI instruction and a supportive work climate that prioritises the change

(Herrington et al. 2009; Noesgaard 2014). The initiation of change depends heavily on the level of **trust** the employee perceives to be present at her workplace. Experiences of incompetence occur when initiating change in behavior, and practitioners are reluctant to adopt new practices unless they feel certain they can make them work (Guskey 2002). If an organization punishes those who make mistakes and take risks, the employees will, thus, be reluctant to initiate change (Kousholt 2009). Trust has been overlooked in work situations but is a significant factor in PDI persistence and learning (Short 2014).

In step three, **individualization** of the learning objectives and content becomes critical for employee motivation. The employee needs to find a meaningful blend of the PDI proposed changes and the specificities of the individual work context to advance her work performance. Hence, it can be reasonable to allow employees to define their own goals and both challenge and support them when doing so (Blondy 2007). Employees do not transfer learning directly to their work practices (Noesgaard & Ørngreen 2015). Consequentially, insisting on transfer per specification may prove to be counterproductive for employee motivation to change.

2.4 Step 4: Motivation to Sustain Change

The fourth step turns initial change into sustainable change. This part of the change process is based on Thomas Guskey's model for teacher change (Guskey 2002), in which he shows that practitioners commit to PDIs and change practices sustainably only when they experience positive **results** from the initiated change. This runs counter to a general understanding that practitioners commit to changing work practices during PD (Guskey 2002). Instead, it is the unpredictable on-the-job reactions to the initial change, fx students' inactivity or a customer's increased engagement, that determine whether or not the employee finds **meaning** in the initiated change and consequently sustains it.

Numerous epistemologically diverse theories of learning underline how accommodating our habits and beliefs to new evidence not only makes creativity, learning, and change possible but can also be a very difficult, frustrating, and painful process (fx Engeström & Sannino 2010; Mezirow 1997; Cohen & Sherman 2014). Through the lens of frustration theory, employees become frustrated when they anticipate positive results in their practices after PDI but find none. Frustration left unmanaged easily obstructs initiated behavior change (Amsel 1992). It often entails an element of discomfort when an employee is led to question his practice as the most fruitful way to foster student learning or business results. Thus, employees may also become frustrated and disengage, because the initiated change conflicts with their beliefs and current practices; thus, posing an identity threat. Self-affirmation theory specifies how the individual needs to uphold his sense of **self-integrity**; to perceive oneself as morally and adaptively adequate: *"the self-integrity motive is so strong that even mundane events can threaten the self as well as instigate defensive responses to protect it"* (Cohen & Sherman 2014, p.335). Providing self-affirming interventions, which focus the individual's attention on his values and capabilities unrelated to the changing work tasks, may ensure the employee's self-integrity and openness to change.

2.5 Empirical Example of the Model: Advancing Science Teaching

The chart below (Figure 2) is a snippet of data from a study of an e-learning intervention intended to improve Danish K-6 science teaching. Ann, Lillian, and Julia (pseudonyms) are middle-school science teachers at the same school. They participated in a research study on the implications of an e-learning PDI, which was conducted at three schools from February 2014 to June 2015 with a follow-up survey six months later (more on this study in Noesgaard & Ørngreen, 2015).

Observation and survey data were gathered in identical ways and weight before (PRE) and after (POST) the teachers interacted with the e-learning (eL). In the chart (Figure 2), each value on the x-axis (PRE1-4, eL, POST1-4) represents the teachers' weekly 90-minute science teaching, in which the classroom observation took place. The curves show the teachers' performance on behavioral learning objectives based on observation protocols and video recordings. The control line represents the other teachers in the study, who did not complete the same course as Ann, Lillian, and Julia but were evaluated on the same objectives. The e-learning intervention included step 3 of the model (Figure 1) as the learning process alternated between a) instruction with theoretical knowledge, exercises, and practical tools; b) guided preparation for classes; and c) actual teaching, in which the change was initiated.

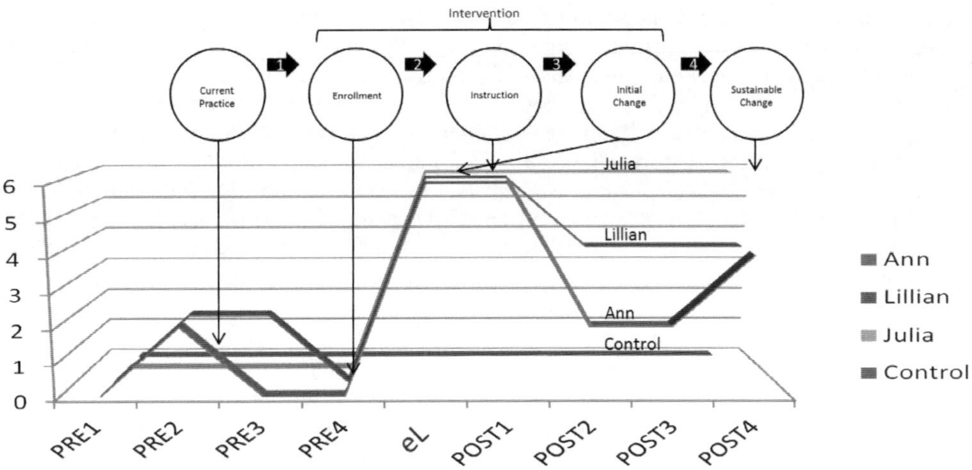

Figure 2. Exemplifying the model: e-learning for science teachers

In the PRE phase (Current Practice, Figure 2), Anna and Lillian performed on a few elements of the objectives, though the general picture shows little to no performance on the objectives. During the eL, the three teachers fully performed on the learning objectives in their teaching. In the POST phase, the e-learning had been completed, and there were no requirements for the teaching, but the classroom observation continued.

The differences in the POST phase were surprisingly apparent—also for the other teachers—despite high levels of similarity in teacher and contextual characteristics measured by self-efficacy, learning outcome, satisfaction, relationship with management, and approach to the PDI. Julia experienced a positive impact on the students during the in-class application and continued to use her new skills after completion, even applying her new questioning technique in her history classes. The follow-up survey indicated that Julia has sustained the change in her teaching. Lillian, conversely, became frustrated as her students reacted to the change in her teaching with inactivity. Both Lillian and Ann continued to apply only elements that were easy to assimilate to their current practice. The follow-up survey indicated that neither Lillian nor Ann is teaching as per the course objectives any longer. Hence, these seemingly similar teachers in very similar contexts, who completed an intervention based on transfer research, underwent very different levels (Figure 2) and kinds of change. This is an example that supports Guskey's argument that sustainable change and commitment only occur when the initial change yields positive results.

3. WHAT IS NEEDED TO ENSURE CHANGE TO WORK PRACTICES?

In PD, there is often a gradual attrition of participants from enrollment over completion to change in work practice (fx. in Marsh et al. 2001; Maloney et al. 2011). Attrition need not be negative; the content may prove irrelevant to the employee after enrollment (step 2), or he immediately finds the exact advice needed. In such instances, the continuation of the PDI could be a waste of time. Many employees who disengage somewhere along the change process could, however, have benefited from persisting. The gradual attrition calls for increasing support throughout the change process, because it becomes increasingly difficult to persist as more motivational drivers are required. Simultaneously, the level of support decreases; often, there is no PDI-related support after the instruction is completed. Thus, the need for motivational support increases the further the employee gets in the change process.

Employees need support that is highly individualized, because they vary greatly in terms of their ability to self-regulate: to control thoughts and actions despite the presence of disruptive impulses. An individual's level of self-regulation applies not only to current situations but may "*also influence the decision about whether to enter into various situations or not in the first place*" (Baumeister et al. 1993, p.141). Highly self-regulated employees may persist through formalized learning and, consequently, advance work practice without additional support. Many employees will, however, disengage when the PDI, for example, proves more time-consuming than anticipated (priority–step 2 driver) or poses a threat to their professional identity (self-integrity–step 4 driver). In frustrating situations of feeling incompetent due to no or negative impact on practice, even highly self-regulated individuals find reason to return to the status quo.

The increased need for individualized support makes scaffolding an effective strategy. Scaffolding is providing support at the individual level of the employee's current skill while she is carrying out the task, and then gradually fading out the support (Järvelä, 1995). "*A scaffold is, by definition, a temporary entity that is used to reach one's potential and then is removed when learners demonstrate their learning*" (Lajoie 2005, p.542). Inspired by Vygotsky's (1978) conception of the zone of proximal development, individuals are viewed as having learning potential that is immediately outside of their comfort zones and that can be reached through competent scaffolding by, for example, managers or coaches.

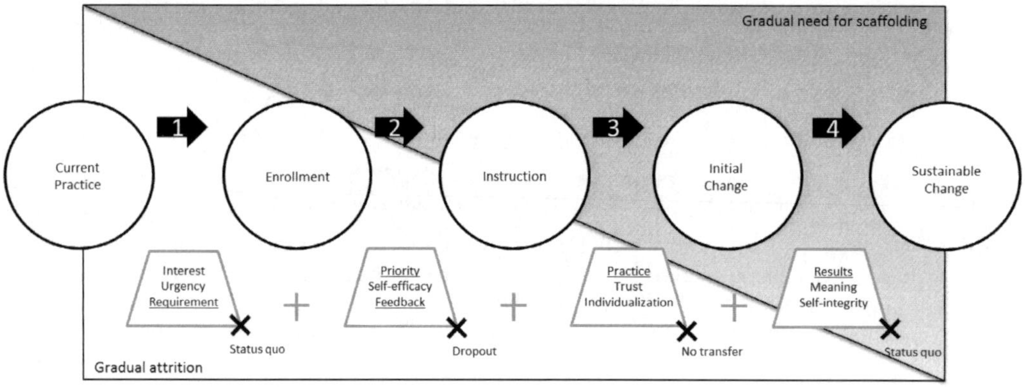

Figure 3. Gradual attrition vs. gradual need for scaffolding

In the above model (Figure 3), a rectangular background to the four-step change process has been added. It illustrates how resistance to gradual attrition requires increasing levels of scaffolding. This relationship is naturally simplified and is unlikely to be linear. In addition, attrition is relevant at the group level, while the change process highlights individual motivations. Nevertheless, scaffolding, which is competently directed at the drivers, is likely to have a positive impact on employee persistence because the extent, length, and technique of support can be tailored to levels of self-regulation and individual motivation (Lajoie 2005).

PDI aims to positively impact complex real-world settings and *"isolating the effects of a single program or activity under such conditions is usually impossible*" (Guskey 2002, p. 50). On-the-job scaffolding will, thus, not inevitably ensure advancements but may contribute positively to employees' change efforts.

4. WHICH ROLES CAN E-LEARNING PLAY IN THE CHANGE PROCESS?

Compared to face-to-face interventions, e-learning persistence is extra challenging due to the need for self-regulation combined with low entry and exit barriers. Looking at learning potential, however, several studies find that self-paced e-learning can effectively convey material for lower-level learning, such as memorization and procedural knowledge (Hofmann 2006). Even in processing difficult material, e-learning can assist through worked examples that provide structure and sequence, thereby reducing employees' cognitive load (Kachelmeier et al. 1992). Hence, stand-alone e-learning can offer inspiration, information, and standardized feedback, extending knowledge on subject matter, processes, and procedures. Therefore, e-learning can be an assimilative learning catalyst that effectively preps the ground for changes in practice.

This paper has argued that e-learning is unlikely to result in changes to work practices on its own, not because it is e-learning but because formal instruction in any modality cannot stand alone in change efforts. However, when organizational decision makers assume that well-designed instruction will advance work practices on its own, investments in scaffolding initiatives are logically considered an expensive noncritical add-on to training and, consequently, cut off the intervention chain. Ideally, the costs of scaffolding employees to sustainable change should, however, not be compared to the costs of stand-alone instructional initiatives, which, in themselves, rarely advance work practices. Acknowledging this premise, some suggestions for lowering the direct and alternative cost of scaffolding may include 1) using the majority of PDI investments on on-the-job scaffolding instead of lengthy formal instruction; 2) using e-learning snippets for retention and assimilative learning purposes; and 3) investing in scaffolding of employees' change processes for business-critical or strategic change initiatives.

At face value, on-the-job scaffolding is not scalable. Despite breakthroughs in machine learning and artificial intelligence, the in-person commitment (supporting persistence) and individualization (supporting meaningful change) cannot be fully and meaningfully turned into algorithms. As such, only incremental cost cuts can be obtained. Scaffolding may, however, become simultaneously effective and cost-efficient through the use of technology. Online coaching and follow-up has been effective in completion of PD tasks and achieving work-related goals (Poepsel 2011). Mobile probes, which are personal text messages with questions or tasks, can provide a scaffolding experiences of *"gentle, but also disciplinary, reminders to act and reflect"* (Ørngreen et al. 2016, p.8). In addition, scaffolding and assessment are two sides of the same coin; employees are continuously assessed to determine what type or level of scaffold is sufficient to help them reach their potential (Lajoie 2005). Hence, formative digital assessment tools could advance both scaffolding and learning evaluation. These technological tools cannot ensure performance increases in isolation, but as elements in adaptive learning technologies, they may prove the value of less instruction and more just-in-time and just-for-me performance support.

Broadening its definition to include scaffolding technologies, e-learning can be the provider of critical content *and* scaffolding in a multitude of fashions. When we start thinking of e-learning in these ways, we are closing in on answers to employee growth and performance in both meaningful and scalable ways.

5. CONCLUSION

This paper investigated the assumption that e-learning is as effective as face-to-face interventions when stimulating change. A four-step change process was presented illustrating key challenges and vulnerabilities of intervention-based change. E-learning can play an important role in the change process, though it highlights that sustainable change requires more than the formal instruction of any modality. Instead of evaluating e-learning in the light or shadow of its instructional alternative—face-to-face-instruction—the paper suggests that educators, managers, and employees themselves focus on the change needed and the motivational means to accomplish it. This change in perspective can open up to potentially simple and financially feasible technologies that scaffold employees to continuously advance their work practices.

PDIs do not change practice; people do. Therefore, this paper has focused on individual motivations for change. A key argument has, however, been that change does not occur in a vacuum that we can control or design. Thus, an extension of the paper would benefit from elaborating on group dynamics and from adding theoretical models of organizational learning and change. In addition, further research and technological developments can investigate the extent to which in-person situated scaffolding can be digitalized to advance work practices, thus finding scalabilities in and around the seemingly non-scalable.

ACKNOWLEDGEMENTS

This research is funded by the KATA Foundation, Denmark and Innovation Fund Denmark. I am grateful to Professor Rikke Ørngreen for her careful reading and insightful comments on a draft of this paper.

REFERENCES

Amsel, A., 1992. Frustration theory: Many years later. *Psychological Bulletin*, 112(3), pp.396–399.

Bandura, A., 1982. Self-efficacy mechanism in human agency. *American Psychologist*, 37(2), pp.122–147.

Baumeister, R.F., Heatherton, T.F. & Tice, D.M., 1993. When ego threats lead to self-regulation failure: Negative consequences of high self-esteem. *Journal of personality and social psychology*, 64(1), pp.141–156.

Blondy, L.C., 2007. Evaluation and application of andragogical assumptions to the adult online learning environment. *Journal of Interactive Online Learning*, 6(2), pp.116–130.

Cohen, G.L. & Sherman, D.K., 2014. The psychology of change: Self-affirmation and social psychological intervention. *Annual Review of Psychology*, 65(1), pp.333–371.

Engeström, Y. & Sannino, A., 2010. Studies of expansive learning: Foundations, findings and future challenges. *Educational Research Review*, 5(1), pp.1–24.

Guskey, T.R., 2002. Professional development and teacher change. *Teachers and Teaching*, 8(3/4), pp.381–391.

Guskey, T.R., 2002. Does it make a difference? *Educational Leadership*, 59(6), pp.45–51.

Halawa, S., Greene, D. & Mitchell, J., 2014. Dropout prediction in MOOCs using learner activity features. *eLearning Papers*, 37(March), pp.1–10.

Hattie, J. & Timperley, H., 2007. The power of feedback. *Review of Educational Research*, 77(1), pp.16–7.

Herrington, A. et al., 2009. Transfer of online professional learning to teachers' classroom practice. *Journal of Interactive Learning Research*, 20(2), pp.189–213.

Ho, Maris; Jones, M., 2015. *2015 State of the industry*. Alexandria, USA: ASTD DBA Association for Talent Development (ATD).

Hofmann, J., 2006. Why blended learning hasn't (yet) fulfilled its promise. In C. R. Bonk, C. J. Graham, ed. *Handbook of Blended Learning: Global Perspectives, Local Designs*. San Francisco, USA: Pfeiffer Publishing.

Hoskins, S.L. & Van Hooff, J.C., 2005. Motivation and ability: Which students use online learning and what influence does it have on their achievement? *British Journal of Educational Technology*, 36(2), pp.177–192.

Jackson, T.W. & Lichtenstein, S., 2011. Optimising e-mail communication: The impact of seminar- and computer-based training. *International Journal of Internet and Enterprise Management*, 7(2), pp.197–216.

Kachelmeier, S.J., Jones, J.D. & Keller, J.A., 1992. Evaluating the effectiveness of a computer-intensive learning aid for teaching pension accounting. *Issues in Accounting Education*, 7(2), p.164.

Kaiden, R., 2002. Lessons from the cyberspace classroom: The realities of online teaching. *The Internet and Higher Education*, 5(1), pp.71–74.

Kousholt, B., 2009. *Forandringsledelse og forandringskommunikation*, Frederiksberg: Samfundslitteratur.

Lajoie, S.P., 2005. Extending the scaffolding metaphor. *Instructional Science*, 33(5–6), pp.541–557.

Lee, Y. & Choi, J., 2011. A review of online course dropout research: Implications for practice and future research. *Educational Technology Research and Development*, 59(5), pp.593–618.

Lobato, J., 2006. Alternative perspectives on the transfer of learning : History, issues, and challenges for future research. *Journal of the Learning Sciences*, 15(4), pp.431–449.

Maloney, S. et al., 2011. Effectiveness of web-based versus face-to-face delivery of education in prescription of falls-prevention exercise to health professionals: Randomized trial. *Journal of Medical Internet Research*, 13(4).

Marsh, C.M. et al., 2001. Design and effectiveness of a computer-based continuing education program for orthodontists. *The Angle Orthodontist*, 71(1), pp.71–75.

Mezirow, J., 1997. Transformative learning: theory to practice. *New Directions for Adult and Continuing Education*, 1997(74), pp.5–12.

Miller, L. et al., 2014. *2014 State of the Industry*. Alexandria, USA: ASTD DBA Association for Talent Development (ATD).

Noesgaard, S.S., 2014. Supporting transfer of learning: Practice-based considerations on the applicability of transfer literature in online design. In *Proceedings of Designs for Learning 2014*. Stockholm, pp. 1–5.

Noesgaard, S.S. & Ørngreen, R., 2015. The effectiveness of e-learning : An explorative and integrative review of the definitions, methodologies and factors that promote e-learning effectiveness. *The Electronic Journal of e-Learning*, 13(4), pp.278–290.

Ørngreen, R., Jørgensen, A.N. & Noesgaard, S.S., 2016. Mobile probes: A scaffold for peer and self-regulated learning. In *Proceedings of Designs for Learning 2016* (accepted). Copenhagen.

Palloff, R.M. & Pratt, K., 2001. Learning lessons from the cyberspace classroom. *17th Annual Conference on Distance Teaching and Learning*, pp.1–5.

Poepsel, M.A., 2011. *The Impact of an Online Evidence-Based Coaching Program on Goal Striving, Subjective Well-Being, and Level of Hope*. Capella University.

Short, H., 2014. A critical evaluation of the contribution of trust to effective technology enhanced learning in the workplace: A literature review. *British Journal of Educational Technology*, 45(6), pp.1014–1022.

Vygotsky, L.S., 1978. Interaction between learning and development. In *Mind in Society: The Development of Higher Psychological Processes*, pp.29–36.

Wahlgren, B. & Aarkrog, V., 2012. *Transfer: Kompetence i en professionel sammenhæng*. Aarhus Universitetsforlag, Aarhus.

Zimmerman, B.J., 2000. Self-efficacy: An essential motive to learn. *Contemporary Educational Psychology*, 25(1), pp.82–91.

A PRACTICE OF MOBILE LEARNING BASED ON CLOUD COMPUTING

Wu Heng and Dong Zhong
Tianshui Normal University

ABSTRACT

Information and communication technology are well known rapid growing industry in this decade. That is nearly the same as fast as growth in costs in education. Therefore, many people have been forced to find alternative ways to meet their education needs. Innovations of distance education create a new way to provide learning content, unlimited participation and open access through Massively Open Online Courses(MOOCs) via the web. In the addition, mobile learning centered research are sprouting out, anytime, anywhere, anyone learning is becoming what people aspire to. The published papers introduced mobile native applications, web applications and hybrid applications in order to enhance mobile learning. However, scalability becomes a common issue among all the solutions. In this paper, we tackle the scalability, collaboration, and content delivery problems by using cloud computing method aimed at making best effort to MOOC in mobile devices. Therefore, a practice of mobile learning is well designed and implemented based on cloud computing.

KEYWORDS

Cloud computing; mobile learning; mobile computing; mobile application

1. INTRODUCTION

MOOC, is one way of learning in networked world, has been around us for a while. A Mooc is a course, its open, participatory and distributed. It supports lifelong network learning that is education for all ages. MOOC is built for a world where information is everywhere. It is not just online course but a path to connect and collaborate while developing digital skills to waive engaging in the learning process[1]. In November of 2012, the New York Times declared 2012 “the Year of MOOC”. MOOC even had been touted as the first serious bit of competition of universities in the past thousand years. The main reason why MOOC become so popular is education cost grows too fast. For example, the growth in price of a college education has grown faster than prices in many other categories. People’s hunger of professional skills and knowledge from top academic intuitions also play important role in the blooming of MOOCs. It is maybe one of the most important events around which people who care about a topic can get together in work and talk about it in a structured way. Most likely, people have to pay to get the credit through an institution, but they are not willing paying for participating in the chargeable MOOC courses.

This is a new way that people really master knowledge because that all the work gets done in areas accessible for people to read and reflect in and comment on. It is also mean that all the people take the material put together by the facilitators and the work done by the participants, learners have to keep their work in order to share with others. People become part of the course by engaging with other people’s work. Participants are not been asked to complete specific assignments but rather to engage with the material with each other in with other material that may find on the web. MOOCS fits very well to several area knowledge and offers practice-oriented learning[2]. All of these features embrace MOOCs as a path toward professional skills and high-paying jobs without college degree approaching and paying for.

There are almost as many cell-phone subscriptions (6.8 billion) as there are people on the earth(seven billion) according to United Nations’s telecommunications agency[3]. In another words, it is almost everyone has a mobile phone. The phone like smartphone has already become the main information process device. When mobile phone first came out, it was the communication device that only manage wireless phone calls and text messaging. With the rapid development of telecommunication, the cell signal covers almost every corner in the world. The smart phone can be used to watch videos with Youtube, make social network with Wechat and dealing with email. In fact, 21.6% of globe web page views goes through mobile device, and most of those users hardly use computer.

People has concerned about mobile device as the new media with very high expectation. It should be competent for learning content delivery, collaboration between participants and publishers, live streaming, survey, homework marking and so on. Mobile learning solution needs to take into consideration of all aspects of system with scalable, cross-platform design. Mobile device are born with these defects but not limited: bandwidth is narrow, easy loss, small screen and easily interfered signal. Mobile device manufactures also create some flaws: fragmentation of mobile phone operation system(OS) and hundreds of different screen sizes. Therefore, to produce one unique solution in order to integrate all sorts of OS and all kinds of different technique seems very complicated.

This paper introduce a mobile cloud computing solution to solve above problems by employing Cloud computing. The cloud computing based solution unleash the power of mobile device and ease publishers, developer and learners by reducing the cost of online resource. Some necessary tools also have been brought up that enable system with live stream, survey, file sharing capabilities. This is a highly scalable, reliable, and cross-platform solution. For demonstration, we designed a mobile learning MOOC course to practice the method of this paper.

The paper is organized by following structure: part II describe mobile learning at present, then we analysis mobile learning with cloud computing in part III; in part IV we dive deeply into cloud computing and come up with solution; part V compare the advantages and disadvantages among other available cloud computing platforms then design a demonstration in part VI and end up with VII.

2. RELATED WORK

Now, most of learning application running on the computer, therefore, it is not only a modification of the configuration files but also a redesign in order to run the program on mobile device. In mobile application development, there are two points: the first is mobile native app and the second is mobile web app. The realization of two methods is not the same with its own advantages and disadvantages. The mobile native app is an app that is built using native stack.

2.1 Advantages of Native app but not limited

2.1.1 Higher User Engagement

Native apps live on a user's home screen and it can be used offline. It also allows users to use apps in a more personal and interactive manner on a regular basis with little difficulties. Native apps have the ability to send push notifications and reminders to users, furthermore, increasing the possibility of brand interaction.

2.1.2 Smoother Experience

Native apps respond more fluidly to user, it gives better user experience.

2.1.3 Integration with Hardware

GPS or Motion detector modules can be directly integrated into hardware.

2.1.4 Commercialization is Easy

In-app billing, app payment and free options are available for mobile native apps.

2.2 Things need to be concerned for Developers

2.2.1 Mobile Native Apps are not Cross-Platform

It has to be designed for certain platforms that sometime become enormous time-consuming and over the budget. Although there are certain cross-platform development tools available in public, for example Xamarin, its high license price just reject most individual developers.

2.2.2 Updating is not Easy

Native app updates need lot of effort on developing and testing to program, and it needs to be downloaded and installed by clients to take effect.

As earlier mentioned, the alternative way is mobile web app. A web app is an app that built using HTML, CSS and Javascript for most part. Web apps have the following pros[4]: It is almost cross-platform, web app runs in multiple environment with the idea "write once, run everywhere"; No need to send updates through the app store, updates can be published anytime; Faster to prototype in HTML/CSS/JAVASCRIPT than native apps. Space saving; All the materials are downloaded from the web, saved mobile limited space.

Web apps have following cons:Web apps will never be as perform as it' s native counterpart; Executing code in a browser-context is slower than the native context; There are so many limitations in mobile device comparing computer web browser; Web apps need to be online to run properly; The communication between web app and integrated hardware is a pain, and not elegant.

To solve all the above-mentioned issues, integrate the ability of cloud computing into mobile devices and maximum the advantages of mobile devices, there are some solutions produced by published papers. Using [5], author confirms some requirements and key technologies to implement cloud computing with mobile device. In paper [6], author illustrate MOOC as a revolutionary force that disrupt traditional higher education by expanding access and reducing costs. Using [7], a virtual cloud computing platform based on mobile device is shown, which is consist of nearby mobile devices by assembling a Ad Hoc network.

However, the collaboration between developers and learners is not included in those solutions. Therefore, this paper introduce a fine designed cloud computing solution that host data and applications within sina cloud computing platform. In helping collaboration, the solution with integration of mobile cloud computing can easily solve scalablity problems which was still bottleneck in other platforms.

3. MOBILE LEARNING AND CLOUD COMPUTING

People may have different points of view in mobile learning, but the center idea of common points is learning activities should be available anytime in any locations. Mobile learning is the intersection of mobile computing and e-learning, and mobile learning is defined as resource access with no location limitation, powerful search engine, efficient study, easy evaluation[8]. The mobile learning system is aimed to satisfy learner's anywhere, anytime studying style with open, easy access, massive knowledge.

The very basic objective of mobile learning is: 1)Open educational resources, sufficient course materials, effective evaluation[9]. 2)Learners should be more proactive in their education and in building their personal learning networks, they need to participate to get the most out of a MOOC. 3)The system has the ability to analysis the need of learners. 4)Cut down the cost to the bottom. 5)Delivery of learning, education or learning support everywhere. 6)Reforming traditional education, learner only focus on the interesting knowledge. 7)Improving the communication between learners and facilitators.

To achieve these mobile learning goals must rely on scalable, powerful, efficient computing network which is cloud computing technology. The main purpose of this paper is how cloud computing use in mobile learning, but not cloud computing itself. The content will refer some key technologies of cloud computing, exploring how those technologies were functioned in the mobile computing.

In brief, cloud computing is the practice of using a network of remote servers hosted on the Internet to store, manage, and process data, rather than a local server or a personal computer[10]. Cloud computing comes in four forms: 1) Public cloud. Public services provider offer the services and infrastructure off-site over the Internet with the high level of efficiency in public cloud; however, they are more vulnerable than private clouds. 2) Private cloud. Comparing public cloud, A private cloud is maintained on a private network. These clouds offer the greatest level of security and control, but they require a carefully planning of company. 3) Hybrid cloud. A hybrid cloud inherit a variety of public and private advantages with multiple providers. It is the trend of cloud computing in the future. The downside is that you have to keep track of multiple different security platforms and ensure that all aspects of your business can communicate with each other[11]. 4) Community cloud. A community cloud is a multi-tenant infrastructure that is shared among several organizations from a specific group with common computing concerns[12]. Such concerns might be related to regulatory compliance, such as audit requirements, or may be related to performance requirements, such as hosting applications that require a quick response time, for example[12].

Figure 1.Three different type of Cloud computing services

There are three different type of Cloud computing services:1) Software-as-a-Service(SaaS):is defined in [13], some defining characteristics are: web access to commercial software; Software is managed from a central location; Software delivered in a"one to many" model; Users not required to handle software upgrades and patches; Application Programming Interfaces (APIs) allow for integration between different pieces of software. 2) Platform-as-a-Service(PaaS): brings the benefits that SaaS bought for applications, but over to the software development world. PaaS can be defined as a computing platform that allows the creation of web applications quickly and easily and without the complexity of buying and maintaining the software and infrastructure underneath it.PaaS is analogous to SaaS except that, rather than being software delivered over the web, it is a platform for the creation of software, delivered over the web[14]. The example of PaaS include SAE, Amazon and so on. 3) Infrastructure-as-a-Service(IaaS):Infrastructure as a Service (IaaS) is a way of delivering Cloud Computing infrastructure – servers, storage, network and operating systems – as an on-demand service. Rather than purchasing servers, software, data center space or network equipment, clients instead buy those resources as a fully outsourced service on demand[15].

4. SINA CLOUD COMPUTING

Sina cloud computing platform is the leading PaaS platform in China, it is been chosen to represent cloud computing in this paper for instantiation. Applications are created and implemented in the cloud facilities by developers over the Internet. It is supplier's responsibility to keep the whole system running successfully, therefore, the cost of hardware purchasing and service maintain from content provider is almost reduced to zero. Publisher will have more energy to produce better MOOC materials and delivery better content. For a education institution, to run a web server not only need to configure web server to setup, but also, the internal and external firewalls have to be configured properly. Administrator of the web server have to make certain computer program running environment according to clients application design programming language. This will increase the size of technical team and operation cost of institution. According to the supplier's policy, education related applications have more privileges than applications other categories. Cloud builder wants to put best effort to delivery better online course to hungry for knowledge of the students. The hardware, software, services are well designed to work together, for example, load balancing, cache and storage, each of them has the most popular scheme. Some unique features of Sina Cloud engine is the reason why we gave up other platform:

4.1 Multiple Programming Language Support

Cloud Computing platform support some most commonly used programming languages, such as PHP, PYTHON, JAVA. Any of them can be used to create fascinating applications for background data process or web pages for mobile web apps with modern interfaces. Each programming language has its own SDK and documents.

4.2 Distributed Implementation

Application code is distributed to web servers in different locations. If one server power down or stop servicing, clients requests will automatically forward to the rest servers, client feels nothing. This improves user experience dramatically.

4.3 Efficient Load Balancing

By using “7 layer” load balancing technology, gateway server will analysis clients request content, and forward the request to the lowest load server. “7 layer” is a reverse proxy technology, which handle clients requests and check the backend server constantly in order to forward request only to the health one.

4.4 Sandbox

The sandbox attempts to isolate processes to protect process and whole system. Sandbox increase the value of application by isolating other user to read application.

4.5 Relational Database and No-Sql Database Support

By default, it support MySQL database. With the fashion of nosql, the system supports KVDB. Third part database management software can be use to manage MySQl even without modify one single line. In addition, database uses mater-slave prototype, this makes best effort of preventing data lost.

4.6 Multi-layer Security

The security is consist of sandbox, application firewall, password protection.

4.7 Powerful Service

The platform comes with some powerful services to developers. STROAGE handles big files, CDN speed up clients access based on the geographic locations of the users, MEMCACHE offers distributed cache service.

5. ADVANTAGES AND DISADVANTAGES IN MOBILE LEARNING

Cloud platform satisfy all different need of mobile learning, including mobility, learners interaction, communication between learners and facilitators, file sharing, live stream and so on, and this is why we recommend education institutions use SAE as mobile learning solution.

5.1 Advantages

5.1.1 It can integrate with Sina’s other Service, meet Different Need of Developers

Sina Email: Sina email service is one of earliest email providers, there are millions users on the web. It is convenient to use sina email because of large users and similarity. Sina vDisk: Sina vDisk is where documents, comments, pictures, ebooks, all sorts of electronic resource to save and share and it comes free to use. Weibo: Like Twitter© in the US, Weibo has the same influence in China. Weibo can be seamlessly embed into other suppliers services. Weibo is the best way for students to participant MOOC topics. It can publish learner’s thoughts and comments other peoples ideas which in turn helps deepen the learning experience.

5.1.2 Highly Scalable

When clients number jumps from millions to billions, system can smoothly shift up.

5.1.3 Server Management

Server management, data distribute, load balancing are all responded. Education institution only focus on the content of resource.

5.1.4 Security

Sandbox means the high security, data confidential, and reliability.

5.1.5 Multiple Language Support

At present, there are three programming languages available in SAE, they are: PHP, PYTHON and JAVA. Document of those three languages is also available.

5.1.6 Cost

It is absolutely free to start. When traffic and load among certain level, publisher will need to pay for the platform.

5.1.7 Easy to develop

In order to attract more developers and learners, its official website have tons of nice tutorials, it ease the development process. Developer will create fantastic application only need nice ideas.

5.1.8 High Reliability

For non-profit or commercial use, cloud can guarantee 90% of online time.

5.2 Disadvantage

5.2.1 Portability

Application configurations must meet cloud platform specific properties. When transform a application from Sina into other platform, application sometime need to be redesigned and plan.

5.2.2 Need More Support Language

As everyone know, the programming language like C is used so wildly. The lack of C programming language make this cloud platform less popular in certain developers. SAE has the right to support other common languages like, C#, Ruby.

5.2.3 Lack of In-Built Billing System

There is no in-built billing system, you have to employ this method by other third part company.

5.2.4 No Advertisement Publish

Most mobile application is free, developers use advertisement to gain incoming, the cloud platform should have this system to enhance application and increase incomes.

6. EVALUATION

In order to demonstrate the idea, we use two classes for experimental. One with traditional teaching method and another one with mobile learning method. Therefore, we name traditional teaching method class as Group A, and another one as Group B. Both of the classes use exactly the same syllabus, same content, same exercise, same teaching period and same lecturer.

However, Group B students have to watch tutorial video before the class and join the class conference in the middle of the class. Also, they need to post feedback on mobile learning conference website after class. The group A student will skip the part.

We carefully create a web app that contains all course related materials and conference website that receive and post all students feedback. All content of course is coded in HTML, CSS and Javascript. Study session could be established at anytime, with all different device. The content is optimized to adjust narrow screen and full screen. It is running in practice, hosted within Sina Cloud computing platform. The snapshot of web site is shown below in figure 2:

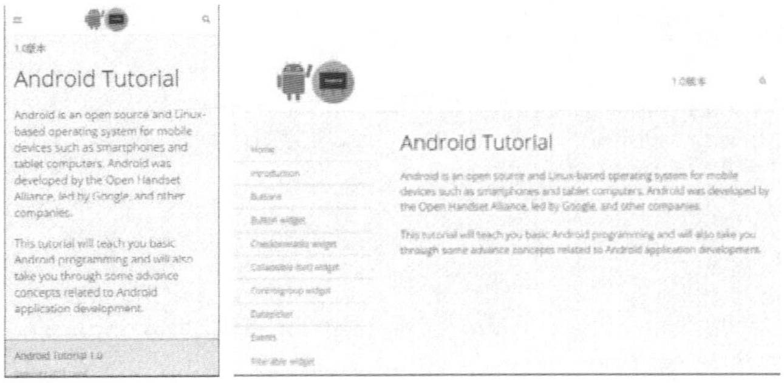

Figure 2. Same content in Samsung Galaxy IV and Galaxy Tab with different display. The navigation will be automatic hide if screen is not big enough. The MOOC course can be view from: http://kennyandroidtutor.sinapp.com

By tracking the content view history, it shows us the learners study anytime at convenience and access from all different location. Flexible access enable users no longer to rote, however, every topic can be viewed as many times as they wish.

The following table shows some analysis data between Group A and B students.

Table 1. Data analysis between Group A and B students

	Group A	Group B
Students number	53	49
Average score	62	78
Exercise number	14	17
Study hours/week	2	9
Feedback number	2	70
Wish to continue Android advanced study	5	23
Study evaluation	78%	90%

The average score between Group A and B is up to 16 that clearly shows Group B students have between study effect. However, in order to achieve higher score, the Group B students spend more than four times of Group A do.

The two groups have slightly difference in assignment numbers. Exercise effect do not strongly depend on mobile learning method.The most impact is continue learning influence. Almost half of the Group B students wish to carry on advanced study in the future comparing only 10 percent in Group A student wish to study further.

According to feedback, review video is the most popular feather in mobile learning method. Students have better understanding and interesting with review video capacity.

These result easily shows that a carefully designed website, mature course material and elegant tutorial videos combined mobile learning method with cloud computing implements improve study effect remarkably.

Figures should de numbered consecutively as they appear in the text.

7. CONCLUSION

In this paper, we have seen the benefits of cloud computing as a scalable solution for mobile learning. Mobile learner can study anytime, anywhere without computer limitations. The mobile solution fit all mobile learning requirements. Social apps and most available internet tools make cloud computing more powerful to collaborate and communicate. By employing cloud computing , education institution really cut down the cost and leave the hash of scalability. This is a right solution that can be implemented with great success by any institutions that would chose a cross-platform compatible approach to educational content delivery through the cloud to mobile learners. Finally, we implement this method in practice by setting up a online MOOC course and demonstrate the idea by data analysis.

ACKNOWLEDGEMENT

This work was partially supported by GOOGLE 2015 industry-university collaboration for discipline reform program "Mobile Application Development Teaching methods on MOOC".

REFERENCES

1. A. Tabot, M. Hamada, "Mobile Learing with Google App Engine", 2014 IEEE 8th International Symposium on Embedded Multicore/Manycore SoCs.
2. Garcia, F. (Electr. & Comput. Eng. Dept., Spanish Univ. for Distance Educ., Madrid, Spain); Diaz, G.; Tawfik, M.; Martin, S.; Sancristobal, E.; Castro, M. Source: 2014 IEEE Global Engineering Education Conference (EDUCON), p 969-74, 2014
3. http://qz.com/179897/more-people-around-the-world-have-cell-phones-than-ever-had-land-lines/W.-K. Chen, *Linear Networks and Systems.* Belmont, CA: Wadsworth, 1993, pp. 123–135.
4. http://tilomitra.com/web-vs-native/
5. K. Kaur , S. Sharma, M. Arora, "Mobile Cloud Computing Techniques: A Review, " International Journal of Advanced Research in Computer Engineering & Technology (IJARCET)Volume 3 Issue 4, April 2014.
6. N. Mallikharjuna, C. Sasidhar, V. Satyendra, "Cloud Computing Through Mobile Learning," Available at arxiv.org/pdf/1204.1594.
7. H. Gonzalo, L. Dongman, "A Virtual Cloud Computing Provider for Mobile Devices," ACM Workshop on Mobile Cloud Computing & Services: Social Networks and Beyond. MCS'10, June 15, 2010, San Francisco, California, USA.
8. Crompton, H. (2013). A historical overview of mobile learning: Toward learner-centered education. In Z. L. Berge & L. Y. Muilenburg (Eds.), Handbook of mobile learning (pp. 3–14). Florence, KY: Routledge.
9. http://www.explorance.com/blog/2013/11/4-ways-evaluate-massive-open-online-courses-moocs/
10. https://www.google.com/?gws_rd=ssl#newwindow=1&q=cloud+computing+definition
11. Judith Hurwitz, Comparing Public, Private, and Hybrid Cloud Computing Options (2012),http://www.dummies.com/how-to/content/comparing-public-private-and-hybrid-cloud-computin.html
12. http://searchcloudstorage.techtarget.com/definition/community-cloud
13. http://en.wikipedia.org/wiki/Software_as_a_service
14. http://www.rackspace.com/knowledge_center/whitepaper/understanding-the-cloud-computing-stack-saas-paas-iaas
15. http://diversity.net.nz/wp-content/uploads/2011/01/Moving-to-the-Clouds.pdf

GUIDELINES FOR CONDUCTING A POST-GRADUATE MODULE WITHIN A BLENDED SYNCHRONOUS LEARNING ENVIRONMENT, FACILITATOR AND STUDENT PERSPECTIVES

Christopher Upfold
Rhodes University, South Africa

ABSTRACT

Technology facilitated teaching and learning can now influence the way both lecturers and students collaborate. The problem is that many of these interventions are conducted in a non-systematic ad-hoc way. There are concerns that merely adopting a traditional lecturing approach to a technology based environment provides little if any advantage to the education processes resulting in no manifest difference.

During 2013 and 2014, an attempt was made to offer a virtual collaboration (VC) module blending a traditional face-to-face approach with a blended teaching approach by adding a synchronous virtual classroom environment. The VC module had previously been offered to Information System honours students in a traditional face-to-face environment only. An action research methodology was deemed the most appropriate and in the first year, a conservative, phased approach was adopted to mitigate risk to both students as well as the lecturer concerned. After attempting a traditional lecturing style within the virtual environment, it was quickly realized that a facilitative role is necessary to achieve the potential of a virtual classroom. During the first year, data was collected from students as well as a virtual participant. The lecturer maintained a detailed log of experiences as well. During the second year, major process changes reflected the lessons learned from year one. This also resulted in six (6) guidelines believed to be appropriate for conducting a post-graduate module within a blended synchronous learning environment. The most significant contribution, however, is believed to be in the realization of what a virtual classroom environment means to an extended learning community and the value of providing a collaborative learning environment and encouraging students to engage with external stakeholders.

KEYWORDS

Blended learning, virtual collaboration, extended learning communities, community of enquiry

1. INTRODUCTION

Technology pervades most universities with high speed data line connectivity providing both wired and wireless computer access and internet connectivity. It is not surprising then that tertiary institutions have been exploring ways to leverage information and communication technologies (ICTs) in support of teaching, learning and administration (Draper and Brown 2004; Corlett , Sharples , Bull and Chan, 2005; Oliver, 2006). From an education perspective, ICTs are already influencing and indeed disrupting the traditional business as usual approach to course delivery (Stensaker, Maaseen, Borgan, Oftebro and Karseth, 2007).

During 2011, a new two-week elective module titled Virtual Collaboration (VC) was offered to Information Systems honours students at a South African University. The intention was to expose students to virtual collaboration under three banners, eLearning, Social Networking and Virtual Business. The idea was to provide students with a theoretical and a rigorous practical perspective on virtual collaboration by taking both a business as well as an educational perspective. The module was well received by students and after experimenting with virtual classroom technology as part of the 2011 and 2012 VC module, it was decided that during 2013 and 2014, an attempt would be made to adapt and re-design the VC for a blended synchronous environment supported by the blackboard collaborate virtual classroom environment. The open source course management system (CMS) Moodle had been used at the outset of the module in 2011 and was continued during 2013 and 2014. To cater for technical uncertainties including bandwidth concerns, the

2013 module combined a conservative equal measure of traditional classroom contact with virtual classroom contact. Based on lessons learned during 2013, the 2014 module was almost entirely conducted within the blackboard collaborate environment.

Lecturer and student experiences and perceptions captured during the two years, have resulted in several guidelines which are suggested for adapting an existing face-to-face module for delivering a post-graduate module within a blended synchronous learning environment.

2. BLENDED LEANING

Blended Learning (BL), the focus of this paper, is about blending traditional classroom instruction with online learning activities using both asynchronous communication as well as real-time synchronous communication modes (Lin and Overbaugh, 2009). Blended learning may include any combination of learning delivery methods which normally include face-to-face instruction with asynchronous and or synchronous computer technologies (So and Brush, 2007). An essential component of most online learning systems including blended learning systems is a software application for the administration, documentation, tracking, reporting and delivery of electronic educational technology, called a Learning Management System (LMS) (Ellis and Ryann, 2009). As suggested, the open source Moodle LMS was used during this research and played an important anchoring role in both asynchronous and synchronous delivery.

Much research has been undertaken to demonstrate "achievement gains of technology-facilitated learning over conventional methods of teaching" with limited regard for understanding how and why the gains might have been realised (Herrington, McKenney, Reeves, and Oliver, 2007). There are concerns that merely adopting a traditional lecturing approach to a technology based environment provides little if any advantage to the education processes rendering "no significant difference" resulting in a "pseudoscience" (Reeves, 2011 in Teras and Herrington, 2014).

An area considered important in the context of blended learning is understanding the student, the extended learning community and the engagement that takes place between all stakeholders. The Community of Inquiry (CoI) framework (Figure 1) which was created by Garrison and Vaughan (2008) is intended to guide the practice and research of online learning.

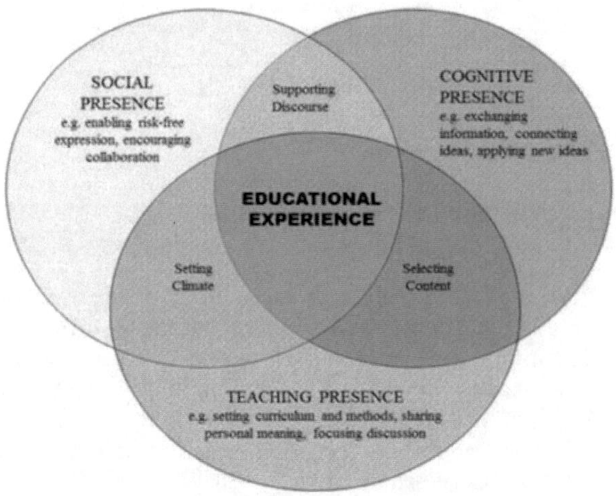

Figure 1. Community of Inquiry Framework (Garrison and Vaughan, 2008)

The CoI framework covers two critical areas in higher education, community and inquiry. Garrison and Vaughan (2008) suggest that reflection and discourse play a critical role in a "meaningful education experience". They argue that successful blended learning design must incorporate the careful integration of online learning and face-to-face learning "for better reflection and discourse" and also that blended learning design must revisit and rethink "the learning and teaching to optimize student engagement" (Garrison and Vaughan, 2008 in Chew et al., 2008). In essence, the CoI framework has as its foundation Dewey's constructivist paradigm arguing that educational inquiry is not about memorizing nor attempting to reach final answers, but rather about a practical process to investigate problems and issues. They argue that ideally "knowledge is shaped and constructed through social interaction and collaboration". While Garrison and Vaughan (2008) promote the use of research into technologies to enhance the educational experience, their major focus is on learning supported by and taking into account, Social Presence, Cognitive Presence and Teaching Presence (Chew et al., 2008).

Through what may be described as a fairly naïve and immersive approach to the research, the researcher discovered that Social Presence, Cognitive Presence and Teaching Presence were core to the success of the blended learning intervention. By involving industry experts, students were able to meet with and debate various theoretical issues pertaining to the selected topics in support of the outcomes of the module. Providing the appropriate learning outcomes and affording students the opportunity to research and debate various issues not only amongst themselves but within a virtual environment consisting of remotely based academics and industry professionals, was illuminating.

An additional component believed to be equally important in informing a successful blended learning approach, is focusing specifically on the student. DeTure (2004) suggests that cognitive style and self-efficacy needs to be understood in order to predict student success in online education. Cognitive style refers to the "cognitive, affective, and physiological traits that serve as relatively stable indicators of how learners perceive, interact with and respond to the learning environment" (Keef, 1998). Self-efficacy refers to a student's confidence and ability to complete tasks or research goals (DeTure, 2004).

Student generational theory can provide some useful insights into understanding cognitive style and self-efficacy. Generation Y, enter higher education with "very different learning backgrounds, experiences, preferences, attitudes and skill sets" and respond best within an experiential learning environment with the dominant pedagogy being hands on and interactive assignments and in class activities, "team-work" and "collaborative presentations". Also, the level of connectedness is critical to this generation who display a lot of technical savvy, and partake in high levels of virtual collaboration and embrace entertainment and excitement. (Shih and Allen, 2007).

3. METHOD

An action research method was chosen in which the lecturer initiated a practical, reflective as well as iterative approach to the blended learning module intervention. Parsons and Brown (2002) suggest that in order to be an effective educator a lecturer should be an "active participant" in the teaching and learning process, This includes active participation in the classroom, observing, analyzing and interpreting information. Baskerville (1999), Derntl and Motschnig-Pitrik (2004) concur with this view suggesting that action research is increasingly accepted as an appropriate methodology for introducing new media into innovative teaching. They argue that pioneering teachers are likely to introduce new media into teaching and learning as a combination of practical research and deliberate reflective processes. This was certainly the approach taken with regards this research.

3.1 Additional Research Context

During the first two years, 2011 and 2012, the VC module was offered as a traditional face-to-face module only. Students were organized into three teams and these consisted of an eLearning team, a social networking team and a virtual business team. Team topics were arranged around specific module outcomes. The lecturer provided scene-setter lectures at the start of each new section and students were required to research and prepare presentations intended to address their specific outcomes. Classwork assessment included; individual topic presentations (style and content), team text book contributions and technology intervention presentations. Detailed assessment criteria were provided for each component. Students were required to sit a final case based exam during the formal University examination period. A Moodle based CMS was used for all module related material including detailed assessment rubrics.

3.2 Introducing a Virtual Classroom in 2013

Twenty one (21) IS honours students selected the VC module at the start of 2013. As usual, IS honours students were provided with personally assigned workstations and in addition, a webcam with headset. The University has a division known as the Centre for Higher Education Research, Teaching and Learning (CHERTL) which is a central service provided to all faculty. CHERTL lease a 50 user Blackboard Collaborate license which faculty can then access. CHERTL provided initial Blackboard Collaborate support. Excitingly, an eLearning expert based in a different province agreed to participate virtually in the module.

Besides some minor pedagogic revisions, the VC module retained a similar structure to the face-to-face module delivered during 2012. The significant change being to conduct at least 50% of the module online with the introduction of the synchronous virtual classroom.

The module was launched in a lecture venue. The module outcomes, assessment strategy and blended learning strategy were explained in detail. Students were also introduced to the module CMS implemented via Moodle. This was followed by Blackboard Collaborate familiarity training. From then on, lectures ran as either traditional or virtual depending on the pre-planned module schedule.

3.3 Data Collection

Students were tasked to email the lecturer their perceptions of the virtual classroom experience after each session. Students had the opportunity to relate their experience as both module participant and a content presenter. The eLearning expert who participated in the module agreed to provide feedback as well. The lecturer also kept a personal detailed log of all experiences and impressions as the module progressed.

As student data were received, a content analysis was conducted extracting certain themes that emerged throughout the two weeks. These included: the need for additional time to get used to extended functionality within the virtual environment, the need to introduce greater engagement in order to maintain student involvement and interaction, the need to compensate for the lack of visual cues and feedback.

3.4 Lessons Learned in 2013

- Less than ideal bandwidth is a major impediment and may result in compromised video and audio quality from time to time, impacting some of the core functionality within the virtual classroom.
- Lack of familiarity within the Blackboard environment resulted in sometimes muddled usage of the tool and limited usage of some features included in the tool.
- On occasion it took upwards of 20 minutes to get everyone into the virtual classroom. It is essential that all participants start the process at least 25 minutes prior to the scheduled start time.
- The lecturer MUST facilitate the process. This is a key observation and requires very deliberate planning prior to the launch of a particular course or module. Attempting to a traditional face-to-face lecture is not appropriate in a virtual classroom and results in a boring experience for all concerned.
- The millennials involved in the course were excited about exposure to a virtual learning environment, especially given the opportunity to prepare short presentations as part of their group contribution to the module.
- A guest lecturer provided a highly valuable eLearning perspective.

3.5 Revisiting the VC module in 2014

The 2013 VC module received encouraging reviews and the decision was taken to offer it again in 2014 Twenty-four (24) students registered. In planning the 2014 VC module, it was decided to try and attract several guest lecturers and to use the virtual classroom for most planned contact time. The willingness by industry professionals and external academics to give of their time was overwhelming.

The three (3) main focus areas were narrowed to two (2), eLearning and Virtual Business. Social networking was incorporated in both these topics. As before, students would each deliver and facilitate their module content by way of 15 minute virtual lectures. Two case studies served as an addition to the 2014 VC module. One case study was designed for the eLearning group and the other for the Virtual Business group.

The University's Moodle based CMS was again selected for hosting all module material. The module was again, launched with a face to face session in a lecture venue, this time incorporating lessons from 2013.

Changes included:

- Etiquette and politeness within the virtual classroom environment.
- In preparing material, it is essential to include and require interaction from your participants. Questions must be asked. Quizzes must be administered. Ideally break out rooms should be invoked.
- Develop your best "radio voice" as it will make a big difference. You need to sound enthusiastic especially when you have limited visual feedback. Web cams are supported in the Collaborate environment but are usually left off to preserve bandwidth.
- Students were informed that they would need to complete a short daily questionnaire on Moodle indicating their experiences of what they liked and disliked about the module.

Again, a familiarization session was conducted. The session was a lot more structured and involved participants actually trying out functionality themselves. Some guest lecturers participated or at least observed the training as well. The session was better structured and created a sense of anticipation. I personally found the blackboard collaborate session a valuable refresher.

3.6 Lessons Learned in 2014

- The University had switched to a high speed network providing far greater local bandwidth. This made a difference to the overall virtual classroom experience.
- A detailed face-to-face module launch lecture is vital for setting expectations and specifying required conduct.
- A more structured and thorough virtual classroom familiarisation experience for students resulted in less confusion within the environment.
- By adopting a far greater facilitative role, the lecturer provided much improved structure to the module. This also resulted in far greater use of features of the system.
- By far the most encouraging change in 2014 was the sense of learning community that formed between students, the module lecturer / facilitator and the numerous guest lecturers. Not only were guests happy to provide a themed guest lecture, but a few of them expressed interest in participating in other guest as well as student presentations. Students seemed to "raised their game" accordingly.

As a result of the experiences gained during the two (2) years, the following section proposes guidelines for implementing a virtual classroom environment within a post-graduate module.

4. GUIDELINES FOR IMPLEMENTING A VIRTUAL CLASSROOM ENVIRONMENT AS PART OF A BLENDED LEARNING APPROACH TO A POST-GRADUATE MODULE

Given the 2013 and 2014 experiences of adapting and delivering a traditional face-to-face honours module within a virtual learning environment, the following guidelines are proposed:

4.1 Module Planning

It is critical to plan well ahead of time to ensure that you have determined learning outcomes, assessment strategy both formative and summative, blended learning strategy and finally a strategy for creating an extended learning community.

4.1.1 Comments

While planning is critical to the success of any University module, a blended learning environment offers so many creative opportunities for engaging with all stakeholders in a variety of different ways. Without the appropriate planning, so much will be lost.

4.2 The use of a Leaning Management System such as Moodle is Essential

It is invaluable to use a CMS as a central repository for all course content.

4.2.1 Comments

Given the blended nature of a module delivered using a virtual classroom environment, all stakeholders but especially remotely located contributors will depend heavily on a "central" repository for uploading and downloading module content, presentations, scheduling information etc.

4.3 Module Launch

It is critical to plan and deliver a well-planned high impact module launch including module outcomes.

4.3.1 Comments

Based on experience, a blended learning environment is a very different learning environment for students. They need to understand what is expected of them in terms of interaction and how to communicate for greatest impact and clarity. The launch discussion should include blended learning etiquette such as how to behave online when perhaps the technology responds in a strange way and how to behave as an ambassador for the Department / University given that guest lecturers and even remote participants may be part of such a program, possibly even internationally.

4.4 Virtual Classroom Training

It is imperative to conduct at least one (1) highly structured initial training session introducing participants to the virtual collaboration environment. This should include guests if at all possible. The training must include the vital role of facilitation. Presenters of sessions must understand that the environment demands a facilitative approach.

4.4.1 Comments

There was a real sense of excitement amongst the millennial students involved in this research who were keen and excited to experience the virtual classroom. In some respects, it is possible to do more in a blended learning environment than in a traditional classroom. It is essential that training emphasizes the need for presenters and facilitators to explore the rich features of the technology and to make the most of the environment.

4.5 Inclusion of Guests / Lecturers

Using a virtual classroom opens many valuable opportunities in terms of attracting guest contributors and even remotely located students. Ultimately this can lead to an extended learning community which is extremely difficult to achieve in a traditional lecture venue based module, especially at a remotely located university, as said.

4.5.1 Comments

Experts were willing to provide guest lectures and to contribute and interact online with students and with other experts in the virtual classroom environment. Not only has this extended the reach to outside expertise, but it has also created an extended learning environment. During the 2014 module, an unexpected benefit was that some of the guest lecturers expressed a keenness in attending sessions presented by other guests and even student presentations. It was fascinating to witness the effect this had on students who were quite happy to enter a debate and to discuss various topics. Many of the students rose to the occasion and discussed and debated topics.

4.6 Feedback

It is essential that you monitor student and guest lecturer experiences to improve the process.

4.6.1 Comments

During the Virtual Collaboration module, communicating with all stakeholders in an attempt to gauge what was working and also what needed improving was invaluable. Quite often really good ideas / suggestions / insights can arise from simply chatting to students and guest lecturers.

5. CONCLUSION

After two years of successfully conducting a Virtual Collaboration module with Information Systems honours students using a traditional face-to-face contact approach, it was deemed appropriate to experiment within a virtual classroom environment, in essence creating a meta-model in which to explore the theoretical and practical application of virtual communication focusing on eLearning and Virtual Business.

Initially a conservative approach was taken to protect students in the event that the technology did not live up to its potential. Besides some minor challenges, the technology worked reasonably well and the decision was taken to extend the use of the virtual classroom during the second year of the virtual intervention. By carefully documenting all stakeholder experiences, learning some core facilitation lessons and immersing himself in the research process, the lecturer was able to reflect on and refine the adoption processes, producing six (6) guidelines for implementing a Virtual Classroom environment as part of a blended learning approach to a post-graduate module.

The most significant and least expected benefit was, however, the value and contribution made by expanding the learning community to include remotely located experts and academics who engaged willingly with the students and likewise who were engaged by the students participating in the VC module, resulting in an extended and enthusiastic virtual learning community.

REFERENCES

Baskerville, R., 1999. "Investigating information systems with action research." Communications of the AIS 2.3es (1999): 4.

Chew, E., Jones, N. and Turner, D., 2008. Critical review of the blended learning models based on Maslow's and Vygotsky's educational theory. In Fong, J.; Kwan, R. and Wang, F. L. (eds.) Hybrid Learning and Education, First International Conference, ICHL 2008 Hong Kong, China, August 13-15, 2008 proceedings, Lecture notes in computer science. Theoretical computer science and general issues, 5169. Berlin: Springer, pp: 40-53.

Corlett D., Sharples M., Bull S. & Chan T., 2005. Evalua tion of a mobile learning organiser for university students. Journal of Computer Assisted Learning 21, 162–170.

Derntl, M and Motschnig-Pitrik, R 2004. The role of structure, patterns, and people in blended learning. The Internet and Higher Education, volume 8, Issue 2, 2nd Quarter 2005, Pages 111–130

DeTure, M. 2004. Cognitive style and self-efficacy: Predicting student success in online distance education. The American Journal of Distance Education, 18 (1), 21-38.

Draper S. & Brown M., 2004. Increasing interactivity in lectures using an electronic voting system. Journal of Computer Assisted Learning 20, 81–94.

Ellis, R and Ryann K., 2009. Field Guide to Learning Management Systems, ASTD Learning Circuits. Available through: https://www.td.org/~/media/Files/Publications/LMS_fieldguide_20091. [Accessed 02/09/2015]

Garrison, R. and Vaughan, N., 2008. Blended Learning in Higher Education, Framework, Principles and Guidelines. John Wiley & Sons 2008. ISBN: 978-0-7879-8770-1.

Herrington, J., McKenney, S., Reeves, T. and Oliver, R. 2007 Design-based research and doctoral students: Guidelines for preparing a dissertation proposal. In: World Conference on Educational Multimedia, Hypermedia and Telecommunications (EDMEDIA) 2007, 25 - 29 June 2007, Vancouver, Canada pp. 4089-4097.

Keefe, J., (1998) Profiling and Utilizing Learning Style. Reston, VA: National Association of Secondary School Principals, 1988.

Lin, K. and Overbaugh, R., 2009. Computer-mediated discussion, self-efficacy and gender. British Journal of Educational Technology, 40(6), 999-1013.

Oliver R., 2006. Exploring a technology-facilitated solution to cater for advanced students in large undergraduate classes. Journal of Computer Assisted Learning 22, 1–12.

Parsons, D., and Brown, K., 2002. Teacher as reflective practitioner and action researcher. Belmont, CA: Wadsworth/Thomson Learning, 2002.

Reeves, 2011 in Teras, H and Herrington, J., 2014. Neither the frying pan not the fire: In search of a balanced authentic e-Learning design through an educational design research process. The International Review of Open and Distance Education (IRRODL), Vol 15, No 2 (2014).

Shih, W. and Allen, M. 2007. Working the generation-D: adopting and adapting to cultural learning and change. Library Management, Vol.28 Nos 1-2, pp.89 – 100.

So, H and Brush, T., 2007. Student perceptions of collaborative learning, social presence and satisfaction in a blended learning environment: Relationships and critical factors. Computers & Education 51 (2008) 318-336. [Accessed 12/09/2015]

Stensaker, B., Maaseen, P., Borgan, M.,Oftebro, M and Karseth, B., 2007. Use, updating and integration of ICT in higher education: Linking purpose, people and pedagogy. Springer Higher Education (2007) 54:417–433.

IT TOOLS IN INITIAL TEACHER TRAINING

Prof. dr. Dorin Herlo
"Aurel Vlaicu" University of Arad
Bd. Revolutiei, nr.77, Arad, Romania

ABSTRACT

In initial teacher training, the call to use IT tools, and to integrate them into the virtual learning space, is not conjectural but is an example of introducing new technologies in the complexity of educational sciences. For this reason we approached the use of new technologies in the courses and seminars of subjects from the curriculum of training the future teachers, other than Computer Assisted Instruction (CAI) or Information and Communication Technology (ICT). Thus, as a solution for interactive learning, we have integrated, in other several courses, the smart board "eBeam Engage" linked to a laptop, a projector and a surrounding sound system and computers connected to the internet, therefore IT tools. By embedding them in the act of learning it was watched: overcoming communication barriers facilitate engagement of students in designing and supporting transformative learning activities by using this type of IT instruments in various learning situations; increasing their attendance to courses and, to emphasize the formed skills of the students and to form new competences to them, thus increasing their responsibility for their own becoming. For observing their personal development in these directions observation sheets, questionnaires, e-portfolios and the exams as evaluation instruments were used. After processing the data collected by means of these evaluation instruments, our expectations on enhancing intellectual quality product of the work of the students were justified.

KEYWORDS

Integration of IT tools, eBeam Engage smart board, blended learning, transformative learning.

1. INTRODUCTION

In the knowledge society we live in, we are challenged to use new technologies and the virtual space in all fields. This challenge is even more accentuated in education.

In initial teacher training programs, the use of IT tools and virtual space for training is not conjectural and "appropriate to times", but it is an example of introducing new technologies in the complexity of educational sciences, in the traditional content of pedagogy. Theoretical and practical supports of pedagogy are not put aside, but they are combined with the IT tools, making thus possible the agglutination of information into knowledge, acting as a procedural tool and as a method (such as CAI). It is obvious that the teaching-learning-evaluation methodology undergoes changes when IT tools, which will ensure the unity between technological and didactic-informational aspects of educational relation, are integrated.

We approached the use of new technologies in the courses and seminars of topics from the curriculum of training the future teachers, other than Computer Assisted Instruction (CAI) or Information and Communication Technology (ICT) where they are a sine qua non condition, such as: Theory and Methodology of Curriculum, Intercultural Education (Bachelor level) Docimology – comparative perspective, e-Learning in Teacher Training, Advanced Study of Education in the Community, Quality Management in Educational Organizations (Master level).

Why? As students were less and less interested in learning, in developing their personality based on true values and not of the moment ones, we bent over the things that "fill their day", draws their attention, captivates and motivates them – technology.

So, we have introduced an innovative IT tool, the *eBeam Engage Smart Board*, the most complete multimedia instrument that transforms any flat surface (wall or anything else) into an interactive training space, to make the students more motivated to attend the process of their own becoming and to improve their competencies by using a didactic tool offered by new technologies.

So in the text below we will show a short description and the capabilities of *eBeam Engage*, a few methods of the integration of IT tools in initial teacher training and their benefits for the students.

2. INTEGRATION OF IT TOOLS IN INITIAL TEACHER TRAINING. METHODS. RESULTS

As we have presented in the introduction, having noticed students' smaller interest in learning and participating in academic didactic activities, we decided to increase the integration of the IT tools into their learning process, to give them satisfaction.

By observing students' interest in new technologies and frequent use of their devices on one hand, and pursuing formation of competent future educators, we launched the **hypothesis**: *the introduction in academic didactic activities of IT tools on a larger scale, by using the already known interactive methods but shaped according to new technologies, will lead the students' motivation towards a responsible approach of learning and it will transform them in their formation as specialist in education.*

Due to the technical capabilities and operational flexibility of smart board *eBeam Engage*, we integrated this IT tool [1], connected to a laptop, a projector and a surrounding sound system in the courses and seminars of topics from the curriculum of initial teacher training, others than CAI or ICT (above mentioned, in introduction).

2.1 "eBeam Engage" Smart Board and its Associated Tools

So, taking notice of the existence of *eBeam Engage Smart Board* [2] - one of the next generation of interactivity with its built-in high fidelity JBL speakers and microphone, one-touch recording, wireless keyboard, intuitive scroll knob and interactive stylus -, we proceeded to inquire of its characteristics and possibilities of integration in university's courses and seminars for initial teacher training academic program.

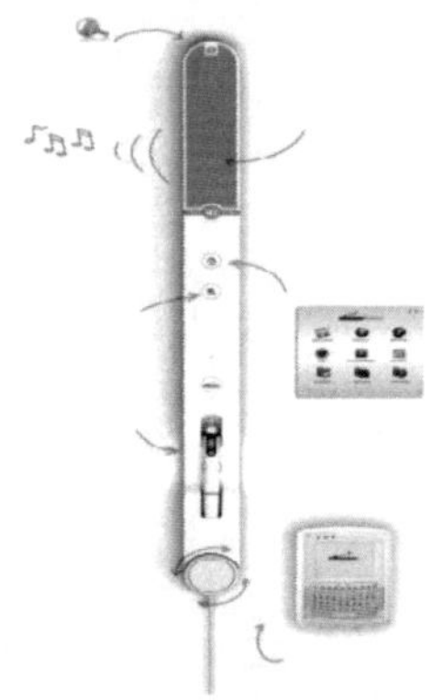

Figure 1. eBeam Engage
(http://www.e-beam.com/support/ebeam-engage/overview.html)

In the superior part of the eBeam there is a *built-in locking feature*, which keeps in security everything exactly where was it left.

JBL Speaker produces and reproduces the sound intensity according to the Volume Control's central button and the two flaps (+) and (-).

eBeam Home Button manages the quick access to the files and personalizes our eBeam experience. When it is pushed, in the surface of the whiteboard it is seen a window with different icons such as: Scrapbook, Web resources, eBeam education suite, Web Browser, Encyclopedia Britannica, Power Point, My Scrapbook, My Recording and Lesson Exchange.

With a *One-Touch Recording Button* (when pushed) and built-in Microphone, it's easy to record audio and video in real time (records, at the same time, what is on the screen and the sound). The built-in microphone has the capability to capture the sounds from the environment, clearly enough.

Interactive stylus, as a component of eBeam Engage (mightier than the sword), allows write and draw with it, use it as a mouse with three-button (including left and right click) which eases the instant access to eBeam software tools. With interactive stylus it can be calibrate the work area of the whiteboard as big as 213 x 152 cm, touching each dot from the working space projected by the eBeam software, when the smart board is active.

Tool palette – which appears on the surface of the smart board when it presses the round button of interactive stylus – allows selecting different kinds of items: the highlighter tool, the pen tool, the text tool, the on-screen keyboard tool, the eraser tool, the mouse tool, the snapshot tool and the zoom tool. The four main places that we can use the Tool Palette are: in PowerPoint, in Scrapbook, on top of all applications (in Screen Annotation Mode) or outside of any application.

Scroll Knob makes easy the navigation into the files uploaded on the computer and shown on the whiteboard surface. Scroll knob lets us navigate everything from PowerPoint and Keynote Presentations to our favorite website, without blocking the display area.

Wireless Keyboard lets us control content from anywhere in the room without missing a beat, having at the disposal a keyboard, a touchpad and the ability to page up and page down, to enter text and navigate the computer attached to the eBeam Engage.

One can say that *eBeam Engage* quickly transforms our aula, seminar room or conference room into an interactive multimedia experience. No more running back and forth between the computer, sound system and other devices. *eBeam Engage* puts everything we need at arm's length keeping presentations and courses/seminars delivery seamless and fun.

2.2 "eBeam Engage" Smart Board, Capabilities

The *eBeam Engage*, being at this moment „the world's only complete multimedia interactive whiteboard attachment, which features a speaker, a one-touch recording mechanism, a magnetic wireless keyboard and a lightweight stylus integrated into a single console for seamless presentations" as it say by the American producers [3], we proceeded to include it in our initial teacher training programs (bachelor and master level), in order to add value to student-centered learning, and mostly to induce transformative learning.

Connected to a laptop or a computer (uploaded with a specific and adequate software for *eBeam Engage*) and at the same time to a video projector, *eBeam Engage* whiteboard offers more hope and help than hype in the process of learning.

Why? Because:

1. *it can provide a nice and easy management of the files* (.doc, .docx, .ppt, .pptx, .xls, .pdf, .jpg, .gif, .avi, .wmv etc) with learning purpose, designed by professor and uploaded in My Scrapbook, for example;
2. *it can develop diverse educational themes into the Scrapbook*, having different kind of tools at disposal, such as: text tool, snapshot tool, marker tool, highlighter tool, eraser tool, shapes tool, select tool etc.
3. *has a huge range of access to the Web Resource* and can connect the interest of the students and professors for the same subject;
4. *it can design a new PowerPoint presentation during the course or seminar*;
5. *can record part or whole course or seminar*, with all the information, written and/or spoken, *which afterwards could be delivered*, all sessions digitally, *to the absent students*;
6. *tutorials are easier to be created;*
7. *it is easy to "wipe the board" without losing any of the content;*
8. *allows to invite participants to log into a shared Scrapbook meeting;*
9. *the voting system allows participants to respond to electronic testing, formative assessments, surveys, opinion polls, games and questions posed by the presenter. The data collected from these keypads is immediately transmitted to the presentation, giving the presenter a better understanding of comprehension;*
10. *let us carry on the way we've always taught and it enhances our teaching.*

We have taken into consideration these capabilities of the smart board and we have mounted it on a wall, thus proving that *eBeam Engage* turns any flat surface into an interactive multimedia environment.

2.3 Methods of Integration IT Tools in Initial Teacher Training

Taking into consideration the capabilities of the smart board and computers' educational software we proposed to facilitate the interactivity and communication of the users, whoever they are, students or professors, challenge and request from the users a proactive, creative, even imaginative attitude, allowing their intellectual development into a "multimodality, adapted to different psychological profiles of those who learn, a perceptive multimodality, coherently shaping the image, the color and sound in composite representations" structure (Ionescu M., Bocos M., 2009) [4]. Of course, the micro-informatics is added to all these characteristics of a multimedia product, the one that ultimately "animates" everything, which makes possible the mixing of things mentioned above into a ready to delivery product, qualitative validated and accepted by the users eager to learn.

By integrating the IT tools with their capabilities in initial teacher training, correlated with the interactive methods, one can move from a transmissive or transactional towards a transformative learning. Knowing that Merizow, the father of Transformative Learning Theory (Merizow J., 2000) provides the existence of three stages [5] in this type of training – critical reflection, development of a reflective discourse and action – our concern was to ensure the framework for such an approach - to offer the students support in transformative learning, such as:

- to benefit the full necessary information, either directly (professor) or indirectly through search (informational and communication technology)
- to have access to IT tools;
- not to be subject to coercion;
- to have equal chances to assume different roles;
- to encourage them to state critical reflections on working hypothesis and solutions;
- to have the will to synthesize different point of views;
- to ensure them the environment to become good listeners and to have empathy.

How have we accomplished these desiderates?

We have proposed the following methodology (see below, dotted) for offering to the students the opportunities to state critical reflections on certain concepts and/or theories, to implement these concepts integrating IT tools at the same time, and to evaluate the outcome of their application in real learning situations, in other words, to produce transformative learning.

A. Access to the all facilities of the Lab of Didactical Technology – computers, *eBeam Engage* smart board (with all the devices), educational software, etc., – from our University;
B. The full necessary information consisting of:
   - electronic course support;
   - Power Point presentations of the learning situations, with tasks to be solved during their daily activity or to be solved separately or in groups during future activities;
C. Approaching the blended learning strategy which has consisted also in integration of IT tools:
   - In face-to-face situations:
     - ➢ use of *eBeam Engage* smart board for showing some metaphors, PowerPoint presentations or video clips in the beginning of the learning activity (ice breaking) – related with the content of the course – by professor;
     - ➢ involvement of *eBeam Engage* smart board into presentation of prepared files by professor or made by the students, on the basis of which it has been possible, during the course, to highlight relevant issues (key words) with intelligent stylus (underlining or marking them), to modify the content (after reflecting and using the critical thinking) with the wireless keyboard, or to record them;
     - ➢ *eBeam Engage* smart board connected to laptop, projector and surround sound system, to "save" and then present the information processed within a team, information that give answers to given or assumed tasks and thus turning them into knowledge;
     - ➢ use by the students of the *Gallery* from *Scrapbook* of *eBeam Engage* smart board for building some models or figures;

- ➢ possibility to audio and video recording during different learning sessions with the smart board and laptop web cam, in order to resume and refine them, saved in *My Scrapbook* in the folder of each year of study, subject of that year of study, respectively;
- ➢ use of computers by the students during the courses or seminars for preparing the files on .docx, .pdf, .pptx format with the possibility to underline, to modify them and even to intake them as image and sound, to process them immediately, at home or in a future activity;
- ➢ a continuous coaching offered by the professor using: heuristic conversation, reflection, demonstration, exercises, problem solving, brainstorming, modeling, etc., for providing "the agora" for all the students without coercion;

- In e-learning (virtual environment) situations:
  - ➢ possibility to search for information on the internet, others than the ones provided by the professor, but related to the given themes or tasks;
  - ➢ facility to remote educational data transfer (the activities performed or even registered) by *eBeam Engage* smart board;
  - ➢ opportunity for the students, in groups of two, to write an essay under Google docs, for improving collaborative and cooperative learning and to form the spirit of the team working;
  - ➢ exploitation of our University's Moodle platform or "Performer" project platform (for students of "Teacher training for early childhood and small age education" master study program), to store through LMS (Learning Management System) all files requested by a professor and assumed by the students, as a responsibility for forming and developing the competencies for teaching career.

D. The agreement done at the beginning of each semester with students, regarding the percentage from the final grade for attendance in f2f activities, for e-learning activities and for final exam has proven beneficial for the students.

By including all these points (and especially IT tools) in the academic activity, we determined the student to be in situations of interactive learning, of intense dialogue with himself and with the others, of analysis, decision and applied external action, thus in transformative learning.

Comparing our approach in integration of IT tools in learning situations with the approaches of other authors like Tom Barrett [6], Olimpius Istrate [7], Gabriela Noveanu [8] or Kaye Thorne [9], we can state that our approach is related more with its effect in students' personal development under learning umbrella, than only their ability to use the IT tools.

2.4 Results/Effects of integrating IT Tools in Initial Teacher Training

By using observation sheets, questionnaires, e-portfolios and exams as evaluation instruments, we have gathered and processed the data of this research, in order to establish the effects and results of integrating IT tools in initial teacher training.

We would like to start with a first effect seen from the observation sheets. The increased motivation of the students to take part in face-to-face activities that integrated the IT informational and communication technology, as seen on the average presence of the students (percentage) versus the students enrolled.

Table 1. Percentage of students participating in face-to-face activities versus the number of students enrolled

No.	Subject	Students attending %	No. of student enrolled
1	Theory and Methodology of Curriculum	76	155
2	Intercultural Education	54	128
3	Advanced Study of Education in a Community	67	50
4	Docimoloy – comparative perspective	72	50
5	Quality Management in an Educational Organization	48	50
6	E-learning in Teacher Training	84	25
		66.83%	**458**

Comparing the average percentages for students' presence at our courses and seminars that have integrated IT tools – 66.83% - with the average percentage for other subjects which didn't use IT tool – 48.27% - according to the timesheets held by my colleagues who proposed other courses for the same students, one can notice a significant increase, which we presume is due to the extrinsic but also intrinsic motivation of the students. The extrinsic motivation of students does not mean only initiating questions, exercises or problems, but mostly the use of an interactive methodology, in which computed technology (in this study *eBeam Engage* smart board first of all) finds its useful and active role and can attract the student in the process of his becoming as a professional in education, transforming him.

Another effect of integrating IT tools was the overcoming of the communication barriers professor-student and student-student. By providing them an "agora" necessary for free but responsible expression of thoughts, of discursive reflections, students lost their inhibition to ask questions, to actively listen to the answer, to debate others' hypothesis or ideas with arguments, to think and act constructively as a result of deep reflection, which indicates the clear presence of elements of transformative learning. The students' interventions in the learning situations of the professor in face-to-face (f2f) situations, counted in observation sheets, gave an average of 21 interventions / 2 hours course activity – in average, every 5.23 minutes something was debated – and 32 interventions / 2 hours seminar activity – every 3.43 minutes there was a dialogue –, which means a real progress in professor-student communication. The communication student-professor was at the opposite pole. Student's interventions with questions for the professor, an average of 6 questions per course and 11 per seminar, prove that there is still a lot to work on the communication student-professor. The student-student communication was natural, exciting and constructive, especially when they were asked to work on groups or teams.

But in the virtual communication student-professor the situation is totally changed, positive, students losing their inhibition, emotion and maybe frustrations, giving answers to the professor or easily asking him, within the communication frames, previously agreed upon by both sides. Thus, by e-mails with or without attached files (Word, Power Point, etc), or by messages on Moodle platform or chat, the communication student-professor was easily made. The other types of communication taken into consideration, professor-student and student-student obviously worked very well but, we would like to remind again, within the communication frames agreed upon between the parties. So, the f2f communication and the virtual one at the level professor-student, student-student and student-professor were much improved by integrating the IT tools in the educational process.

We also found that students are learning much better if the teaching activities are enriched with visual images, graphical organizers, than receiving the information in "lecture format". Visual images, animated or not, accompanied by sound or not, displayed by means of IT tools (computer, laptop, interactive board, projector, audio system) and graphical organizers (comparative, descriptive, sequential, cause-effect or problem-solution type) projected with the help of MindMaster software had a major impact in the engagement of student in structuring advanced capabilities of thinking. Including "eBeam Engage" in learning situations, students were able to share, to shape, to prove what they have learned, thus transforming the learning situation the professor proposed, into learning experience gained presented by them.

The presentation made by students, as a result of accomplishing the work tasks, have been another gain for them because, proving a great desire to engage themselves in using the new "eBeam Engage" interactive tool, they asserted their learning sequences in front of their colleagues, analyzing and debating them, under the professor' guidance, which lead to a real/authentic learning. More than that, certain sequences presented by the students were audio and video recorded (or the images of the learning sequence projected on the interactive board were saved) in order to become an example (positive or negative) for a future didactical activity, through the profound implication of the student and creation of transformative learning.

On the other hand, these students' presentations, either learning sequences for themes of the curriculum (Bachelor level, 1st year), Intercultural Education (Bachelor level, 2nd year), Docimology (Master study, 1st year), Education and Community (Master study, 1st year), or a 2.0 Web tool used in education on their choice (for e-Learning for Teacher Training, Master study, 2nd year), have contributed to the development of the content of courses and seminars. Thus, this is another benefit of integrating IT tools in training.

Another result of the impact of introducing IT tools, especially the *eBeam Engage* smart board, was the increased quality of the students' product of intellectual work – their e-portfolios. They contained about 7-9 "products" that were evaluated during the semester, through a constant professor-student communication and at the end of semester, before the final evaluation. Going through the contents of the e-portfolios for each topic, we found that students were concerned to meet the demands expressed by the professors in elaborating and presenting their thoughts in a fair and responsible way. As the evaluation of e-portfolios represented 35% of the entire grade at the end of the semester, it had a mobilizing effect on the students, their grades ranging from 8 to 10, as follows:

Table 2. Grades obtained at the final evaluation of e-portfolios

No.	Subject	Grade 8	Grade 9	Grade 10	Total
1	Theory and Methodology of Curriculum	32	71	52	155
2	Intercultural Education	41	47	40	128
3	Advanced Study of Education in a Community	13	14	23	50
4	Docimoloy – comparative perspective	12	18	20	50
5	Quality Management in an Educational Organization	16	20	14	50
6	E-learning in Teacher Training	4	7	14	25
		118	**177**	**163**	**458**

The final grade consisted of 35% for the e-portfolios, and the rest of the grade consisted of, with the consent of the students, 15% contribution to courses and seminars (which included using eBeam Engage) and 50% in the exam. This consent between the parties (professor-students) led to the increase of their self-esteem and of their motivation to study the topics in a responsible, non-constrictive manner.

The criteria assumed by students in the format:

Table 3. Final evaluation criteria, their percentages and details

Attendance – 15%		E-portfolios – 35%		Exam -50%	
Presence	Scores	Grade	Scores	Grade	Scores
10 ---------	1.5 points	10 --------	3.5 points	10 --------	5 points
9 ---------	1.35 p	9 --------	3.15 p	9 --------	4.5 p
8 ---------	1.2 p	8 --------	2.8 p	8 ---------	4 p
7 ---------	1.05 p	7 --------	2.45 p	7 ---------	3.5 p
6 ---------	0.9 p	6 --------	2.1 p	6 ---------	3 p
5 ---------	0.75 p	5 --------	1.75 p	5 ---------	2.5 p
4 ---------	0.6 p	4 --------	1.4 p	4 ---------	2 p
3 ---------	0.45 p				
2 ---------	0.3 p				
1 ---------	0.15 p				

led to a final grade, as a sum of points obtained for each criterion, on a certain topic.

At the end of the semester, we had the following situation, as a result of this type of evaluation, the results/topic of study, grades and percentage and per all topics, sum of same grade and average value of percentage of a certain type of grade:

Tabel 4. Final grades of the students based on the 3 criteria (attendace, e-portfolios, final exam)

No.	Subject	Grade 7	Grade 8	Grade 9	Grade 10	Total
1	Theory and Methodology of Curriculum	24 15%	32 21%	51 33%	48 31%	155 100%
2	Intercultural Education	-	47 37%	54 42%	27 21%	128 100%
3	Advanced Study of Education in a Community	2 4%	14 28%	26 52%	8 16%	50 100%
4	Docimoloy – comparative perspective	-	13 26%	20 40%	17 34%	50 100%
5	Quality Management in an Educational Organization	4 8%	12 24%	19 38%	15 30%	50 100%
6	E-learning in Teacher Training	-	-	11 44%	14 56%	25 100%
		30 **6.55%**	**118** **25.76%**	**181** **39.52%**	**129** **28.17%**	**458** **100%**

Of course that it is satisfactory both for students and professors to have such a situation, compared to the students' results in other topics where neither the interactive methods nor IT tools were used during the courses and seminars. We can state that by using computers with a proper software, the eBeam Engage smart board with its laptop, projector, audio-video system and LMS Moodle platform, the students increased their achievements in learning activities, as a result of hard work of all those implied in the process.

3. CONCLUSION

Because nowadays, youth grow in a digital world and its technological tools, we need to make important changes in our approach of the teaching methods, to include technology-based instruction, learning inducing a transformative learning, a challenge that was at the base of this study.

There is a real need for the professors to play an active role in specifying the ways in which these more and more powerful IT tools can be chosen and used in order to be harnessed in education and for the education. That is why we have decided not only to understand the usefulness of IT tools in initial teacher training, but to study the winning ways to make learning be attractive and alive for most of the students and the ways it can increase the interactivity of courses and seminars, so that it lead to transformative learning.

As *eBeam Engage* smart board, together with its associated tools, proved to be collaborative/interactive tools for data/information gathering, for content creation, for their presentation, and we used it within these parameters, we believe that all these gets us closer to the validation of their effectiveness and efficiency.

On the other hand, from our study results that the blended learning strategy, which combines f2f activities, in which using the already known interactive methods shaped according to new technologies, with e-learning activities, in which IT tools are integrated, is proper.

In this condition, we can notice that the hypothesis launched is validated, namely: the introduction in academic didactic activities of IT tools on a larger scale, by using the already known interactive methods but shaped according to new technologies, led the students' motivation towards a responsible approach of learning and transformed them in real thinker for their formation as specialists in education.

Based on the ways presented here and the students' results, we cannot but recommend the use of IT tool – in this case eBeam Engage smart board and its connected tools – in initial teacher training, and in academic didactics, in general.

REFERENCES

[1] Herlo., D., 2014. Integration in academic activities of "eBeam Engage", *the 10th International Scientific Conference eLearning and Software for Education*, Bucharest, April 24-25, 2014, in *Volume II, "Let's build the future through learning innovation"*, pp. 232-237, Ed. Universitară, Bucharest, ISSN 2066-026X

[2] http://www.e-beam.com/support/ebeam-engage/overview.html

[3] http://www.e-beam.com/education/products-overview.html

[4] Ionescu M., Bocoş M., (coord.), 2009. *Tratat de didactică modernă.* Ed. Paralela 45, Piteşti, Romania

[5] Mezirow, J., 2000. *Learning as Transformation: Critical Perspectives on a Theory in Progress*. Jossey Bass, San Francisco, USA

[6] Barrett, T., *56 Interesting ways to use the interactive whiteboard in the classroom* https://docs.google.com/presentation/d/1IpRaaQvSLl5Q7pj91D2jSRn3sFSX4QOYOYAR8JzvCA0/present?slide=id.i0

[7] Istrate, O., 2010. Efecte si rezultate ale utilizarii TIC in educatie, *Lucrarile Conferintei Nationale de Invatamant Virtual, Editia a VIII-a, Tehnologii Moderne in Educatie si Cercetare*, Editura Universitatii din Bucuresti

[8] Noveanu, G.N, Vladoiu, D., 2009. *Folosirea TIC in procesul de predare-invatare* , Educatia 2000+, Bucuresti

[9] Thorne, K., 2007. *Blended Learning: How to Integrate Online & Traditional Learning*, Kogan Page Publisher

APPLICATION OF A REFERENCE FRAMEWORK FOR INTEGRATION OF WEB RESOURCES IN DOTLRN – CASE STUDY OF PHYSICS – TOPIC: WAVES

Fabinton Sotelo Gomez and Armando Ordóñez
Intelligent Management Systems
University Foundation of Popayán
Popayán, Colombia

ABSTRACT

Previously a framework for integrating web resources providing educational services in dotLRN was presented. The present paper describes the application of this framework in a rural school in Cauca – Colombia. The case study includes two web resources about the topic of waves (physics) which is oriented in secondary education. Web classes and educational resources are designed for a group of 35 tenth graders using the LMS. The academic performance was compared with a second group of 35 students oriented in the traditional way. The objective is to compare the academic performance and effectiveness of using LMS during the educational process.

KEYWORDS

E-learning; services; integration; reference framework; Web resources; learning management system

1. INTRODUCTION

The progress of information and communications technology (ICT) in education has led to the emergence and positioning of Electronic Education or E-learning [2] supported by learning management systems (LMS). An LMS is a tool that performs among other functions: mediation of knowledge appropriation, administration of such mediation, access to educational and communication tools. By using LMS, educational institutions provide distance learning courses and educational services to more students. This online education facilitates access to those who cannot move to the physical classroom classes [3]. In our region, universities provide support for undergraduate and graduate courses using diverse technologies: the University of Cauca for example uses "dotLRN"[1], and the University Foundation of Popayan uses Moodle[2].

Two of the most used LMS are Moodle and dotLRN [17]. Moodle is a free software package based on pedagogical principles and allows the construction of online learning communities. dotLRN is a "business" free software platform to support e-learning and virtual communities. Although the best platform for an depends on the requirements of each institution [4], dotLRN offers many advantages associated with its business approach [5] [6]

The integration of Web resources within LMS allows reuse of content available online and promotes the quantity and quality of educational services that can be provided by the LMS. Likewise, the integration of Web resources avoids student distractions as they don't need to surf the internet searching other educational web resources. If web resources are integrated into the LMS, the students don't need to leave the platform during the learning process, and consequently, the students may stay focused and save time. Numerous studies exist on the integration of Web resources such as educational services in Moodle platform. However, few works integrating Web resources in dotLRN can be found [1]. This integration presents significant challenges because of the architecture and the programming language used in dotLRN. Previously, a review of the state of the art on the different technologies to integrate Web resources in dotLRN was presented [7].

[1] http://dotlrn.org/
[2] https://moodle.org/?lang=es

Equally, the framework for integrating Web Resources in dotLRN and the architectural guidelines to incorporate web resources are described elsewhere [8]. This framework has been tested in other areas [20]

In this article, the implementation of this framework for integrating web resources as e-learning services in dotLRN in the topic waves (Physics course) is presented. The paper is organized as follows. Section 2 presents a summary of the Framework. Section 3 describes the case study. Section 4 and 5 depicts the results and conclusions.

2. FRAMEWORK FOR INTEGRATION SERVICES WEB RESOURCES AS E-LEARNING IN DOTLRN

2.1 Learning Management System dotLRN

DotLRN focuses on facilitating communication between actors in the learning process. DotLRN users can share documents, manage users and communities. One important element of our research is that dotLRN platform offers many tools to interact with external agents. This functionality opens the possibility of interaction with other LMS and external Web resources [9] [10] [11]. The framework for the integration of web resources such as e-learning services in dotLRN [7] defines the requirements and architectural guidelines for integrating web resources within dotLRN. DotLRN offers the following services [12]: Calendar, Blog, Documents, Wiki, community management, content repositories, forums [13], Member List, FAQs, Internationalization i18n, Authentication [14] [15], tasks, tracking, object repository, Photo Album, WebDAV, E- Commerce, Wysiwyg - web editor, AJAX [16].

2.2 Web Resources

In the context of the present research these three concepts are defined:

Framework: Articulation of three elements: 1. A conceptual framework; 2. Architectural Guidelines 3. Validation of these guidelines through a case study.

Resource Web: elements identified by a URI (uniform resource identifier) hosted online and accessed using a version of the HTTP protocol according to the ISBD ER (Standard International Bibliographic Description) and W3C (a consortium of the network around the world).

E-learning services, information services under service architecture (e.g., Google Docs or Google Forms or other Web 2.0 as a platform for educational activities) [18] [19].

Most of the Web resources are accessed using HTTP protocol. This feature allows interacting with different technologies such as flash, java, javascript, HTML, html5, Web 2.0, etc. Due to the fact that many educational resources based on HTTP can be found, it is necessary to set minimum requirements to ensure integration with dotLRN [8].

During a course, a teacher may see the need to include services not present in the LMS. DotLRN solves this need by using applets, portlets, and packages. For this reason, the integrating of Web resources in dotLRN is based on these three elements: 1: Package: Contains the data model, the logic and the operation of the package. Equally, it integrates the user interface of the package. During the integration, in this element, the programming is done to reference the URL of the Web resource. 2: Portlet: Provides the user interface for the portals of the platform. In this element, the graphical interface of the package and its management is defined describing the Web resource linked to the package. 3: Applet: Uses the interface of the portlets and set the properties for the dotLRN portal. This functionality allows administrators and teachers to add applications to the course.

2.3 Reference Framework

This section describes the clue aspects of the framework for the integration of educational web resources dotLRN. The detailed description, as well as the validation, may be found elsewhere [8]:

2.3.1 Requirements for the Integration of Web Resources into dotLRN

The requirements to ensure the integration of web resources dotLRN are the following:

1) Resources must be identified by a URL. 2) The whole Web site to which the resource belongs shouldn't be integrated. 3) The displaying size of the resource must be considered. The resource must be incorporated into the Web site dotLRN, and limited space is available. 4) Extra features (flash, java, javascript, html5, Web 2.0, etc.) must meet the above requirements. 5) Web browsers must support the necessary plugin to run Web resources. 6) The Web resources must provide learning functionalities to the dotLRN course.

2.3.2 Architectural Guidelines for the Integration of Web Resources in DotLRN

The guidelines to be followed for the integration of Web resources that provide services e-learning in dotLRN are the following: 1) Create the package using the Package Manager, 2. Program the package to reference the Web resource to integrate. 3) Create portlet directories and applet. This task is done automatically using Nima Mazloumi script. 4) Set the portlet to describe the Web resource and link to the package. 5) Set the applet only if necessary. 6) Install the applet and the portlet through the installation tool dotLRN software. 7) Finally, the application is available to be added in a course from the option "*Manage applets.*"

2.4 Implementation of the Reference Framework

Two educational web resources associated with the topic of Waves (Physics) were integrated and evaluated during the case study. For purposes of this implementation, it has created a virtual course, a teacher and 35 students on the platform. Table 1 shows the verification of the requirements to integrate services performed since it is the first thing that must be done to comply with the framework:

Table 1. Verification of integration criteria - Web Resources

#	Criteria Integration	Web Resources	
		1	2
1	The resource has a URL	Yes	Yes
2	Identification of the URL of the resource	Yes	Yes
3	display size checked	Yes	Yes
4	Compatible functionality with HTTP	Yes, .swf, simulator	Yes, .swf, simulator
5	Compatibility with most browsers	Yes	Yes
6	The resource supports a learning process	Yes	Yes

2.4.1 Execution of Architectural Guidelines for the Integration of Web Resources dotLRN

The following steps were performed according to the guidelines previously described:

1) Create the package using the Package Manager: The package name was "Física_Décimo (Physics 10th grade in English)" and aims to integrate two web simulators in the LMS. 2) Program the package to point to the web resource: Here the necessary files are created in the package directory "ondas" (Waves in English) (... / Física_Décimo / www / ondas). 3) Create directories portlet and the applet using the script (code to run) Mazloumi Nima. After running the script, the directories generated (/ usr / share // packages) were copied taking into account the privileges of reading, writing and owner of the operating system. After this step, the package directory contains three application directories (Waves, Waves-portlet, and dotLRN-ondas).

4) Set the portlet to describe the web resource and link the package. 5) Set the applet only if necessary. For this case, it is not required since the applet generated meets the requirements worked in the portlet. 6) Install the applet and the portlet: Through the software installation tool of dotLRN in InstallFrom Local option -> Service -> ondas applet selection. 7) Finally, the application is available to be added in a course from the Manage applets option on the Admin portal course by the teacher in charge.

2.5 Verification of the Implementation of the Framework

After an implementation of software (dotLRN) in the hardware (server), it is necessary the verification using the client access (teacher and student):

1) Verify that the new applets appear in the list of available applets. 3) Verify that the *Waves educational web resource* appears on the course home page. 4) Verify that the *portlet package management* appears in the course administration page. The two web resources integrated into the case study are simulators. The students can interact to strengthen their knowledge regarding concepts of tension, damping oscillation pulse amplitude, among others, the figure 1 and 2 the two integrated web resources.

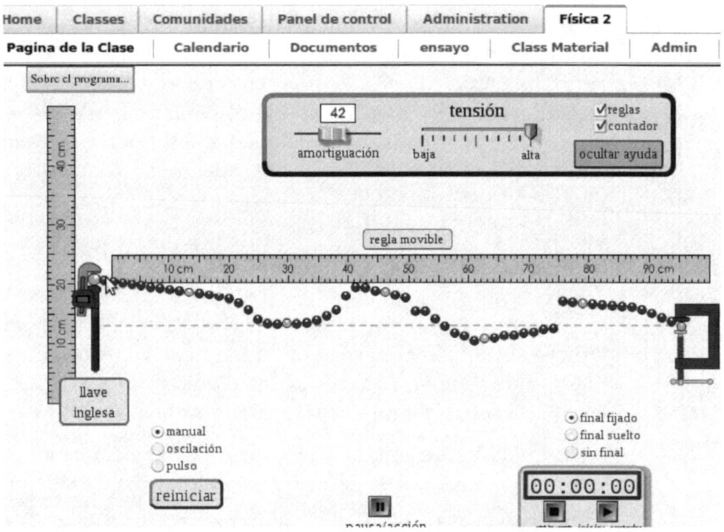

Figure 1. Web Resource 1

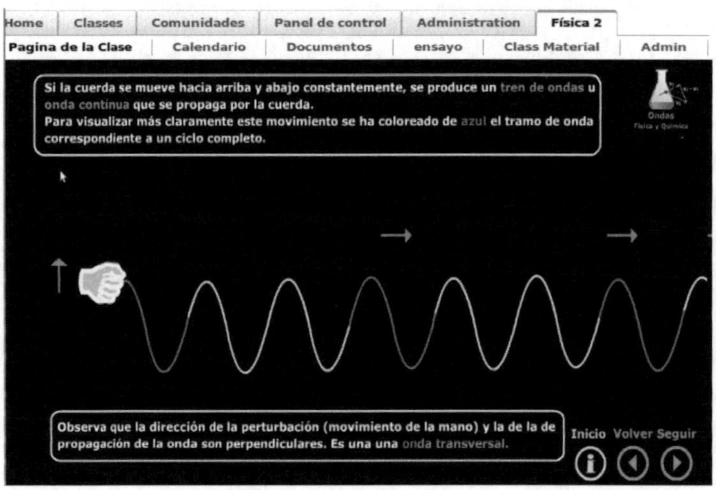

Figure 2. Web Resource 2

3. CASE STUDY

3.1 Context of Study

The implementation was done in the Jose Maria Cordoba school. This school is located in Mondomo, municipality of Santander de Quilichao (Cauca Colombia). The emphasis of the school is environmental and business education. It has approximately 600 students from sixth to eleventh grade. The proposed framework was used in a physics course for 10th Grade. The course has a total of 70 students. 35 students were guided in mode B-Learning (Group A), and the other 35 were guided using traditional methods (Group B). The evaluation was done to compare the academic performance and verify the impact or of the use of Web resources during the student learning. This process is done by working sessions of the research team, faculty, administrators, and students.

3.2 Implementation of the B-Learning Process

3.2.1 Day 1: Management of the Platform

With the teacher: some details about the platform and the Web resources are described. Equally, a basic training about dotLRN is oriented. The elements covered were: access to the platform, registration, login, available courses. Equally the basic elements of courses: activities, forums, materials, assessments, calendar, email, students, and integration of educational web resources by aggregating applets.

With students: training is done to register on the platform, access and interact with courses and Web resources. Equally, some training was done about forums and online questionnaires solution.

3.2.2 Day 2: Definition of the Teaching Methodology

The methodology to be applied to Group A is defined. It is intended that the methodology was close to the methodology used daily in the classroom, thus the research group and teaching methodology CONCERT the following steps:

• The course platform is named according to the subject to which it applies: Décimo_Física

• The teacher explains the theory of the subject in a conventional manner (board, beam video, exposure, and interaction with the student).

• In the virtual course, the courses and web resources are integrated. These contain textual, multimedia information, practical and simulates an interactive process with the student.

• A reasonable time is given to the student to interact with resources. These resources support the conventional educational process.

• A forum activity is proposed on the platform.

• The teacher proposes a workshop with a series of questions on the subject. This workshop is solved with the help of educational resources.

• The teacher reviews the workshops, socialize and clear up doubts.

• An activity examination is implemented as assessment. This evaluation is based on evidence-based know 11 (knowledge measurement system applied by the Colombian Ministry of Education). The assessment questions have single or multiple answers

• Finally, the results of the evaluation are analyzed and compared with students who did not receive B_Learning method.

3.2.3 Day 3: Application of the Proposed Methodology

The class was developed during 3 hours in the computer room where each one of the 35 students has a computer connected to the LMS.

Relevant classroom observations regarding students: increased attention, concentration, interaction, less indiscipline, greater participation, a fluid management platform and its modules required (e-learning resource, forum, and evaluation). Students were enthusiastic about the two simulators; they mention that the topic is clear, and the resources help to clear up doubts.

Relevant classroom observations regarding the teacher: from the responses in the forum, the teacher observes that the students were more efficient, fast and motivated. The 35 students developed the workshop correctly.

The teacher expresses: "optimizing the understanding of students is very important, the assessment using the forum allows know the learning of each student and his motivation. The results are satisfactory compared to those obtained in a conventional manner. "

At the end of the day, a survey was applied to students to determine the satisfaction and efficiency of the approach.

100% of the students like to use the computer in the learning process. 90% considered easy to enter to the platform. 100% considered easy to find the resource suggested by the teacher; this issue avoids distraction and greater concentration. 80% considered easy to integrate the LMS service. 100% understood the topic. 100% would like that all teachers will use this tool to their classes. 85% consider excellent the use of ICT in education and see the need for more computers and higher bandwidth.

4. RESULTS

4.1 Evaluation of Results

This section describes the results obtained in the case study. The following tasks were accomplished:

Platform installation, the creation of students and teachers, integration of two web resources, no performance drawbacks or technical platform were presented, good management of the platform is performed by students and teachers for each one of the functions needed.

On the other hand, an impact analysis in academic performance with the teachers involved in the two subjects in a fourth day is done.

4.1.1 Day 4. Analysis of Assessments

The results of the student assessment groups A (B_Learning) and B (conventional classes) are shown in Table 2.

Rating Scale: 1 to 5: Low: 1.0 to 3.0; Medium: 3.1 to 4.4 High: 4.5 to 5.0

Table 2. Students assessment analysis

Group	Evaluation (# of Students)			Percentage performance analysis (%)		
	Low	Medium	High	Low	Medium	High
A	5	7	23	14%	20%	66%
B	12	16	7	34%	46%	20%

In Figure 3 the percentage analysis of student assessment according to the scale used (low, medium, high) is presented

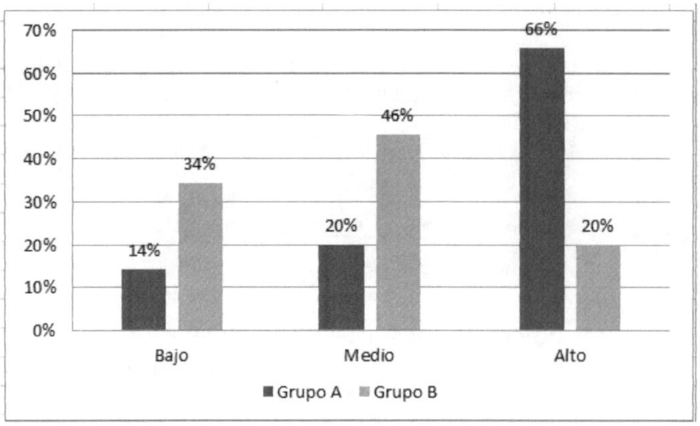

Figure 3. Percentage analysis evaluation

Table 3 shows the results of the approbation by group of the 70 students.

Table 3. Students approved or not approved

Group	# approved	% Approved	# Not Approved	% Not Approved
A	30	86%	5	14%
B	23	66%	12	34%

In Figure 4 the percentage of students who passed is plotted and who failed

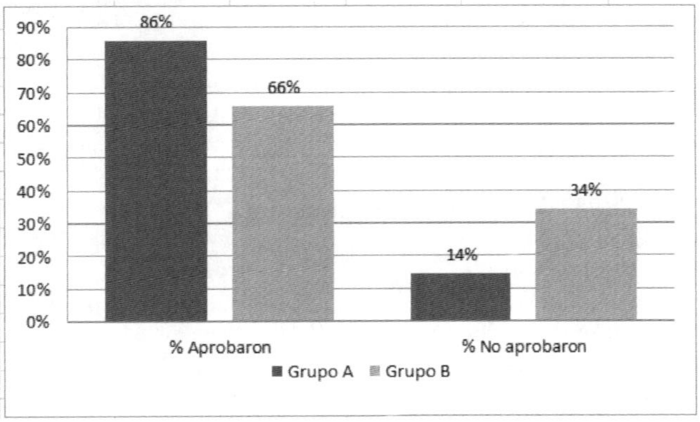

Figure 4. Percentage analysis of students approved or not approved

4.2 Performance Analysis

70 students were divided into two groups, Group A: use the LMS with the web resource being integrated, and B. Group receives traditional instruction. In group A, only 14% had a low performance while in group B 34%. In group A, 20% had an average performance while the B 46%. In group A, 66% get high evaluation while in group B only 20%. In summary, 86% of students in group A passed the assessment, while in group B only 66%. In group A, only 14% did not approve the assessment while in group B 34%.

5. CONCLUSIONS AND FUTURE WORK

The use of the LMS integrating Web resources has been well received in the educational community (teachers, students, and managers) of the school of the case study. The approach attracted high interest. The teacher says that improved performance is evident in students using the platform. The academic impact of students is positive in those who used the platform compared to those who did not use it. With the integration of resources greater concentration of students is obtained since it is not necessary to leave the platform to use other Web resources. The framework for integrating external services in dotLRN allows reusing more and better resources in the platform supporting educational processes. Future work will focus on integrating Web resources into other LMS, such as Moodle. Additionally, the framework will be implemented in other educational institutions with different students, such as indigenous [21], Afro-Colombian and urban.

6. FINANCING

This article is part of the MsC thesis in Telematics from the Universidad del Cauca called: "Framework for the Integration of Web Resources and Services E-Learning in dotLRN." This thesis is part of the SOLITE project ("Free Software in Teleformación") funded by Ibero-American Science and Technology for Development CYTED in the area of Information Technology and Communications.

ACKNOWLEDGMENTS

The authors thank for funding received from CYTED, Research Groups in Telematics Engineering of the University of Cauca; Intelligent Management System - IMS University Foundation of Popayan and the Teacher Edwin Martinez.

REFERENCES

[1] Sotelo, F., Ordóñez, A., Solarte, M. (2013) "Marco de Referencia para la Integración de Recursos Web como Servicios de E-Learning en .LRN," Universidad del Cauca, Popayán, Tesis de Maestría en Ingeniería Telemática.

[2] Cabero, J. (2006) "Bases pedagógicas del e-learning. Revista de Universidad y Sociedad del Conocimiento RUSC", Revista de Universidad y Sociedad del Conocimiento (RUSC)., Vol. 3, no. 1, Abr.

[3] Boneu, J. (2007) "Plataformas de e-learning para el soporte de contenidos educativos abiertos", Revista de Universidad y Sociedad del Conocimiento (RUSC).

[4] Martin, L., Martinez, D. Revilla, O,. Aguilar, M., Santos, J. O. C., and Boticario, J. (2008) "Usability in e-Learning Platforms: heuristics comparison between Moodle, Sakai and dotLRN. In The 7th Europian Conference on e-Learning," Agia Napa, Cyprus, February.

[5] Santos, O. C., Boticario, J., Raffene, G., and Pastor, R. (2007) "Why using dotLRN?," UNED use cases. In Proceedings of the FLOSS (Free/Libre/Open Source Systems) International Conference, pp. 195-212.

[6] Martin, S. (2013) "Interoperability between the new open e-learning platforms: an intelligent answering machine," Universidad Nacional De EducaciónADistancia, España, 2007.

[7] Sotelo, F. and Solarte, M. (2014) "Revisión de tema para la incorporación de recursos Web como servicios de e-learning al sistema de gestión de aprendizaje dotLRN," Revista TECNURA de la Univerisdad Distrital José Francisco Jose de Caldas, Vol. 18, No. 39, pp. 165-180, enero – marzo.

[8] Sotelo, F. and Solarte, M. (2015) "Hacia un Marco de Referencia para la Integración de Recursos Web como Servicios de E-Learning en .LRN," Revista TECNURA de la Univerisdad Distrital José Francisco Jose de Caldas, en proceso.

[9] dotLRN. (2005) About dotLRN - Learn, Research, Network. Retrieved from http://dotlrn.org/about/

[10] dotLRN.(2010) About-Openacs.Retrieved from http://dotlrn.org/about/openacs/

[11] tWSDL Project. (2010) Tcl WSDL Client/Server. Retrieved from http://code.google.com/p/twsdl/

[12] San Cristobal, E. (2010) "Metodología, Estructura Y Desarrollo De Interfaces Intermedias Para La Conexión De Laboratorios Remotos Y Virtuales A Plataformas Educativas," Tesis Doctoral, Universidad Nacional De Educación A Distancia, España,

[13] Matesanz, M. and Lopez, M. (2009) "Las plataformas de aprendizaje: del mito a la realidad". Revista de innovación educativa, Univercidad de Valencia (3), 146-148.

[14] MIT. (2013). Kerberos: The Network AuthenticationProtocol. Retrieved from http://Web.mit.edu/kerberos/

[15] IETF. (2013) The Secure Sockets Layer (SSL) Protocol Version 3.0. Retrieved from http://tools.ietf.org/html/rfc6101

[16] Eguiluz, J. (2007) Ajax. Retrieved from http://www.librosWeb.es/ajax/

[17] Romero, L. and Troyano, J. (2010) "Análisis Comparativo entre las Plataforma de más Frecuente Implantación en los Sistemas Virtuales de Formación frente a un Modelo: Proyecto Sakai (Comparative Analysis between the most Common Platform in the Virtual Training Systems against a Model: Sakai Project)", Conferencia EATIS Panama 2010, Septiembre 22.

[18] De la fuente, L. (2011). *Orchestration of learning activities through the integration of third-party services in IMS Learning Design.*(Tesis doctoral). Universidad carlos III de Madrid, España.

[19] W3C. (1999). *Web Characterization Terminology & Definitions Sheet*. Retrieved from http://www.w3.org/1999/05/WCA-terms/#Resource

[20] Sotelo, F. Ordonez, A, Solarte, M. (2015). Evaluation of the reference framework for integration of web resources in DotLRN. Proc. IEEE Computing Colombian Conference. (Bogotá, Septiembre 2015), 470-477

[21] Ordonez, A. (2014) Including user devices and context into STEM education for minorities. Proc. IEEE Integrated STEM Education Conference. (NJ, February 2014), 1 -5.

[22] Sotelo, F. Ordonez, A, Aplicación del marco de referencia para la integración de recursos web en Dotlrn en la asignatura de Física - Temática Electricidad. Proc. TISE 2015.(December, Chile) 724-729

CREATING MICRO-VIDEOS TO DEMONSTRATE TECHNOLOGY LEARNING

Mark Frydenberg[1] and Diana Andone[2]
[1]*Computer Information Systems Department, Bentley University, Waltham, MA 02452*
[2]*eLearning Center, Politehnica University of Timisoara, Timisoara, Romania*

ABSTRACT

Short videos, also known as micro-videos, have emerged as a platform for sharing ideas, experiences, and life events on online social networks. This paper shares preliminary results of a study involving students from two universities who created six-second videos using the Vine mobile app to explain or illustrate technology concepts. An analysis of their videos shows that the six-second constraint often inspires creativity and critical thinking, as students need to carefully consider the message they wish to convey, and how they can do so effectively in a compelling micro-video. The creation of such videos provides a way to demonstrate student learning.

KEYWORDS

Micro-Videos, Vine, Creativity, Digital Story Telling

1. INTRODUCTION

Micro-videos, or short-length videos, have become a popular form of creative expression in online social networks and digital media sharing sites. The wide availability of mobile devices and the ability to record and share short videos on platforms such as Vine and Instagram have encouraged a new genre of multimedia communication where videos lasting for matter of seconds convey powerful messages.

One of the most popular websites for hosting and apps for creating micro-videos is Vine, a sharing platform owned by Twitter, acquired in October, 2012. Vine launched on January 24, 2013 as an app for iOS mobile devices, and an Android version followed shortly afterward. With the Vine app, users create short videos ("vines") by tapping on a mobile device's screen to record video content for a short duration. They may stop and start recording, capturing one or several scenes to compose a six-second video.

Vine's video player plays each vine repeatedly; a characteristic of vines (and a measure of their popularity) is the number of loops which viewers watched them. Repeated playing of micro-videos can be compelling, as was the case with one of the first viral Vine videos created from news footage of the Boston Marathon bombing in 2013 (Lorman, 2013). It since has reached over 645,000 loops.

1.1 Creativity in Micro-Videos

From its very beginning, Vine was intended to encourage creativity. Just as Twitter has a limit of 140 characters on Tweets, Vine founder Dom Hoffman said in an inaugural post on the Vine blog, the six-second "constraint inspires creativity" (Hofmann, 2013) when developing videos that will resonate with their audience.

Poulaki (2015) distinguishes between looping background videos, such as waves crashing in the ocean or logs burning in a fireplace, and looping foreground videos, which communicate thoughts and feelings. The former have "less creative potential" than looping foreground videos, which often "reproduce a gesture or incident, an event. They often contain a distinctive action, or a curious object and its transformation." (Poulaki, 2015, p. 93).

Redi. et al (2014) developed criteria used to analyze over 3800 Vine videos to ascertain the level of creativity they demonstrate. They define a video as creative if it presents ideas in a novel and unexpected way, and that it has aesthetic value. A creative video is "unique in a significant way, or it expresses ideas in an unexpected or surprising manner." (Redi, O'Hare, Schifanella, Trevisiol, & Jaimes, 2014, p. 4273).

1.2 Vine Usage

The Pew Research Center for Internet, Science, and Technology reports that 24% of American teens between ages 13 and 17 use the Vine app on their mobile devices as a social media platform. (Lenhart, 2015). Of its 200 million monthly users, 71% are millennials. (Lella, 2015)

Yarosh studied the types of videos created by youths and adults, and found that youth see online video as a stage to capture their own performances rather than archiving memories. (Yarosh, Bonsignore, McRoberts, & Peyton, 2016) Vine is a "playground for teenagers" (Yarosh, Bonsignore, McRoberts, & Peyton, 2016, p. 1434) that offers a platform for creative expression.

For undergraduate college students, video sharing services like YouTube, and micro-video blogging services like Vine are among the tools that promote "user generated content, sharing, and social commentary, which have been found to encourage student expression and participation, as well as foster social learning theory." (Buzzetto-More, 2014)

Given this acceptance of micro-videos by millennial students and the creativity that many micro-videos display, higher education institutions have begun including Vine, Instagram, and similar platforms in their marketing and outreach to college students via social media. In addition, some creative educators are beginning to incorporate micro-videos in the classroom, as the next section describes.

2. MICRO-VIDEOS IN AN EDUCATIONAL CONTEXT

Secondary and tertiary institutions have begun to make use of micro-videos in educational contexts as a means for students to express their own creativity and mastery of subject matter. At a high school in Pennsylvania, in the United States, Hilton and Oldakowski (2015) studied the vines of students in a literature class that demonstrated their understanding of Aldous Huxley's *Brave New World*. They found that students, through the use of social media, increased their engagement and understanding of the text. Over the course of reading the book, students created six video interpretations its themes at regular intervals. The investigators noticed progression from earlier vines to later ones, and saw that the more meaningful vines contained several quick scenes rather than one longer recording.

Mozdzer Gil (2014) describes how journalism students create micro-videos with Vine or Instagram to engage their audiences in digital stories. "The demand for short videos creates a challenge for journalists to be efficient with images, words, and their audience's time." Students "dissect, evaluate and emulate good video blurbs" (Mozdzer Gil, 2014, p. 1) from micro-video sharing platforms before they embark on creating their own videos.

Students at Babson University integrate social media tools into their marketing courses to learn how to present products effectively. (Bal, Grwal, Mills, & Ottly, 2015) They create a Facebook page for a company, and then use a social media photo or video sharing service such as Instagram or Vine to enhance the company's online presence, and demonstrate their understanding of social media marketing and analytics.

The process of creating vines may improve learning outcomes by engaging students with digital and social media (Bal, Grwal, Mills, & Ottly, 2015), and help them develop digital literacy skills. "To become digitally literate means a disruption of traditionally passive notions of the use of texts and textbooks for understanding, and moving toward a more active approach in which digital classroom texts and technology are used to provide new opportunities for understanding, exploration and engagement." (Hilton & Oldakowski, 2015, p. 935) "The active engagement and critical thinking skills encouraged by multimodal activities can have substantive benefits for students. To begin, activities focused on the application of digital literacy require greater cognitive effort on behalf of students, who must simultaneously learn both the content and the digital medium" (Hilton & Oldakowski, 2015, p. 936)

This study extends the use of Vine in education, by having students produce micro-videos using Vine to illustrate or explain technology concepts. As with the examples cited, students must create an engaging presentation that is succinct in its message. The study considers the following guiding questions:

- Does the process of creating micro-videos encourage creativity?
- Does the process of creating micro-videos demonstrate student learning about a topic?

3. METHODS

Students from an American university and a Romanian university participated in this exercise as members of international teams in a collaborative project called TalkTech. (Andone & Frydenberg, 2014) The project matches first year business students in IT 101, an introduction to technology concepts course at Bentley University, a business university in the United States, and Bachelor in Telecommunications engineering students in the Technologies of Multimedia (TMM) course in their final year at Politehnica University Timisoara in Romania. 34 American and 41 Romanian students participated in the TalkTech 2015 project. All of the students who participated spoke English with fluency. The American students were all an average of 19 years of age; the Romanian students were about 4 years older than American partners.

Both IT 101 and TMM teach students basic digital literacy skills, including creating and posting videos, making personal web pages, interacting with social networking sites, and using a search engine as a research tool. Students also learn to develop new media and use Internet technologies for communication and collaboration. The TalkTech project give students the opportunity to develop and demonstrate their skills in these areas, as they must become facile with creating, consuming, posting, and embedding multimedia, using the web as a research tool, and communicating online using appropriate tools.

Students formed groups of three or four by selecting a topic shown in Table 1.

Table 1. TechTalk 2015 Topics

TalkTech 2015 Topics
1. How is augmented reality being used in various businesses or industries?
2. How does social media influence customer experiences?
3. What are the most popular messaging apps, and who uses them?
4. What are the biggest cybersecurity threats facing Internet users today?
5. How does streaming audio and video impact the entertainment industry?
6. How do mobile technologies and the Internet enable new business models through crowd sourcing?
7. Are MOOCs threatening the future or value of a traditional university education?
8. Are wearable devices a fad, or the future direction for staying healthy?
9. Should you license your photos using Creative Commons on media sharing sites?
10. Does information privacy matter in the age of big and open data?
11. When it comes to the Internet of Things, are we there yet? If not, what is possible in the future?
12. How smart are Virtual Personal Assistant apps such as Siri and Cortana?
13. What factors are most important in increasing the adoption of mobile payment technologies?
14. How do personal live streaming video apps change the way information is shared over the Internet?
15. What features do open-source mapping apps have over Google or Bing Maps?

Each group worked together for a period of six weeks to research the topic, and share their findings by preparing a variety of multimedia artifacts. Among the artifacts required, each student needed to prepare a micro-video to illustrate some aspect of the topics, and group members could discuss their ideas for the videos with each other. The assignment given was for each person to create his or her own original Vine video to present some aspect of the topic. The instructors provided no further qualifications or requirements for their videos. The instructors demonstrated Vine in class, and asked their students to install the app if they had compatible mobile devices, but did not provide any further instruction on how to use it. When some students (mostly Romanian) were not able to use Vine, the instructors added the option of creating a micro-video on YouTube as an alternative. The YouTube videos were generally one or two seconds longer than the Vine videos because of no enforced time constraint, and they did not play in a loop, as Vine does.

68 of the 75 participants successfully created micro-videos as part of this project. 21 of the Romanian students used YouTube rather than Vine to create and share their videos, mostly because they did not have a smartphone that could run the Vine app. Three students removed their videos at the end of the semester, so

they were not considered in this study. After reviewing the 68 videos, and based on concepts of video creativity in (Redi, O'Hare, Schifanella, Trevisiol, & Jaimes, 2014) and (Poulaki, 2015), the authors identified broad categories into which each video falls: definition, demonstration, skit, slide show, or removed (for those videos which were created during the semester and removed immediately afterward.) Table 2 summarizes each category and the number of vines created in each as part of TalkTech 2015.

Table 2. Categorizing educational micro-videos

Category	**Description**	**Number of Videos**
Definition	The video contains a student reading a definition	14
Skit	The video contains a skit where student(s) act out some aspect of the concept	16
Demonstration	The video contains screenshots or some other demonstration of the concept, with voice-over narrative	29
Slide Show	The video contains an animation or a slide show showing series of words or images in succession to describe the concept	6
Removed	Students removed their videos after the semester ended	3

Demonstration videos were clearly the most popular among this cohort, and in many cases required the greatest amount of technical expertise in order to complete. In this small sample, 51 of the 65 videos created, or 78% demonstrated creativity beyond simply reading a definition into the camera. As an example of a creative Demonstration video, consider the five-frame Vine video described in Figure 1 that one student created to explain the concept of popular messaging apps. (Karpowicz, 2015) This vine shows screenshots of five different messaging apps, one in each frame. Each app displays part of the sentence "These are the most popular messaging apps!" The sentence appears one or two words at a time as a message on one of five popular messaging apps. Upbeat music plays throughout in the background.

1. iMessage

2. SnapChat

3. Skype

4. WhatsApp

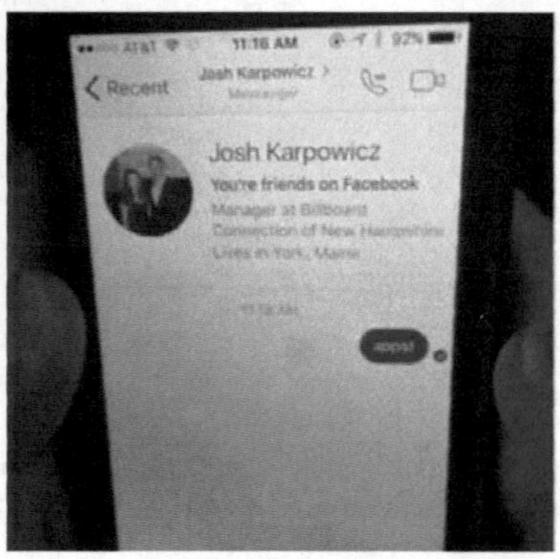

5. Facebook Messenger

Figure 1. Screenshots of five messaging apps make up a Vine on messaging apps

Skit videos were the second most popular type of Vine videos created among this cohort, and demonstrated creativity in capturing the essence of the topic. As an example, a five-scene micro-video about MOOCs shows (a) a student discarding her textbooks and (b) packing them away; (c) opening her laptop, (d) searching for online courses, and (e) visiting the Coursera website. These five scenes convey basic information and understanding about the topic.

Most of the skits and demonstrations met the requirements for creativity by Redi et. al (2014) as students set up specific scenarios to illustrate their assigned technology trends and concepts in unexpected ways. In order to create the messaging apps demonstration video shown in Figure 1 above, the student had to research the most popular messaging apps, install each one on his mobile device, become proficient at using them, ask someone to help record the video, and upload it online. Illustrating the concept of messaging apps by demonstrating five messaging apps to form a message one word at a time is a novel and unexpected approach, and seeing all of them in rapid succession in the video adds an aesthetic value to the viewing experience. To create the MOOCS skit, students needed to understand what MOOCs are, name a MOOC provider, and convey the motivation for taking a class online, all in six seconds.

The number of scenes in a micro-video often hinted at its complexity and the number of different ideas that the students are trying to convey. Most videos only had or two scenes. The messaging app and MOOCs micro-videos described previously has five scenes; that is, recording started and stopped five times when creating each video. Figure 2 notes the frequency of the number of scenes in each of the 65 videos considered in this study.

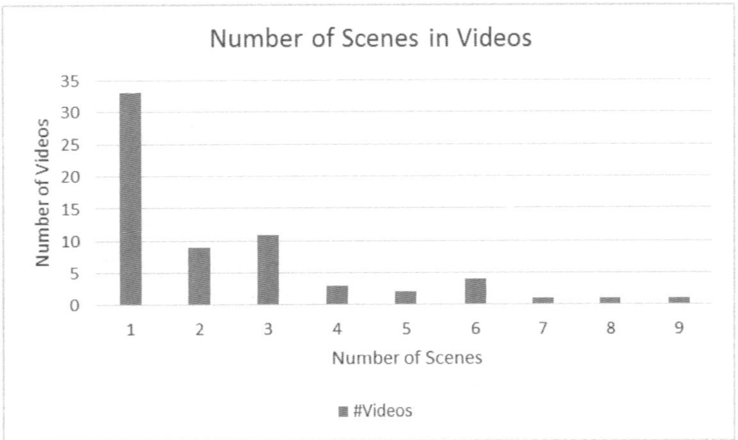

Figure 2. Number of scenes in TechTalk 2015 micro-videos

It is worthwhile to note that videos with more than six scenes were created using additional software, rather than simply tapping on the Vine app running on a smartphone screen for a second at a time to record one scene before setting up the next.

All 14 of the student-created micro-videos that fell into the Definition category had one scene containing the student reading or reciting a definition while looking in the camera, as if taking a video selfie. While the majority of the micro-videos had one, two, or three scenes, several videos had more than six scenes. Two groups used mobile apps such as Flipagram, to create micro-videos from their photos and videos, and set them to music.

4. ANALYSIS

This study implemented several evaluation methods. The authors relied on interviews and team blogs during the project to understand the student experience better, and to learn how students interacted with each other in their teams. Students voluntarily completed an anonymous online questionnaire based on the ZEF method (Selkava, Ronkainen, & Alasaaraela, 2011) at the conclusion of the project.

Students involved in this project have significant previous experience using a variety of digital and social media tools, although most had not used Vine regularly before this project, as shown in Figure 3.

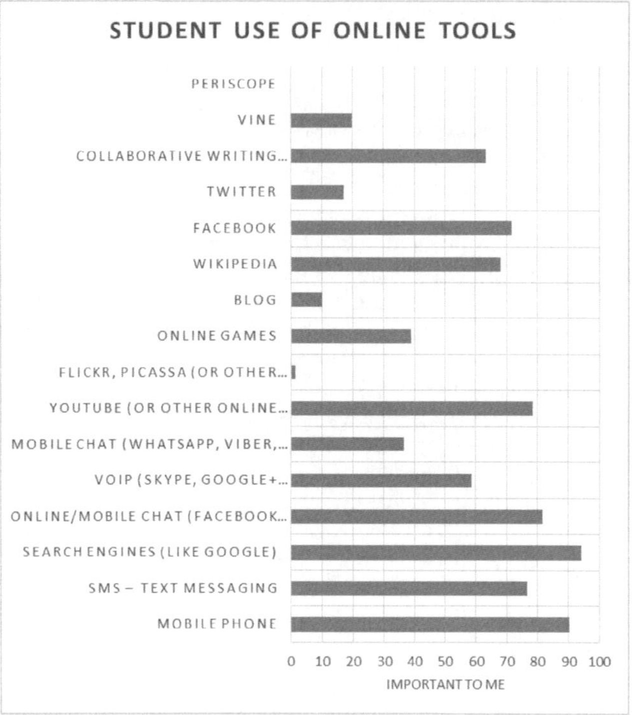

Figure 3. Student use of Online and Social Media Tools

Groups met using live communication (Skype, Google Hangouts, etc.) to talk about various approaches and tools for making their Vine videos. In an open-ended question at the end of the project, five of the students said that "making the Vine" was the part of the project that they enjoyed the most. One student shared with her group on their blog, "I used Flipagram to create a picture slideshow, and then uploaded it to Vine." Said another, "I made it in (Adobe) Premier and recorded myself as doing some buying over the Internet, and then got hacked."

When asked the extent to which they agree with the statement, "Using Vine, I was able to express a complex topic in a simple way" the mean answer was 45.9% answer, with a distribution of responses as shown in Figure 4:

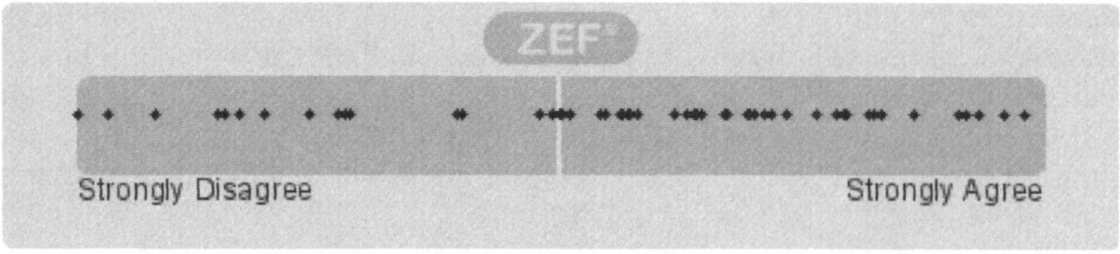

Figure 4. Using Vine, I was able to express a complex topic in a simple way

This median score suggests that it may have been difficult for many students to express a complex topic in a micro-video. Some students found the open-ended nature of this assignment to contribute to the challenge of completing it, remarking that they weren't sure how much information they "were supposed to" convey in their videos. In future iterations of this project, the instructors may suggest that students create a story board for their videos, requiring them to more formally list the scenes and concepts they wish to include in their videos. In some cases, the simplest appearing videos were the most complex to create. For example, in one demonstration of the Internet of Things, students set up a scenario where a smartphone controlled a sensor on another object. The behind the scenes work of preparing this demonstration showed student understanding of the topic, and made for an engaging video to the viewer because of its simplicity.

When asked which tools allowed them to be most creative, 72% listed Vine as at tool that allowed them to be creative, as shown in Figure 5.

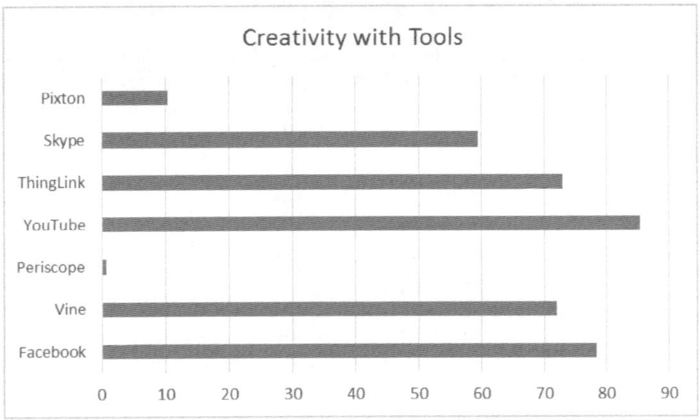

Figure 5. Creativity with Online Tools

The time constraint contributed to the need to be creative. As for Vine's six-second limit, many students agreed with the sentiments that "You have to think hard about what you're going to say and how you can say it in six seconds."

The project showed that micro-videos provide a creative way for students to share their cursory knowledge of a topic in six seconds. Students found that it is difficult, if not impossible, for a six-second video to convey much depth about a particular topic, but they were able to convey the essence of their topics effectively in this short timeframe.

5. CONCLUSION

The TalkTech 2015 project introduced the task of creating micro-videos to illustrate technology concepts as one of several multimedia deliverables. A future study could examine the motivation and process students used to create Vine videos, and approaches to conveying the essence of a complex topic in a micro-video. Although some students were familiar with Vine, for many, the task of creating micro-videos was new, and for all, the challenge of capturing and conveying the essence of a technology concept in six seconds proved to be a challenging exercise in critical thinking and planning. While some students simply read a definition of their topic, the majority chose to present their understanding of an aspect of their topic in ways that were innovative and creative.

As tools and social media platforms may change frequently, this exercise exposed students to new ways to express themselves and think creatively. The use of micro-videos in the classroom can extend to many disciplines, and further projects might involve students critiquing each other's videos, or having groups of students create micro-videos, that when viewed together, present a mini-series about the topic. The task of creating micro-videos proved to be engaging, encouraged creativity, and provided a new way for students to demonstrate what they learned about current technology trends and developments.

REFERENCES

Andone, D., & Frydenberg, M. (2014). Becoming Creative Creators: Simulating a Global Workplace using Computational Thinking Practices. *Proceedings of Ed-Media World Conference on Educational Media and Technology, 1*, pp. 564-571. Tampere.

Bal, A. S., Grwal, D., Mills, A., & Ottly, G. (2015). Engaging Students with Social Media. *Journal of Marketing Education*, 1-14.

Buzzetto-More, N. A. (2014). An Examination of Undergraduate Student's Perceptions and Predilections of the Use of YouTube in the Teaching and Learning Process. *Interdisciplinary Journal of E-Learning and Learning Objects, 10*, 17-32. Retrieved from http://www.ijello.org/Volume10/IJELLOv10p017-032Buzzetto0437.pdf

Hilton, J., & Oldakowski, T. (2015). Brave New World: The Use of Popular Social Media for Multimodal Literary Analysis. *Proceedings of EdMedia 2015*, (pp. 935-943). Montreal.

Hofmann, D. (2013, January 24). *Introducing Vine*. Retrieved from Vine Blog: http://blog.vine.co/post/55514427556/introducing-vine

Karpowicz, J. (2015, December 2). *Messaging Apps Vine*. Retrieved from Vine: https://vine.co/v/iWnHjT0UQaQ

Lella, A. (2015). *The 2015 U.S. Mobile App Report*. comScore. Retrieved February 21, 2015, from http://www.comscore.com/Insights/Presentations-and-Whitepapers/2015/The-2015-US-Mobile-App-Report

Lenhart, A. (2015, April 9). *Teens, Social Media, and Technology Overview 2015*. Retrieved from Pew Research Center Internet Science, and Tech: http://www.pewinternet.org/files/2015/04/PI_TeensandTech_Update2015_0409151.pdf

Lorman, D. (2013, April 15). *Boston Marathon explosion from the news*. Retrieved from Twitter: https://twitter.com/Doug3P0/status/323878851803496448

Mozdzer Gil, J. (2014, Fall). Using Short-Form Video in the Multimedia Journalism Classroom. *Teaching Journalism & Mass Communication, 4*(2), 1-5.

Poulaki, M. (2015). Featuring shortness in online loop cultures. *Empedocles: European Journal for the Philosophy of Communication, 5*(1+2), 91-96.

Redi, M., O'Hare, N., Schifanella, R., Trevisiol, ,. M., & Jaimes, ,. (2014). 6 Seconds of Sound and Vision: Creativity in Micro-Videos. *Proceedings of the IEEE Conference on Computer Vision and Pattern Recognition* (pp. 4272-4279). IEEE.

Selkava, A., Ronkainen, S., & Alasaaraela, E. (2011, April). Features of the Z-scoring method in gaphical two-dimensional web surveys: the case of ZEF. *Quality & Quantity, 45*(3), 609-621.

Yarosh, S., Bonsignore, E., McRoberts, S., & Peyton, T. (2016). YouthTube: Youth Video Authorship on YouTube and Vine. *Proceedings of CSCW '16* (pp. 1423-1437). San Francisco: Association for Computing Machinery.

AN ANALYSIS OF STUDENTS ENROLLED TO AN UNDERGRADUATE UNIVERSITY COURSE OFFERED ALSO ONLINE

Nello Scarabottolo
Dipartimento di Informatica – sede di Crema – Università degli Studi di Milano
Via Bramante, 65, 26013 Crema (CR), Italy

ABSTRACT

This paper analyzes the main characteristics of the students enrolled to a three-years undergraduate course on Security of Computer Systems and Networks, offered in traditional, classroom based fashion as well as online at the University of Milan (Italy). This allows to compare classroom and online students from several points of view, and gives useful information to institutions willing to exploit e-learning as a vehicle for extending the enrollment to already existing traditional courses.

KEYWORDS

E-learning, online bachelor degree, online students, classroom students.

1. INTRODUCTION

As deeply discussed in Milani (2014) and Damiani (2005) the "Corso di Laurea in Sicurezza dei Sistemi e delle Reti Informatiche" (from here on denoted as SSRI) is a three-years undergraduate course (bachelor level) on Security of Computer Systems and Networks, activated by the University of Milan (Italy) in a campus located in Crema (a small city 40 kilometers east of Milan) in academic year 2003/04 as a traditional, classroom based university degree and offered also online since 2004/05.

The online version of SSRI has been implemented through a design process which required a deep revision of all teaching materials already prepared for classroom lectures by teachers – as suggested e.g. in Anderson (2008) – to obtain the best possible result in terms of students learning.

This revision – coordinated by CTU (the e-Learning Centre of the University of Milan) and initially supported by consultants from Isvor Knowledge System (an Italian company specialized in the production of e-learning courses) and described in details in Milani (2014) – can be summarized as follows:

- online courses are structured in modules composed by different activities: lectures, exercises, tests;
- lectures are mainly constituted by slide sequences and/or desktop capturing synchronized with teacher's voice, or blackboard-like effects recording teacher's voice and handwriting (almost no teacher's video recording);
- as suggested e.g. in Salmon (2000) and Rivoltella (2006) students tutoring has been carefully considered, and SSRI online is supported by:
  - one Course expert tutor for each single course of SSRI and for each group of 40/50 students;
  - a Process tutor, who acts as e-moderator, process facilitator, adviser/counsellor for the whole community of online students, as recommended e.g. by Berge (2000) and Moisey (2008).

The following sections of this paper compare the two "families" of SSRI students (i.e., classroom students physically following lectures at the university campus vs. online students accessing e-learning materials through the web platform implemented by CTU) to evaluate their most important characteristics and to identify possible critical aspects to be considered when planning the e-learning offer of a complete university degree.

2. PERSONAL CHARACTERISTICS OF SSRI STUDENTS

In academic year 2009/10, SSRI has been partially re-designed, both to tune the curriculum on the basis of the results of the first five years of its offer, and to be compliant with the new recommendations coming from the Italian Ministry of University. Such a renewed version of SSRI has been furtherly modified in academic year 2014/15, again to be compliant with additional requirements coming from the Ministry.

For these reasons, in Sections 2. and 3. we restrict our analysis to students who enrolled to SSRI in the five-years period beginning with academic year 2009/10 and ending with academic year 2013/14. Moreover, we include in our analysis only students who started their university studies enrolling to the first study year of SSRI, thus not considering students already enrolled in other university courses who decided to move to SSRI with some exams already registered and validated.

2.1 SSRI Student Population

The number of students enrolling to the first study year of SSRI in the considered period is given in Table 1. As it can be seen, the two populations (classroom and online students) are almost equivalent except for academic year 2013/14, when online students doubled the classroom ones: this is mainly due to an initiative aimed at publicizing the existence of SSRI (the unique Italian undergraduate course dedicated to computer security) through social networks: as a result, several people decided to take the opportunity of the online version to enroll to SSRI.

Table 1. Total number of students enrolling to the first year study of SSRI

Academic year of enrollment	Classroom students	Online students	**Total**
2009/10	57	59	**116**
2010/11	67	56	**123**
2011/12	45	51	**96**
2012/13	32	46	**78**
2013/14	46	98	**144**
Total	***247***	***310***	***557***

An interesting characteristic of SSRI students is their age when enrolling, represented in Figure 1, where enrollments have been grouped by age intervals.

As it can be seen, more than two thirds of the classroom students (68.8% of them) are "conventional" students, entering the university just after finishing their high schools; there is a significant number of students between 21 and 25 years old (24,3%) but looking in details most of them are 21 and 22 years old, thus again students entering the university soon after finishing their high schools, maybe with some delays due to repeated high school years.

On the contrary, online students are definitely "unconventional" students, coming back to university far after the completion of high schools. In fact, almost half of them (44,5%) are more than 30 years old, and just 10% of them can be considered "conventional" students aged 18 to 20. It seems then very reasonable to conclude that SSRI online is selected by just few young students living far from Crema, while it attracts mainly older students, most likely characterized by a job position and interested in improving it through a course that gives the advantages of a final university degree without requiring physical presence.

In fact, a questionnaire distributed in 2014 showed that 73.9% of online students are full time employees (vs. 5,9% of classroom students) and most of them decided to enroll to SSRI online both for its utility in the job they already have and for the possibility of studying while working.

From the above, we can then state that the e-learning version of a classroom university course does not "compete" with its traditional, classroom version in terms of enrolling students: on the contrary, it attracts a significant number of additional students that would never come to the university without the chance of distance learning. In other words, the investment necessary to implement such a distance learning environment is rapidly compensated by the additional incomes deriving from tuition fees of online students, as quantified in Milani (2014).

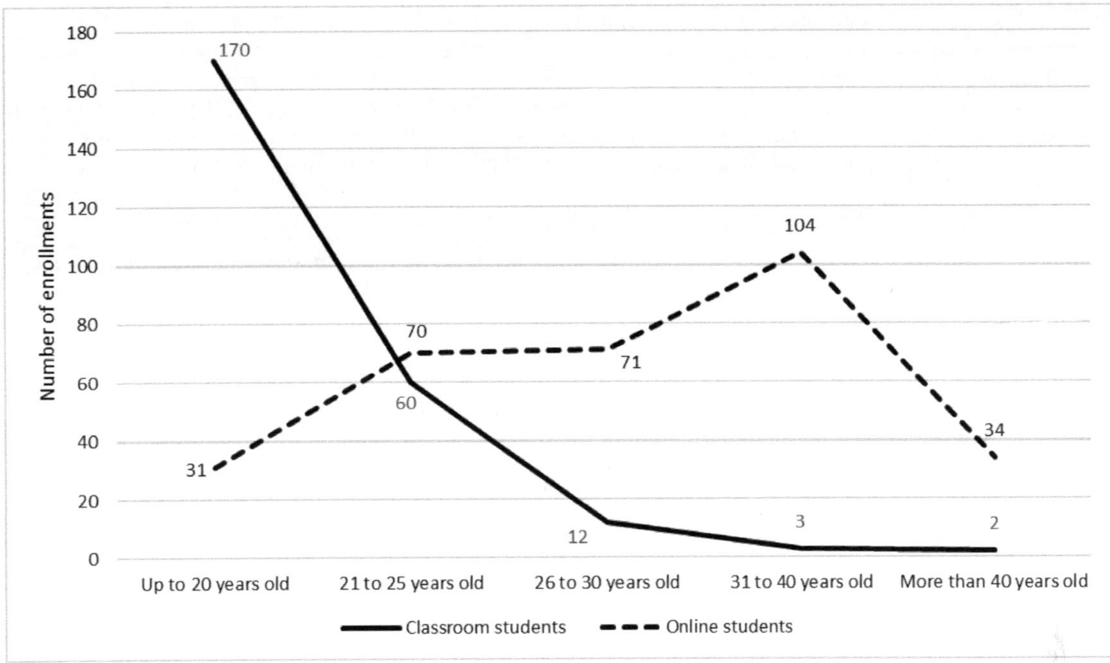

Figure 1. Age of students enrolling to SSRI

2.2 Economic Situation of SSRI Students

A first look at the economic situation of SSRI students can be derived from Table 2., reporting their average economic indicator. This indicator (called ISEEU: Equivalent Economic Situation Indicator for University enrollment) is used to compute the actual fee each student is expected to pay each year to the University of Milan. It takes into account not only the total incomes and properties of the family the student belongs to, but also the number of persons and their job position (worker, retired, full time student, etc.).

It seems reasonable to have lower indicators for "conventional" students (usually living with their parents) with respect to online students, whose age suggests they are people already occupied and with their own family, most likely smaller and younger.

However, it must be noticed that students enrolling to SSRI online have to pay an extra fee of 1,500 euros per year with respect to classroom students (for the extra services provided online, like tutorship, exams during weekends to facilitate workers, etc.). This can to some extent justify higher economic indicators for students able of affording the online extra costs.

Table 2. Economic indicator of students enrolling to SSRI

Academic year of enrollment	Classroom students	Online students
2009/10	€ 25.492	€ 30.410
2010/11	€ 21.970	€ 27.165
2011/12	€ 26.256	€ 27.356
2012/13	€ 25.745	€ 33.639
2013/14	€ 25.644	€ 26.524
Total	***€ 24.720***	***€ 28.533***

2.3 Previous Studies of SSRI Students

As far as the type of high school attended by SSRI students is concerned, we may refer to Figure 2. In this case, the two populations (classroom and online students) show a very similar behavior: most of them (around 40%) come from Industrial Technical Institutes (where ICT is frequently a fundamental topic) and summing up also Commercial Technical Institutes (preparing accountants) and other types of Technical Institutes the total exceeds 70%.

Only around 20% of SSRI students come from Scientific Lyceums: the general-purpose high school preparing to scientific university courses. This is a common problem for ICT university courses, whose scientific aspects are usually underestimated. A very small minority comes from Classical Lyceums.

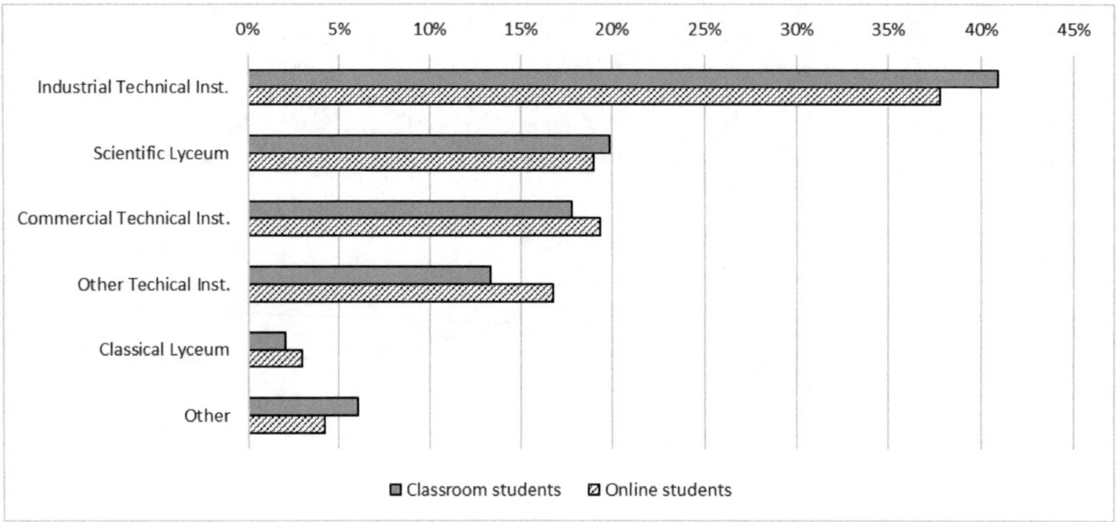

Figure 2. Type of high school attended by SSRI students

3. STUDY PERFORMANCE OF SSRI STUDENTS

3.1 Graduation

A first, rough indication of the performance of SSRI students about their studies is given in Figure 3., where four possible student situations are shown:

- students already graduated, i.e., who obtained the final degree ("laurea");
- students still enrolled and "active", taking exams at their own pace;
- students who decided to quit SSRI feeling it too difficult, probably after failing the first exams;
- students who moved to other undergraduate courses, at the University of Milan or elsewhere.

If we consider that – for students enrolled in 2009/10 – the last opportunity for graduating "in time" (i.e., without having to register for one or more extra years) was spring 2013, the percentage of classroom students already graduated is very low, but extremely low for online ones. The result is not surprising: Italian students enrolled in ICT university courses frequently start having some occasional work opportunities before graduating; moreover, since – as already discussed (Section 2.3) – they have in general a technical background, theoretical exams often cause unexpected delays in their career. Finally, online students already employed have to study during evenings and weekends, thus forcedly reducing their study performance.

However, if we concentrate on graduated students, we obtain the results shown in Table 3. It may be seen that for the first years of enrollment – when the numbers of graduated students are statistically more significant – the final marks (on the Italian scale in one hundred and tenths, where the maximum mark is 110/110) are definitely higher for online students.

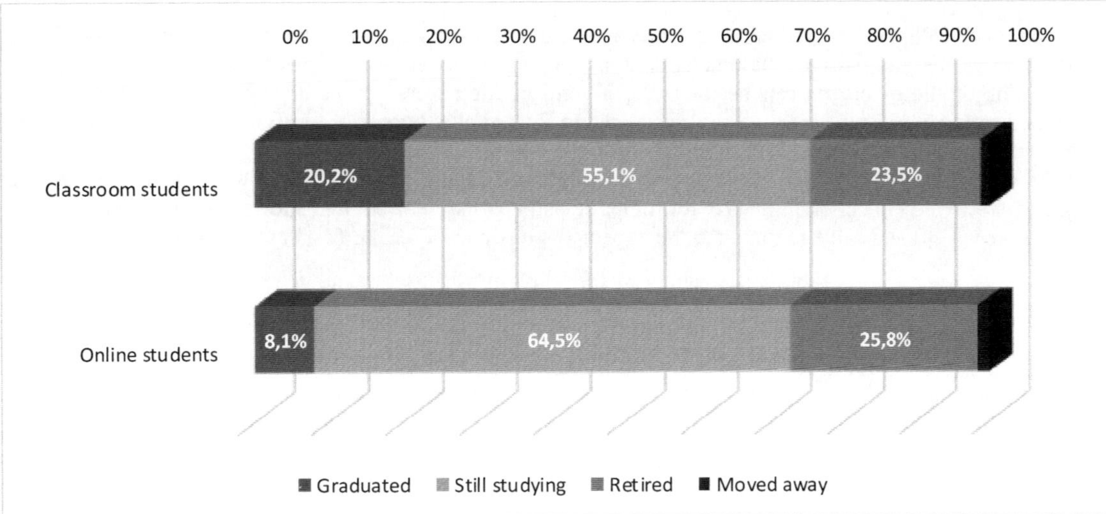

Figure 3. Present situation of SSRI students enrolled from 2009/10 to 2013/14

Table 3. Final marks of SSRI graduated students

Academic year of enrollment	Classroom students		Online students	
	# of graduations	average mark	# of graduations	average mark
2009/10	19	93,53	8	96,88
2010/11	15	93,13	9	102,78
2011/12	10	93,60	4	93,50
2012/13	6	103,50	4	100,50
Total	***50***	***94,62***	***25***	***99,04***

A possible explanation of the above is the fact that online students capable of finishing their studies without delays even while working – thus drastically reducing free time available for family and hobbies – have to be particularly motivated, high-quality students, comparable with their classroom counterparts.

3.2 Results in Exams

The considerations just made about the final graduation mark can be repeated if we look at the marks obtained by SSRI students when passing their exams during the course, as summarized in Table 4.

It is easy to see that the average mark for online students (on the Italian scale in thirtieths, where the maximum mark is 30/30 and the minimum mark for passing an exam is 18/30) is more than 1.5 higher than the one of classroom students (corresponding to 13% of the mark interval 18÷30 for passed exams).

Table 4. Average marks obtained by SSRI students during the course

Academic year of enrollment	Classroom students	Online students
2009/10	23,0	24,9
2010/11	22,8	24,3
2011/12	22,8	24,4
2012/13	23,7	24,0
2013/14	22,4	24,8
Total	***22,9***	***24,5***

A better insight into student behavior can be obtained by considering the mandatory courses offered at the first year of SSRI, namely: Computer architecture (6 credits) Computer law (6 credits) Discrete mathematics (9 credits) Mathematical analysis (12 credits) Computer programming (12 credits) Probability and statistics

(6 credits) and Physics (6 credits). The 3 missed credits necessary to reach the standard amount of 60 ECTS credits per academic year are obtained by demonstrating a B1-level knowledge of the English language.

Exams of these courses can be taken at the end of their offering period. For classroom students, the academic year is organized in two semesters, while for online students – deserving to concentrate on fewer topics at a time – it is organized in three four-months periods.

As shows in Table 5., the percentages of classroom students who passed these exams are reasonably regular, while they lower significantly for the online student population, that shows an immediate decrease in the number of students able to maintain the expected study pace after the first study period.

Table 5. Behavior of students regarding first year exams of SSRI

1st year courses	Classroom students			Online students		
	year period	passed exams	av. mark	year period	passed exams	av. mark
Computer architecture	1st semester	55,1%	24,3	1st period	38,4%	25,9
Computer law	1st semester	78,1%	23,2	1st period	40,3%	24,7
Discrete mathematics	1st semester	53,8%	22,4	2nd period	30,3%	23,9
Mathematical analysis	2nd semester	51,0%	23,1	2nd period	31,9%	23,7
Computer programming	2nd semester	44,5%	24,6	2nd period	22,9%	25,2
Probability and statistics	2nd semester	42,9%	25,4	3rd period	19,7%	26,8
Physics	2nd semester	48,2%	21,2	3rd period	21,3%	23,3

But if we consider the time elapsed between the beginning of the first year (September 1st) and the date when the exams are passed – as shown in Table 6. – we found a similar behavior of the two populations of SSRI students (with the exception of Probability and statistics, for some reason significantly delayed by classroom students). In other words, online students capable of quickly adapting themselves to the required study pace are able to pass exams as their classroom counterpart, and e-learning materials designed for the online version demonstrate their quality and effectiveness.

Table 6. Days between beginning of first year and passing date of first year exams

1st year courses	Classroom students	Online students
Computer architecture	387	338
Computer law	252	311
Discrete mathematics	325	574
Mathematical analysis	471	403
Computer programming	462	505
Probability and statistics	1189	797
Physics	599	682

4. A LOOK AT GRADUATED STUDENTS

To complete our analysis, we can now consider SSRI students graduated from 2010 to 2013 and interviewed one year later to know their experiences after graduation. A first aspect – shown in Table 7. – regards the work condition of SSRI students during their university course.

As expected, most of the classroom students had no or little work experiences during their studies (less than 20% of them had full time employments) while more than two thirds of the online students had a full time job even following the university course. This confirms the results already outlined in Section 2.1: the two student populations have significant differences in terms of age and work position when enrolling to SSRI.

Table 7. Work condition of SSRI students during their studies

Work condition	Classroom students	Online students
Full time employed	19.4%	70.9%
Part time employed	36.1%	16.4%
Unemployed	44.4%	12.7%
Total	***100%***	***100%***

Another confirmation of the above comes from the monthly salary declared by graduated students, given in Table 8. Classroom students can clearly be defined as "fresh" workers, who entered the job market after graduation and earn salaries generally lower than 1,500 euros per month. On the contrary, a large part of online students is already present in the job market, thus their salaries are significantly higher.

Table 8. Monthly salary of SSRI students one year after graduation

Monthly salary	Classroom students	Online students
Less than 1,000 euros	30,0%	4,9%
Less than 1,500 euros	53,3%	31,7%
Less than 2,000 euros	16,7%	41,5%
Less than 2,500 euros		17,1%
More than 2,500 euros		4,9%
Total	***100%***	***100%***

We may also consider in Figure 4. the level of satisfaction of SSRI graduated students about:

- the coherence between topics studied during SSRI and competences required by the job;
- the adequacy of the level of preparation acquired during SSRI to the job requirements;
- the general satisfaction about the present job.

In general, SSRI graduated students are very or enough satisfied about their study experience related to the job they found. And – even more encouraging – online students are more positive than classroom ones regarding the competences acquired during SSRI, thus implicitly asserting the high quality of the e-learning approach.

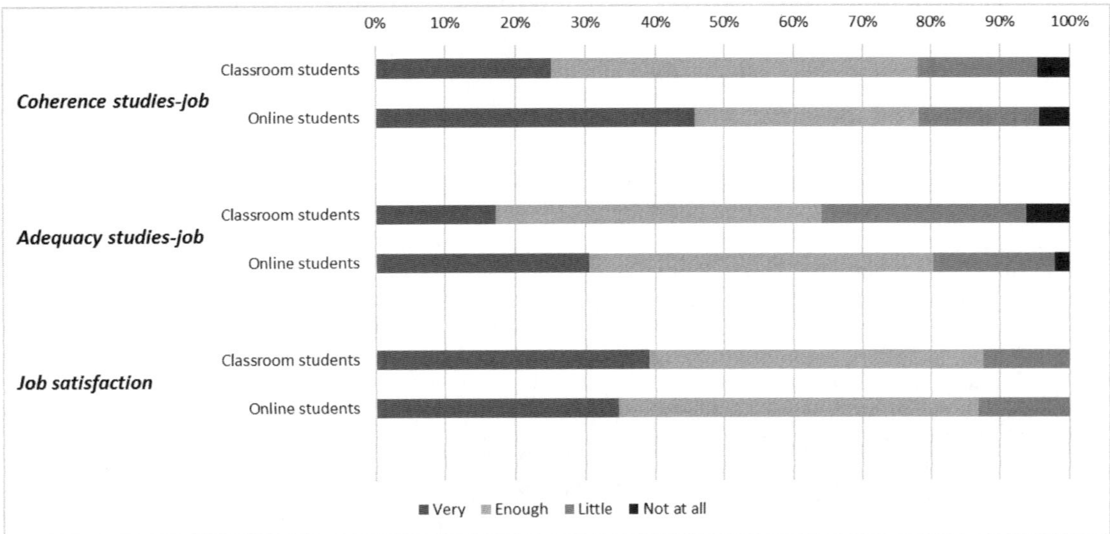

Figure 4. Level of satisfaction of graduated SSRI students

A feedback about the quality of the teaching material provided to online students – deeply discussed in Milani (2014) – can be derived also from the opinions collected from graduating students about their university experience: all online students are fully or enough satisfied of the choice they made, and 80% of them (vs. 76% of the classroom students) would repeat the same choice.

5. CONCLUSIONS

In this paper, we analyzed the characteristics of students enrolled from the first year to the undergraduate course on Security of Computer Systems and Networks (SSRI) offered both in classroom based fashion and online at the University of Milan, and some information given by graduated students one year after obtaining the final degree. Main conclusions we can draw from such analysis are the following.

Students enrolling to the online version of SSRI are definitely different from "normal" students following lectures in classroom; in fact:

- online students are significantly older;
- they are in general already occupied in a job when enrolling and during the course;
- they show a better economic situation;

thus there is almost no overlapping between the two student populations, and no "competition" between the two versions of the course. This means that the activation of an e-learning version of a university course does not steal students to the traditional, classroom version.

For several reasons – all related to their personal situation – the progression in studies of the online students is definitely slower than the one of classroom students, even if the best and most motivated online students show results in line with the classroom counterpart. This suggests the opportunity to concentrate on didactic supports aimed at helping online students to keep the correct study pace since the beginning of their university experience.

The opinions of graduated students show – perhaps surprisingly – a better feeling about the quality of the university course by people who followed the online version: this is a very positive message about the possibility of building a successful complete university course in e-learning. A better insight about the cognitive ability of both classroom and online students, their motivation, the factors that influence the effectiveness of the two modes of learning will be the subject of a future investigation.

ACKNOWLEDGEMENT

The author would like to thank Dr. Silvia Spazzacampagna from the University of Milan, and Dr. Claudia Montalbetti from CINECA, for their assistance in the retrieval of student data necessary to perform the analysis reported in this paper.

REFERENCES

Anderson T., 2008. Teaching in an online learning context. *Theory and practice of online learning*, Athabasca University Press, USA

Berge, Z.L., Collins, M.P., 2000. Perceptions of e-moderators about their roles and functions in moderating electronic mailing lists. *In Distance Education, Vol.21, No. 1, p.p.81-100*

Damiani E. et al, 2005. SSRI online: first experiences in a three-years course degree offered in e-learning at the University of Milan (Italy). *11th International Conference on Distributed Multimedia Systems*. Banff, Canada, pp.65–70.

Milani M. et al, 2014. Organisation and management of a complete bachelor degree offered online at the university of Milan for ten years. *International Conference E-Learning 2014*. Lisbon, Portugal, pp.87-94.

Moisey S. D, 2008. Supporting the online learner. *Theory and practice of online learning*, Athabasca University Press, USA, p.p.419-439

Rivoltella, P. C., 2006. *E-tutor. Profilo, metodi e strumenti*. Carocci.

Salmon, G., 2000. A model for CMC in education and training. *E-moderating. The key to teaching and learning online. London: Kogan Page*

HOW DO WE KNOW WHAT IS HAPPENING ONLINE?: A TRIANGULATED APPROACH TO DATA ANALYSIS

Marina Charalampidi and Michael Hammond
Centre for Education Studies, University of Warwick
Coventry, CV4 7AL, United Kingdom

ABSTRACT

This paper discusses the process of analysing online discussion and argues for the merits of mixed methods. Much research of online participation and e-learning has been either message focused or person focused analysis. The former covers methodologies such as content and discourse analysis, the latter interviewing and surveys. The paper discusses the strength and weaknesses of these approaches in the context of a study of an online social educational network for gifted students. Here interviews, questionnaire survey and content analysis were all used in order to explore the process of online discussion and the experience of taking part. The paper argues for a mixed approach in which different types of data can be compared and contrasted. Such triangulation is time-consuming but it allows for a comprehensive picture of the use of the network and the experience of online participation.

KEYWORDS

Online discussion, triangulation, data analysis, learning.

1. INTRODUCTION

There has long been interest in developing forms of online collaborative learning in both formal and informal contexts. These developments have provided researchers with the challenge of describing and evaluating the learners' experience of participation and the online archives that they create. In addressing this challenge researchers have developed a range of methodologies and methods, many of which can be divided between *focus on message / focus on participant*.

Message focused analysis includes content analysis (e.g. De Wever et al. 2006); conversation analysis (e.g. Stahl, 2005) and discourse analysis (e.g. Littleton &Whitelock 2005; McConnell 1994). In addition, archives have frequently been analysed and described in respect to number of messages and breakdown of messages by sender and by group (e.g. gender or cohort in formal learning). There have been attempts to provide social network analyses too (e.g. de Laat et al. 2007; Rabbany et al. 2013) and more recently learning analytics (e.g. Agudo-Peregrina et al. 2014). In contrast to message analysis, person focused analysis has typically included interviews and surveys of learners' attitudes to online participation, their backgrounds and their evaluation of their experiences online. At times, more ethnographic approaches have been undertaken, most notably Lindtner et al. (2008).

Both approaches, and the particular methods within each, have their own advantages and disadvantages. For example, it is an obvious step to provide data on numbers taking part in online debates and the frequency with which individuals or groups post as these will say something about the intensity of the discussion. However, it is not straightforward to explore the relationship between participation and learning and a particular challenge that has dominated research has been content analysis of messages. Clearly the automatic archiving of messages has given almost unique opportunities for researchers to explore interactive learning, but making sense of these archives is open to different types of interpretation (De Wever et al., 2006). In-depth content analysis was introduced by Henri (1992) and taken forward by, amongst others, Gunawardena et al. (1998) who developed a model to judge the quality of online interaction and of the learning experience. Yet, while researchers have claimed an objectivity in their analyses doubts remain. For example, Naidu and Järvelä (2006, p. 101) note that "keeping the complex characteristic of human learning in mind, it is never possible to find full evidence of learning from 'traces', such as computer notes of discussion threads". Hammond (2015, p. 229) also questioned the assumptions made about participation arguing it was "easy to be sanguine about the affective and motivational gains from participation in these contexts and to identify a process of 'knowledge building' without asking difficult questions as to the status of that knowledge."

A further problem in over focusing on message analysis is that this may lead to the erroneous assumption that those who did not send messages gained nothing from reading / reflecting on others' messages. 'Quiet participation' (or so called 'lurking') may be important to the maintenance of community and may be not just tolerated but welcomed by some active participants - something that would not be uncovered without directly interviewing members of forums (e.g. Takahashi et al. 2003). In contrast, by themselves surveys and interviews may offer rather misleading findings on participation. For example, they typically show a great deal of generalised support for the idea of collaborative learning which may not borne out by rates of participation in particular forums.

Of course the argument for a mixed methods approach in social research has long been made (e.g. Johnson & Onwuegbuzie, 2004) and Dennen (2008) and Naidu and Järvelä (2006) amongst others have noted that those studying online learning need not stick to one method of analysis. Mixed methods enhances the trustworthiness of research findings by providing confirming, complementary and contrasting sources of data. For instance, Wee and Looi (2009) provided an example of the social construction of mathematical knowledge that included comparison of the researchers' analysis to the participants' own interpretations. de Laat et al. (2007) explained how they used content analysis, interviews and social network analysis to investigate a networked learning community, noting the value of both data and methodological triangulation. Schrire (2006) incorporated content analysis into a case study methodology as it helped address 'what' and 'how' research questions. Hammond and Wiriyapinit (2005) carried out an interpretive case study using a variety of methods including questionnaire survey, text analysis and interviews. However, though there is, at least on intuitive grounds, much to recommend it, triangulation is not a routine strategy and there have only been sporadic attempts to reflect on its methodological possibilities. This paper then addresses a gap by looking at the use of a mixed methods approach to describing 'what was going on' in one online community.

2. THE STUDY

This research involves a social educational online network, namely IGGY. IGGY was created in the UK by the University of Warwick for academically gifted young people, aged 13 to 18. According to IGGY's database, the network currently has around 7000 active members. IGGY has members from all over the world, though most live in the UK (n = 6547). Around 60% are 16 to 18 years old and the rest 13 to 15 years old. Four tenths of the total number of active members are female, 15% are male (45% did not provide this information). An important feature of IGGY is the high level of participation safety - for example the network is closed to non-members and non-disclosure of personal information is ensured through regular monitoring of communication by organisers. IGGY can be regarded as an unusual or unique online network offering a hybrid of social and individual learning. It feels open in that members tend not to know each other in person, but closed as students usually need to be recommended by a teacher in order to join the network (for a more detailed explanation, see Charalampidi et al., 2014).

The IGGY network consists of five sections; *Profile, Members, Debate, News and Events, Knowledge*. Of particular importance to the members are the Debate and the Knowledge sections.

The *Debate* section is broad and may include anything that might be of interest to the members. Debates can be initiated by members or mentors (these are local university students or members of the IGGY staff). Debates are moderated and, reflecting the ethos of IGGY, while they tend to be conversational they are also discursive and are seen by members as different from the everyday social networking sites in which they participate. Meanwhile, the *Knowledge* section contains learning material grouped around academic categories such as Maths, Science, History and Politics, and Creative Writing. IGGY does not offer its members a guided programme, rather members are expected to identify for themselves relevant challenges. These cover topics of interest to the community but are not matched against any particular awarding body's programme of study. Participation in challenges is not formally assessed but is led by members of the IGGY team, the mentors or invited academics.

Researching IGGY may throw light on online participation and interaction patterns alongside the potential educational and/or affective benefits from participation. It also throws interesting light on the notion of giftedness. Underlying the various questions we posed while researching IGGY laid a wider question of how we could describe what was going on online. To address this question we decided to employ a mix of methods, including interviewing, questionnaire survey and content analysis, on an expectation that our understanding of IGGY would be strengthened by the unique contribution of each method.

The approach was an iterative one. For example, in the early stage of the research, questionnaires were sent via email to a few members, who were then interviewed. More interviews followed which yielded significant findings in relation to the experience of participation (see Charalampidi et al., 2014). However, more data were needed and a revised questionnaire was prepared and uploaded on the network for a period of approximately eight months. Throughout this period a content analysis of messages from discussion forums was undertaken. There is not the space to present all the findings to date from our exploration of this network, instead this particular paper focuses on the methodology. It considers: the methods used; examples of using the methods; the benefits of a triangulated approach.

3. THE METHODS USED TO ANALYSE PARTICIPATION

In line with our earlier categorisation we look here at message focused and person focused analysis.

3.1 Message Focused Analysis

Analysis was carried out on posts found in the debate section of the network. IGGY had designated 16 broad topics for debate at the time of our analysis: *Writing wrongs essay competition; Unitracks; University offer holders; Homework help; IGGY community hub; Help and feedback; Student mentors; Careers and personal development; What's it like to be gifted; Education and the internet; Science; Maths; History; English and creative writing; Politics; Law.* These we grouped into four categories: *cognitive; social / moral / political; personal development; administrative.*

The most popular of these debates were identified through analysis of numerical data including the number of posts and views. Some of these debates required short, quick answers such as *Three Word Story?*, *First Thoughts in Mind* but others were discursive covering questions such as *Who Believes in Evolution and Why/Why not?*. We decided to apply a more fine grained analysis to some of these debates including *Is Homework A Waste Of Time?, What Is The Best Place You've Ever Been To On Holiday?, How Do You Tell If Someone Is Gifted?* and *Studying Law At University.* These debates were representative of the cognitive, social / moral / political, personal development categories mentioned above, but not the administrative category. A further criterion for selecting debates was that they evidenced the participation of members who had been interviewed by the researchers. This meant that in interviews we could refer back to examples of debates and of participation.

After considerable trial and error, our content analysis focused on analysing large units of meaning. The coding scheme was finalised after several false starts, and contained the key codes *Triggering a discussion (T), Inviting a response (R)* and *Stating (S)*, and several sub codes (see Table1). We wanted a scheme which would not be overcomplex and thus we limited our focus to just three main codes. Within our scheme we wanted to identify situations in which interaction was invited (the T and R codes) as interaction has been central to claims made about the value of online discussion (e.g. Swan, 2002). We also wanted the scheme to help us identify how members justified their opinion and made claims to knowledge. As classroom teachers we realised that we spent a great deal of our time asking learners about the moral, practical and academic basis for the judgements they reached and we wanted to examine how this was done online and how sources of knowledge were evoked in different contexts. Thus our subcategories directed us to look at how participants responded to particular texts and drew on external sources, general knowledge, accepted facts, their own experience and own value judgements to support their arguments.

Table 1. Codes used in content analysis

Codes	How achieved (sub codes)	Examples
Triggering discussion – T	*Introducing, Maintaining, Asking, Acknowledging*	(T/Introducing) "There are a lot of stereotypes surrounding intelligent people. How true do you find them?" (T/Maintaining) "This is really nice. Thanks."
Stating – S	Appeal to: *Reading, General knowledge, Facts, Value judgements (Aesthetic, Moral), Own experience, No reason given*	(S/General knowledge) "Driving less can have enormous benefits for the environment, while walking and bicycling can also improve your health." (S/Value judgement) "I think academically gifted is showing ability in many academic subjects; talented is in one."
Responding – R	*Disagreeing, Agreeing, Resolving, Expanding on previous comments* plus Appeal to: *Reading, General knowledge, Facts, Value judgements (Aesthetic, Moral), Own experience, No reason given*	(R/Disagreeing by appeal to own experience) "But in my school we usually spend so much time checking everyone has handed the h/w, we might as well have done the work it that time!!" (R/Agreeing but no reason given) "I agree nebiyah!"

Apart from analysing the debate transcripts in terms of functions of posts, we identified who interacted with whom.

3.1.1 Examples of Message Focused Analysis

Message focused analysis began by reading the forums and getting a feel for them. This was beneficial in three ways: it provided access to tangible examples of knowledge claims made by earlier interviews; it enabled the identification of debates that were of particular relevance to our study, and it stimulated the formation of interview questions that examined various aspects of these debates in more detail.

Selected examples of debates analysed thoroughly are now presented. The first debate invited members to share their opinion regarding the best holiday destination they had ever been to. The second concerned the significance of homework and the third encouraged members to put forward any questions they might have had regarding studying law at University.

Table 2 summarises the number of units of analysis labelled as interactive or non-interactive. These raw totals informed us about participation practices in respect to different debates. Each debate had particular characteristics: the first triggered a sharing of personal experiences, the second triggered particularly strong interaction and the third generated many information requests. This suggested that different topics provoked different forms of cognitive engagement.

Table 2. Number of functions per debate

Debate	Functions	
	Interactive	Non-interactive
What is the best place you've ever been to on holiday?	T = 4 R= 6	S = 23
	Total = 10	Total = 23
Is homework a waste of time?	T = 38 R = 199	S = 105
	Total = 237	Total = 105
Studying law at University	T = 8 R = 2	S = 1
	Total = 10	Total = 1

Visualisation diagrams (Figures 1, 2 and 3) enabled us to identify the pattern of interactions within the discussions and the key participants around which discussions evolved. In the figures, the square nodes represent learner members of IGGY, the circles represent mentors or members of the IGGY staff, and the lines represent connections between the nodes. The size of the nodes is proportional to the number of their connections. The octagon signifies those messages that did not address a particular discussant but rather all discussants in the debate. Using these diagrams we could explore whether online participation could be better described as 'many to many' interaction or one to many or as simply chaotic.

It was interesting to observe that even though all messages revolved around the initial post, the participant who triggered the discussion in all three debates did not contribute further to it. It was also clear that the mentors in the first and second debate (see Figure 4) were particularly active in sending messages and were frequently addressed when members replied. This suggested that the mentors' contribution in encouraging further interaction among discussants was significant. The second debate is of particular interest as it has been one of the most popular in IGGY. In this debate, 122 students and 9 mentors participated. Figure 3 shows that apart from the main discussion, several subgroup discussions were developed. Many messages were also directed to the group as a whole. This suggested that discussants in this debate were not only interested in the topic as such, but also in the opinions expressed by others.

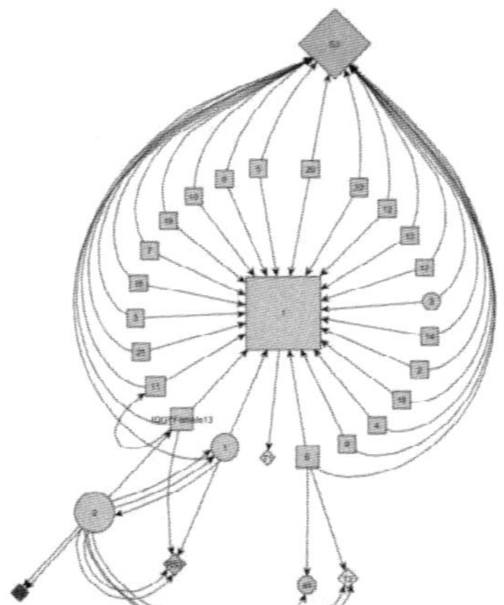

Figure 1. 'What is the best place you've ever been to on holiday?' – representation of interactions and functions of posts

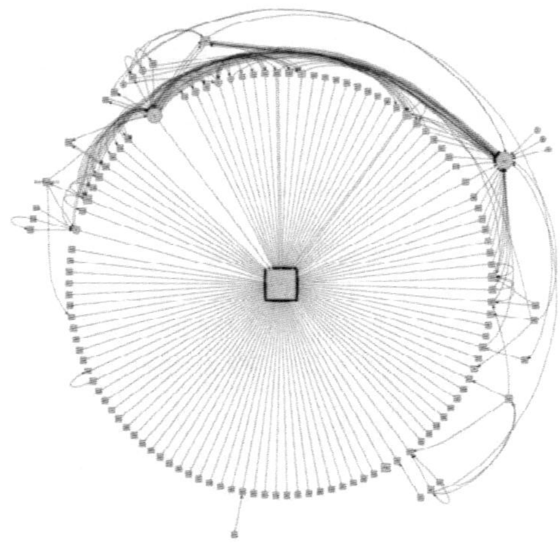

Figure 2. Is homework a waste of time – representation of interactions

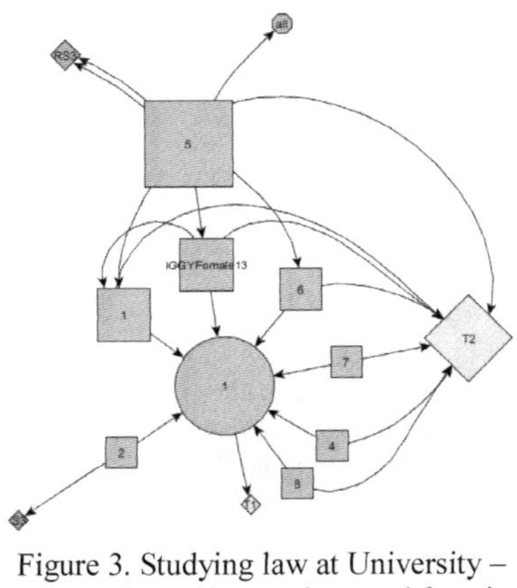

Figure 3. Studying law at University – representation of interactions and functions of posts

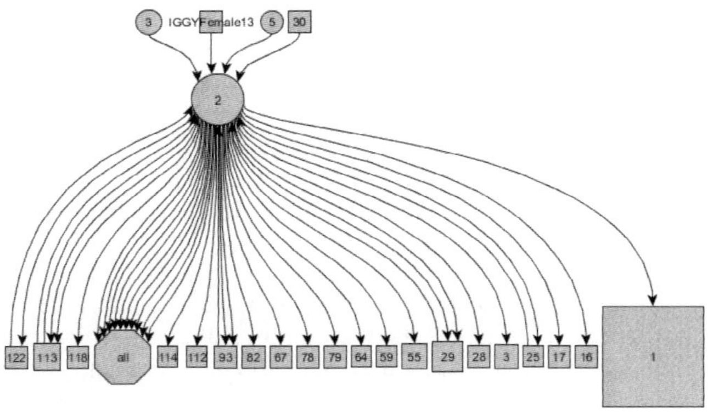

Figure 4. Is homework a waste of time – representation of M2's connections

3.2 Person Focused Analysis

A survey (n = 76 responses) was carried out comprising of 25 questions; 22 closed questions, 2 open-ended questions and 1 question that invited students to opt in for an interview. The closed questions included Likert scales, yes – no questions and multiple choice questions. The questions were broadly divided in two categories; questions about the students' profile (e.g. gender, age etc.), and his/her online experience. The latter covered the themes of online behaviour and forms of engagement and provided quantitative data on issues such as membership duration, the frequency of accessing the network, the time spent using the network during a typical week, and the frequency of engagement with various types of activities. It also examined the members' preference over interactive or non-interactive activities, perceived benefits and reasons for using IGGY, feelings towards the community, constraints and suggestions for improving the online experience.

The use of the network was further explored through a series of semi structured interviews (n = 12). Key themes that emerged concerned the users' profiles (hobbies, family, friends), the idea of giftedness (conceptions of giftedness, the label, feelings and/or problems related to it), their use of technology in general, their use of IGGY (expectations, why join, why use, what do you do, benefits, online relationships and community, facilitators, constraints, suggestions for improvement). In the latest round of interviews we also used one strategy, stimulated recall, which enabled us to discuss intentions and composition with some interviewees in relation to particular debates.

The questionnaire survey presented us with an overview of the use of IGGY. From the survey we found that members carried out a variety of activities in IGGY but the favourite ones were reading and/or replying to debates and doing quizzes. Members used IGGY for a number of reasons: to address lack of challenge at school, to access learning resources, to meet new people, to communicate with other members, and to learn about other cultures. Many members stated that they experienced both educational (i.e. vocabulary development), cultural (i.e. knowledge of other cultures) and affective benefits (i.e. confidence in expressing their opinion) through their participation. In general, IGGY was seen as an educational community within which members felt trust, empathy and respect. The main constraint in using IGGY was lack of time and learning to navigate the network.

Interviews provided the detail for this general picture. For example, one interviewee (coded in our study as IGGYFemale13) was classified as a frequent user of the network as she accessed it daily, spending between one and two hours in it. IGGYFemale13 provided explanations and examples to support her idea that the network was helpful and valuable for her. She also expanded on debates to which she had contributed, read or initiated. She participated when she found the topic important and challenging, as in the second debate above. She was led to contribute further when different views were expressed:

"*Yeah that homework is really important for our learning to progress. I just thought that I tried to make people see different views. People who thought that it wasn't important I tried to make them see that it actually is really important.*"

Notably, she replied to posts when she felt she had something to add to the conversation. Yet, even when she remained quiet, she did read and contemplate the messages giving us insight into the process of quiet participation:

"*I just wanted to push it as far as possible so that they thought of different ways, but the others were so thought through I didn't know what to answer. There was nothing I could say, because it was just so well written and so well researched. I did look at them, I did come back to it.*"

"*... on the most serious debates I do tend to read every single one to see just the different opinions. I don't always post in them but I read other peoples' experiences.*"

The interview allowed this IGGY member to reflect on the size of debates (small versus large scale) and type (i.e. fun versus serious). She felt that a debate that generated carefully considered replies was successful even if the number of replies was limited. Additionally, she valued any type of debate, being fun or more serious, if they had something to offer her:

"*... there weren't that many replies but the replies that were there were really thorough and thought through so that is what I was trying to get people to do, to think about it and give me an honest answer.*"

"*I like the ones that really challenge my way of thinking, people who try to convince me that their way of thinking is better because I can argue with them. They sometimes even convince me! I also like the ones that are fun because it's just really nice to take some time out of serious things and just have fun even though it still brings something to me.*"

She also shed further light on facilitators of participation and referred to the importance of social presence. She believed that replying to specific members was useful in making them feel both accepted and confident as "*it shows that somebody has actually taken the time to read their message*". She explained that she "*... really enjoyed the year and a bit now (she) spent on IGGY and (she) want(ed) as many members to feel welcome to the community as (she) was.*"

The interview confirmed the earlier finding regarding the importance of the mentors' participation. IGGYFemale13 commented on this role and stated her appreciation of their contributions. She even referred to two specific mentors, one of whom was the mentor (M2) who stood out in the second debate above:

"*I think they bring a high level of sophistication and a lot of intelligence to IGGY and their posts are really interesting. One of the usernames (...) I think that's her name, always wrote specifically to someone for example she put a username and answered, and there could be 5 messages for different members on one debate and I think that was really good that she took the time to answer.*"

Finally, via the interview we were able to reach an understanding of what online learning meant to the members. IGGYFemale13 felt that online learning included the exchange of different views and the stimulation of rethinking about one's own ideas. Hence, she did perceive her participation in debates as learning, including debates on less academic topics:

"*I'd say it is because, from other peoples' experiences and other peoples' views it just brings on a whole other way of your thoughts and maybe you thought one way but somebody else thought another way and it just makes you think, so it is challenging your brain which is what my definition is of learning and, just some debates do relate a lot to learning but other debates are slightly more like fun and I think they are also important. One of the debates, I think it's "Five random facts about you", you just say the five first things about you that pop into your head and it's just funny to see what people write but others like the one about geeks and nerds, they just really make you think, make you learn and share experiences.*"

One obvious limitation of the interviews and even the survey was that of sampling. Not surprisingly those that volunteered to be interviewed tended to be among the most active of members and their experiences might not be representative. The survey was likely to be more representative but to date take up has been less than we would like.

4. CONCLUSIONS

The paper began by noting the variety of approaches to analysing online participation. Two main approaches were identified; message focused and person focused analysis. In our study we combined these approaches to exploit the opportunities afforded by each. We drew three key conclusions from this attempt to apply a triangulated approach to understanding 'what is going on online'.

First, different sources of evidence provide different insight. In particular, the message focused analysis informed us about the structure of debates and showed how debates were triggered, who triggered them, who contributed and how. The analysis gave clues as to how discussions were sustained and pointed to the key role of moderators. Our content analysis gave us insight into the different sources of knowledge and claims to knowledge and how these differed depending on the nature of the discussion. This was important as a claim to academic knowledge needed to be founded on more than personal experience and should consider appropriate evidence. However, such analysis did not provide access to the participants' perceptions about what is happening online but rather an interpretation from an 'external' point of view. Thus the need for interviews, to allow an in-depth exploration of the participants' experiences and offer answers to 'why' questions. Interviews have the additional potential of informing researchers about 'hidden' or 'quiet' participation. Alongside interviews, surveys can enable access to a wider population and provide background information, both quantitative and qualitative. This can be beneficial in examining individual members or in identifying subgroups with common characteristics.

Second, the analysis of an online environment should not be treated mechanistically. For example, coding for content analysis was not chosen 'off the peg' but rather developed by ourselves to fit around the questions we wanted to ask. More importantly while we used familiar methods of contrast, consistency and complementarity to triangulate findings this required a continual cross checking of different data rather than a simple aggregation. Indeed, based on constant comparison of data we were able to reach the conclusion that IGGY can be described as an educational community in which, through participation and interaction, members experience learning benefits, albeit with constraints on members' participation and differentiated patterns of participation.

Third, a triangulated approach is intensely time consuming and perhaps this explains its uneven use in the field. Yet the approach is a valuable one and we are in danger of making misleading claims about online learning if we rely on only one source of data.

REFERENCES

Agudo-Peregrina, Á. F., Iglesias-Pradas, S., Conde-González, M. Á., & Hernández-García, Á., 2014. Can we predict success from log data in VLEs? Classification of interactions for learning analytics and their relation with performance in VLE-supported F2F and online learning. *Computers in Human Behavior*, Vol. 31, pp. 542-550.

Charalampidi, M., Hammond, M., & Boddison, A., 2014. Exploring aspects of participation in an international online network for 'gifted' students - A research in progress. *Proceedings of EDULEARN14 Conference*. Barcelona, Spain, pp. 6250-6259.

de Laat, M., Lally, V., Lipponen, L., & Simons, R.-J., 2007. Investigating patterns of interaction in networked learning and computer-supported collaborative learning: A role for Social Network Analysis. *Computer-Supported Collaborative Learning*, Vol. 2, No. 1, pp. 87-103.

De Wever, B., T., S., Valcke, M., & Van Keer, H., 2006. Content analysis schemes to analyze transcripts of online asynchronous discussion groups: A review. *Computers and Education*. Vol. 46, No. 1, pp. 6-28.

Dennen, V. P., 2008. Looking for evidence of learning: Assessment and analysis methods for online discourse. *Computers in Human Behavior*, Vol. 24, pp. 205–219.

Gunawardena, C. N., Lowe, C. A., & Anderson, T., 1998. Transcript Analysis of Computer-Mediated Conferences as a Tool for Testing Constructivist and Social-Constructivist Learning Theories. *Distance Learning 1998. Proceedings of the Annual Conference on Distance Teaching & Learning*, Madison, Wisconsin, USA, pp. 139-145.

Hammond, M., & Wiriyapinit, M., 2005. Learning through online discussion: A case of triangulation in research. *Australasian Journal of Educational Technology*, Vol. 21, No. 3, pp. 283-302.

Hammond, M., 2015. A Habermasian perspective on joint meaning making online: What does it offer and what are the difficulties? *International Journal of Computer-Supported Collaborative Learning*, Vol. 10, No. 3, pp. 223-237.

Henri, F., 1992. Computer conference and content analysis. In A. R. Kaye (Ed.), *Collaborative Learning Through Computer Conferencing*, Springer-Verlag, Berlin, pp. 117-136.

Johnson, R., & Onwuegbuzie, A., 2004. Mixed methods research: a research paradigm whose time has come. *Educational Researcher*, Vol. 33, No. 7, pp. 14-26.

Lindtner, S., Nardi, B., Wang, Y., Mainwaring, S., Jing, H., & Liang, W., 2008. A hybrid cultural ecology: world of warcraft in China. *Proceedings of the 2008 ACM conference on Computer Supported Cooperative work*, San Diego USA, pp. 371-382.

Littleton, K., & Whitelock, D., 2005. The negotiation and co-construction of meaning and understanding within a postgraduate online learning community. *Learning, Media and Technology*, Vol. 30, No. 2, pp. 147-164.

Mcconnell, D., 1994. Managing open learning in computer supported collaborative learning environments. *Studies in Higher Education*, Vol. 19, No. 3, pp. 341-358.

Naidu, S., & Järvelä, S., 2006. Analyzing CMC content for what? *Computers & Education*, Vol. 46, No. 1, pp. 96-103.

Rabbany, R., ElAtia, S., Takaffoli, M., & Zaïane, O. R., 2013. Collaborative learning of students in online discussion forums: A social network analysis perspective. In A. Peña-Ayala (Ed.), *Educational Data Mining: Applications and Trends*, Springer-Verlag, Berlin, pp. 1-30.

Schrire, S., 2006. Knowledge building in asynchronous discussion groups: Going beyond quantitative analysis. *Computers & Education*, Vol. 46, No. 1, pp. 49-70.

Stahl, G., 2005. Group cognition in computer-assisted collaborative learning. *Journal of Computer Assisted Learning*, Vol. 21, No. 2, pp. 79-90.

Swan, K., 2002. Building learning communities in online courses: The importance of interaction. *Education, Communication & Information*, Vol. 2, No. 1, pp. 23-49.

Takahashi, M., Fujimoto, M., & Yamasaki, N., 2003. The active lurker: influence of an in-house online community on its outside environment. *Proceedings of the 2003 international ACM SIGGROUP conference on supporting group work*, Sanibel Island, Florida, USA, pp. 1-10.

Wee, J. D., & Looi, C.-K., 2009. A Model for Analyzing Math Knowledge Building in VMT. In G. Stahl (Ed.), *Studying Virtual Math Teams*, Springer, New York, pp. 475-497.

ANALYSIS OF 3D MODELING SOFTWARE USAGE PATTERNS FOR K-12 STUDENTS

Yi-Chieh Wu, Wen-Hung Liao, Ming-Te Chi and Tsai-Yen Li
Dept. of Computer Science, National Chengchi University, Taipei, Taiwan

ABSTRACT

In response to the recent trend in maker movement, teachers are learning 3D techniques actively and bringing 3D printing into the classroom to enhance variety and creativity in designing lectures. This study investigates the usage pattern of a 3D modeling software, Qmodel Creator, which is targeted at K-12 students. User logs containing participants' operations were recorded and analyzed. We expect the results to be instrumental to the developers of Qmodel Creator regarding future enhancements of the software. Moreover, by observing operation behaviors of K-12 students, lesson plans for 3D printing can be tailored to fit the needs of users of different education levels.

KEYWORDS

3D modeling software development; Qmodel Creator; K-12 education; STEM lesson plan; User behavior analysis

1. INTRODUCTION

3D Modeling software has become popular in recent years due to advances in 3D printing technology as well as affordability of 3D printers. According to a research report by Gartner, 2016 shipments of 3D printers will exceed 490,000 units. The report also stated that major clients for products below $2,500 are schools and universities that need to lower procurement costs (SC, 2015). Many training courses in several professional areas, such as medicine (Mahmoud & Bennett, 2015), architecture (Cesaretti *et al*, 2014), and machinery (Gonzalez-Gomez *et al*, 2012), often incorporate 3D printing in their lecture cases. An increasing number of teachers in elementary education also plan to learn 3D-related techniques and apply 3D printing directly in their courses (Irwin *et al*, 2014).

The overall process of 3D manufacturing includes the following stages: 1) modeling using software or scanning, 2) editing and refining and 3) printing using additive or subtractive manufacturing. There is no doubt that 3D printing is beneficial for K-12 education as it ignites children's imagination and creativity. It is also critical to include modeling concepts in STEM courses. However, current K-12 lecture cases focus too much on the printing phase of the process, possibly due to the complexity of 3D modeling and editing software. To ease the learning curve of modeling for K-12 students, we have developed Qmodel Creator, a cubic style modeling software with an intuitive user interface that quickly converts 2D drawings into 3D models. Figure 1 shows how the 3D model of a snail is generated using very simple sketches.

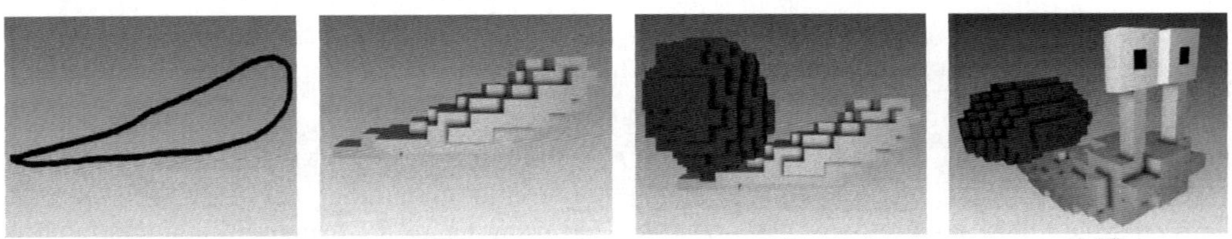

(a) (b) (c) (d)

Figure 1. Demonstration on how to create a snail using Qmodel Creator. (a) Sketch a contour, (b) System generates a rough model with thickness adjustment, (c) Sketch another part then combine all components into one, (d) Adding details to the model

In order to understand the user behavior and provide feedback for updating the user interface and functions of the application, we recorded operation logs of participants who tried out Qmodel Creator in several workshops. The following questions were posed and answered based on the analytical results derived from the recorded information:

- For models created with Qmodel Creator, what is the degree of completion?
- Which function is used more frequently: intuitive modeling or traditional 3D editing (such as adding and deleting voxels)?
- When users create models, is the process smooth? Is trial and error needed?
- How long does the user take to finish a modeling task?

In this paper, firstly, we found that there is detectable distinction in the detail of the finished models for users from different skill level groups. Furthermore, our analysis indicated that students with different backgrounds have respective preferences on particular functions of Qmodel Creator. At last, we examined the operation logs and concluded that Qmodel Creator is a suitable 3D modeling software for all ages of K-12 students.

The remainder of this paper is organized as follows. In Section 2 we outline related works on lesson plans, user interface design, and user behavior analysis research. Section 3 elucidates our experiment process and methodology, as well as the indicators we used for evaluation. In Section 4, we respond to the above questions according to our analysis of user behavior. Section 5 concludes this paper and outlines future work.

2. RELATED WORK

Thornburg *et al.* (2014) demonstrated excellent examples in introducing 3D printing technology to the classrooms. In their book, half of 18 projects begin with 2D Inkscape drawing, and OpenSCAD is then used for 3D modeling, following the easy-to-difficult order for designing lectures.

Shneiderman *et al.* (2010) inducted the 'eight golden rules of interface design'. The second rule: 'cater to universal usability' suggested that we should provide the appropriate user interface for various user conditions. Therefore the design of a user interface has to retain a certain degree of flexibility.

Dreyfus *et al.* (1986) presented a phenomenology of skill acquisition of humans, and offered a theoretical explanation for it. Based on subjective and objective results, they presume that the learning process goes through five stages: novice, advanced beginner, competent, proficient, and expert. The process from novice to expert is universal and applicable in many fields. According to their research, we assume a model that formulates the process of skill acquisition from novice to advanced beginner, and so on, as depicted in Figure 2.

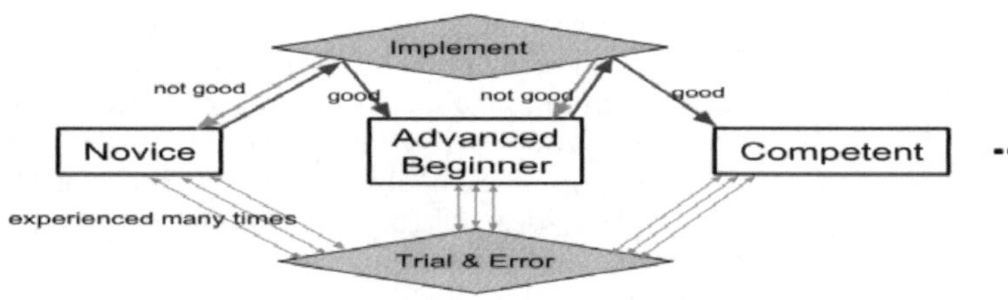

Figure 2. Skill acquisition model based on Dreyfus *et al.*'s work

3. USER LOG ACQUISITION AND ANALYSIS

This section describes the format of user logs recorded using Qmodel Creator and the subsequent analysis procedure. 3D models made by K-12 participants have been collected for experts to evaluate and judge users' competency level. Selected evaluation indicators are also presented and discussed.

3.1 UI and Log of Qmodel Creator

Figure 3(a) shows the Qmodel Creator user interface. For all participants, we recorded each operation along with the corresponding timestamp for subsequent calculation of operation time span. We stored the information in a log file: the first field is the timestamp, and the second field is the operation event. Figure 3(b) presents a snapshot of the Qmodel Creator log file.

In Qmodel Creator, traditional 3D modeling functions such as adding and deleting voxels require more steps than intuitive modeling. Certain function keys are shared (e.g., Clean/Undo/Redo). The following list contains operations that are classified as 'intuitive'. The rest are regarded as traditional 3D operations.

- Change mode to 'Draw Simple'
- Change mode to 'Draw Symmetry'
- Start drawing
- End drawing
- Click OK

As shown in Figure 3(b), drawing operations come in pairs, with "Click OK" as the operation logged after "Adjust Thickness" and "Click Confirm".

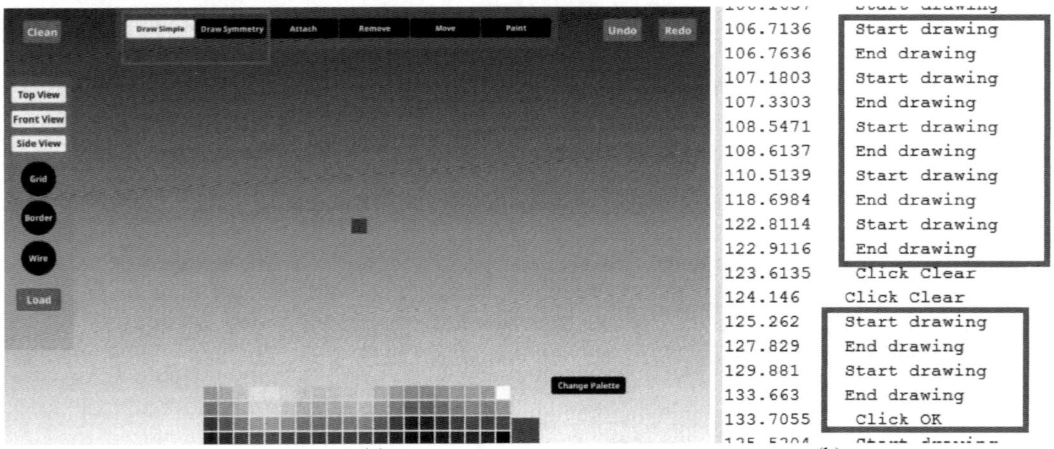

(a) (b)

Figure 3. User interface and log of Qmodel Creator. (a) Interface; red square indicates two intuitive modeling functions: Draw Simple and Draw Symmetry. (b) Snapshot of Qmodel Creator log file. Red frame indicates intuitive operations

3.2 Data Collection

We have hosted two workshops to introduce Qmodel Creator to K-12 students and collected user logs for future analysis. The data collection processes are described below.

1. Lanyu Primary and Junior High School: The experiment involved 62 students aged from 9 to 15. The experiment was separated into three sessions. Of the 62 students, 49 used Qmodel Creator on an iPad and 13 did so using an Android tablet. In order to motivate students' interests, we prepared 3D printed models as gifts to active participants. All the students have no prior experience in 3D modeling software.

2. Sanchong High School: The experiment involved 8 students aged from 16 to 17. All the students tried Qmodel Creator on an iPad. These students have solid training in arts. They have been instructed to create 3D models using TinkerCAD and Sculptris. However, Qmodel Creator is a first time experience for them.

3.3 Users' Skill Level Identification

In keeping with the aforementioned skill acquisition assumption, there is a need for an evaluation system to gauge if the students' modeling competency for Qmodel Creator is at the novice stage. To judge the quality of 3D models in the two experiments, we designed a web interface and asked three experts (our researchers in the study) to label the model as bad or not. If a model received more than half the 'bad' votes, it was classified as a bad model. Therefore, if a model was judged as bad, the student's modeling skill was deemed to be at novice level. Figure 4 illustrates some evaluation results. The consensus rate among three experts is 82.86% (58/70).

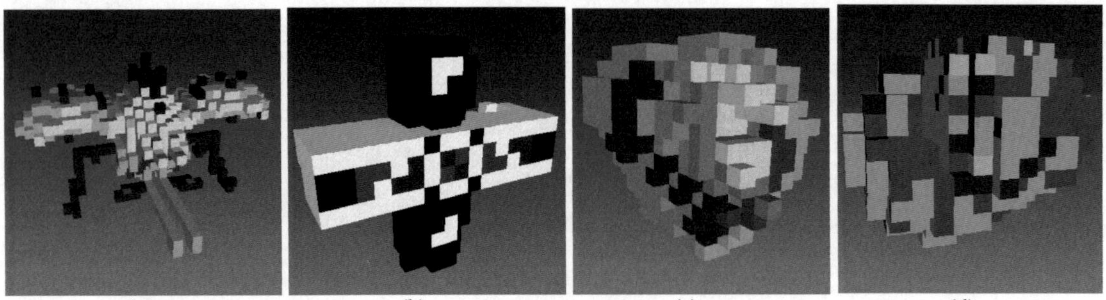

(a) (b) (c) (d)

Figure 4. Examples of evaluation. According the votes by experts, we classified (a)(b) as advanced group, and (c)(d) are classified as novice group. (a) 0 bad vote (b) 1 bad vote (c) 2 bad votes (d) 3 bad votes

3.4 Indicators of User Behavior

To respond to the questions raised in Section 1, we propose the following indicators which can be derived from operation logs.

1. Mean and standard deviation of Step Period: In the log files, each operation has a timestamp. Therefore, we can compute the period from the previous operation to the next, thus fully reflecting the student's situation. If the student left, thus interrupting his/her operation, then the mean and standard deviation would be larger.

2. Effective Operating Period (EOP): We estimated an effective operating period that excluded daze, idle, or disturbed period, with threshold defined as 5 seconds.

3. Trial and Error Period (TEP): Operations in this period do not affect the final outcome. In log files, we check for operator "Click Clear" or "Click Undo", then label the related operators and do the calculation.

4. Implementation Period (IP): We defined the duration of a set of operations that resulted in the creation of a model as the Implementation Period. Actually, we can define Trial and Error Period, Implementation Period, and Effective Operating Period relations as Eq. (1).

$$TEP + IP + \Delta t = EOP \tag{1}$$

where Δt is the total switching cost between TEP and IP.

5. Mean and standard deviation of Trial and Error Period step: Represents an overview of a student's operating speed during the Trial and Error Period.

6. Mean and standard deviation of Implementation Period step: Represents an overview of a student operating speed during the Implementation Period.

7. Degree of Detail (DoD): We discovered that if the surface to volume ratio is larger, there are more details in the model, representing a higher surface area percentage. Moreover, in order to exclude size factor, we multiply an approximate side length of the model. Thus we compute the value named as *degree of detail* as the following formula.

$$Degree\ of\ Detail = (Surface/Volume) \times (Average\ Side\ Length/6) \tag{2}$$

where *Average Side Length* is the average side length of the bounding box of the model. Using Eq. (2), a cube model with dimension N will have a DoD equal to 1.

$$Cube\ DoD = (6 \times N^2/N^3) \times (N/6) = 1 \tag{3}$$

From the above result, we know that if the DoD of a model is closer to 1, this model is more similar to a cube. Fig. 5 listed some user created models and their corresponding DoDs.

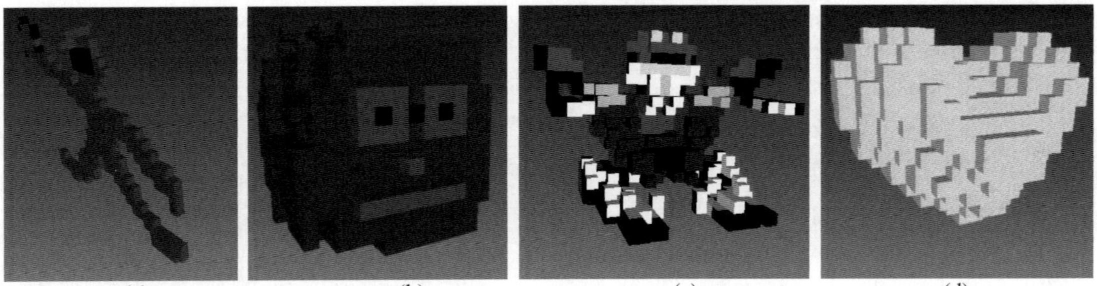

(a) (b) (c) (d)

Figure 5. Models with different *degree of detail*. (a) maximum of Lanyu: 9.81 (b) minimum of Lanyu: 1.46 (c) maximum of Sanchong: 6.61 (d) minimum of Sanchong: 1.89

Based on the above 7 quantitative indicators, the tendency to use intuitive modeling can be observed. Students were categorized into two groups with experts' evaluation of model completeness, making comparisons between groups possible.

4. RESULTS AND DISCUSSION

After defining quantitative indicators, analytic results were used to answer the questions posed in Section 1. Based on the evaluation procedure outlined in Section 3.3, of the 62 students from Lanyu Primary and Junior High School, 20 were novices while the other 42 had advanced skill. As for the 8 students from Sanchong High School, only 1 was categorized as a novice. The other 7 were categorized as advanced. Statistics of the computed indicators are summarized in Tables 1 and 2.

Table 1. Statistics of TEP, IP, EOP, DoD and intuitive operation ratio from Lanyu dataset

Gender /Age	**Advanced Group**											
	TEP (s)			***IP (s)***			***EOP (s)***			***DoD***		***n***
	Mean	***SD***	***I-r (%)***	***Mean***	***SD***	***I-r (%)***	***Mean***	***SD***	***I-r (%)***	***Mean***	***SD***	
Female	226.255	264.27	44.02	246.889	217.961	22.21	480.393	299.246	31.86	2.574	0.863	20
10	0	0	0	860.703	0	3.44	860.703	0	3.44	1.459	0	1
12	125.235	130.633	42.81	139.045	113.760	37.4	265.985	235.485	45.02	3.114	0.912	4
13	212.08	244.372	40.86	251.652	179.516	15.23	469.330	261.76	24.61	2.478	0.841	7
14	574.326	370.376	40.37	258.506	133.74	6.37	837.361	239.751	25.91	3.168	0.81	3
15	163.325	66.746	58.19	196.763	191.165	33.1	377.163	174.44	40.73	2.144	0.185	5
Male	374.27	356.160	39.73	269.195	252.103	31.62	657.111	453.428	35.57	3.822	1.764	22
9	462.108	0	73.26	197.096	0	35.17	667.905	0	62.37	4.067	0	1
10	524.143	499.9	41.08	422.832	256.818	10.47	965.773	556.165	27.48	3.32	1.2	4
12	201.532	0	38.85	251.168	0	20.22	478.078	0	27.24	3.065	0	1
13	225.255	189.515	48.59	197.165	124.130	20.28	425.808	142.094	28.96	4.427	2.73	6
14	370.339	366.052	29.83	312.392	316.138	37.46	702.954	532.925	39.26	3.801	1.308	8
15	579.74	281.478	39.06	50.289	16.931	88.53	634.448	265.078	47.61	3.352	0.127	2
Total	303.786	324.294	41.25	258.573	236.723	27.14	572.96	397.65	33.8	3.228	1.541	42
Gender /Age	**Novice Group**											
	TEP (s)			***IP (s)***			***EOP (s)***			***DoD***		***n***
	Mean	***SD***	***I-r (%)***	***Mean***	***SD***	***I-r (%)***	***Mean***	***SD***	***I-r (%)***	***Mean***	***SD***	
Female	52.962	22.805	49.68	136.636	14.692	34.07	194.977	5.8	42.44	3.024	0.169	2
12	30.157	0	39.03	151.328	0	50.06	189.177	0	49.61	3.193	0	1
13	75.767	0	60.32	121.943	0	18.07	200.777	0	35.27	2.856	0	1
Male	282.867	297.739	42.37	153.126	143.606	26.68	440.799	370.201	34.67	2.65	1.094	18
10	858.644	0	9.79	358.143	0	3.15	1219.82	0	7.81	4.834	0	1
11	319.225	15.519	48.79	259.133	241.133	45.96	583.047	256.962	41.55	3.432	0.317	2
12	321.257	352.815	65.04	170.474	105.758	14.29	497.778	370.598	38.75	2.172	0.483	6
13	109.174	142.872	24.74	97.899	115.192	20.26	211.149	252.693	28.88	2.157	0.221	6
14	446.987	245.724	52.23	100.006	74.039	41.98	551.177	170.869	43.02	2.143	0.586	2
15	117.947	0	12.15	69.608	0	93.92	192.555	0	41.39	5.751	0	1
Total	259.876	290.849	43.1	151.477	136.405	27.42	416.217	358.868	35.45	2.688	1.045	20

Table 2. Statistics of TEP, IP, EOP, DoD and intuitive operation ratio from Sanchong dataset

Gender /Age	Advanced Group											
	TEP (s)			*IP (s)*			*EOP (s)*			*DoD*		*n*
	Mean	***SD***	***I-r (%)***	***Mean***	***SD***	***I-r (%)***	***Mean***	***SD***	***I-r (%)***	***Mean***	***SD***	
Female	180.024	186.275	58.01	168.77	162.887	46.86	355.036	169.262	47.84	3.258	1.089	5
16	223.033	184.728	66.53	144.767	174.025	56.24	374.352	184.246	56.94	3.094	1.16	4
17	7.992	0	23.96	264.782	0	9.35	277.774	0	11.4	3.918	0	1
Male	52.87	24.635	53.34	57.116	24.053	62.77	110.836	0.565	65.28	5.653	0.958	2
16	77.505	0	79.88	33.063	0	58.8	111.401	0	73.77	6.611	0	1
17	28.235	0	26.8	81.169	0	66.75	110.271	0	56.78	4.696	0	1
Total	143.695	168.1	56.68	136.869	147.177	51.41	285.265	180.649	52.82	3.943	1.51	7

Gender /Age	Novice Group											
	TEP (s)			*IP (s)*			*EOP (s)*			*DoD*		*n*
	Mean	***SD***	***I-r (%)***	***Mean***	***SD***	***I-r (%)***	***Mean***	***SD***	***I-r (%)***	***Mean***	***SD***	
Female/16 (Total)	501.232	0	53.05	365.887	0	4.31	881.933	0	31.94	1.894	0	1

4.1 For models created with Qmodel Creator, what is the Degree of Completion?

The proportion of advanced group in Lanyu dataset is 67.7%, while the proportion of advanced group in Sanchong dataset is 87.5%. It specified the degree of completion using Qmodel Creator in the two datasets. We then compared these two groups (novice and advanced) using models' degree of detail, as shown in Figure 6. We found that the models created by advanced group possessed higher degree of detail after analyzing the Lanyu dataset with F test and 1-tailed T test.

However, we were concerned that frequent use of intuitive modeling functions may affect the DoD measure. To clarify this, we compared DoD, intuitive modeling operation time and ratio during Implementation Period (IP) according to intuitive operation span defined in Section 3.1. The results are shown in Figure 7, indicating that use of intuitive modeling functions is not relevant to resulting model degree of detail, but rather dependent on the characteristics (sense or skill level) of the individual user.

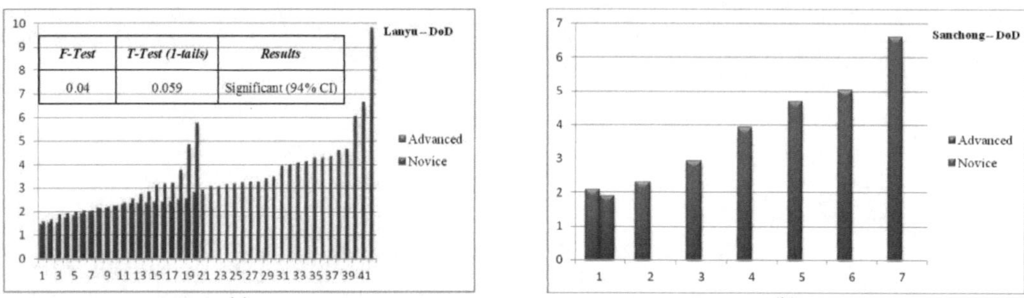

(a) (b)

Figure 6. Degree of detail comparison between the different skill level groups. (a) Lanyu Primary and Junior High School, (b) Sanchong High School

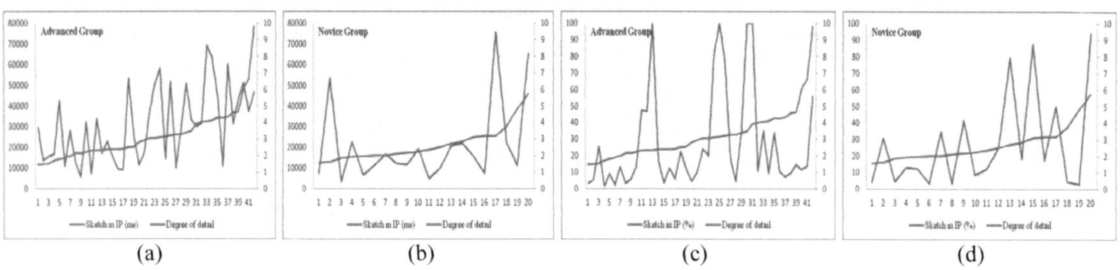

(a) (b) (c) (d)

Figure 7. Comparison of relationship between degree of detail with Implementation Period of intuitive modeling using data of Lanyu Primary and Junior High School. (a) IP of advanced group in milliseconds (b) IP of novice group in milliseconds (c) IP ratio of advanced group (d) IP ratio of novice group

4.2 Which is used more frequently: Intuitive Modeling or Traditional 3D editing?

Using the conditions in Section 3.1, effective operation time span for intuitive modeling, trial and error time span, and implementation time span were calculated. As the time required for each operation is different, operation counting is not employed. Instead, we adopted operation time span, and observed the ratio of operation time span to total time span. Tables 1 and 2 show two groups of Lanyu Primary/Junior High School and Sanchong High School, as well as comparisons of ratio of those who used the intuitive modeling functions.

The results indicate that not all the students used the intuitive modeling function frequently, so traditional 3D editing functions are still necessary. However, when comparing both groups between TEP and IP in Lanyu dataset, we discovered that a considerable proportion of the users decrease the use of intuitive operation during IP in both groups, as illustrated in Table 3. Although they use intuitive modeling less in Implementation Period, the average ratio of intuitive operation of IP are more than 25%. For comparison, the average ratio of intuitive operation of IP in advanced group of Sanchong dataset is more than 50%. Therefore, high-school students who have used other modeling software and understood basic 3D space concepts use intuitive modeling functions more frequently, while primary and junior high-school students who create 3D models for the first time prefer traditional 3D editing functions.

Regarding this phenomenon, we propose a possible explanation as follows. Intuitive operations require users to have some 3D concepts beforehand in order to gain the confidence to create models in accordance with their expectation. Because Lanyu students are willing to try out unfamiliar functions, the average ratios of intuitive operations of TEP are more than 40% in both groups. However, the main purpose of this event is to submit a finished model, so the primary and junior high-school students prefer complicated but controllable operations by adding and removing voxels incrementally.

Table 3. Comparison for the ratio of intuitive operation between TEP and IP in Lanyu and Sanchong dataset

Trend	Lanyu				Sanchong			
	Advanced Group		Novice Group		Advanced Group		Novice Group	
	Count	*Ratio*	*Count*	*Ratio*	*Count*	*Ratio*	*Count*	*Ratio*
Decrease	31	73.81%	13	65%	4	57.143%	1	100%
Increase	5	11.905%	5	25%	3	42.857%	0	
No TEP	6	14.285%	2	10%	0		0	

4.3 When users create Models, is the process Smooth? Is Trial and Error needed?

We have calculated values of mean and standard deviation of Trial and Error Period step and Implementation Period step. Because the series of TEP and IP were retrieved from the same student, they should be considered as two distributions having the same variation. Thus we can adopt 2-tailed T test to examine if the operation speed were consistent during TEP and IP.

The 2-tailed T test results confirmed that the means of the TEP and IP steps were unequal, as shown in Table 4. The test results also indicated the direction of shifting means in the same tables. If the mean of IP step was sufficiently less than the mean of TEP step, then we call this case "speed up", and vice versa.

Table 4. T test significant results in Lanyu and Sanchong dataset

Trend	Lanyu				Sanchong			
	Advanced Group		Novice Group		Advanced Group		Novice Group	
	Count	*Ratio*	*Count*	*Ratio*	*Count*	*Ratio*	*Count*	*Ratio*
Speed Up	13	30.952% (13/42)	10	50% (10/20)	2	28.571% (2/7)	0	
Slow Down	4	9.524% (4/42)	2	10% (2/20)	1	14.286% (1/7)	1	100% (1/1)
Total	17	40.476% (17/42)	12	60% (12/20)	3	42.857% (3/7)	1	100% (1/1)

α=0.05

In Table 4, we found that users in the novice group tended to speed up in Implementation Period in Lanyu dataset. This could be due to external reward or deadline pressure to complete the model-making quickly. It is suggested that these factors should be taken into account when designing lecture plans for 3D modeling.

It is worth noting that few users of Lanyu skipped Trial and Error. All cases are listed in Table 5. We also observed that some students have their own patterns of Trial-and-Error, such as using 'remove voxels' to delete content entirely. The operation counts are also included in Table 5. After excluding these cases, the remaining contained models of relatively low degree of detail, and low Implementation Period (less than 90 seconds).

Table 5. The cases of no Trail-and-Error in Lanyu dataset

Advanced Group			Novice Group		
DoD	***IP (s)***	***Remove count***	***DoD***	***IP (s)***	***Remove count***
1.459	860.703	485	2.356	40.452	0
1.507	249.554	108	2.517	39.864	0
1.976	214.154	63			
2.328	72.6	0			
3.152	14.378	0			
6.045	439.217	7			

Here, we offer several possible reasons regarding why the students skip Trial and Error, irrespective of whether they were classified as novices or advanced users:

- They are not familiar with the Clear and Undo functions, and use other buttons (e.g., remove) to purge their trial model(s). Such cases, however, still belong to the Trial and Error Period.
- They just want to finish the model quickly (e.g., to get reward).
- They have previously used similar 3D modeling applications, or have learned advanced 2D graphics software.

According to the above results, we believe that users need to be given sufficient time for trial and error. The finished models will contain more details, which means that users will have better achievements in the learning process.

4.4 How long does the User take to finish a Work?

To answer this question, we used Trial and Error Period, Implementation Period, and Effective Operating Period to evaluate the performance. In these two datasets, the longest EOP is 1,748 seconds (nearly 30 minutes), and the shortest EOP is 14 seconds. Detailed statistics have been reported in Tables 1 and 2, from which we discovered that the advanced group of Lanyu spent slightly more time to create their models than the other groups for all three sessions. Table 6 lists the F and T-test of operation periods from three user groups, namely, novice group from Lanyu, advanced group from Lanyu and advanced group from Sanchong. The result shows only the advanced group of Lanyu has a significant Implementation Period gap between the novice group of Lanyu.

Table 6. F and T test between three groups of Lanyu and Sanchong dataset

Period	***Lanyu Advanced & Lanyu Novice***			***Lanyu Advanced & Sanchong Advanced***			***Lanyu Novice & Sanchong Advanced***		
	F	***T (2-tails)***	***Results***	***F***	***T (2-tails)***	***Results***	***F***	***T (2-tails)***	***Results***
TEP	0.67	0.614	Not significant	0.14	0.217	Not significant	0.222	0.345	Not significant
IP	0.012	0.031	Significant	0.305	0.203	Not significant	0.617	0.82	Not significant
EOP	0.692	0.146	Not significant	0.075	0.072	Not significant	0.122	0.382	Not significant

$\alpha=0.05$

From above results, we can conclude that the operation of advanced group of Lanyu is significantly slower than novice group of Lanyu, suggesting that advanced group of Lanyu is more careful in creating models. Furthermore, when comparing datasets from Lanyu and Sanchong, the three periods (TEP, IP and EOP) exhibit no detectable difference. Consequently, we believe that Qmodel Creator would make an easy start for 3D model creation for all ages of K-12 students.

5. CONCLUSION AND FUTURE WORK

In this study, we investigate the usage patterns of a 3D modeling software to understand user behavior and requirements. Operation logs of Qmodel Creator have been recorded and analyzed. Characteristics of different user groups have been observed using the quantitative measures derived from the log file. The result shows that there is no significant difference in operation period between students of Lanyu Primary and Junior High School and Sanchong High School, making this software an easy-to-use tool for all K-12 students.

Designing suitable 3D modeling software for children is a challenging task. According to user behavior analysis, Qmodel Creator's intuitive modeling function greatly eases the learning curve for K-12 children. If complemented by suitable lesson plans, this software could be widely adopted by elementary school students.

We will survey other suitable 3D modeling software for the K-12 lesson plans in the near future. The quantitative indicators developed in this research could be applied to the evaluation of other 3D modeling software, as well as serve as a reference for designing lecture cases.

ACKNOWLEDGEMENT

This work is supported by Ministry of Science and Technology, Taiwan under MOST-104-2218-E-004-003.

REFERENCES

STAMFORD, Conn.(SC), 2015. *Gartner Says Worldwide Shipments of 3D Printers to Reach More Than 490,000 in 2016*, [Online], Available: http://www.gartner.com/newsroom/id/3139118 [05 Feb 2016].

Mahmoud, A., & Bennett, M., 2015. Introducing 3-Dimensional Printing of a Human Anatomic Pathology Specimen: Potential Benefits for Undergraduate and Postgraduate Education and Anatomic Pathology Practice. *In Archives of pathology & laboratory medicine*, 139(8), pp. 1048-1051.

Cesaretti, G. *et al*, 2014. Building Components for an Outpost on the Lunar Soil by Means of a Novel 3D Printing Technology. *In Acta Astronautica*, 93, pp. 430-450.

Gonzalez-Gomez, J. *et al*, 2012. A New Open Source 3D-Printable Mobile Robotic Platform for Education. *In Advances in Autonomous Mini Robots*, pp. 49-62. Springer Berlin Heidelberg.

Irwin, J. L. *et al*, 2014, June. The RepRap 3-D Printer Revolution in STEM Education. *In 121st ASEE Annual Conference & Exposition.*

Thornburg, D. D., *et al*, 2014. *The Invent to Learn Guide to 3D Printing in the Classroom: Recipes for Success*. Constructing Modern Knowledge Press.

Shneiderman, B. and Plaisant, C., 2010. *Designing the User Interface: Strategies for Effective Human-Computer Interaction: Fifth Edition*. Addison-Wesley Publ. Co., Reading, MA.

Dreyfus, H. L. and Dreyfus, SE., 1986. *Mind over Machine. The Power of Human Intuition and Expertise in the Era of the Computer*, P.50. The Free Press, New York.

A DISTRIBUTED INTELLIGENT E-LEARNING SYSTEM

Terje Kristensen
Bergen University College, Department of Computing, Mathematics and Physics
Inndalsveien 28, 5020 Bergen, Norway

ABSTRACT

An E-learning system based on a multi-agent (MAS) architecture combined with the Dynamic Content Manager (DCM) model of E-learning, is presented. We discuss the benefits of using such a multi-agent architecture. Finally, the MAS architecture is compared with a pure service-oriented architecture (SOA). This MAS architecture may also be used within E-health.

KEYWORDS

E-learning, MAS, JADE, DCM, Intelligent Tutoring, E-health

1. INTRODUCTION

Traditional classroom learning is mostly based on behavioural learning theories where the learner is the object of assessment. The teacher initiates the learning process and the learner responds. Another learning approach, constructivism, focuses on the learner's abilities to develop her own mental models and learning concepts [Kichin, 2000], [Hay, Kichin, 2000], [Kichin, Hay, Adams, 2000], [Novak, Canãs, 2006/2008]. This approach has more and more become accepted to be a more relevant method to promote learning, even at the university level.

E-Learning may be categorized into two different classes, *asynchronous* or *synchronous* learning [Graziadei, et al. 1997]. Classical classroom learning is an example of synchronous learning. The student has to stay in the classroom when the lecture is given, synchronized with the tutor and the class. If the students are not in the classroom at the same time as the lecture is given, they will miss the lecture. We now understand that the phrase "Learn from anywhere at any time" does not include synchronous learning. However, it includes asynchronous learning. The student does not have to be synchronized with the tutor or the class in order to participate or access the learning scenario. In a discussion group, users post their responses when they have available time. The course might require the student to read about a topic, and then do different activities before taking a test.

By use of Internet, people around the world may study on their own without having to worry about the time differences. By using asynchronous E-Learning the student and the teacher do not have to be in the same room or virtual chat room at the same time during the learning process. The student may fit to the study and at the same time being in a job situation. Being able to study at anytime across the Internet, the student may also reduce his travel time expenses. E-Learning is not just about delivering information and knowledge, but also how it is presented to the student.

2. AGENT TECHNOLOGY

Agent technology provides excellent methods for dividing problems into sub-problems and building component based software. Each agent operates independently and each sub-problem can be solved in a structured way. The agent framework infrastructure makes the agents to communicate and cooperate and the solutions of the sub-problems may be conveniently put together to form a global solution. A software agent acts autonomously within some environment. The software runs on a machine and the agent may perceive and act in the environment. For an agent to act it will need to have some actuators. An agent needs to perceive the environment in case of changes so it can act adequately. An agent designed to automatically park a car, needs to look at its surroundings, in order to identify obstacles, other vehicles or pedestrians.

Each agent acts on behalf of one or more clients. Because the agent acts autonomously, the client does not have to tell the agent how to do the task. He just needs to inform the agent of what he wants, to do it. For instance, Bob has delegated the task of retrieving the latest episode of his favorite podcast to an agent. He knows that his agent can act autonomously, so he does not need to explicitly tell his agent how to do it.

Autonomous agents decide what to do at run-time as opposed to having all the decisions hardwired when they are designed. The fact that software agents are autonomous and not hardwired, is one of the reasons why they differ from regular software. Agents also differ from objects by each agent has at least one thread of control, instead of using object methods. The agents are associated with behaviours to identify different models of the agents [Wenger, 1998]. The behaviours are ranging from the simplest model, where the agent only reacts to its environment, to more intelligent models of proactive agents that work towards a common goal or maximizing their utility.

2.1 JADE

The JADE framework provides an agent platform where the agents are situated. Each agent has to be instantiated in an agent container. The platform has a main container with an Agent Management System (AMS) agent providing the naming service for the other agents on the platform and a Directory Facilitator (DF) agent, with a *Yellow Page service*, helping the agents to get access to services provided by other agents. The first JADE instance automatically creates the main container and later instances create normal containers for the agents. JADE is implemented by using the FIPA standards [FIPA, 2013], and makes it possible for JADE agents to interact with any other agent framework implementing these standards.

A platform may have multiple containers, but only have one main container. The other containers can either run on the same machine or on other machines. This makes it possible to create distributed agent platforms. Agents living on the same platform can easily communicate with each other, and the MST (Message Transport Service) uses the Internal Message Transport Protocol (IMTP) for delivering messages. Figure 1 shows a platform with multiple containers, one main container and a set of containers running on other machines.

The IMTP requires full IP connectivity between the machines. This means that the machine where container 1 is running must be able to contact the main container on the server, and vice versa. The main container also holds three important tables, the Global Agent Descriptor Table (GADT), the Local Agent Descriptor Table (LADT) and the Container Table (CT). The CT contains information about all the containers connected to the actual platform, their names and addresses. In Fgure 1 we see three connected containers. Their addresses would be stored in the CT of the main container. Information about all the agents connected to the platform is stored in GADT. It also holds information about each agent's status and location. The GADT is managed by the main container. This information is used when agents exchange messages with other agents on different containers.

2.2 Agent

The JADE platform takes care of managing and keeping track of the agents, as well as enabling the agents to communicate. However, JADE also contains an API for programming our own agents. Each agent runs in its own separate thread within a container. This means that a multi-agent system is also multi-threaded. Agents act by executing behaviours. To add the behaviour to our agent, we add an instance of this behavior by calling the *addBehaviour()* method with our new behaviour as an argument. There are also more complex behaviours available, and some of the more interesting ones are those that implement the different FIPA interaction protocols. The most used *FIPA Contract Net Interaction Protocol* can easily be implemented as a behaviour by extending a certain class. Sometimes it is difficult when we need to know if some information gained in one behaviour should also be available at a specific time in another one [Bellifemine, Caire, Greenwood, 2007].

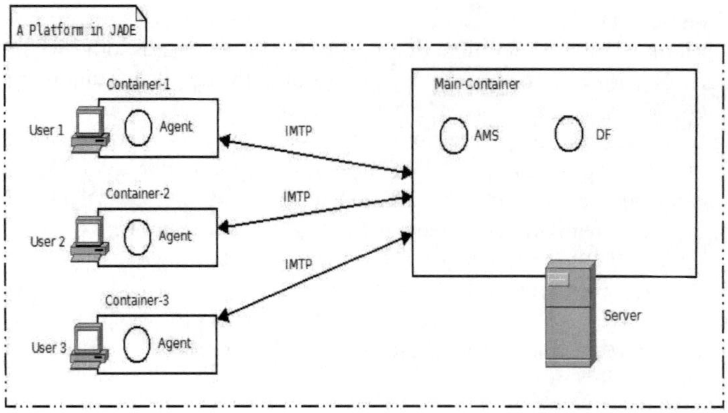

Figure 1. A platform with multiple containers

2.3 Agent Communication

Agents communicate by sending messages. Agents send messages by calling the send() method. A message between agents uses a special Agent Communication Language, ACL [Wooldridge, 2009]. An ACL message has only one mandatory property, a *performative*, identifying the communication type of the message. The use of performatives is closely connected to *speech-act theory* [Searle, 1969], [Austin, 1962] where communication is regarded as actions, and thus having the ability to make physical changes to the environment. A speech-act or performative is a verb describing it. A valid speech-act believing that the hearer has the ability to perform the action. Five classes of performatives are identified: Inform, request, promise, thanks and declaration. The performatives defined by FIPA represent a collection of standards which are intended to promote the interoperation of heterogenous agents and the services they represent. Only two performatives are needed in the system we have designed, INFORM and REQUEST.

2.4 Agent Ontology

For agents to be able to understand each other, they need to agree on the meaning of different concepts. An ontology defines the set of concepts within a specific domain. If an ontology is selected for a message, the conversations between all the participants have to know this ontology. The ontology includes a set of components that describes the concepts and their relations. Different concepts are described by class concepts, and they are ordered in a tree structure with classes and subclasses. Such concepts maybe described by a "is-a" relation as shown in Figure 2.

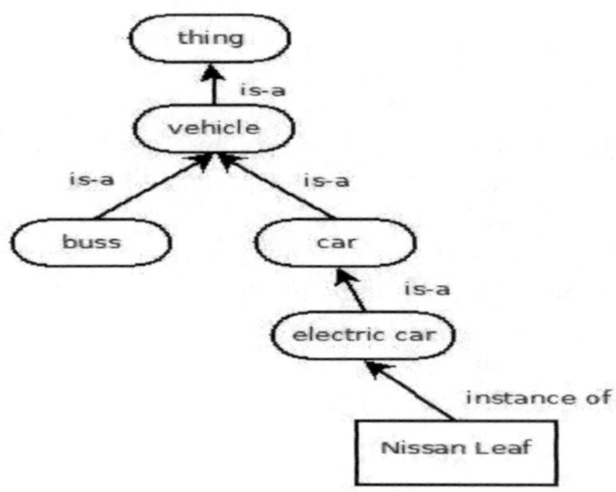

Figure 2. An ontology example

The agents use this structure to get information about the object Nissan Leaf. It finds that it is not a buss, but in fact an instance of an electric car. If the classes have different properties, the object Nissan Leaf would inherit from its parents. To access these properties, the agent traverses up the subclass relation tree to find all the properties of Nissan Leaf. Some classes will also have value restrictions on certain properties, for instance, who owns the car since we know that a car only may have one owner. These are mostly actions the agents may perform and concepts used to reason about their actions.

3. MOBILE AND TUTORING AGENTS

Our E-learning system has two specific types of agents, *mobile* agents and *tutoring* agents. A mobile agent can be used in different ways. Since mobile agents may move between computers, the agent may move to the data, instead of moving data to the agent. This is very efficient in cases where the data is much bigger in size than the agent. Another example is if the agent needs to call a lot of services on a server, then we can just move the mobile agent to the server to call it locally.

The tutoring agent is an agent created to help the student in the learning process. In learning of programming, a tutoring agent may, for instance, help students learning parameter passing in Java [Naser, 2008]. In our system we would like to connect tutoring agents to different activities. If a student have difficulties completing a task, a tutoring agent could give hints and help the student to solve the problem. An agent may also be used to decrease / increase the difficulty of the task depending on how well the student performs. By using tutoring agents that move to the client, we would have more resources available for the agent. This may sound strange. However, a student may only be running one activity at a time, so there will only be one tutoring agent running as a client at a given time, as opposed to tutoring agents running on the server. GUI may also be available to mobile tutoring agents through an interface. In a multi-agent environment, agents can delegate tasks to other agents. They work together in order to achieve common goals. Agents in such environments usually have different roles depending on their purposes. By defining several agent roles, the agents may be assigned to different skills and permissions [Wooldridge, Jennings, Kinny, 2000]. Agents may not only use their own skills, they may also be able to find an agent with the right skill and request its service.

3.1 Why use Multi-Agent System

Why do we want to design an E-learning system based on MAS? According to Wooldridge [Wooldridge, 2009], there are four factors that determine if an agent-based architecture is suitable to be used to design a system

- Dynamic or complex environments
- Agent as a metaphor
- Distribution of control, data or expertise
- As interface for legacy systems

The environment of our e-learning system is not very complex or dynamic. The system may contain one server and a set of clients connecting to it. In this case we do not need any distributed control since there is only one server. This system will not connect to any legacy systems either. In some environments it would be natural to model the entities as a society of agents and an agent-based architecture should be suitable. A commercial environment is a good example of such a society. The agents buy and sell, and compete with each other, just as in the real world. This is very difficult to model in an object-oriented system.

In an intelligent tutoring system the agent is also a natural metaphor to use. Different types of activities would need different kinds of tutoring agents, each one with a certain ability. The tutors are modelled as mobile agents. When a student accesses an activity, a tutor is transferred to the student in order to help her with the actual problem. A multi-agent system may also be used because it is flexible, extensible and fault-tolerant [Shenghuau, Kungas, Matsin, 2006]. Agents are autonomous and are designed to react to its environment. The more intelligent they are, the more flexible they should be.

By creating an E-learning system as a MAS it should be more scalable. Distributed systems can easily be scaled by adding more nodes. The possibility of creating mobile tutoring agents, makes it possible to transfer an agent to the student to help him to do some activity. This implies that the load of the processing is moved from the server to the individual clients. We believe that an E-learning system designed as a MAS will be more extensible, fault tolerant and scalable than a conventional system. In addition, by using also interface agents we may tailor a special interface to the user.

So why are we using agents? The brain is a highly parallel dynamical system able to solve a wide range of tasks. Neuroimaging has shown us that different brain areas are active during execution of certain tasks. So we may argue that the learning process itself is highly parallel and similar to biological learning [Hodgkin, Huxley, 1952], [Kristensen, McNearney, 2013]. By using a sequential model it is difficult to simulate such independence since the only way for interaction to happen between objects is by letting one object performing an operation on another. Autonomy, reactivity and social abilities are important properties of software agents. These properties are also important properties of the biological neural networks in the brain when we are learning [Kristensen, Johansen, 2006]. Biological neural networks in the brain are autonomous to a certain degree. We may then argue that that such a software model therefore also has a biological foundation.

4. THE DCM MODEL

The Dynamic Content Manager (DCM) model is a new pedagogical model for E-Learning that focuses on concept maps and reusable learning objects [Kristensen, et al., 2006-2011]. The model is designed to make it easier for teachers to collaborate when creating learning material, but it also gives the students a more flexible learning experience. Together with the idea of intelligent tutoring agents, it should be possible to create a system that will give the students more flexible learning experience. It may then be natural to design the system as a MAS architecture since we want to include tutoring agents into the learning model. The most important property of the DCM model is the ability to reuse learning content. For content to be reusable, it is important that the content is separated from the presentation. A web application, where the learning content is created as HTML files, is an example where reusing content may be difficult. The reason for this is that an HTML file contains both the content and the code how it is going to be presented to the user. If we want to reuse this learning content in another application that does not use the web pages, we would have to manually strip out the content from the presentation within the HTML file. PowerPoint is also often used as a rapid E-Learning tool to quickly create learning content [Kuhlmann, 2012]. But again, the content is coupled with the presentation in a PowerPoint file. This makes it difficult to reuse the content.

The DCM model solves this by storing the content in a content unit, a collection of resources used to teach a specific theme. The content unit is a reusable element and is not tied to any form of the presentation to be reused in different courses and situations. The business logic of the application decides how to present the content unit. Another property of the DCM model is that the learning process itself is modelled by the content unit. This is done by creating a map that guides the student through the different resources and evaluations. In the DCM model the learning maps represent courses. The possibility of having multiple paths in the learning map, gives the learner the flexibility that the contents of a course may have different approaches. The DCM model consists of four important concepts:

- Content unit
- Learning map
- Knowledge map
- Student map

In our system the agents will have to know different concepts of the DCM model. All the domain specific knowledge needs to be part of the ontology. The agents should know that a learning map contains a set of content units and the way they are organized. However, the agents also need to know about some application specific ontology, described by an ontology language.

4.1 Content Units

The content unit is an atomic unit of knowledge element, often also called a learning object. Each content unit will help the student to acquire knowledge about a specific theme. A content unit contains a combination of resources and evaluations. These resources can be anything the teacher finds useful to represent as knowledge of a theme, and is used to teach the student important aspects of a specific field. This could be explained in a text, an image, a video or a combination of them. However, a resource could also be an activity that the student has to do. Activities can be anything from small exercises to small games that simulates concepts while requiring input from the student. A content unit should also have evaluations. These are used to assess the student, to see how much she has learned of the actual content unit. Each evaluation has a value to describe how much it counts on the final score of the content unit. Content Units consists of:

- *Theme(t,w,v,pv):* theme t, weight w of the content unit. The version v and the version of parents
- *Resources:* a list of resource elements. Resources have a name and a type.
- *Evaluations:* a list of evaluations, where each evaluation has a name, weight and a type. The weight defines the importance of the given evaluation compared to the other evaluations of this content unit.
- *Prerequisites:* a list of prerequisites, describing the paths between resources and evaluations within the content unit.

The prerequisites list acts as edges between the resources and evaluations. This may be visualized as a map. This map of resources and evaluations corresponds to the learning process of the actual content unit. The learning process itself may be modelled in the DCM model. It may then be natural to place the pedagogical philosophy of the teacher in the content unit.

4.2 Learning Map

In the DCM model, courses are represented as learning maps. A learning map contains content units that the students will access to get knowledge. The teacher design the pedagogical philosophy used in the course by adding prerequisites between different content units. This may then create a map structure with a set of paths between the content units. Learning maps may have multiple paths, so the student may select optional ways to learn. The map structure also limits the available new content units of the user. Available content units depend on what content units the user has already completed. By finishing one of the available content units, new paths will be opened in the map, and new content units will be available for the student to access.

To give an example: if theme B requires that the student knows about concepts explained in theme A, it is the teacher's job to design this into the learning map so that the student does not begin on theme B before theme A. This is done by setting theme A as a prerequisite for the theme B. By using the combinations of prerequisites and content units we have created a learning map. The pedagogical philosophy the teacher wants to emphasize in the course, is then expressed by the map structure created by prerequisites between the content units. A Learning maps consists of

- *Course(n,w):* the course name n and the weight w of the learning map
- *Content units:* a list of the content units used in this learning map
- *Prerequisites:* a list of prerequisites describing the prerequisites between the content units

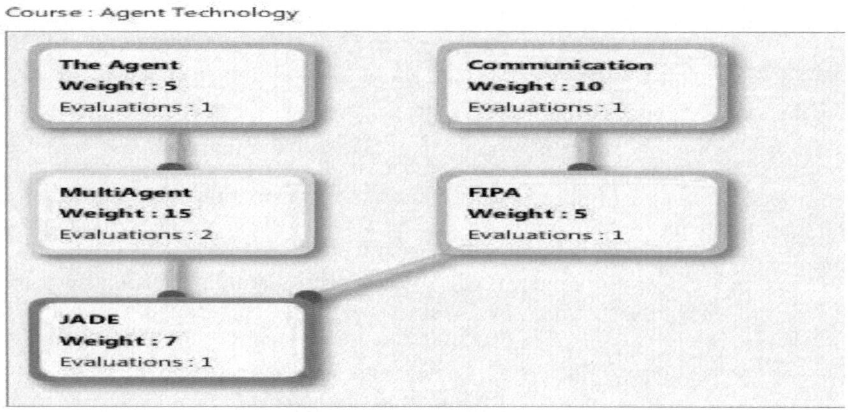

Figure 3. A Learning map example

We have decided that only other content units can be made prerequisite to a given content unit. The reason is that content units are atomic units and should be used as a whole. If we only want to use parts of a content unit, we should create a new content unit. By storing the content unit as a new version unit the original one is left intact.

A learning map is basically a graph consisting of nodes and edges where the content units are the nodes and the prerequisites of the content units are the edges. The edges make the different paths a student may select. A content unit without any prerequisites is a source node in the graph. A learning map needs at least one source node. Otherwise the student cannot access any content units. In addition the graph cannot contain any cycles. The maps have to be directed acyclic graphs (DAG) to make sense. In Fgure 3 we see that there are two source nodes. They are both colored green, meaning that they have both been completed by the student. In this example the content unit "FIPA" has also been completed. The only available content unit is MultiAgent with weight 15. The student has to complete two evaluations before making JADE available. In addition, showing completed, available and unavailable content units, the system also shows the prerequisites in the map. In this learning map, the content unit "Communication" is the prerequisite of "FIPA".

4.3 Student Map

The knowledge map contains all the available knowledge of the system. The map contains information about how the content units are structured in the courses. A key point of this map is to make it easier for teachers to reuse content units. When creating a new learning map the teacher can add previously created content units from the knowledge map to create the new learning map. If there is a content unit related to a specific theme a teacher wants to use, she may find it in the knowledge map instead of creating a new content unit from scratch. As more content units are created, the knowledge map will grow bigger. In a large knowledge map it may be difficult to find the most appropriate content units that we are looking for. To solve this problem, it should be possible to filter the map by searching using different keywords. The knowledge map could also be visualized as a map to make the structure clearer to the teacher. The content units could be displayed in the same way as in a learning map. However, this may also become a problem when content units are used in a lot of different learning maps. The map would then have a lot of edges, and it will be difficult to get any useful information from it. It is therefore highly important that there is a way to visualizing the importance on the edges between different content units. We could solve this by adding a weight to the edges. Such a weight could for instance depend on the relative frequency the edge occurs in the different learning maps of the actual content unit. Edges with low weights could then not be included in the learning map, and by making the edges thicker one could illustrate their importance. When a student is taking a course we may want to know his progression, the score on evaluation tests, which questions she failed on and the path of the student through the learning map. The progression of the student is important for both the teacher and the student. The student wants to see what courses she has completed, and also what content units are available next time. The teacher might want to look at the overall progress in a course, to identify if some students are falling behind. The scores on the evaluations could for instance count as the student's grade of a course. This depends on how well the student has been doing (scored), the weight of the evaluation and the type of the content unit. However, student maps may also be used to identify possible problems in the course. If all the students get a very low score on some evaluation, the teacher should make the resources of the content unit more clear and informative.

To identify what problems of a content unit, the teacher may observe which questions the students failed on. Courses may have multiple paths. If for instance, the content units have been presented in the wrong order we may have a didactical problem. By combining information about the paths of the student and their scores in a learning map, the teacher may be able to identify the problem. This means that the student map is also an important tool for the teacher, in order to improve the teaching of a course. A student map keeps track of the progression of a student in a course. There is one student map for each course a student is taking. A student map contains information about the resources and completed evaluations with all the answers on a test taken by the student. Each student map consists of:

- *Student:* the map of an actual student
- *Course:* the course to which map it is related
- *Completed content units:* an ordered list of the content units the student has completed
- *Completed resources and evaluations:* an ordered list of completed resources and the answers of the on the evaluations of the content unit

5. THE DISTRIBUTED MODEL

The DCM platform may be distributed, with multiple containers running on other locally connected computers. This enables us to scale the system horizontally by adding more computers, each containing a set of agents. These agents are registered with the main container and communicate with the AMS and DF agent through an intra-platform communication using the IMTP (Internal Message Transport Protocol) [Bellifemine, Caire, Greenwood, 2007]. When a user requests a service, the DF will provide a list of agents capable of carry it out. Some of the agents will be running in added computers and may therefore reduce the load of the agents on the main container. An important requirement of the system is that it should be easy to access the user services. The functionality of the system is defined by the different services provided by different server-agents. The user may request one of these services. The server-agents are designed using the Gaia methodology [Jennings, Wooldridge, Kinney, 2000]. We analyzed and identified some of the important roles in the system by using the roles model given in Gaia. For the system to be able to handle create, read, update and delete (CRUD) operations on the different concepts of the database we defined database handler roles. By using GUI a user may interact with the DCM system and may be able to create and take courses by using this client. Users may access the client in different ways. We believe that the system is more user-friendly when the users access the system through a web page. To start the client application, the user first click on the “Start DCM Client” link where the application is available provided by the Java Web Start framework. The DCM system does not have its own a web server, but colleges usually have their own, from which the client is available. Another option is to download the client and use it as a standard desktop application. The client consists of two parts, the GUI and the agent container. The username is also used to identify the agent platform.

5.1 The Client Agents

The client should be easy to use. This quality has been expressed in multiple use case scenarios. A navigation tree has also been developed, so the user may be able to quickly navigate between learning maps, content units and resources. The navigation tree may be used to select the different courses as well as navigate directly to a specific resource or an evaluation of a course. A learning map may be expanded to show all the content units in the navigation tree. The user can then click on the desired content unit in order to view it. In Fgure 4 we see that the user has expanded the course Agent Technology given by the five themes of the course. The theme Communication is also expanded, and two resources are here available. The user may now easily select one of the content units or one of the resources in the Communication theme.

The GUI displays the learning maps, content units and resources and handles input from the user. We have used the MVC (Model, View, Controller) pattern to create the GUI. Figure 4 shows an overview of the client. The GUI consists of views and controllers. As an ontology language we have used Protégé [Wooldridge, 2009]. The models consist of different ontology classes generated from Protégé such as LearningMap, ContentUnit, Evaluation, etc. The views are responsible for showing content, text and images, one view for each of the different models. The GUI also consists of buttons and other controls so the user may interact with the system in a nice way. The clientAgent is also responsible for updating the GUI when it receives information messages from the server. If the system is extending to handle mobile tutoring agents by using an IPMS (Inter-Platform Mobilitty Service) plug-in, these agents are transferred to the client. When a user is starting an activity, the client receives a corresponding tutoring agent. The agent will then run inside the client's agent platform where it will support the user doing some activity. The mobile tutoring agent will interact with the GUI using an interface specifically designed by the tutoring agents.

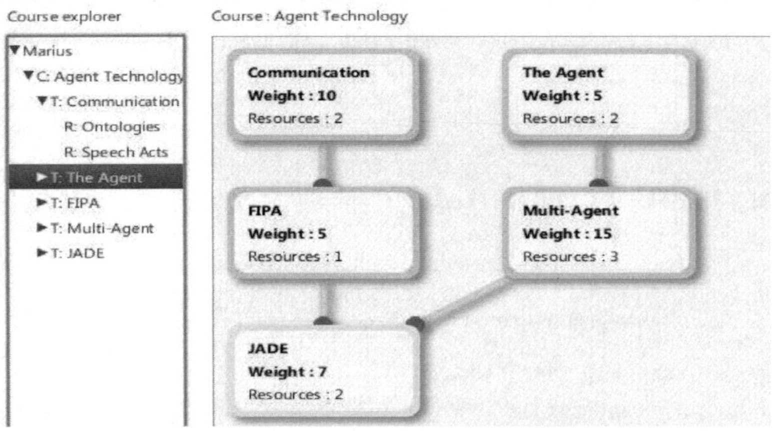

Figure 4. GUI screenshot - viewing a course / learning map

In Fgure 4 the user has selected the Communication content unit, and is now viewing the map made of the two resources. An interactive graphical view of the maps makes it easier to understand the structure of a course and the learning process of a theme. Both learning maps and content units are displayed by the GraphView tool of the client. The colours show the difference between completed, available and unavailable content units/resources. The user may also navigate by clicking on items in the map. When clicking on a vertex it will open the view to display the content of that model.

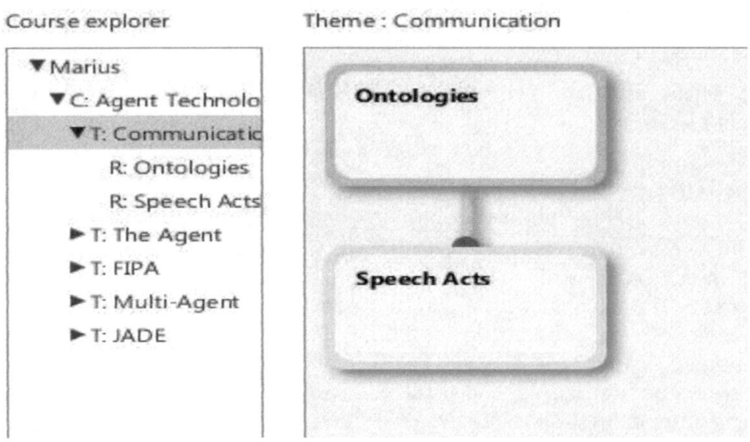

Figure 5. GUI screenshot - viewing a theme/content unit

6. CONCLUSION AND FUTHER WORK

In this paper we have focused on creating a new architecture of an E-learning system based on the DCM model and MAS. It is shown how the Knowledge Map may be used to structure the content of a course. The approach is flexible in respect to organising the content of a course. The content includes learning resources, practical tasks and evaluations. The Learning Map is created by the professor to design a course. It describes a selected scenario as a path through the content. The actual Learning Map may vary between different professors, even in courses with the same content and syllabus. This is due to the individual didactical understanding of each professor. The Student Map is created by the system, based on the results and weights of the Evaluations. It represents a model of the learning progress of individual students taking the course. The Student Map may be used by the educator to monitor the learning progress. A platform is created for e-learning as a distributed system by combining such a model with MAS.

In a Service-Oriented Architecture (SOA) [Pautasso, Zimmermann, Leymannn, 2008] we add more services to create new functionality. Systems using such an architecture are easy to extend. A SOA application usually creates web services that the client may access via a HTTP connection. Since all interactions are initiated by the client of the service, the result of the service is sent in response to a HTTP message. This means that we can easily access web services from behind a gateway. However, by using of MAS architecture we have to initiate a conversation between a pair of agents. In our system we have used the *FIPA SL Content Language* [FIPA, 2013]. We create messages that conform to the FIPA SL Content Language. As far as the agents have access to the same ontology, the agents connected to the server understand the messages, no matter from which platform they were sent. A SOA system may also have the property of loose coupling. There are different ways for a system to be loosely coupled. Web services make the system loosely coupled with respect to time/availability, location and service evolution. A Multi-agent system also has the same properties. We may easily modify and develop services that agents provide without directly affecting the clients that request the services..

6.1 Further Work

More time is needed to implement optimal functional requirements of the system. The functionality we have developed has been related to create learning maps and content units. The prototype lacks functionality with respect to the scores of the students, the courses taken and their evaluations. We then need to focus more on the implementation part of Student maps and add agents that provide services, related to the statistics of the courses the students have taken. An important aspect of this E-learning system is the creation of mobile tutoring agents related to the individual learning process of the student. This is a very interesting and important aspect and is domain specific. The students also need to create their own maps to describe their conceptual understanding of the subject and to create their own teaching scenarios. In this way the students gain experience with (Meta) modelling. By using a system as DCM, based on Knowledge map, Learning map and Student map, one adapts the e-learning system to the learning process itself, in contrast to traditional learning management systems where the learning process must be fitted to the management system. Such an architecture may also be used to design an intelligent distributed E-health system of autonomous interacting components (agents). In this case, the knowledge repository may consist of atomic knowledge elements taken from the health sector. The learning map may then indicate different ways a patient may be treated. The tutoring agent in this case may be a patient agent following the individual patient.

REFERENCES

Book

Austin, J.L. 1962. How to Do Things with Words. Oxford University.

Bellifemine, F., Caire, G., Greenwood, D. 2007. Developing multi-agent systems with JADE. Wiley.

Graziadei, W.D. et al. 1997. Building Asynchronous and Synchronous Teaching-Learning Environments: Exploring a Course/Classroom Management System Solution. State University of New York, NY USA.

Novak, J., Canãs, A. 2006/2008. The theory underlying Concept Maps and how to construct them, Technical report, IHMC CMaps Tools, Florida Institute for Human and Machine Cognition, USA.

Searle.J. 1969. An Essay in the Philosophy of Language. Cambridge University Press. 203 pp.

Wenger, E. 1998. Communities of Practice. Learning,, Meaning and Identity. Learning in Doing: Social, Cognitive and Computation Perspectives. Cambridge University Press, UK.

Wooldridge M. 2009. An Introduction to Multi-Agent Systems, Wiley.

Journal

Hodgkin, A.and Huxley, A. 1952. "A quantitative description of membrane current and its application to construction and excitation nerve". In J. Physiol., 117, pp. 500-544.

Hay, D., Kinchin, I.M. 2000. Using Concept Mapping to Measure Learning Quality. Education & Training, pp 167- 182.

Kinchin, I.M, 2000. Using Concept Maps to Reveal Understanding: A Two-Tier Analysis, In School Science Review. 81:296, pp 41-46.

Kinchin, I.M, Hay, D., Adams, A. 2000. "How a qualitative approach to concept map analysis can be used to aid learning by illustrating patterns of conceptual development, in Educational Research.

Kristensen, T., Dyngeland, M., Bech, Ø. 2013. Towards a Multi-Agent E-learning Platform. Journal of Computer Engineering and Informatics. Volum 1.(2) pp. 64-81, Hong Kong, China

Kristensen,T., McNearney,D. 2013. Simulating Spiking Neurons by Hodgkin Huxley Model. International Conference on

Bioinformatics & Computational Biology, BIOCOMP'13, July, Las Vegas, CSCREA Press, 2013, USA.

Wooldridge, M., Jennings, N.R, Kinny, D. 2000. The Gaia Methodology for Agent-Oriented Analysis and Design. Journal of Autonomous Agents and Multi-Agent Systems.

Conference paper or contributed volume

Kinney, D., Georgeff, M., Rao, A. 1996. A methology and modeling techniques for systems of BDI agents. In Van de Velde, W. and Perram, J.W. Editors, Agents Breaking Away. Proceedings of the Seventh European Workshop on Modelling Autonomous Agents in Multi-Agent World, pp.56-71. Springer verlag, Berlin Germany.

Kristensen. T. 2011. The Dynamic Content Management System. IEEE Explorer Digital library, pp.1-8, 2011.

Kristensen, T, Johansen, J. 2006. Simulation of Attentional Networks in the Brain – an Agent based Approach. Proceedings of European Simulation and Modelling Conference, ESM'2006. Toulouse, France.

Kristensen, T., et al. 2009. Dynamic Content Manger – a New Conceptual Model for e-Learning. In Proceedings of International Conference on Web information System and Mining,WISM'09, Shanghai China, Springer Lecture Notes in Computer Science.

Kristensen, T., Hinna, K., Hole, F.O, Lamo, Y. 2007. Different E-learning paradigms - a Survey. In Proceeding of MIT-LINC (MIT Learning International Network Consortium 4.th International Conference: Technology-Enabled Education: a Catalyst for positive Change), Amman, Jordan.

Kristensen, T., Lamo, Y., Mughal, K., Tekle, K..M., Bottu, A.K. 2007. Towards a dynamic, content based e-learning platform. In V. Uskov, editor, Computers and Advanced Technology in Education. ACTA Press, pp 107–114, Beijing, China.

Kristensen, T., Lamo,Y., Mughal. K. 2006. E-learning Systems in the Bergen Region, Norway - an Overview, Proceedings of the IRMA International Conference, Washington DC, USA.

Naser, S.A. 2008. An Agent Based Intelligent Tutoring System for Parameter Passing in Java Programming. Journal of Theoretical and Applied Information Technology.

Shenghuau, L., Kungas, P., Matskin, M. 2006. Agent-Based Web Service Composition with JADE and JXTA. International Conference on Semantic Web and Web Services.

FIPA ACL. 2013, (http://fipa.org).

Short Papers

USING COGNITIVE MAPS TO PROMOTE SELF-MANAGED LEARNING IN ONLINE COMMUNITIES OF INQUIRY

Dr Susi Peacock and Professor John Cowan
United Kingdom

ABSTRACT

As online learners become more diverse and less well-prepared individually, particular help is required when transitioning into new, online learning environments, requiring engagement in collaborative, community-based educational activities. Cognitive maps provide one tool for tutors to support individuals in navigating the unfamiliar maze of online education and promote self-managed learning. Such maps, developed and offered at induction by the teaching team and linked to throughout the course, describe the territory that learners may wish to explore, signpost possible activities providing landmark knowledge, and encourage the development of cognitive and interpersonal abilities required for online learning. The contents of such maps may include the location of key sources, study guides, and provision of advice to beginners on how to handle the profusion of online material. They may feature a tutor-developed diagrammatic representation of the course, showing links between the different themes, and signposts to appropriate resources for further study and support. Tutors may also encourage learners to refine their own cognitive maps by adding further links to useful sources and materials which they have identified. Such enriched maps could be shared with the community for feedback, allowing for the comparison and contrasting of learners' journeys during their online studies. Working in groups, learners may, for instance, develop their maps to include accounts of group work.

KEYWORDS

Cognitive maps; communities of inquiry; self-managed learning

1. INTRODUCTION

Continuing interest in online higher education has led to a rapid growth in its number of programmes and learners (Allen & Seaman, 2013). Some now assert that it has become the ". . . preferred or 'new normal' mode of study throughout the world" (Brown, 2015, p. 1). Many of these online offerings, taking a collaborative, community-based approach to learning, may be informed by the Community of Inquiry Framework (CoIF), which is arguably the most prominent, detailed and cited model of online learning. The CoIF's purpose, Garrison declares (2011), is the development of a quality, educational experience, within an online community, where learners engage in collaborative educational activities and conversations.

There has, however, been an ambivalent response to these innovative developments, with some questioning if learners are ready and prepared, for the transition from the more traditional, didactic face-to-face learning experiences to learner-centered online activity (Akyol, 2013). Thus many learners expect to take a "lone wolf" approach to their online studies and as one of the learners from Baxter's study (2012) in the UK explains:

I thought I'd be on my own, then I realised that for some assignments I would actually be working with other students, sort of like in a group. That was so different to what I thought this would be.

Learners in Taiwan, for instance, appeared to exhibit high levels of readiness in computer/internet self-efficacy and motivation for learning and communicating online, but had lower levels in self-directed and self-managed learning - essential attributes for successful online learners (Hung et al. 2010). Our emergent work focuses on the development and provision by tutors of cognitive maps, assisting learners in the planning of their joint studies designed to promote self-managed learning in community-based, collaborative learning environments.

2. COGNITIVE MAPS SUPPORTING SELF-MANAGED ONLINE LEARNING

The concept of cognitive maps, introduced by Tolman (1958), was based upon his work with rats, investigating how they navigate a maze. Cognitive maps in education can be one valuable resource for human learners who are transitioning into unfamiliar learning landscapes. Access to, and use of, a well-designed cognitive map can help learners navigate the maze of such landscapes to good purpose, by providing "landmark knowledge" supporting and nurturing their learning (Li et al. 2013). Such maps will not only show where learners can make their start towards desired progress, but can also indicate the routes they can use - depending on what is, and is not, important to each individual learner and their community. The contents can be of many different forms and types, and could indicate:

- The location of key sources – seminal papers in the subject area, recent literature surveys providing an overview of publications, concepts, issues and findings, regulations if applicable, and even definitions of key terms.
- Recommended guides – to the basics such as searching in this field, tools of inquiry and how to use them, the approach to be followed in effective online learning and collaboration, and the issues, especially affective ones, likely to emerge in group learning.
- Relevant work in progress; key personalities in the field.
- The level of source material; too deep may be more than the learners seek or can cope with; too shallow is best avoided.
- Advice to beginners on how to handle the profusion of online material, in the unfamiliar digital form, and how to establish their own landmarks, as described for example by Li et al (2013).

3. COGNITIVE MAPS AND ONLINE COMMUNITIES

A cognitive map helps online learners to identify and record where they have reached at any point in time, where they could go next, and generally how they might profitably progress in this maze of the new learning environment, in pursuit of their desired learning (Garrison and Akyol, 2013). Such maps usually developed and offered at induction by the teaching team, describe the territory that learners may wish to explore, signpost possible activities providing landmark knowledge, and encourage the development of cognitive and interpersonal abilities required for online learning. Cognitive maps will identify the location of materials to assist with the development of much needed learner abilities, particularly in the cognate area. They may feature a tutor-developed diagrammatic representation of the course, showing links between the different themes and signposts to appropriate resources for further study and support. Comprehensive cognitive maps should assist learners in going beyond themselves and well into their Zone of Proximal Development (Nicholl, 1998).

An important element of cognitive maps will be pointers towards guidance for those new to the online environment, regarding working online and working collaboratively. Maps may identify, locate and even commend short videos of learners discussing why they became active and collaborative participants in a community, rather than feeling isolated individuals in pursuit of their own individual knowledge acquisition.

Examples of individual and group work could be pinpointed to enable learners to appreciate the differences in the level and type of work they could develop. The aim of this area of a cognitive map should be to broaden and deepen learners' conceptualisations of their imminent online learning, and to assist them in engaging effectively.

Learner discomfort in online discussions is well-documented; for many learners, the very nature of 'posting' to an online space housing thoughts that will be read critically by unknown peers and tutors is alien, threatening and impersonal. This often-unexpected demand of online learning becomes even more daunting for the learner when the communication tools provided by the institution are cumbersome and difficult compared to the more familiar social network tools such as Facebook. Cognitive maps may suggest guides about the purpose of online discussions, with hints and tips about using the tools, exemplars of different types of postings, and the location of videos that demonstrate how to use these tools and links to support services within the institution.

Cognitive maps may also usefully identify sources of helpful guidance on how students can manage their emotional responses in the online learning environment. It is important for tutors and learners to recognise the affect for its vital role in developing, though sometimes hampering, online learning. Whilst some learners have positive response to online offerings, including joy, enthusiasm and excitement, all too often learners report feelings of fear, anxiety, alienation, guilt and stress (Zembylas et al. 2008). Learners may need to develop coping mechanisms such as increased awareness of the different avenues available for support. Cognitive maps can link to different available help services that learners can use throughout their studies. Xu, Du, & Fan (2013) conclude that the tutor will "... want to promote a culture of help-seeking, encouraging students to learn how to ask for assistance from multiple sources (for example, the instructor, peers and friends) through multiple channels (for example, email, web chat, and video conferencing) when they confront personally challenging tasks and perceive the need for help." (p.7).

4. THE TUTOR AND THE COGNITIVE MAP

Once a map has been prepared and made available, the tutor should concentrate on having learners and the community use the map, use it well, and to good effect. In the introductory weeks of a programme of study, tutors will typically encourage learners to make self-managed use of their cognitive map by linking introductory activities, for example in the ice-breaker activities in the online discussions, to the map. Later tutors will promote specific links when reminding learners of the landmark knowledge available from the cognitive map. From time to time, tutors may advise individual learners how to use other such maps to guide and shape periods of study away from the group.

5. LEARNERS CONTRIBUTIONS TO DEVELOPMENT OF COGNITIVE MAPS

Whilst teaching teams will have developed a cognitive map in the planning stages of setting up their online communities, tutors should also encourage learners to refine their own individualised cognitive maps by adding further links to useful sources and materials which they have identified. Such enriched maps could be shared within the groups or the wider community for feedback, allowing for the comparison and contrasting of learners' journeys during their online studies. Working in groups, learners may, for instance, develop their maps to include accounts of their group work. Such maps, with their accounts of learning journeys, may also be gathered for tutor feedback and used, with learner agreement, for future iterations of the module. Maps developed during one course may also be used by learners to navigate their own further online studies and support continuing professional development.

6. CONCLUSION

The purpose of cognitive maps is to meet the navigational needs of self-directed online learners. As communities of online learners become more diverse and often less well-prepared individual learners, particular help will be required by learners in transitioning to, and through, online learning. Cognitive maps provide one tool for tutors developing and maintaining online learning communities to support individuals in navigating the unfamiliar maze of online learning seeking to promote and nurture deep learning.

Confronted with the immense assembly of virtual resources available on Internet and beyond, today's self-directed learner can feel as forlorn as someone to whom the doors of an immense international library have generously been thrown wide open. The naïve online learner knows for certain that what they require is in there - somewhere on the array of crammed shelves. They need helpful suggestions and pointers, framed with their current area of interest in mind, to help them in deciding which shelf they should go to, what item should have their first attention, and then, how to progress. A cognitive map, distinct from a course guide which would of course be mapped within it, should provide learners with suggestions, coupled with enough information about highlighted items to inform their decision-making as they journey through the new online learning environs.

We submit that every course team developing online collaborative, community-based learning should give careful attention to formulating and providing an effective cognitive map for use by their self-managed learners. Their tutors should monitor its effectiveness in use, and use individualised maps to record accounts of their learners' journeys, and diversions, so that the next edition of the map can be enhanced for future learners.

REFERENCES

Allen, E. and Seaman, J., 2013. *Changing course: ten years of tracking online education in the United States*. Babson Survey Research Group.

Akyol, Z., 2013. Metacognitive development within the Community of Inquiry. In: Z. AKYOL and D.R. GARRISON, eds. *Educational Communities of Inquiry: theoretical framework, research and practice.* Hershey: IGI Global, pp. 30-44

Baxter, J., 2012. Who am I and what keeps me going? Profiling the distance learning student in higher education. *International Review of Research in Open and Distance Learning*. vol. 13, no.4, pp.108-129. BROWN, M. 2015. Stories from students in their first semester of distance learning. *International Review of Research in Open and Distrubted Learning, vol. 16*, no.4, pp.1-17.

Garrison, D.R., 2013. Theoretical foundations and epistemological insights of the community of inquiry. In: Z. AKYOL and D.R. GARRISON, eds. *Educational Communities of Inquiry: theoretical framework, research and practice.* Hershey: IGI Global., pp. 1-11.

Garrison, D.R., 2011. *E-learning in the 21st century: a framework for research and practice.* 2nd ed. New York: Routledge.

Hung, M. et al., 2010. Learner readiness for online learning: scale development and student perceptions. *Computers & Education.* vol. 55, no. 3, pp. 1080-1090. LI, LIANG-Yi et al., 2013. Construction of Cognitive Maps to Improve E-Book Reading and Navigation. Computers & Education, vol. 60.

Nicholl, T., 1998. *Vygotsky* [online]. [viewed 6 February 2015] Available from: http://www.massey.ac.nz/~alock/virtual/trishvyg.htm

Tolman, E. C. 1958.. Cognitive maps in rats and men. *Psychological Review.* vol. 55, pp. 189-208.

Zembylas, M. et al, 2008. The role of emotions in the experience of online learning: challenges and opportunities. *Educational Media International.* vol. 45, no. 2, pp. 107-117.

AUTOMATION IN DISTANCE LEARNING: AN EMPIRICAL STUDY OF UNLEARNING AND ACADEMIC IDENTITY CHANGE LINKED TO AUTOMATION OF STUDENT MESSAGING WITHIN DISTANCE LEARNING

Dr Hilary Collins, Dr Hayley Glover, Fran Myers and Mor Watson
Open University Business School, Milton Keynes, UK

ABSTRACT

This paper explores the unlearning and learning undertaken by adjuncts (Associate Lecturers) during the introduction of automated messaging by the university as part replacement of adjunct pastoral support for students. Automated messages were introduced by the University to standardize the student experience in terms of qualification communications, for example, reminders of forthcoming assessment deadlines. This change in communicative strategy is due to shifting power from a collegial to a managerial culture and practice in supporting distance learning students effectively. This is a university-wide initiative in a bid to improve progression and completion in an increasingly cost-focused higher education environment. The introduction of automated messaging requires adjuncts to learn new processes, and thus unlearn previous organizational routines which impacts upon their academic identity and perceived power within their roles.

KEYWORDS

E-learning; automation; academic identity; organizational routines.

1. INTRODUCTION

Within Higher Education Institutions (HEIs) and particularly within distance learning providers, there is an increased emphasis on the use of technology to improve retention, progression and completion cost effectively. Cost drivers, coupled with a drive to improve the student experience and qualification completion rates, prompted the Open University to introduce an Information Technology system to target e-mail communications to predefined student groups. The attractiveness of these systems is indicated by reports on technologically-driven retention activities, which have multiplied; from Government perspectives e.g. Browne et al. (2008), and from individual HEIs, for example, Long and Siemens (2011), Ferguson (2012), Slade and Prinsloo (2013). Much emergent literature appears aligned to institutional perspectives and student experience rather than narratives grounded in the lived experiences of lecturers. Changes to practice are being imposed, impacting established teaching-related routines (Akgün et al. 2007), learning and unlearning, identity and relationships between adjunct faculty, administrators and management.

2. LITERATURE REVIEW

2.1 Learning and Unlearning

Research on learning and unlearning (Hislop et al. 2014, Tsang and Zahra 2008) stems from initial work by Garfinkel (1967), Hedberg's (1981) subsequent article "How organizations learn and unlearn" and Giddens' structuration theory (1984). These contributions and others form two intertwining bodies of work regarding learning and unlearning; organizational, and individual, as tabulated by Hislop et al. (2014: 543).

Tsang and Zahra (2008) point out that although Hedberg (1981) stresses unlearning as well as learning, the overwhelming content of his discussion, as supported by other authors (e.g. Wang and Ahmed (2003)) focuses on learning to the detriment of a more full exploration of unlearning as a process.

Literature indicates that organizational unlearning impacts processes as part of change, although for a mature organization routines are indicated as entrenched. Tsang and Zahra (2008: 1442) state that: "managers cannot always make clear causal links between unlearning and the acquisition of new skills or improvements in organizational performance". They continue with individuals' unlearning being restricted to fading and wiping, and little evidence that deep unlearning occurs despite Hedberg (1981:3) arguing that "...this discarding activity – unlearning – is as important a part of understanding as is adding new knowledge".

In their typology, Tsang and Zahra (2008) set out three distinct types of change which they characterized as; episodic change which was infrequent and discontinuous, ostensive change via a set of written procedures and practices, and performative change to actual routines of implementation. Hislop et al. (2014: 547), and Turc and Baumard (2007), underpin through early works of Nystrom and Starbuck (1984) and Hedberg (1981); all observe close links between organizational change including unlearning phases, which are essential for facilitating adaptive behavior. Hedberg (1981:18) expresses this directly by saying that "organizations learn and unlearn via their members". The impact of individual level unlearning on organizations can, however, be perceived as "difficult, challenging and time consuming", Hislop et al. (2014: 548).

2.2 Academic Identity

A key concept for evolving academic identity is the link to developing managerialism in Higher Education. Berg et al. (2013:383) write "...private sector practices of accountability, audit, control and surveillance have proliferated in the public sector". Traditional ideas of academic identity and associated ways of working have been challenged, not least by recent changes in the university environment (Collins, 2013) and the introduction of new procedures (e.g. automated messaging) eroding collegiate culture. An earlier study of new managerial approaches in Higher Education by Goolnik (2012:19), explored feelings of mistrust and of a professionally and personally unfulfilled self. Recent developments in the study of identity work include paying attention to alternative selves (Obodaru, 2012), threatened selves (Petriglieri, 2011) and narrative selves (Ibarra and Barbulescu, 2010). As Clarke and Knight (2015:15) assert "instead of presenting 'resistant' selves, academics are inclined to comply with or conform to the demands of the performance culture..."

Increasingly, academics are under pressure to alter their ways of thinking and behaving in an evolving managerial culture, and to concern themselves with the organizational aspects of how tutoring is delivered (Hinings, 2005).

2.3 The Research Gap Addressed

As distinct from much of the research around organizational unlearning and identity, our research was undertaken within an HE institution. The majority of extant research proposed theoretical typologies, in contrast this study is empirically based. There is therefore, an identified gap in investigating how managerially imposed change shifts power, affects the process of individual learning and unlearning (e.g. Hislop et al. 2014), and impacts academic identity in a mature HE context.

2.4 Approach Taken / Methods of Analysis

The aims of this research are to add to emerging literature by examining the process of unlearning using a sample of teaching faculty within Business and Law. Impressions were collated over a 12 month period whilst the HEI introduced automated student support systems. The objective was to evaluate, using qualitative methodologies, adjuncts' perceptions of potential impact on and changes to both their role and identity, and the learning and unlearning around automated interventions and its associated impact on student retention.

Themed focus groups were selected as an appropriate method of eliciting views on tutors' work in supporting students and possible impact of new learning interventions on the tutor role as well as on student experience. A group of six Business and Law tutors representing introductory undergraduate modules were engaged with the project. The participants were experienced, and held substantive contracts with the HEI. Opinions were explored through a series of telephone and online interviews and face-to-face focus groups. Discussions evolved depending upon interviewees' experiences, producing data around topics including student focus, changes to tutor role, managerial communication, student services, and evaluation. Verbatim transcripts were subsequently coded and evaluated independently by four researchers, to identify dominant themes with the results then synthesized into a group response. Analysis was grounded in the words and reported experiences of participants. Miles and Huberman's (1994) framework was adopted to support theme triangulation, qualitatively evaluating perceptions of potential impact on and changes to their role around automated student interventions, both in the lead up to, and following, the introduction of these interventions.

2.5 Main Findings

Discussions centered around various ways that adjuncts could learn new processes/procedures in the future, meaning that they had to undertake 'wiping', also known as 'directed unlearning' or 'behavioral unlearning', Rushmer and Davies (2004). These methods included working with automated interventions, mentoring other adjuncts, peer monitoring, working with Blackboard Collaborate recordings, adjunct staff development events, and networking. In the past, participants reported sending out their own emails if a student failed to submit an assignment on time; however, with the confidence that the organization would send a reminder intervention message, adjuncts chose to call or text as alternative use of their time. As one respondent commented: "*...it's quite a job of work for me to go through each of these interventions [for] modules and carefully think about what I actually want to say to supplement those messages and not duplicate them, because I read a few of them and I thought oh well that means I don't have to send this in now*". As this research was undertaken early on in the change process, there was little evidence at this point to suggest fading or deep unlearning. Our findings suggested that episodic change was limited to support for student queries rather than teaching and assessment practice which appears unchanged for adjuncts at this time. Adjuncts were given strategic and operational documents as part of the investigation and invited to share their opinions for the first time via the research process, which can be seen as an example of ostensive change in itself; this was very well received, for example the opportunity to input in "any meaningful way" rather than just report back.

Adjuncts indicated their academic identity might start to fracture as a result of imposed automation and the perceived loss of pedagogic support routines and pastoral care, as discussed by Goolnik (2012). One respondent feared lessening ties and a severed relationship with a student, stating: *"I'm going to have to change my practices so that L1* [introductory level] *don't become overwhelmed (by email). I am just a bit worried about where students will feel guidance should come from".* Adjuncts also became aware of their changing academic role as more management structures were put in place, thus supporting the work of Berg et al. (2013) and their focus on the impact of managerialism on academic identity: "*I think it is important, this balance between SST* [Student Support Team] *and AL* [Associate Lecturer] *intervention, and as an AL we do need to become clear on what our role is and what the role is of the new evolving SST... I think it's not 100% clear at the moment where levels of responsibility lie".* And, another respondent's insight: "*...people will worry their pastoral side... is being slowly taken away from them*".

Due to the diversity of the adjuncts' backgrounds, their views on the impact of increased managerialism on their professional/commercial/traditional academic selves varied. One respondent commented: *"You will have ALs who are practitioners who will not have any experience of an HE environment whatsoever. Yes it's easy to assume it runs like a large business*". Notably, it was acknowledged that taking part in the research itself could be seen as a means of greater engagement with the change processes and routines, thus reinforcing organizational and individual (un)learning and identity.

We have drawn upon the work of Petriglieri (2011) by paying close empirical attention to *how* the tensions of a productive, adjunct identity are reproduced in the adjunct role. In contrast to Petriglieri (2011), however, our findings and analysis suggest that in interaction our identities are always, at least potentially, under threat from competing and alternative possible identities; however, these are managed discursively so that a coherent (in the moment) identity is (re)produced.

3. CONCLUSION

This paper has sought to provide empirical evidence of effects of organizational change from a collegiate to managerial culture in a HE context more specifically adjunct academic identity, unlearning and learning as transformed in response to the introduction of automated student messaging. The processes of learning and unlearning new practices have been found to impact adjuncts' perception of their academic identity and behavior, although we have been unable to establish the extent to which this occurs over a longer time frame.

Our work concurs with Clarke and Knights (2015) who state that "Identity management often manifests itself in contemporary academia.[...], as a response to the performative demands of managerialism". Although they characterize this as "instrumental game-playing", in our work we viewed this as evidence of the adjuncts' need to negotiate academic identity initiated by the learning and unlearning work. The difference may be explained by comparative insecurity in part-time adjunct as opposed to tenured faculty roles.

A further longitudinal study is planned to observe evolving adjunct academic identities in response to continual changes instigated by the shift from collegial to managerial culture within HE institutions. Further research could include comparative studies between distance learning and traditional face-to-face pedagogy, or comparative studies taking a cross-cultural perspective.

REFERENCES

Akgün, A. et al, 2007. Organizational unlearning as changes in beliefs and routines in organizations. *Journal of Organizational Change Management*, Vol 20, 6,794-812.

Berg, E. et al, 2013. Introduction to special issue - 'biting the hand that feeds': reflections on power, politics, identity and managerialism at work in academia. *Workplace rights*, Vol. 17(3-4), 383-388.

Browne, T. et al, 2008. 2008 Survey of Technology Enhanced Learning for higher education in the UK, UCISA <http://www.ucisa.ac.uk/publications/~/media/290DD5217DA5422C8775F246791F5523.ashx> [Accessed 29 September 2013].

Clarke, C. et al, 2015. Careering through academia: Securing identities or engaging ethical subjectivities? *Human Relations,* 68: 1865-1888.

Collins H., 2013. Transition identity: the role of communication tools. *EGOS conference 2013*. Montréal, Canada, July.

Ferguson, R., 2012. Learning analytics: drivers, developments and challenges. *International Journal of Technology Enhanced Learning*, 4 (5/6), 304-317.

Garfinkel, H., 1967. *Studies in Ethnomethodology.* Prentice Hall.

Giddens, A., 1984. *The Constitution of Society: Outline of Structuration Theory.* Cambridge, Polity Press.

Goolnik, G., 2012 Change Management Strategies When Undertaking eLearning Initiatives in Higher Education. *Journal of Organisational Learning and Leadership*, Vol 10, No 2, 16-28.

Hinings, C.R, 2005. Changing nature of professional organizations, *Oxford handbook of work and organization*, 405-424.

Hedberg, A., 1981. How organizations learn and unlearn. In: Nystrom, P. and Starbuck, W.H. (eds), *Handbook of Organizational Design.* Vol 1, Oxford, Oxford University Press, 3-27.

Hislop, D., et al, 2014. The Process of individual unlearning: A neglected topic in an under-researched field. *Management Learning*, Vol 45 (5), 540-560.

Ibarra, H. and Barbulescu, R., 2010. Identity as narrative: Prevalence, effectiveness and consequences of narrative work in macro work role transitions. *Academy of Management Review*, 35 (1),135-154.

Long, P. and Siemens, G., 2011. Penetrating the fog: analytics in learning and education, *EDUCAUSE Review*, 46, 5:31-40.

Miles, M.B. and Huberman, A.M., 1994. *Qualitative Data Analysis, 2nd edition.* Sage, Beverly Hills, CA.

Nystrom P.C. and Starbuck W.H., 1984. To avoid organizational crises, unlearn. *Organizational Dynamics* 12, 53-65.

Obodaru, O., 2012. The self not taken: How alternative selves develop and how they influence our professional lives. *Academy of Management Review*, 31 (1), 34-57.

Petriglieri, J.L., 2011. Under threat: Responses to and the consequences of threats to individuals' identities. *Academy of Management Review*, 36(4), 641-662.

Rushmer, R. and Davies, H., 2004. Unlearning in healthcare: *Quality & Safety in Health Care,* 13, 10-15.

Slade, S. and Prinsloo, P., 2013. Learning analytics: ethical issues and dilemmas. *American Behavioral Scientist*, 57 (10), 1509-1528.

Tsang, E. and Zahra, S., 2008. Organizational Unlearning. *Human Relations*, 61 (10): 1435-1462.

Turc, E. and Baumard, P., 2007. "Can Organizations Really Unlearn?" in McInerney, C.R. and Day, R.E. (Eds.). Re-thinking knowledge management: From knowledge objects to knowledge processes. Berlin: Springer-Verlag, 125-146.

Wang, C. and Ahmed, P., 2003. Organizational learning: a critical review. *The Learning Organization,* 10:1 8-17.

DEVELOPING THE 1ST MOOC OF UNIVERSITY OF PORTO: CHALLENGES AND STRATEGIES

Isabel Martins, Nuno Regadas and Margarida Amaral
University of Porto
Pç Gomes Teixeira – 4099-002 Porto, Portugal

ABSTRACT

This article is a case study on how the educational technologies unit of the Digital University describes the experience of thinking, creating multimedia contents and training teachers regarding the development of the first MOOC of University of Porto (U.Porto).
Upon describing this experience, we focus on the most relevant topics such as how the university regards MOOCs, our previous experiences and on our role as facilitators and producers of the first MOOC.of the university. This experience challenged us to define newer and better strategies regarding content production. We ended this first experience valuing AV professionals when recording educational videos in order to have good quality in final products, which was afterwards confirmed by the MOOC participants when replying the final satisfaction questionnaire.

KEYWORDS

MOOC; education; pedagogy; multimedia; educational video

1. INTRODUCTION – THE UNIVERSITY OF PORTO

The University of Porto (U.Porto) is a benchmark institution for Higher Education and Scientific Research in Portugal and one of the top 200 European Universities according to the most relevant international ranking systems (U.Porto website).

The growing investment that the University has done in the modernization of pedagogical paradigms and informal education is also achieved by encouraging teachers in the development of MOOCs.

Being this the first MOOC of the University of Porto, it has increased the importance of being able to establish itself as an example that can be taken by other teachers who are developing this type of courses. (Azevedo, 2014)

At U.Porto the unit for educational technologies, has the mission of promoting and supporting the usage of a vast array of technologies in learning and education on "b" and "e-learning" contexts. We help both academics and support staff, regardless their area of knowledge. Each member of the team helps teachers to put into practice their ideas into an online learning journey, guiding them through the design, development and delivery stages of an online course. This unit exists since 1998 and now is evolving with new challenges specially those centered in the use of video material in distance learning courses. It is important to point out that U.Porto is a traditional face-to-face university with no intention of being a distance/online university. This involvement is seen as a challenge for the academic staff and an opportunity to explore new T&L paradigms.

When developing a MOOC, the educational technologies team plays a key role, acting as an interface between the platform that hosted the course and staff. On top of that we also help with the recording, production and editing of all the videos, providing also advice and information about various aspects of creating a MOOC. All of this work is free of charge for the academic staff.

2. STATE OF THE ART

Right before engaging on this MOOC initiative, at U.Porto we actively worked to get involved with the biggest players in this industry, learning by sharing ideas and methods. Following this idea, in November 2014 we hosted at U.Porto the HOME (Higher education Online: MOOCs the European way) conference "Mapping the European MOOC Territory".

This event gathered many of the HEI that produce MOOCs and a statement was drafted "on how European institutions, governments and the European commission should react on the opportunities and threats of MOOCs" (EADTU, 2015). The Porto Declaration on European MOOCs (Porto Declaration) was signed and paved the way to ensure that European MOOCs keep following the upward movement they have been on: "MOOCS have continued to attract considerable media coverage as governments and universities respond to the open and online education movement. MOOCs are, at this moment, seen as a disruptive force and an important driver for change—for both better and worse.

The growth of MOOCs has helped to make institutions, governments and societies at large more aware of the possibilities of open and online education." (EADTU, 2015).

Another landmark was the Seminar "Criando um curso MOOC - da ideia ao ensino" - Creating a MOOC course - from the idea to teaching" promoted by ET unit with keynote speakers from the Universitat Autònoma de Barcelona. The turnaround was very interesting and we could feel a shy, but existing buzz around this subject at U.Porto.

From some empirical standpoint, teachers still feel uneasy with MOOCs and how to implement them. In Portugal, many of the so called MOOCs are still following a structure more commonly used on online distance courses. The focus is still not on video production like many of the examples we can see from reference institutions.

This lead to the development of U.Porto's vision for MOOCs, where video quality and a strong multimedia production play vital roles. One of the first items addressed was the necessity of implementing guidelines to support staff on every aspect of thinking, creating and producing a MOOC.

3. GUIDELINES FOR MOOCS

We defined several guidelines for the MOOCs implementation. All these guidelines were created and analyzed by a multidisciplinary team of teachers, technical and pedagogical specialists, that worked together, and created a positive engagement in the organization regarding this new learning experience.

These resources were made available at the elearning website (https://elearning.up.pt/mooc/recursos/) and had information on "How to get started", but also resources about the pedagogical model for MOOCs, an excel spreadsheet for content planning and some recommendations for video pre-production.

All of these guidelines were always followed by a close watch and guidance from our team.

4. U.PORTO FIRST MOOC

4.1 MOOC Framework – Financed Project

Entitled "Climate changes in the school media" (https://miriadax.net/web/as-alteracoes-climaticas-nos-media-escolares), the first MOOC of University of Porto is dedicated to the topic of climate changes and the usage of digital media in the classroom, as a way of engaging students to learn more about this topic.

The target audience of this course was primarily consisted of primary and secondary school teachers in the fields of science, to those responsible for school's media and to anyone interested in this topic.

At the moment, climate changes are a global issue, but schools are failing in teaching the theme to participants. This MOOC intends to innovate in this field, by providing teachers with a set of strategies and soft skills they can use in the classroom setting to convey, through the media, information on climate changes such as what is happening in the climate and its causes, impacts and possible solutions. All of this would be achieved by using a more familiar language, some skilled teachers would learn upon learning how the media works.

This MOOC was an output of a bigger project, Clima@EduMedia (http://climaedumedia-en.weebly.com/), developed by the Faculty of Arts of the University of Porto under the Programme "AdaPT - Portugal Adapting to Climate Changes" and financed by the EEA Grants.

4.2 Summary of the MOOC: Topic, Content and Target Audience

Climate changes are a recurrent subject on the media. To make a critical interpretation of the information submitted it's necessary to understand the basics of the climate system (such as weather, climate or greenhouse gas effect). The advantages of using media such as writing news, infographics, audio and video, to teach climate changes are explored in this MOOC.

The course is divided into five modules taking place during five weeks. Each week trainees are given specific tasks to complete, for example: view the two videos of the module; analyze the proposed teaching strategies for classroom and complete a self-assessment.

Additionally, participants have the opportunity to engage in discussion forums, analyze the support manuals, for a further view on the topics covered by the videos; and have access to a references section, which allows participants to explore the subjects according to their interest.

Given that the target audience of this MOOC is composed almost entirely of full-time workers and the subject was related to the use of new technologies in education, this MOOC became a flagship for U.Porto to explore massive and global education scenarios, supported by good quality audiovisual content. For this, a fairly known TV journalist was hired to present all the contents that have been previously scientifically validated. The iterative process of creating the videos started with writing the scripts. Soon after the scripts were adapted to a more appealing video language that made full use of the journalist's expressiveness, video and motion graphics. The goal was to create interesting as well as scientifically correct videos. The journalist was key to make the videos appealing and the video production easier and more cost effective. His previous experience working with this subjects made him very at ease with the process and his inputs regarding how to convey information the best way possible were always regarded and validated by the teachers responsible. MOOC.

4.3 MOOC: Facts And Figures

The MOOC had 723 people enrolled, in which 90% were Portuguese and the remainder from Brazil, Spain and other portuguese speaking countries - PALOP. Of this number, about 549 (75.9%) started the course and 311 (43%) have completed it, which shows a higher rate of completion than average in MOOCs.

Most of the participants were teachers (80%), which showed great interest in the MOOCs pedagogy and also in the educational resources available on the course (videos, support manuals and educational strategies proposals).

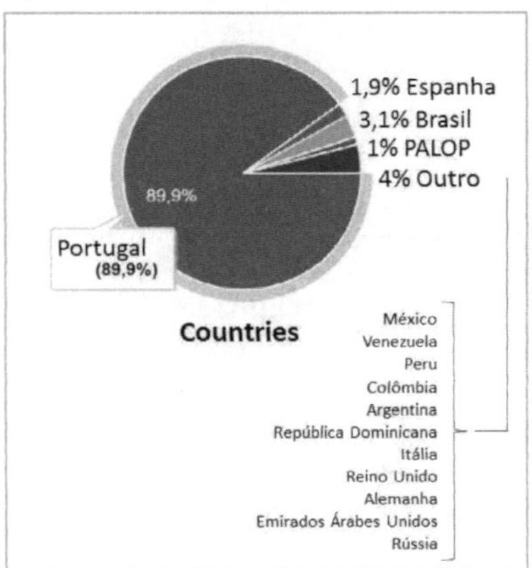

Figure 1. MOOC community: countries

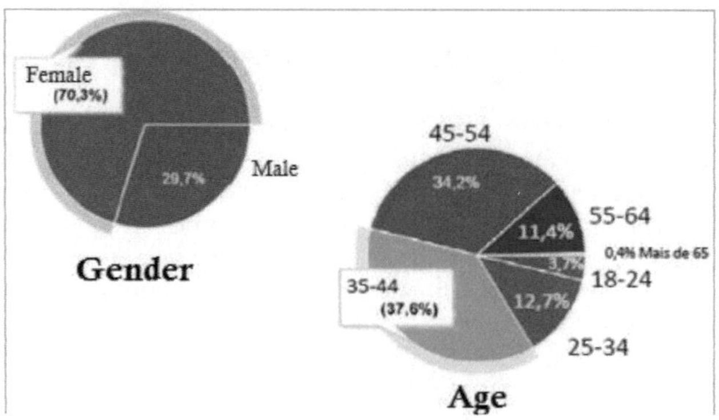

Figure 2. MOOC community: gender and age

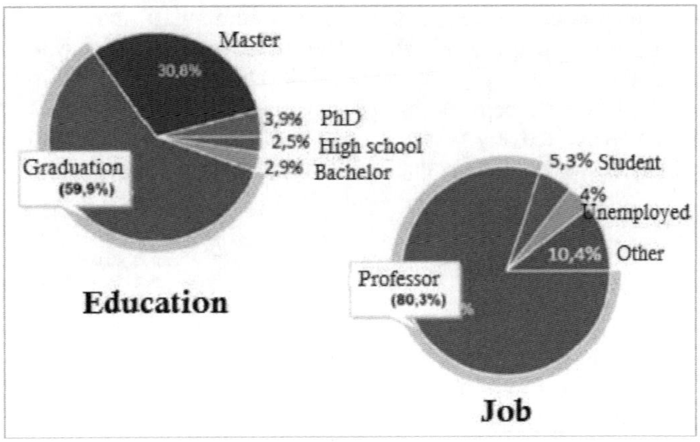

Figure 3. MOOC community: education and occupation

The MOOC started on 5 October 2015 with an introductory week, called "Presentation module".

During the first week, "the participants were asked to give some elements of their profile, such as their geographic origin and their scientific and professional background, among others to check to which point the actual audience fitted the expected one. During this week they could get familiar with MOOCs rules, platform's tools and basic vocabulary." (Soares-Frazão, F. et al, 2005).

4.4 MiríadaX Platform

The chosen platform to offer the MOOC was MiriadaX (http://www.miriadax.net), promoted by Telefónica - a company specialized in offering integral solutions of online learning and training for education - and Universia, the largest network of Spanish and Portuguese speaking universities whose purpose is to foster diffusion of open knowledge in the ibero-american higher education space (MiríadaX website).

The platform is widely spread in the ibero-american community and has 3 years old, 2 million of registered users, 64 universities represented and 1469 professors enrolled. Currently the MiríadaX community have 338 courses with about 600,000 peer review activities.

These figures put MiríadaX on the 5th place in the ranking of MOOC platforms most commonly used in worldwide. (ICEF Monitor, 2015)

5. CONCLUSIONS AND FUTURE WORK

The University of Porto first MOOC attracted a large number of participants and the tutor's interventions on the course were focused on how to create an effective learning community, mainly by encouraging the use of these tools and strategies in classrooms.

Participants highlighted as crucial for their registration and continuity in the MOOC the following items: interest in the topic, considered innovative by combining climate changes and media; quality of the resources presented; flexibility allowed - online course without synchronous moments; opportunity to interact with a large number of people with similar interests, allowing for the exchange of experiences and ideas.

As we know, from other experiences, the innovative conception behind this MOOC and "the process of its creation has offered to all team an invaluable opportunity to reflect about the way MOOCs offer some answers to the challenges of the European higher education system today." (Prades, G. et al, 2005).

With the development of this first MOOCs it became clear that group dynamic is very important for the design, development and execution of a MOOC. A multidisciplinary team was assigned to create and develop this course and its success is the direct result of everybody's inputs. Producing high quality audiovisual content, after this experience, is even more important than before. We used every facility at our disposal such as the University's TV production studio and their sound and video technician. For the voiceover parts we used an experienced voiceover artist. Every step we took was to make sure that both audio and video could be the best at the time of production. Our team, despite being small, managed to overcome some of the technical challenges faced during the production. The pedagogical support was also determinant for the success of this MOOC. Summing up, the team used over 400 hours to produce this course.

This first experience leads us to believe that the University of Porto's policies on MOOCs could also be improved upon and we will be actively working on this topic. Currently we have in production two more MOOC courses and there are some others being developed as projects.

REFERENCES

Azevedo, S.F. 2014 *Rector action programme for University of Porto 2014-2018* (website accessed on 08.02.2016) http://reitor.up.pt/wp-content/uploads/2014/09/Programa_Acao.pdf

EADTU, 2015 (website accessed on 08.02.2016) http://www.eadtu.eu/home/policy-areas/open-education-and-moocs/news/251-porto-declaration-on-european-moocs

ICEF monitor (2016) *MOOC enrolment surpassed 35 million in 2015*. http://monitor.icef.com/2016/01/mooc-enrolment-surpassed-35-million-in-2015

MiríadaX platform (website accessed on 05.02.2016) https://miriadax.net/web/guest/nuestra-filosofia

Porto Declaration (website accessed on 08.02.2016) http://www.eadtu.eu/images/News/Porto_Declaration_on_European_MOOCs_Final.pdf

Prades, G. et al, 2005. An Unconventional MOOC as a Solution for Short Budgets and Young Researchers in Europe. *Proceedings of the European Stakeholder Summit on experiences and best practices in and around MOOCs*. Mons, Belgium, pp23-27.

Soares-Frazão, F. et al, 2005.Collaborative MOOCs: a challenging experience. *Proceedings of the European Stakeholder Summit on experiences and best practices in and around MOOCs*. Mons, Belgium, pp32-36

U.Porto in international rankings (website accessed on 08.02.2016) https://sigarra.up.pt/up/en/WEB_BASE.GERA_PAGINA?p_pagina=uporto-nos-rankings-internacionais

INFORMAL LANGUAGE LEARNING IN AUTHENTIC SETTING, USING MOBILE DEVICES AND SNS

Ruthi Aladjem and Bibiana Jou
Tel Aviv University

ABSTRACT

One of the challenges of teaching a foreign language in non-immersive contexts, is extending the exposure of learners to the target language, beyond school hours. Since it is quite common to find linguistic and cultural exponents of foreign languages, in authentic contexts (i.e., the "Linguistic Landscape"), those exponents may serve as triggers for students to interact and engage with the foreign language, on a daily basis. Using mobile devices and social media to increase awareness to the exponents, may facilitate foreign language learning outside the classroom and across settings. This paper describes an approach for designing an informal, contextual, foreign language learning experience. Students were encouraged to utilize their mobile devices in order to document the presence of Spanish exponents in their surroundings and to share them in a dedicated Facebook group. The findings suggest that this approach may hold the potential to increase learner awareness to language learning opportunities, thus supplementing formal learning in the classroom and encouraging a continuous learning process.

KEYWORDS

Mobile Learning, Informal Learning, Linguistic Landscape, SNSs.

1. INTRODUCTION

When learning a foreign language, students should get as much exposure to the target language as possible. This is especially important when learning takes place in non-immersive contexts, where the target language is not prevalent. Furthermore, language learning encloses much more than just learning the formal aspects of the language and hence, pragmatic and socio-cultural aspects should become an integral part of the language learning curriculum (Verhelst et al., 2009).

Technology has the potential to support language learning opportunities in versatile ways (Lai & Gu, 2011). Learning theories have stressed the importance of learning in authentic, relevant, contexts (Lave & Wenger, 1991) and ubiquitous mobile devices may support such contextual learning in authentic settings. Mobile technologies can further support learning by allowing for learner immersion, enhancing engagement and increasing the motivation for learning (Dieterle & Dede, 2007; Sharples et al., 2007). Social network sites (SNSs), such as Facebook, cab be used for educational purposes by serving as informal learning environments and as supplemental tools for formal learning (Dabbagh & Kitsantas, 2012). SNSs may facilitate a collaborative process of knowledge building, by creating a sense of community and encouraging discussion (Wodzicki et al., 2012; Zhang, 2010).

The task described in this paper was designed with the intention of raising student's awareness to language exponents in their daily surroundings, by using the "Linguistic Landscape" (LL) as an input source. Initial definitions of the LL were quite restrictive and referred mainly to the "visibility and salience of languages on public and commercial signs in a given territory or region" (Landry & Bourhis, 1997). However, more recent studies point out the necessity to go beyond this definition and to "include images, sounds, drawings and movement, in line with current theories about multimodality" (Shohamy, 2012). Past research on the potential of the LL for language learning had suggests that the LL could contribute to language learning by serving as a source of authentic input for the development of pragmatic competence and literacy skills, as well as for raising student's language awareness (Cenoz & Gorter, 2008). The objective of the current pilot study was to encourage a continuous interaction with the target language (Spanish), by increasing awareness to Spanish exponents in the LL and also, to create a flow between the classroom, the daily surroundings and the digital sphere, which serves as the informal learning environment. Language awareness is a complex construct which requires a holistic approach, in this paper we refer to awareness in the context of language learning, as "the learner's knowledge or subjective experience that he/she is detecting a stimulus" (Al-Hejin, 2004). The stimulus in this case, is the language exponent, found in the LL. From this perspective, capturing and sharing an exponent suggests that there is awareness to its existence. Taking a soci-constructivist perspective, learning is viewed as a social process, resulting from an active participation in a collaborative creation of knowledge. This knowledge can, in turn, serve as a basis for other learners in their learning processes (Scardamalia & Bereiter, 2003; Stahl, 2000).

2. STUDY APPROACH

The study was conducted over a period of a full school year (two-semesters) but participation in the task was not mandatory. Students were asked to capture Spanish related exponents, as they encountered them in their daily surroundings and share them on a dedicated Facebook group with a short description, in Spanish. Thus, participants were essentially interacting with the foreign language in both a receptive (capturing the exponents) and a productive (sharing and adding information and description) manner, as well as interacting with the other participants in the group. The task was intentionally loosely defined and open-ended in order to allow as much room as possible for student expression and for interaction. In this sense, the task was mainly designed to create opportunities to experience unplanned encounters with linguistic exponents and to encourage communication and interaction between the participants.

The study takes an exploratory, qualitative approach, focusing on the analysis of the types of exponents that students chose to post, as well as on the resulting interaction patterns.

3. FINDINGS

3.1 Exponents and Student Interaction Patterns

28 students, out of the 52 students who had joined the Facebook group, chose to actively share one exponent or more. A total of 83 exponents were shared, out of which, 59 were photos, 10 links, 11 Videos and 3 were textual status updates. The posts were versatile and included Spanish dishes, photos of signs in Spanish, Spanish and Mexican restaurants names, Spanish related events and more. The content of the exponents can be classified into two groups: textual content (such as street signs or venue names) and visual content (such as photos of dishes or events). The majority of posts (65 out of the 83 posts) referred to the physical surroundings but several students chose to capture digital (as opposed to physical) exponents, such as video clips in Spanish or links to Spanish related commercials.

The exponents shared by students, suggest varying levels of awareness that may go beyond the definition of "detecting a stimulus" (Al-Hejin, 2004) and indicates understanding, noticing, communicating emotions and reminiscing, as described in the following examples:

- One student posted a photo of a venue named *"Alegria"* (joy- in Spanish) and commented *"Alegria!"* (With an exclamation mark) implying not only acknowledgment of the Spanish word, but also an understanding of it.
- A student posted a photo of a coffee cup with *"¡Precaución caliente!"* (Caution hot) warning in different languages, among them Spanish. Indicating awareness to a message, written on a daily item that is normally unnoticed.
- Another student explicitly acknowledged something that she hadn't noticed up until that point- *"no sabia que tenemos..en Israel"* (I didn't know that Spanish ballrooms exist in Israel).

3.2 Instructor Interaction Patterns

Three instructors participated actively in the group. Instructor interaction can be categorized into three main roles- Exemplary role, Supportive role and Instructive role, as detailed bellow.

Exemplary role: In order to kick start the activities and demonstrate the idea of language exponents, the instructors created the first few posts of exponents that they had encountered. In addition, the instructors served as "models" of the culture of the target language by postings exponents from their lives, for example, two instructors posted photos of typical Spanish dishes that they had prepared at home.

Supportive role: Instructors often included emphatic expressions in their comments to posts, such as *"¡qué bueno!" (Great!) or "estupendo"* (wonderful), in order to express support and encouragement and create an environment where students feel safe and secure, even to make mistakes. Instructors also showed encouragement by using the "like" button for each post. In addition, instructions provided affective feedback- for example, one instructor expressed her personal fondness for a location (a bar) that a student had posted *"Uno de mis bares favoritos de los pocos que conozco"*(One of my favorites bars, of the few I know).

Instructive role: Instructors encouraged communication in Spanish and often pointed to formal aspects of the Spanish language. For example, an instructor used one of the posts as a learning opportunity and commented on the correct use of exclamation marks in Spanish in one of the posts *"¡Qué bien! Incluso se ve el signo de exclamación al comienzo y al final."* (That's nice! you can even see the exclamation marks at the beginning and the end). In another case, a student posted a photo of a yacht named "*hispaniola*" and the instructor encourages a discussion by noting the historical context implied by the name of the Yacht *"¿Es tu yate, Roni? Si no, esi nteresante saber quién da a su yate el mismo nombreq ue la isla a donde llega Cristóbal Colón..."* (Is this your Yacht? If not, it would be interesting to know who names his Yacht with the same name as the island where Christopher Columbus arrived at).

4. DISCUSSION AND CONCLUSIONS

Learning a language entails more than just memorizing formal linguistic structures and cannot be separated from social and contextual aspects (Cenoz & Gorter, 2008). By becoming actively aware of language exponents in their surroundings, the participants of this study were effectively acting as active explorers, recognizing and seizing learning opportunities around them in authentic contexts, while being supported and encouraged by the virtual community (Dieterle & Dede, 2007; Lave & Wenger, 1991; Sharples et al., 2007). Mobile technology and social media enabled a seamless and immediate experience by allowing students to capture and upload the exponents, as well as to add information and interact in real time. In reply to a comment on her post, one student noted "a hora est oya quí" (I am here now!), expressing, in this sense, the immediate and authentic aspect of the experience, enabled by the mobile device. The Facebook group provided learners with a space to interact, as they engaged both cognitively and affectively with the task.

The notion of the Linguistic Landscape initially referred to the physical context but was extended beyond its original definition (Shohamy, 2012). Our findings suggest that this concept should be further enhanced to include the **digital** sphere as well. Students, though not explicitly guided to do so, naturally shared exponents from both their physical and digital surroundings. We conclude that the digital sphere has become an integral part of our reality and hence, should be considered a part of the LL.

As for the types of exponents that were located and shared from the LL, we noted that two aspects, critical to language learning, correspond with the two types of exponents that students chose to share; the formal linguistic aspect and the cultural aspect, match exponents containing textual and visual content respectively. Further research should analyze the two types of exponents and possible ways for enhancing learning opportunities that arise from each type.

We found that the participation rate in the group decreased over time, both in terms of the rate of posting as well as the number of views. A possible explanation may be that students were not motivated enough to participate in this non mandatory task and may have lost interest, once the novelty of the task wore off. Holding class discussions related to the posts shared by students, may serve as means for acknowledging the contribution of the students to the learning process, thus increasing motivation for participation in the task. We believe that bringing the informal, digital world into the classroom in such a way, may strengthen the sense of continuity between the classroom and the external assignments, breaking the time-space classroom boundaries. We also conclude from the findings, that facilitation is needed in order to encourage the discussion both in class and on the SNS. Those strategies should be further explored, as well as additional ways for encouraging discussion among students and discussing topics such as cultural and historical aspects of the target language.

This project served as an exploratory task for both instructors and students. Overall, the results appear to be encouraging but there is a need to further investigate, replicate and enhance the experience. We are planning on conducting a similar exercise next year, taking into account the lessons learned from the first year trial and discussed in this paper.

REFERENCES

Al-Hejin, B., 2004. Attention and Awareness: Evidence from Cognitive and Second Language Acquisition Research. Teachers College, *Columbia University Working Papers in TESOL & Applied Linguistics*, 4, pp.1–22.

Cenoz, J. & Gorter, D., 2008. The linguistic landscape as an additional source of input in second language acquisition. *IRAL - International Review of Applied Linguistics in Language Teaching*, 46(3), pp.267-287.

Dabbagh, N. & Kitsantas, A., 2012. Personal Learning Environments, social media, and self-regulated learning: A natural formula for connecting formal and informal learning. T*he Internet and Higher Education,* 15(1), pp.3-8.

Dieterle, E. & Dede, C., 2007. Neomillennial" learning styles propagated by wireless handheld devices. *Ubiquitous and pervasive knowledge and learning management: Semantics, social networking and new media to their full potential.* Hershey, PA: Idea Group, Inc.

Lai, C. & Gu, M., 2011. Self-regulated out-of-class language learning with technology. *Computer Assisted Language Learning,* 24, pp.317-335.

Landry, R. & Bourhis, R.Y., 1997. Linguistic Landscape and Ethnolinguistic Vitality: An Empirical Study. J*ournal of Language and Social Psychology*, 16, pp.23-49.

Lave, J., & Wenger, E., 1991. *Situated learning: Legitimate peripheral participation*. Cambridge university press.

Scardamalia, M. and Bereiter, C., 2003. Knowledge building environments: Extending the limits of the possible in education and knowledge work. *Encyclopedia of distributed learning,* pp.269-272.

Schmidt, R., 1995., Consciousness and foreign language learning: A tutorial on the role of attention and awareness in learning. In *Attention and awareness in foreign language learning*. 9, pp. 1-63.

Sharples, M., Taylor, J. & Vavoula, G., 2007. A Theory of Learning for the Mobile Age. In T*he Sage Handbook of Elearning Research*. pp. 221-47.

Shohamy, E., 2012. Linguistic landscapes and multilingualism. T*he Routledge handbook of multilingualism*, pp.538-551.

Stahl, G., 2000. A model of collaborative knowledge-building. In *Fourth international conference of the learning sciences* (Vol. 10, pp. 70-77). Mahwah, NJ: Erlbaum, 2000.

Verhelst, N., Van Avermaet, P., Takala, S., Figueras, N. and North, B., 2009. *Common European Framework of Reference for Languages: learning, teaching, assessment*. Cambridge University Press..

Wodzicki, K., Schwämmlein, E. & Moskaliuk, J., 2012. "Actually, I Wanted to Learn": Study-related knowledge exchange on social networking sites. *The Internet and Higher Education*, 15(1), pp.9-14.

Zhang, Z., 2010. Feeling the sense of community in social networking usage. *Engineering Management,* IEEE Transactions on, 57, pp.225-239.

ENHANCING THIRD-YEAR MEDICAL CLERKSHIPS: USING MOBILE TECHNOLOGY FOR TEACHING AND LEARNING

Janette R. Hill[1], Michelle A. Nuss[2], Ronald M. Cervero[1], Julie K. Gaines[2] and Bruce Middendorf [3]
[1]*University of Georgia, Athens, GA USA*
[2]*AU/UGA Medical Partnership, Athens, GA USA*
[3]*St. Mary's Hospital, Athens, GA USA*

ABSTRACT

The third year clerkship is one of the most exciting and challenging times for medical students (Cooke, Irby, & O'Brien, 2010) when students spend significant time in clinical settings (e.g., hospitals) assisting in the care of patients on a daily basis. Getting information and resources just-in-time and at point-of-care (Author, 2009) is one challenge faced by supervising doctors and students. Technology has long been used to assist in point-of-care decision-making (Burke & Weill, 2008); mobile technology has added value to this activity. In this study, we explore how mobile technologies (e.g., iPads) were being used to support supervising doctors and medical students. After completing full data analysis of year one of two, results indicate that the faculty and students benefitted from the use of the iPads during the third year clerkship.

KEYWORDS

Third year clerkship, mobile technology, point-of-care, decision-making.

1. INTRODUCTION

The third year clerkship is one of the most exciting and challenging times for medical students (Cooke, Irby, & O'Brien, 2010). This is often the first time that medical students are spending a significant amount of time in real-world clinical settings – hospitals, clinics, and private offices – assisting in the care of everyday patients. A challenge that medical students and their supervising doctors face is one faced in many educational settings: how to access just-in-time resources and information (Author, 2009) to inform evidence-based decision-making while interacting with the patient.

Various computer and information technologies have long been used to assist with patient care (Howell, 1995). Doctors and medical students and interns have made use of technology to guide decision-making. The use of technology to assist with evidence-based decision-making gained traction in the 1990s as medical professionals embraced the use of mobile technology (e.g., laptops). This movement progressed in the last decade as mobile technologies have become more powerful and accessible (Ducut & Fontelo, 2008). Smart phone technology and other tools such as Palm Pilots and iPods have helped medical professionals access information just-in-time to facilitate patient care (see, for example, Embi, 2001). Recently, iPads have gained widespread attention in the medical field as a tool to assist medical professionals in decision-making. The iPad, replete with hundreds of apps accessible literally at the fingertips, has enabled exponentially more opportunities for accessing information, thus increasing the ability to provide evidence-based decision-making just-in-time at the point of care.

Initial reports of iPad use by medical professionals have been promising (see, for example, Patel et al., 2012). That said, there are not many formal research studies that have been completed exploring the use of the iPad by third year medical students during clerkships. Further, our review of the literature indicated that even fewer studies have explored the use of mobile technologies (e.g., the iPad) as a tool to assist or hinder the teaching and learning process as supervising doctors and medical students interact and engage in patient care. We designed a multi-year study to explore the use of the iPad during three important teaching and learning processes: 1) as supervising doctors learn the practice of academic teaching, 2) as medical students learn the practice of doctoring, and 3) as supervising doctors enhance their clinical decision-making process. In the context of this study, the iPad was used in the teaching and learning interactions between physicians and students in the context of seeing patients, by physicians in their own clinical practice, and by students throughout the third year.

The purpose of this longitudinal study was to understand how mobile technology supports supervising doctors' and medical students' learning and professional practice. There were three research questions that guided the study:

1) How does mobile technology support faculty preceptors learning the practice of academic teaching?
2) How does mobile technology support medical students learning the practice of Internal Medicine in third-year clerkships?
3) How does mobile technology support clinical decision-making for faculty preceptors, (i.e., internal medicine physicians)?

2. RESEARCH DESIGN, METHODS, AND PROCEDURES

This exploratory study used a collective case study design. Collective case study enables the researcher to study multiple cases to explore a phenomenon (Stake, 2000). A collective case study is an instrumental study involving multiple cases. As described by Stake, an instrumental case study is used to provide insight into a particular phenomenon. In this study, there are multiple phenomena (teaching, learning, decision-making, use of technology) involving several types of participants (supervising doctors, students). The primary context was the hospital in which the supervising doctors and medical students were working and learning during the Internal Medicine rotation.

Participants in the study included 9 supervising doctors and 36 third-year medical students during their Internal Medicine clerkship rotations at a hospital in the southeast. The students participated in 9 clerkships during the 12-month period, with 8 weeks devoted to the Internal Medicine clerkship. The 4-6 students who were involved in the Internal Medicine clerkship in July and August were involved in additional weekly interviews of 15-30 minutes throughout their other clerkships (e.g., emergency medicine, surgery) to explore if the availability of the iPad changed their learning processes in those clerkships. The 3-4 supervising doctors in the hospital who agreed to more in-depth participation were interviewed for no more than 30 minutes at regular intervals throughout the year (beginning, middle, and end) to get more detailed information related to how the iPad was used to enhance clinical decision-making.

All students and supervising doctors were given a third generation iPad for this project that has been pre-loaded with a variety of applications that allowed them to access medical knowledge resources and productivity tools for clinical decision-making. All students and supervising doctors were provided with initial training in how to use the iPad (30-60 minute sessions respectively). Additionally, a guided overview was provided for each app pre-loaded on the iPad to enable practice with use of the iPad and the apps.

Data was captured in a variety of ways by the research team throughout the year (July to June). Data was gathered via email as well as face-to-face and phone interviews. Weekly observations of the supervising doctors and students as they completed rounds with patients was also captured. All data was kept secure during capturing and analysis, with processes implemented to keep the identity of the participants confidential.

Data analysis was ongoing throughout the study (Merriam, 1988; Miles & Huberman, 1994; Wolcott, 2001; Yin, 2003). A constant-comparative approach (Charmaz, 2006; Glaser & Strauss, 1967; Strauss & Corbin, 1990) was used to analyze the data. Interviews and observations were transcribed as soon as possible following the interview and observations to enable initial analysis. An in-depth analysis was conducted at the conclusion of the year. A cross-year in-depth analysis is on-going; therefore for this paper, only the first year of the study is reported.

3. RESULTS

The first year of the study concluded in June when students completed their third year clerkships. During the 12-months, we completed hundreds of hours of data collection, including interviews and observations, of the medical students as they engaged in the learning process as well as the supervising doctors as they engaged in the process of teaching – some for the first time. It was an exciting year of growth for the medical students as well as the supervising doctors.

Results from year one indicate that the majority of the supervising doctors and medical students made wide and varied use of the iPad during the 3rd year Internal Medicine clerkship. More details are provided in the following paragraphs.

The majority of the supervising doctors used the iPad in a variety of ways to support them in the process of becoming an educator, particularly in their teaching practices. For example, almost all of the supervising doctors modeled the use of the iPad for patient care. One doctor in particular indicated he could not do his work without it. Some supervising doctors also directly asked the student(s) to look up a particular resource or to access information on the patient to help guide decision-making.

The majority of the medical students used the iPad in a variety of ways to support them in the process of becoming a doctor. Like their supervising doctors, most of the students used their iPads during rounds to assist with accessing information on specific patients as well as to gather information for the attending physician. Several students reported regular access to the Electronic Medical Record (EMR) as they gave their daily reports to the supervising doctors. The medical students also reported using the iPads at other times – while working on the hospital floor as well as when they are at home and need to access information related to a particular patient as well as for studying for exams.

The supervising doctors also indicated they used the iPad to support clinical decision-making. For example, almost all of the supervising doctors reported used their iPads while doing rounds with the students so that they could readily access information to help guide patient care. Information accessed included the EMR, x-rays, and lab results.

The additional students interviewed across the year while in other rotations beyond Internal Medicine reported using the iPad to assist with point-of-care decision-making. They also reported using the iPad for patient education. For example, one student reported accessing various apps during his OB/GYN (i.e., women's health) rotation to provide additional information for patients.

While there was a lot of use of the iPads, there was not 100% use – and not everyone found value in the technology. For example, one of the supervising doctors rarely used the iPad while on rounds, reporting that he did not find it to be enough of a value-add to warrant carrying it. Some students shared a similar perspective, reporting that they worried they may lose track of it while going from patient room to patient room.

4. SIGNIFICANCE AND LIMITATIONS OF THE WORK

This study is significant for several reasons. First, there is limited research looking at the interactions of supervising doctors, particularly as they are learning the practice of academic teaching. This study sought to provide insight into this process so to provide suggestions for improving practice.

Second, exploring how students learn the practice of doctoring provides medical educator with insights into how to better support students in this critical activity in their medical education. Finally, there is little research on how mobile technology supports the teaching and learning processes during 3rd year clerkships. This study sought to provide guidance for using mobile technologies to support medical students during their rotations.

There are limitations to the study. First, the data presented is only for one year. Additional analysis of the two years may provide additional insights into how mobile technology can be used more effectively for evidence-based decision-making at point-of-care. Secondly, only one setting was used for the Internal Medicine rotation. Including other hospitals and supervising doctors may also provide additional insights into effective practices for teaching and learning. Finally, the mobile network used by the supervising doctors and medical students was not always running at top efficiency due to overload. Ensuring that a robust wireless network is operational may enable even more use of mobile technology for point-of-care.

5. CONCLUSION

There has been, and the foreseeable future indicates there will continue to be, an exponential growth in the use of technology in clinical medical settings. This study provides some initial insights into the advantages of using mobile technology for both supervising doctors and medical students as they engage in just-in-time, evidence-based decision making at the point-of-care. While promising, there are challenges with the use of the technology (e.g., training, motivation to use) that need to be addressed throughout implementation to help ensure the effective use of the technology. The overall results from this study provide some indication that the benefits of the use of mobile technology in clinical settings outweighs the challenges that may be encountered.

REFERENCES

Author, 2009. Resource-Based Learning Environments In An Organizational Setting: Opportunities For Knowledge Management System Development. *Journal of Korean Human Resource Development,* Vol 4, No. 1, pp. 35-52.

Burke, L. and Weill, B., 2008. *Information Technology For The Health Professionals* (3rd ed.). Upper Saddle River, NJ: Prentice Hall.

Charmaz, K., 2006. *Constructing Grounded Theory: A Practical Guide Through Qualitative Analysis*. Thousand Oaks, CA: Sage.

Cooke, M., et al., 2010. *Educating Physicians: A Call For Reform Of Medical School And Residency*. San Francisco, CA: Jossey-Bass.

Ducut, E., and Fontelo, P. (2008). Mobile Devices In Health Education: Current Use And Practice. *Journal Of Computing In Higher Education*, Vol. 20, No. 2, pp. 59-68.

Embi, P. J., 2001. Information At Hand: Using Handheld Computers In Medicine. *Cleveland Clinic Journal of Medicine*, Vol. 68, No.10, pp. 840-856.

Glaser, B. G., and Strauss, A. L., 1967. *The Discovery Of Grounded Theory: Strategies For Qualitative Research*. Chicago: Aldine.

Howell, J. D., 1995. *Technology In The Hospital: Transforming Patient Care In The Early Twentieth Century*. Baltimore: Johns Hopkins University Press.

Marceglia, S., et al., 2012. How Might The Ipad Change Healthcare? *Journal of the Royal Society of Medicine*, Vol. 105, No. 6, pp. 233-241.

Merriam, S. B., 1988. *Qualitative Research And Case Study Applications In Education* (2nd ed.). San Francisco, CA: Jossey-Bass.

Miles, M. B., and Huberman, A. M., 1994. *Qualitative Data Analysis: An Expanded Sourcebook (2nd ed.).* Thousand Oaks, CA: Sage.

Patel, B. K., et al., 2012. Impact Of Mobile Tablet Computers On Internal Medicine Resident Efficiency. *Archives of Internal Medicine*, Vol. 172, No. 5, pp. 436-438.

Stake, R. E., 2000. Case Studies. In N. K. Denzin & Y. S. Lincoln (Eds.). *Handbook Of Qualitative Research, 2nd ed.*, pp. 435-454. Thousand Oaks, CA: Sage.

Strauss, A. L., and Corbin, J., 1990. *Basics of Qualitative Research: Grounded Theory Procedures And Techniques*. Newbury Park, CA: Sage.

Wolcott, H., 2001. *Writing Up Qualitative Research* (2nd ed.). Newbury Park, CA: Sage.

Yin, R. K., 2003. *Case Study Research: Design And Methods* (3rd ed.). Newbury Park, CA: Sage.

STATISTICAL MEASURES OF INTEGRITY IN ONLINE TESTING: EMPIRICAL STUDY

Tom Wielicki
California State University, Fresno , 5245 North Backer Street, M/S PB7, Fresno, CA 93740-8001, USA

ABSTRACT

This paper reports on longitudinal study regarding integrity of testing in an online format as used by e-learning platforms. Specifically, this study explains whether online testing, which implies an open book format is compromising integrity of assessment by encouraging cheating among students. Statistical experiment designed for this study focused on combining such variables as numerical scores on tests and quizzes with type of feedback received by students during the test and question randomization. Results obtained proved that cheating during well designed online tests is more of a myth than reality.

KEYWORDS

Online testing, integrity of testing, e-learning platform

1. INTRODUCTION

Online delivery of education became a permanent part of educational landscape in spite of many challenges including integrity of online testing. It has been found to be extremely cost effective in delivery of internal corporate training (Zhang, D., Nunamaker, J., 2003) in spite of some evident barriers exhibited especially among SMEs (Anderson, R., Wielicki, T., 2010). The same cannot be said about education – especially higher education, where objectives of instructional activities are broader and more complex then objectives of typical training. Also, universities seem to have more problems with incorporating this new technology into an overall strategy and business processes since – ironically – they are more resistant to change (Jones, N., O'Shea, J 2, 2004).

This may be a reason for apparent differences between number of online credit courses and degree programs offered by lower tier unaccredited institutions and those fully accredited. Accredited degree programs seem to be much more cautious in adopting e-learning format out of concern about quality of education and requirements of accrediting institutions as well as questions about integrity of distance learning. Big part of this skepticism is attributed to legitimate questions about reliability of online testing and assessment, especially at the undergraduate level. Specifically, issue of security or lack of it in a web based testing has been preoccupying researches like Adams and Armstrong (1998) leading to numerous software solutions like their Eval program used for testing at undergraduate level.

However, some studies suggest a negative overall trends in increasing academic dishonesty among new generation of students along with increasing societal permissiveness of our society (Kitahara, R.T., Westfall, F., 2007). Therefore, we should be careful not to attribute problems with integrity of testing solely to an online format of instructional delivery.

Hodgins (2002) in his vision paper developed for the American Society for Training and Development (ASTD) emphasized "Assessment and Certification" as one of the main areas where impact of technology on e-learning has to be closely monitored and controlled. Similarly, Dobbs (2002) in his definition of the state of online learning is concentrating on four fundamental obstacles to high quality of e-learning. Number one problem identified by him is a flawed perception that "reading is learning". He is suggesting that more interaction should be built into the e-learning as well as effective assessment mechanism.

Assessment seems to be an important part of study in the area of designing and evaluating online learning environment like the one proposed by Hoffman and Ritchie (2001). However, its impact on the quality of educational experience is hardly ever measured and assessed in empirical settings.

A serious of quantitative studies based on a solid samples of web based students performance has recently been completed shading more light on the issues of viability of e-learning (see Wei-Fan Chen, 2005).

At the same time some authors warned against Digital Doctrine that greatly overestimates impact of technology on economy and education (see – Albreht and Gunn, 2000). Some anticipate that dot-com bust could be repeated with disappointments in the field of e-learning, due to irreplaceability of some important components of face to face learning process. This study attempts to continue a trend of verifying myths created around e-learning with statistically sound samples of data.

2. METHODOLOGY AND HYPOTHESIS

A sample of 230 students took an upper division undergraduate MIS course, which was delivered fully online using Blackboard LMS – a comprehensive e-learning environment. At the same time another 186 students took the same course with the same instructor and using the same text book but in a web enhanced mode. Web enhanced mode is defined here as a paperless class with all materials, handouts and communication delivered in a digitized form (using Blackboard content), with all tests administered online but with students still participating in a traditional lecture in classroom settings.

Couples of hypothesis were formulated addressing different dimensions of quality of assessment process:

- Online open book delivery format of quizzes and tests is conducive to cheating and abuse, therefore test scores will be impacted by the type of assessment feedback
- Online open book delivery format of quizzes and tests is conducive to cheating and abuse, therefore test scores will be impacted by the level of questions randomization used in the assessment
- Combined impact of type of feedback and question randomization will cause significant difference in the mean scores of online tests and quizzes due to cheating

3. EXPERIMENT DESIGN

A sample of 416 students took 12 quizzes and 2 tests during one semester upper division MIS course. This means that total number of graded assignments (quizzes and tests) used in this study is equal to 5824. It has been insured that the level of difficulty was uniform for all students by using the same pool of questions, the same textbook and the same time frame for the assignments. About a half of the sample were web based students (online course), which had almost no face to face contact with the instructor and each other. The other half of the sample included students that participated twice a week in a regular lecture, knew each other and benefited from instructor's face to face consultation hours.

3.1 Variables and Treatments

Blackboard environment provides numerous settings for designing of an online test. Every design could be more or less conducive to cheating, depending on such parameters as:

- time allocated to every question,
- enforcement of sequential way of answering questions (one at a time) versus scrolling page,
- type of provided feedback (just the score, identification of questions missed and the score, identification of question missed and correct answer)
- questions randomization from a larger pool versus the same set of questions presented to every student

We will define every combination of these parameters as a statistical treatment. For purpose of this study only two of those parameters were used to create treatments in statistical analysis of scores:

- type of provided feedback (3 levels) and
- randomization (2 choices)

Those treatments represented arrangements under which cheating during an open book online quiz or test could be either "very easy" or "very difficult" or anywhere in between. A variable that was measured for every treatment was an average score (class mean) on a given test or quiz with specific format (combination of parameters). It was assumed that - should students abuse an online format of testing – the mean of scores should consistently drop as we move from "easy to cheat" treatments to "difficult to cheat" treatment. In other words – if there was any abuse of online testing among students, it was expected that difference between the mean scores will be statistically significant as we compare different combined setups shown in Table 1 below.

Table 1. Combined setups for delivery of online assignments

SCA-NR	show correct answers (SCR); the same set of questions –NR (not randomized)
DRNA_NR	show missed questions but no correct answer (DRNA); the same set of questions - NR
SCO_NR	show only total score; the same set of questions – NR (not randomized)
SCA-R	show correct answers (SCA); randomized questions - R
DRNA-R	show missed questions but not correct answer; randomized questions - R
SCO-R	show only total score; randomized questions - R

It is reasonable to assume that above formats (assessment setups) represent an increasing degree of difficulty in cheating; therefore treatments from the first row to the last may be viewed as a scale of increasing "degree of difficulty in cheating."

Separate statistical tests were conducted on quiz scores and tests scores due to the difference in settings of the assessment process in both cases. All remaining setup parameters of the assessment process were the same for all collected data: all questions were multiple choice questions, there was always 60 seconds time allocated to every question, and there was always a possibility of answering questions in any order (a scrolling mode enabling student to answer questions in any sequence).

3.2 Statistical Tests

Numerous statistical tests have been conducted to verify some of the hypothesis listed above. Primary focus of this analysis was on the issue of searching for statistically significant difference in the mean scores on online assignments administered under different settings, which were more or less conducive to cheating and abuse by the students.

The first test was conducted using One-Way ANOVA F-test for verification of significant difference among the mean scores on assignments administered with different level of feedback (treatments). Null hypothesis Ho about equal means on scores obtain in assignments delivered with different level of feedback could not be rejected even at alpha = .05 with value of F=1.77 and p-value = .1759 . Post hoc Tuckey analysis of p-values for pairwise t-tests confirmed this result.

Similarly, One-Way ANOVA F-test was used for verification of significant difference in the mean scores obtained on online assignments administered with different form of randomization (treatments). Surprisingly, mean scores on assignments with and without randomized questions shown even more uniformity. Null hypothesis Ho about equal means on scores obtain in assignments delivered with and without randomized questions could not be rejected even at alpha = .05 with value of statistics F=0.60 and p-value = .4406.

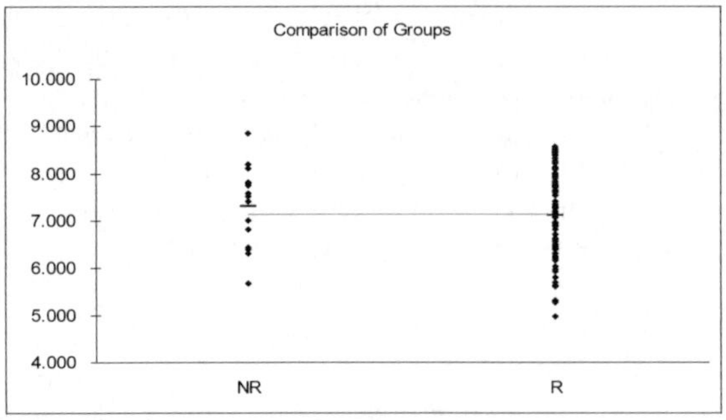

Figure 1. Distribution of means of scores between two types of questions randomization

Lack of impact of questions randomization on the mean score is clearly visible on the Figure 1 above. Post hoc Tuckey analysis of p-values for pairwise t-tests confirmed this result.

The next test utilized Randomized Block Design experiment with blocks identified as two different levels of randomization (R and NR) and treatments as three levels of feedback. Its intention was to remove any variance between investigated means that could be possibly caused by the fact that some assignments used randomized questions and some did not. Again, null hypothesis Ho about equal means on scores obtain in assignments delivered with combined settings of randomization and feedback could not be rejected even at alpha = .05 . Value of F=0.20 for treatments (level of feedback) and F=0.33 for blocks (randomization) with p-values equal respectively 0.83 and 0.62 would clearly indicate statistically solid uniformity of means. Combined and clearly inconsistent impact of feedback and randomization on the means of scores is shown below in Figure 2.

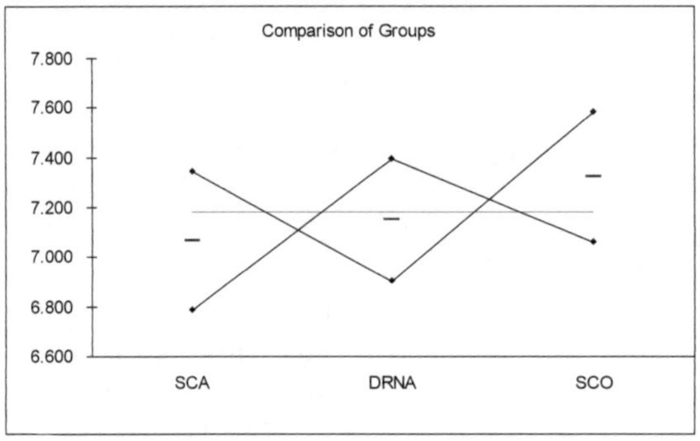

Figure 2. Comparison of impact of feedback and randomization on mean scores

4. SUMMARY OF RESULTS

Preliminary results seem to contradict couple of myths to which academic community often prescribes:

- in general, delivery of quizzes and tests in an online/ open book format does not seem to be conducive to cheating as it does not lead to variations in scores obtained by students under different assessment setups,
- it appears that making answers to questions available to students right after completion of an assessment (treatments SCA) does not have statistically significant impact on average score regardless whether questions were randomized or not,
- randomization of questions when delivering an online quiz or test does not cause statistically significant difference in the means of scores

5. CONCLUSIONS

An overall conclusion should perhaps be formulated in the following way: an average student taking an online class is less mischievous and interested in cheating as he/she is overworked, disconnected and ill organized to be an effective cheater in digital world. Cheating and abusing online testing environment through copying questions, sharing, taking screenshots etc. can be easily made very time consuming and difficult for students by a skillful instructor. Randomization of the questions seems to have a minimal effect on mean scores, whereas revealing answers upon completion of the assignment does not increase possibility of cheating.

REFERENCES

Adams, J.C., Armstrong, A. 1998. Web-based testing: A study in insecurity. *World Wide Web*, Vol. 1, No. 4, pp 193 – 208

Albrecht, K., Gunn, R. 2000. Digital Backlash. *Training and Development*. Vol.11, No.3, 2000, pp. 24-34. ASTD Publications

Anderson, R., Wielicki, T. 2010. Barriers to Application of E-Learning in Training Activities of SMEs. *International Journal on E-Learning*. Vol. 9, No.2, pp.159-167

Chia-I Chang, F. 2003. Quantitative Analysis of Distance Learning Courseware. *Multimedia Tools and Applications*, Vol. 20, No. 1,, pp: 51 - 65

Dobbs, K. 2000. The State of Online Learning – What the Online World Needs Now: Quality. *Training and Development*, Vol. 9, No.2, pp.78-90

Hodgins, W. 2002. Learnativity: Into the Future, in *E-learning Handbook*, McGraw Hill, New York, pp.38-64

Hoffman, B., Ritchie, D. 2001. An instructional design-based approach for developing online learning environment, in Kahn,B. (ed.), *Web-Based Training, Educational Technology Publications*, Englewood Cliffs, NJ, pp.123-156

Jones, N., O'Shea, J. 2004. Challenging hierarchies: The impact of e-learning. *Higher Education*. Vol. 48, No.3. pp. 379 – 395

Kitahara, R.T.,Westfall, F. 2007. Promoting Academic Integrity in Online Distance Learning Courses. *MERLOT Journal of Online Learning and Teaching* . Vol. 3, pp.34-45

Stella, A., Gnanam, A. 2004. Quality assurance in distance education: The challenges to be addressed. *Higher Education*, Vol. 47, No.2, pp: 143 – 160

Wei-Fan Chen. 2005. Effect of web-browsing interfaces in web-based instruction: a quantitative study. *IEEE Transactions on Education*. Vol. 48, No.4; pp. 652- 657

Zhang, D., Nunamaker, J. 2003. Powering E-Learning In the New Millennium: An Overview of E-Learning and Enabling Technology. *Information Systems Frontiers*. Vol. 2, No. 5, pp: 207 – 218

THE COMPLEXITIES OF DIGITAL STORYTELLING: FACTORS AFFECTING PERFORMANCE, PRODUCTION, AND PROJECT COMPLETION

Peter Gobel and Makimi Kano
Kyoto Sangyo University

ABSTRACT

Digital storytelling projects provide a variety of opportunities for learning in the language classroom, but along with these opportunities come a number of challenges for both pedagogy and technology. This presentation describes an ongoing multi-method study into factors involved in task-based learning using digital storytelling. Using intact classes over a three-month period, participants were required to create a series of digital stories and present them to their peers. The stories were quantitatively analyzed using the factors of module (topic), time, medium, and reported technological proficiency. Student attitudes towards the tasks were gauged using and a questionnaire, based on the theoretical framework of Self-determination Theory (Deci & Ryan, 1985), which measured perceived task cost and value, engagement with the task, and expectancy for success on future tasks. The results suggest that digital storytelling can be incorporated into EFL classes for distinct purposes: to reduce foreign language anxiety; provide greater opportunities to use English for lower proficiency learners; and to foster ICT skills, such as knowledge of computers and using software for higher proficiency students.

KEYWORDS

Digital storytelling, action research, learning management

1. INTRODUCTION

In early Computer Assisted Language Learning (CALL) programs the stimulus was in the form of text presented on a screen, and the only way in which the learner could respond was by entering an answer at the keyboard. However, more recent approaches to CALL emphasize more learner-centered, explorative approaches, in contrast to teacher-centered drill-based approaches (Davies, 2000). For example, Ho and Savignon (2013) expound on the advantages of employing face-to-face peer reviewing (FFPR) and computer-mediated peer review (CMPR) for academic writing contexts in CALL settings. Another example of recent approaches to CALL is digital storytelling.

The Center for Digital Storytelling defines a digital story as a short story containing digital images, text, recorded audio narration, and/or music. It allows computer users to be creative storytellers through the process of selecting a suitable topic, writing a script, and developing interesting stories based either on their own experience or the course subject matter. By telling stories with the aid of digital media, students are engaged in learner-centered, authentic tasks. In a digital storytelling project, creating an end product (the digital story) is clearly goal-oriented, and the process itself helps students develop a deeper connection with the subject matter. Robin (2008) suggests that digital storytelling projects provide a strong foundation in many different types of literacy such as digital literacy, global literacy, technology literacy and information literacy. Indeed, the digital storytelling process is an example of a 'multiliteracy' approach. Due to the simultaneous use of a foreign language and technology, students not only are asked to cope with an increasingly globalized society, communicating with other cultures through language, but also are asked to develop communicative competence through new communication technologies.

Digital storytelling (DST) has the potential to help students gain "21st century literacy skills", providing a unique opportunity to acquire new media literacy and IT skills, as well as the standard four skills covered in most language classes. Morgan (2014) reported that digital story projects were beneficial for motivating and helping students improve their writing and reading, because the projects encouraged students to think about how their stories were created. In addition, Kim (2014) suggested that participants in her study were able to develop their oral proficiency. Yang and Wu (2012) have suggested that DST has an effect on both receptive and productive language competences, serving as a transformative technology-supported pedagogy that combines both English language learning in a constructivist/collaborative context, and self-production of authentic materials.

Regarding the educational framework of our study, English as a foreign language (EFL) in Japan, a number of studies have been implemented. Susono (2011) instigated a digital storytelling project at a junior high school for second grade students, finding benefits of the project included a greater understanding of their peers, as well as significant 'knowledge reformation' while writing and rewriting the scripts. Enokida (2015) had students make digital stories about books they had read in an extensive reading assignment and suggested that the stories had a great effect on students' understanding of the content and promoted awareness of story structure. Ono (2014) found that higher proficiency students in his study seemed to feel that their Project Based Learning (PBL) skills, such as computer use, data collection, problem solving, discussion and presentation in the field of foreign language teaching, greatly improved after the project, while the lower proficiency students in the study felt that the main benefit of the project was a reduction in their foreign language anxiety. With the results of these studies in mind, we set out to explore the design and use of DST projects in a content-based framework at the university level.

2. THE PRESENT STUDY

The present research is concerned with the design and implementation of presentation projects for EFL university students majoring in cultural studies. The students were expected to create digital stories/presentations on topics covered in the course texts, and to present them to the class for discussion. It was felt that the digital story projects would allow students to deeply explore the cultural content presented in the course while using English in a focused and purposeful way. The story projects reflect the Content-Based Instruction (CBI) goals of helping students connect meaningful content with language instruction, in an effort to improve their cultural knowledge and language and literacy skills.

Project-based learning tends to be more complicated in nature than more directed forms of task-based learning. Digital storytelling, when used in a project-based learning approach, is an inherently messy process, with the product not always in sync with the original task (Thorne & Black, 2007). Due to the number of steps involved in creating a digital story, and the technical skills necessary, task design is of utmost importance. The researchers are interested in what factors contribute to a successful digital story experience for students. The present research explores the question of task design in digital storytelling, taking into account the context of the task, and the four elements of good task design—purpose, content, activity, and completion— and how they were perceived by the participants. Since task complexity is an important factor to consider in design, both the complexity of the task (in terms of familiarity with the topic and cognitive demands of the task) and required technological proficiency are considered. It is hypothesized that more unfamiliar topics will lead to perceptions of higher cost and less engagement on the part of the participants (Hypothesis 1), and that experience and familiarity with technology needed for task completion will lead to perceptions of those tasks as having greater value and a higher expectancy for success (Hypothesis 2). Also to be considered are the limitations of both technology and technological proficiency when designing a task, since previous research in this area has shown that perceived proficiency has an impact on both product and process (Gobel & Kano, 2013; 2014). To this end, the following research questions were formulated:

1. How do students perceive their technological proficiency?
2. To what extent does project design affect perceived complexity of each project?
3. What were student attitudes towards the individual tasks?

2.1 Methods and Materials

The participants were 18 third-year non-English major university students, studying in the Faculty of Cultural Studies. Their English proficiency, as measured by the TOEFL ITP ranged from (437-515). The participants were enrolled in a compulsory oral skills presentation class which met for 90 minutes a week. All participants had completed a required information technology course in the first year of their studies at university, so all were familiar with using PowerPoint and the school LMS (Moodle).

The course goals centered around developing presentation skills, but as a content-based course the subjects covered in the text and readings focused on the following topics: problems in urban areas; how products are marketed; describing a process, such as how to perform Japanese tea ceremony; comparing cultural differences. Each topic was covered for three weeks, with outside readings provided to supplement the textbook. While studying the text and topic in class, students were asked to prepare a presentation on the topic. This preparation included choosing a topic based on required readings, writing the story, choosing the media, and creating the final product. Students were given 20-30 minutes each week to work with groups to finalize and present their ideas. Table 1 summarizes the topic, style, and requirements of the projects.

Table 1. Project topic, style, and requirements

project	topic	presentation style	requirements
1	city issues	group - in class	visual media, voice recording
2	product critique	group - in class	visual media, voice recording, auto play
3	how to ...	individual - in class	visual media, project sent to instructor as file
4	cultural comparison	individual - watch and respond on LMS	visual media, voice recording, auto play, upload to LMS

At the end of each topic students were asked to present a 1-2 minute digital story on their topic, meant to stimulate a final discussion on the topic. As a result, the projects themselves had a focus on meaning and a non-linguistic outcome. The projects themselves were manipulated to emphasize either familiarity with the topic (topics 1 and 3) or technological and process demands (group work versus individual work, and audio recording versus live presentation, and online submission and online feedback).

At the end of each project, students were given a questionnaire (cf. Appendix). The questionnaire was created with 20 Likert scale items meant to measure perceptions of project design and difficulty (5 questions covering perceived purpose of the project, difficulty of content and project), self-efficacy (6 questions covering perceived performance and perceived technological proficiency), and perceived cost and value of each project (9 questions dealing with actual and expected difficulty of the project, amount of time and effort involved, interest in the project, and expectation for success in future tasks). It was hypothesized that unfamiliar topics would lead to higher cost and less engagement with the project, and that familiarity with technology would lead to greater value and higher expectancy for success in future tasks (Gobel & Kano, 2013; 2014).

3. RESULTS

The projects were assessed based on the rating by the instructor and the impressions of the participants using questionnaires. Instructor ratings for the four projects resulted in the following: Topic 1 (city problems) showed a better use of media and a better presentation of material. There were problems with recording sound; Topic 2 (marketing tricks) displayed less coherence in all stories, with less critical thinking involved, and problems with sound and automatic play functions; Topic 3 (how to) showed a better use of pictures and visual media, clearer story structure, and better presentation of material; Topic 4 (cultural comparison) showed coherent presentations, less critical thinking (a focus on impact rather than logical thought), and problems with sound and automatic play functions and uploading to Moodle and completing forum posts.

After each project, the same questionnaire was administered to elicit participant impressions in four different aspects of the projects: self-efficacy, project design, cost/value of the projects, and presentation and requirement preference. Here are some interesting points we found from the questionnaire, matched with our research questions.

Research Question 1: How do students perceive their technological proficiency?

Student use of computers was rather limited (4 hours per week in average), mostly for school work and searching for information. They reported a mild dissatisfaction with their PC and PowerPoint proficiency, which stayed stable over the projects.

Research Question 2: To what extent does project design affect perceived complexity of each project?

Students were generally satisfied with the projects and what they learned from them, and they felt the projects' purpose became clearer over time. The group work was viewed as being more difficult than the individual work. They found that the presentation demands and use of computer and PowerPoint became more difficult over time. The recording was the most difficult part of the project for the students, especially in the last project.

Research Question 3: What were student attitudes towards the individual tasks?

Student actual and expected difficulties were similar, and the time and effort they put into the projects remained the same, even though they felt the difficulty level of the projects rose over time. As a result, their evaluation of their final product decreased over time, and expectation for success in future projects also slightly decreased.

On the whole, they preferred individual work to group work, and live narration to recording. Manual/auto play preference changed over time. They preferred Moodle upload over class presentation, responding that they didn't have difficulty viewing assignments and commenting on the LMS forum.

4. CONCLUSION

In conclusion, the results show that Hypothesis 1 (unfamiliar topic/cost and engagement) was not supported, while Hypothesis 2 (familiarity with technology/value and expectancy for success) was found to be inconclusive. The results suggest that the more familiar/personal topics resulted in a marginally better product (from the instructor's viewpoint). Students' view of their own skills remained stable throughout the entire study, despite the fact that project demands increased over time. Finally, it seemed that the participants had very little motivation to learn new aspects of technology (auto play function, recoding their voice, Moodle forum). In other words, although the DST projects offered opportunities to learn new skills and master old ones, the students saw the completion of the project (the product) as more important than the creation of the story (the process).

This suggests that, at least with these participants, more support regarding the technical aspects of the DST projects is warranted. Although the students were familiar with most aspects of PowerPoint and the Moodle LMS, it might have been beneficial to review technology and skills throughout the projects, in an effort to build up students' technology skills. Although support was provided in the form of video tutorials and links to 'how to' web pages, it seems that students were not that interested in accessing them or improving their skills.

As with any small-scale intact study, the limitations of sample size and inability to perform meaningful statistical analysis must be noted. With such a small sample size it is difficult to generalize the results in any meaningful way, and he lack of statistical power in the results creates a situation where the findings must be viewed with caution. A future study with a larger population, allowing statistical analysis, should provide more robust results that will add to the body of knowledge in this area. More importantly, the study has suggested a number of areas for future research. Among them are the efficacy of interactive presentations, projects using a variety of formats (movie, chat, Google Maps, etc.), projects using mobile devices, online peer feedback at each step, and the effects of recursive training sessions (teacher or peer-led).

REFERENCES

Deci, E. L., & Ryan, R. M. (1985). *Intrinsic motivation and self-determination in human behavior*. New York: Plenum.

Gobel, P., & Kano, M. (2013). Implementing a Year-long Reading While Listening Program for Japanese University EFL Students. Paper presented at the 15th International CALL Research Conference at Providence University, Taichung, Taiwan. *Computer Assisted Language Learning*, 27, 4, 279-293. DOI: 10.1080/09588221.2013.864314

Gobel, P., & Kano, M. (2014). Japanese teachers' use of technology at the university level. Attitudes to technology in ESL/EFL pedagogy. Arabia TESOL Publications, 36-52.

Ho, M. C., & Savignon, S. J. (2013). Face-to-face and computer-mediated peer review in EFL writing. *CALICO journal*, *24*(2), 269-290.

Kim, S. (2014). Developing autonomous learning for oral proficiency using digital storytelling. *Language Learning and Technology*, *18*(2), 20-35.

Morgan, H. (2014). Using digital story projects to help students improve in reading and writing. *Reading Improvement*, *51*(1), 20-26.

Ono, Y. (2014). Motivational Effects of Digital Storytelling on Japanese EFL Learners. *Proceedings of CLaSIC 2014*, 414-431

Razmi, M., Pourali, S., & Nozad, S. (2014). Digital Storytelling in EFL Classroom (Oral Presentation of the Story): A Pathway to Improve Oral Production. *Procedia-Social and Behavioral Sciences*, *98*, 1541-1544.

Robin, B. R. (2008). Digital storytelling: A powerful technology tool for the 21st century classroom. *Theory into practice*, *47*(3), 220-228.

Susono, H., Ikawa, T., Kagami, A., & Shimomura, T. (2011). Digital Storytelling "Tegami (A Letter to My Future Myself)" Project by Japanese Junior High Students. In *World Conference on Educational Multimedia, Hypermedia and Telecommunications* (Vol. 2011, No. 1, pp. 2324-2327).

The center for digital storytelling. http://digitalstorytelling.coe.uh.edu/index.cfm (Retrieved December 9, 2015)

Thorne, S., & Black, R. (2007). Language and literacy development in computer-mediated contexts and communities. Annual Review of Applied Linguistics, 27, 1-28.

Willis, D. and J. Willis. (2007). *Doing Task-based Teaching*. Oxford: Oxford University Press.

Yang, Y. T. C., & Wu, W. C. I. (2012). Digital storytelling for enhancing student academic achievement, critical thinking, and learning motivation: A year-long experimental study. *Computers & Education*, *59*(2), 339-352.

APPENDIX

Digital Story Questionnaire Items (most set on a four-point Likert scale)

Task design questions (don't agree → agree)

The purpose of the group presentation clear to me.
I learned things from the project.
The topic made the task easy.
The task steps were easy to understand
Rank the difficulty of each part of the task

- Working with others
- Difficulty of the topic
- Finding information for the presentation
- Writing or creating the presentation
- Using computers
- Using powerpoint or prezi
- Recording the presentation
- Finding digital images

Self-efficacy questions (don't agree → agree)

I was able to complete the digital story satisfactorily.
I am proficient at using powerpoint.
I am proficient at using a computer.
I have a computer at home.
How many hours a week do you use a computer?
What do you mainly use it for?

Cost/value questions (not at all/none → very/a lot)

Before starting how difficult did you think the task would be?
How difficult was the task to actually complete?
Did the task take a lot of time?
Did the task take a lot of effort?
Was the task interesting?
Was working in groups interesting?
Did you learn a lot from the task?
Was this task a good way to study?
Do you think you did well on the task?
Do you think you will do well on future tasks?

COLLEGEWIDE PROMOTION OF E-LEARNING/ACTIVE LEARNING AND FACULTY DEVELOPMENT

Nobuyuki Ogawa[1] and Akira Shimizu[2]

[1]*Department of Architecture, National Institute of Technology, Gifu College, 2236-2 Kamimakuwa, Motosu-city, Gifu 501-0495, Japan*

[2]*General Education, National Institute of Technology, Gifu College, 2236-2 Kamimakuwa, Motosu-city, Gifu 501-0495, Japan*

ABSTRACT

Japanese National Institutes of Technology have revealed a plan to strongly promote e-Learning and active learning under the common schematization of education in over 50 campuses nationwide. Our e-Learning and ICT-driven education practiced for more than fifteen years were highly evaluated, and is playing a leading role in promoting e-Learning and active learning. It is essential to do faculty development in order to promote the methods within the college. In this paper we described the actual approaches in our college.

KEYWORDS

e-Learning, active learning, faculty development, Model Core Curriculum

1. INTRODUCTION

In Japan, the former Ministry of Education, now referred to as the Ministry of Education, Culture, Sports, Science and Technology (MEXT), substantially revised the standards for establishing universities in 1991, as Japanese government promoted the decentralization of power by announcing a policy to ease restrictions. In the revisions, the related laws including the School Education Act and the standards for establishing universities were drastically amended, which allowed individual schools to flexibly develop unique education and researches based on its own educational philosophy and objectives, while responding appropriately to advancement of learning and the demands in society. The related legal revisions led to the elimination of the details of the standards including curriculum. (Akiyoshi Yonezawa, 2006.) Under the revisions, the requirements of the standards were eased, on the other hand however, a policy that universities themselves should assure quality of education and research was employed. Consequently, universities were required to conduct self-inspection and assessment of quality of education and researches. Considering the changes related to education, it is a natural tendency to introduce ICT-driven education and e-Learning in Japan, MEXT is also strongly promoting the use of active learning and e-Learning in elementary, secondary and higher education.

In the schematization of education of Japanese National Institutes of Technology (NIT), in addition to showing “Core (a minimum standard)”, the minimum skill level and content to be studied for all the students of NIT, “Model”, a guideline for further advancement of NIT education, is presented to respond to more advanced social request. The curriculum is promoting both “Model” and “Core”, so the name “Model Core Curriculum (MCC)” is used. MCC is organized from the viewpoint of the advancement of NIT to respond to social needs. The direction of NIT is as follows: (1) The fostering of engineers who can be active internationally in response to the globalization of society and industry, (2) The fostering of innovative human resources who can contribute to the sustainable social progress, (3) The expansion into the composite, integrated fields that respond to the needs of the local communities and industries. MCC clearly specifies the targets for students to attain from the viewpoint of 10 items: mathematics, natural science, art and social science, basis of engineering, Specialized Engineering Categorized by Field, Engineering Experiments and Practical Skills Categorized by Field, Substantiation of Specialized Skills, Versatile Skills, Attitude/Orientation, Comprehensive Learning Experience and Creative Thinking Power.

2. SCHEMATIZATION OF EDUCATION AT COLLEGES OF TECHNOLOGY AND THE PROMOTION OF E-LEARNING/ACTIVE LEARNING

2.1 The Promotion of e-Learning and Active Learning

NIT is promoting positive introduction of e-Learning and active learning (e.g. Bonwell, Charles C., and James A. Eison, 1991, Bergmann, J.; Sams., 2012, and Lage, M.; Platt, G.; Treglia, M., 2000.) so that students can attain their target. Several colleges, including our college, are playing a leading role in the field. Our e-Learning and ICT-driven education practiced for more than fifteen years were evaluated, and our program was picked up as a project of the "Acceleration Program for Rebuilding of University Education (AP)" started by MEXT in 2014. (N. Ogawa et al, 2015 and N. Ogawa, A. Shimizu, 2015.) Our AP program, funded by MEXT for five years, is promoting the improvement of the environment for active learning, such as ICT-driven equipment, e-Learning and teaching materials and the implementation of all the above.

2.1.1 The Targets of MCC and its Management by the e-Learning and the ICT-driven System

The teachers are proceeding with the following work, integrating them with each other, in order to meet our targets, following the curriculum created based on MCC: (1) Improvement of lecture and teaching method (Ex. group work, workshop-type learning), (2) Cooperation among teachers, (3) Improvement of educational evaluation and checkup method (Ex. interview and oral examination, portfolio of students and teachers), (4) Development of teaching materials, (5) Activities of Faculty Development (FD) and Staff Development (SD). In order for our college to be a higher education institution that contributes to local industries, it is essential to have a viewpoint of industry-college-government cooperation as well as regional cooperation.

2.1.2 The Development of e-Learning and ICT-driven Education Environment at Our College

As described earlier, our college is leading the way in the promotion of active learning among all the National Institutes of Technology. More precisely, we are improving the environment for active learning including ICT-driven equipment, e-Learning and teaching materials and promoting educational practice with them as the AP, funded by MEXT for five years.

In the academic years of 2014 and 2015, we introduced Projectors with an electronic blackboard system into about three-fifths of all the classrooms through bids at the expense of the AP budget. Furthermore, the wireless LAN device was set up for use in all of the 25 classrooms in all five grades (from the first to the fifth grade) of all the five departments, so that the introduced LMS systems, such as Moodle and Blackboard, can be used in class. STORM Maker, software for making teaching materials, was introduced to make teaching materials for storing in LMS. The special characteristic of STORM Maker, which has an automatic voice synthesis function, simplifies the process of making content based on materials. Therefore, we can easily create teaching materials with voice for e-Learning with the work of entering character, without recording narration voice. Both male and female voices can be synthesized, depending on use and characteristics of teaching materials. Moreover, we introduced more than 160 Tablet computers (Toshiba), 50 notebook PC (Fujitsu) and 20 surface (Microsoft). All of them were introduced for lending and set up for connecting to all the access points of the wireless LAN for e-Learning in class.

The introduction of the electronic blackboard makes it possible to draw and write on its surface with a dedicated electronic pen, without connecting to a personal computer, and digital data of drawing and writing can be recorded and stored in a file server connected to the network. Using the projector control toolbar displayed on the projection screen of the electronic blackboard, teachers can easily select and control students' tablet screen by operating on the screen. (Figure 1).

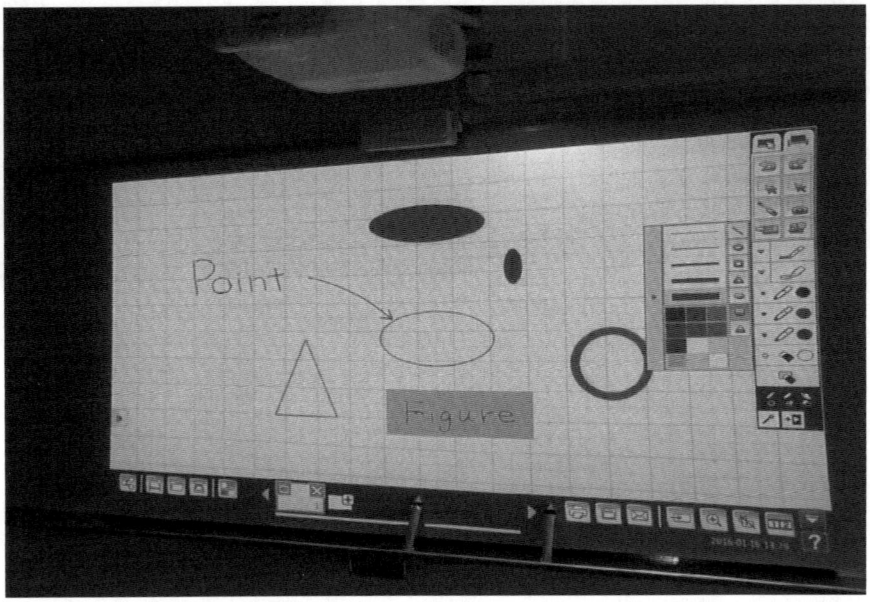

Figure 1. Digital drawing on an electronic blackboard with an electronic pen, without connecting to a PC

It is necessary to consider the following two things for practicing active learning according to MCC curriculum: (1) How to use the e-Learning system and ICT-driven equipment, (2) Educational methods of active learning and e-Learning. The teachers have different degrees of knowledge and skills regarding the two items, so it is important to improve the teachers' knowledge and skills through FD in order to promote active learning and e-Learning within our college. In the next chapter, we will describe the upward spiral of ICT-driven education through FD in our college.

3. UPWARD SPIRAL OF E-LEARNING AND ICT-DRIVEN EDUCATION THROUGH FACULTY DEVELOPMENT

In the 2014 academic year, we established the office for promoting active learning as a collegewide organization and have been practicing active learning. The members of the office consists of the representative teachers of all the departments (Mechanical engineering, Electrical and Computer Engineering, Electronic Control Engineering, Civil Engineering, Architecture, liberal arts, natural science), which makes it possible to exchange information smoothly between the office and each department. This system will be maintained in the future. Also, the members of the office learn newly introduced the e-Learning system, ICT-driven equipment and the approaches of active learning in advance, and each member conveys new information to his/her department. Moreover, the office is playing a leading role in promoting active learning by implementing the following two kinds of FD at every faculty meeting: (A) teaching methods of active learning, (B) How to use the e-Learning system and ICT-driven equipment. In our college, we regard teaching methods of active learning and the use of ICT-driven equipment as important cores, and we have an idea that a variety of active learning can be practiced by combining teaching methods, the e-Learning system and methods of using ICT-driven equipment with each other. Actually, some teachers, inspired by the FD sessions held at faculty meetings, have created and practiced his or her own methods of active learning. Table 1 shows the FD sessions related to e-Learning and ICT-driven education held at our college this academic year. It has been decided that from the next academic year the FD sessions will be held just like this academic year so that the teachers can acquire more advanced skills.

Table 1 shows the dates of the FD sessions held at our college, the type of activity performed, people that the sessions targeted, results and expected effect. It also shows the problems presented through discussion after each session. The measures against the problems were compiled after each discussion. In our college, we are planning to hold similar FD sessions in future academic years in better ways. Therefore, the analysis and proposed coping strategies described in Table 1 will be useful.

Table 1. The content of the FD sessions of our college held in the 2015 academic year

Dates	Type of Activity Performed for Promoting AL	people that the sessions targeted (headcount)	Results, Expected Effect	Problems	Measures against the Problems Described in the Left Column
Faculty Meetings: Apr.1, Jun. 3, Aug. 5, Sep.18, Nov. 18, Feb. 10, Mar.14	Our College, collegewide level (FD on the teaching of active learning and ICT-driven equipment)	All teachers (about 80 people)	The FD lecture sessions are effective because they are held when all teachers get together.	There are different needs, because the teachers have different degrees of skills.	A wide variety of subjects are treated.
FD meetings: May 7, Oct. 14	Our College (collegewide level)	All teachers (about 80 people)	Useful lecture by visiting lecturers	General topics, not concrete content	Concrete content is treated at FD regarding AL conducted at faculty meetings.
(1) May 26-28 Workshop of Blackboard (basic) (2) Jun. 1-3 Workshop of Blackboard (intermediate) (3) Jun. 8-10 Workshop of Blackboard (advanced)	Our College (collegewide level)	All teachers (about 80 people)	To acquire how to use Blackboard (basic, intermediate, advanced) and practice active learning in class)	Some teachers cannot attend workshop because of other school affairs. The teachers have different degrees of skills.	The same content was presented for three days, considering the teachers' schedule. The participants were free to select the level among three (basic, intermediate, advanced).
Workshop of Moodle was held three times in Jun.	Our College (collegewide level)	All teachers (about 80 people)	To acquire how to use Moodle and utilize it in class	Some teachers cannot attend workshop because of other school affairs.	The same content was presented for three days, considering the teachers' schedule.
Jul. 23 (Akashi) Oct. 14 (Gifu) Dec. 3 (Kyoto) Mar. 1 (Maizuru) The 2015 AL promotion study team of the third block	The third block Committee members of AL promotion study team(the colleges that belong to the third block)	The number of colleges that belong to the third block multiplied by two committee members of each college	NIT, Akashi and Gifu Colleges, leading colleges of AL, are supposed to lead the other colleges within the third block to the positive practice of AL.	Each college has a different perspective and degree of penetration of AL, which makes it difficult to have a common understanding of AL.	To respond to diverseness among colleges, first, it is necessary to assess the position of each college by conducting a survey of the teachers who belong to the third block.

Sep. 24: Workshop of projectors which have the functions of electronic blackboards & tablet PC (the fosterage of trainers: for the members of AL promotion WG)	For the members of AL promotion WG of our college	For the members of AL promotion WG(seven people)	How to use projectors which have the functions of electronic blackboards & tablet PC. How to conduct AL classes using equipment.	The teachers have different degrees of skills.	Workshop for the members of AL promotion WG was held, aiming at fostering trainers who would instruct the faculty members. The instructions for teachers by trainers are supposed to be conducted within each department. By doing so, trainers can conduct detailed instructions and respond to different teachers with different skills.
Sep. 25, 28, 29: Workshop of projectors which have the functions of electronic blackboards & tablet PC (for all teachers)	Our College (collegewide level)	All teachers (about 80 people)	How to use projectors which have the functions of electronic blackboards & tablet PC. How to conduct AL classes using equipment.	The instruction of how to use equipment is insufficient for actual use. Some teachers cannot attend workshop because of other school affairs.	In the workshop held at a classroom of each department after school, teachers actually operated projectors which have the functions of electronic blackboards & tablet PC. The same content was presented for three days, considering the teachers' schedule.
Sep. 1-4: Workshop of cybozu	Our College (collegewide level)	All teachers and college staff	To acquire knowledge of procedure/methods for managing various information within college.	Some teachers and college staff cannot attend workshop because of other school affairs.	The same content was presented for four days, considering the teachers' schedule.

4. CONCLUSION

We have come to recognize the importance of diversity through the practice of active learning, e-Learning and various FD sessions conducted in our college. Active learning, which is a flexible way of teaching, adds diversity. Furthermore, since active learning is practiced in all subjects of our college, the existence of a large variety of subjects produces diversity. There are various suitable ways of doing active learning for each subject. In addition to this, the fact that teachers select different ways of active learning for the same subject produces more diversity. Since active learning itself is a flexible, learner-centered approach, focusing mainly on students' initiative and independence, diversity is an important objective of active learning. With the idea that dealing with diversity is important, we are giving detailed responses to the diverse needs of the faculty, shown in the rightmost column of Table 1, when holding FD sessions in our college. Just like students' initiative and independence, the faculty should also learn and develop the content presented at the FD sessions at his/her own initiative. It is essential to seek a better way of active learning and practice it, depending on his/her degree of skills, his/her individuality and the characteristics of each subject.

It is important to enhance teachers' skills for teaching and student counseling/guidance along with systematic curriculum to make collegewide, organizational deployment of education work effective. It is necessary for each teacher to improve not only his or her teaching ability but also his or her skills of using ICT-driven equipment in order to practice education based on e-Learning and active learning. This requires the improvement of the coordinated training system, sharing and publicity of model education examples, and the system of properly evaluating teachers' education examples. Also, it is necessary to introduce the system of teacher evaluations and student counseling/guidance conducted within a campus (peer review). In our college, we consider it important to do continuous improvement performed by sharing and evaluating the education examples, which, we believe, makes high-quality e-Learning and active learning penetrate within the college. These methods work well by both a shared understanding of the objectives of the curriculum and the curriculum itself by teachers and the effort for improving teachers' skills for teaching and student counseling/guidance. Considering the importance of organizational deployment of education curriculum, it is necessary to hold organizational workshops (FD) concerning the objectives of the curriculum, education content and methods, keeping in mind that the characteristics and creativity of education should not be impaired.

REFERENCES

Book

Akiyoshi Yonezawa, 2006, "Japan" in Forest J.F. & Altbach P.G. (eds.) *International Hand-book of Higher Education Part II* pp.829-837, Springer, Federal Republic of Germany.

Bonwell, Charles C., and James A. Eison, 1991, *Active learning: Creating excitement in the classroom.* Washington, DC: School of Education and Human Development, George Washington University, USA.

Bergmann, J.; Sams., 2012, *A., Flip Your Classroom: Reach Every Student in Every Class Every Day.* International Society for Technology in Education. ISBN 1564843157.

Journal

Lage, M.; Platt, G.; Treglia, M., 2000, Inverting the classroom: A gateway to creating an inclusive learning environment. *The Journal of Economic Education.* , vol. 31, no. 1, p. 30-43.

N. Ogawa et al, 2015, Creation of an Environment for Active Learning and its Practices in NIT, GIFU College, *Transactions of ISATE, The 9th International Symposium on Advances in Technology Education*, pp.213-217.

N. Ogawa, A. Shimizu, 2015, Promotion of Active Learning at National Institute of Technology, Gifu College. *Procedia Computer Science*, 60: pp. 1186-1194.

TRAINING PORTUGUESE TEACHERS USING BLENDED LEARNING – A DIFFERENT APPROACH

Bertil P. Marques and Paula Escudeiro
GILT/ISEP

ABSTRACT

The aim of this paper is present a Postgraduate Specialization with a different concept of the traditional ones. Instead of having to follow a curriculum previously established, hard and sequential, time-limited, you can choose the frequency of any course units according to their availability and current needs. It is not a proposal it is already a work in operation, working in Blended Learning. In the chapter of the education in Portugal teachers in primary and secondary education have their activity of teaching is developed in accordance with the fundamental principles enshrined in the Portuguese Constitution and within the framework of the general and specific principles under the Ministry of education. Considering the teachers' training needs to perform in-service training that are intended to ensure the updating, improvement, retraining and support for the profession of teaching staff, aiming at further development objectives in career and mobility under this Statute.

KEYWORDS

Teaching; Education; Training; Blended Learning.

1. INTRODUCTION

A possible solution to the basic and secondary teachers' needs is presented in order to make actions for incrementally training, thus benefiting the teachers for career development. We will see how to proceed to perform this progression and how teachers can benefit from the credits they acquire from completing the modules of the curricular units (CU), not being necessary to sustain the UC in its whole or without having to complete a graduate degree that had been prepared.

Thus this flexibility in the preparation of post-graduations in modular form and semi-in personae, meets the busy day-to-day needs of teachers who do not want to leave behind their career progression.

Nowadays it is a very worrying factor in our country, as there are always a high percentage of not placed teachers in the national teacher selection procedure and every year there are recent graduates in the labour market, not contributing for the improvement of these numbers.

2. TEACHING IN PORTUGAL

In a summarized form, we will try to clarify how the education system in Portugal (basic, secondary and post-graduate degrees) is structured, as well as explain how the career of basic and secondary education teachers develops and give an example of training offer different from standard offerings.

2.1 Educational System Structure

The existing Educational System in Portugal, which has been in force since the 2011/2012 academic year, is represented in **Figure 1**.

The Portuguese Educational System is organized in 4 study blocks:

1St Block: Pre-school education - pre-school education is intended for children aged between 3 years and the entry into compulsory schooling; frequency is optional and is ministered in nursery (Public and Private).

2^Nd Block: Basic education - it has a duration of nine years (1st to 9th grade) and it is organized in three sequential cycles. The 1st Cycle works in a one-teacher scheme (and with resource to expert teachers in certain areas) and it aims at the development of basic skills in Portuguese language, mathematics, Environment Study and expressions.

In the 2.º cycle, the teaching is organized by subjects and multidisciplinary study. In the 3.º cycle, the teaching is organized by subjects. The main objectives of this cycle are the knowledge and skills development, which are necessary to get to active life or to continue studying. In Basic Education, the Vocational Education is embodied in the courses of education and training (EFC) and vocational courses.

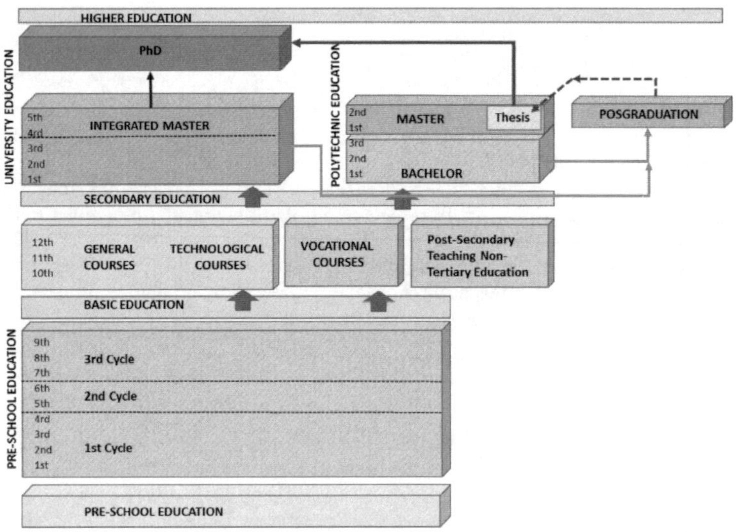

Figure 1. Portuguese Educational System

3^Rd Block: Secondary education - it is oriented for either the continuation of higher studies, either to the world of work. The curriculum of courses secondary level has a referential of three years (10th to 12th form) and it enlarges the following courses: (1) The Scientific-humanistic Courses - essentially for students who want to continue to university-level studies; (2) Professional Courses - essentially for students who want to get to the world of work, also allowing the continuation of higher studies. They are organized by modules in different areas of training; (3) Specialized artistic teaching courses - essentially for students who seek to ensure artistic training specialized in the areas of visual arts, audiovisual, music and dance, allowing the entry into the world of work or the continuation of higher studies; (4) Learning Courses; (5) Education and Training Courses (The CEFs also exist in Basic Education: Type 1, 2 and 3).

Post-Secondary Teaching Non-Tertiary Education - The Technological Specialization Courses (CET) enable specialized training courses in different areas of technology, allowing the insertion in the world of work or the continuation of studies on the upper level. The training undertaken in CET is credited under the upper course in which the student is accepted.

4^Th Block: Higher education - it is structured in accordance with the principles of Bologna and it aims to ensure a solid scientific preparation. The higher education is organized in university education and in polytechnic education, administered by institutions of higher education, namely public, private or cooperatives. In higher education the following academic qualifications are attributed: First Degree (Bachelor), Masters degree (Master) and Doctorate (PHD). This last one (PHD) is only given by university education (but not by polytechnic education).

Postgraduate courses - The courses enable specialized training courses in different areas of technology, allowing the continuation of studies on the upper level. The training is credited under the upper course in which the student is admitted. It is organized in university education and in polytechnic education, administered by institutions of higher education, namely public, private or cooperatives. In Higher education is not attributed the academic degree, but gives a college certificate of skills, and it is the academic basis of the Masters degree (Master).

2.2 Teaching Profession Career Code

The teaching profession career code of childhood educators and teachers of elementary and secondary schools, hereinafter referred to as the Code, applies to teachers, whatever the level, teaching cycle, group of recruitment or area of training, which work in the various forms of education and non-higher education system, and in the context of public establishments of pre-school education and of elementary and secondary schools in the dependence of the Ministry of Education.(DL 75/10, point 1, Art.1, CAP.I) (ECD, 2010).

The teaching staff activity develops in accordance with the fundamental principles recognized in the Constitution of the Portuguese Republic and in the framework of the general and specific principles set out in Articles 2 and 3 of the Educational System Basic Law (ECD, 2010).

For now a little more about the childhood educator, teachers of elementary and secondary schools career, we refer to the Teaching Career Statute some important points for this our implementation (ECD, 2010).

Rights (DL 75/10, Art.4 of Art.9, CAP.II); Duties (DL 75/10, Art.10 to Art.10-C, CAP.II); Training (DL 75/10, Art.11 to Art.16, CAP.III); Teaching career (DL 75/10, art.34, CAP.VII); Career progression (DL 75/10, Point 2.C, Art. 37, CAP.VII); (...) c) Frequency with use of training modules that match, the average number of years of stay in step, 25 hours per year or, alternatively, specialized training courses.

This point (DL 75/10, Point 2.C, Art. 37, CAP.VII) is very important and is one of the reasons which led us to proceed with the provision of training that will present in Section 3 in order that those interested in career advancement could have specialized training offer.

Considering the training needs of teachers in doing continuous training so that they are intended to ensure the update, the improvement, conversion and the support for the professional activity of teaching staff, aiming to further development objectives in career and mobility in accordance with this Code. This continuing training must be planned so as to promote the development of the professional skills of teaching staff.

3. POSGRADUATION IN EUROPEAN UNION AND THE WORLD

Doing research on the concept of posgraduation in the European Union, as well as in the world, we found that the concept is similar to that in Portugal, which is an existing teaching block in higher education and the analyzed literature, it was found that the workings they are similar to undergraduate courses and existing master's degrees in various educational institutions. These are courses that are also regulated/advertised to run in the school year and semester, as well as those found advertised and working in Portugal (Posgraduation, 2015; Posgraduation, 2016).

The main difference of our proposal is that there is the concept for all CUs may be operated simultaneously provided that there is registered students, that is, open the pre-registration is open for all CUs. Once the minimum number of students to particular CU is reached. We Contact the students to perform the actual registration and starts the same. By repeating the process whenever and for the necessary CUs without obeying the rules of the semester and academic year. So is our audience are interested in specialized certifications they will choose when CUs gives them way and according to their needs or training, interest or career. Either theme or temporally.

4. OUR TRAINING OFFER

Therefore, to meet the need of the market in offering graduate in the area of specialization of the primary and secondary school teachers to obtain the credits for career advancement. Post graduations which are teacher tailor-made were created. Thus, the Institute Superior of Engineering of Porto (ISEP) prepared a postgraduate to act in this area, divided into two parts, one, more education and other more technological. An innovative training offer.

What makes these postgraduates different?

- Each CU is independent, Flexibility in CUs frequency, Postgraduate degree, Possibility of enrolling in a branch of IT Engineering Masters.

4.1 Postgraduate Specialization in Technology and IT applied to Education

The structure of these postgraduate specialization offers is distinguished by the flexibility in frequency of different Curricular Units (CU), constituting each one of them as an action of accredited training by the Scientific Council-pedagogical of continuing training (CCPFC). Instead of following a curricular plan previously established, driven and sequential and limited in time, you can choose the frequency of any CU according to your availability and current needs. The course is organized into a total of 60 credits (ECTS), covered with eight CUs. The total number of hours of each CU contemplates classroom instruction and classes in e-learning, thus allowing a more flexible management of the sessions. The trainees can choose to follow the pre-established curricular plan or, alternatively, attend, in separate regime, the CUs that are more adequate to its needs, making the post-graduation conclusion dependent on the completion of all CUs that integrate the correspondent study plan. The course is organized into 2 instruction and e-learning classes, thus allowing a more flexible session management.

Trainees can choose to follow the pre-established curricular plan or, alternatively, attend, in separate regime, the UCs that are more adequate to its needs, making the post-graduation conclusion dependent from the completion of all curricular units that integrate the correspondent study plan.

Aimed to basic and secondary education teachers, to graduates in the education area and other professionals, providing the domain of the technical aspects in the Information and Communication Technologies area, this post-graduation allows the achievement of credits to the progression of the Teaching career, aims the continuous learning in the Information Technologies in education area, allowing the teachers, educators and other professionals specialization in areas and also aims to continuous learning in the area of technologies to support the Education, allowing the specialization of teachers, educators and other professionals in areas related to information technologies, driving innovation of its pedagogical practices, through the use of Information and Communication Technologies, corresponding to a total of 60 ECTS, covered with eight CUs in both postgraduations.

4.1.1 Postgraduate Specialization in Educational Support Technologies

The total number of hours of each CU includes in classroom to educational support technologies, developing innovation of its pedagogical practices through the use of educational practices with technology.

Table 1. Postgraduate Specialization in Educational Support Technologies

CUs	ECTS	T	PL	OT
Information and Communication Technologies in Education (TICE)	7,5	1	3	1
Fundamentals and Power Training Models for Technology (e-Learning) (FTEC)	7,5	1	3	1
Tools to Support the Teaching/Learning Process (FAPE)	7,5	1	3	1
Repository of Educational Resources (RRED)	7,5	1	3	1
Learning Management Platforms (Moodle) (PGAP)	7,5	1	3	1
Project Seminar (SPRO)	7,5	0	4	1
Electives (TWO of the following)				
Interactive Tables in Collaborative Learning (QIAC)	7,5	1	3	1
Digital Arts (ARTD)	7,5	2	2	1
Multimedia Systems in Education (SMED)	7,5	1	3	1
Remote Experimentation in Educational Context (ERCE)	7,5	1	3	1
Image, Audio and Digital Video (IAVD)	7,5	1	3	1
Teaching Art (ARTE)	7,5	2	2	1
Sign Language in Education (LGES)	7,5	1	3	1

T-Theory; **PL**-Practice Laboratory; **OT**- Guidance Tutorial

4.1.2 Postgraduate Specialization in Educational IT

The total number of hours of each CU includes classroom to information technology in education, developing innovation of its pedagogical practices through the use of technology in educational practices.

Table 2. Postgraduate Specialization in Educational IT

CUs	ECTS	T	PL	OT
Educational Software Engineering (ESED)	7,5	1	3	1
Image, Audio and Digital Video (IAVD)	7,5	1	3	1
Web Programming (PWEB)	7,5	1	3	1
Network Administration (ADMR)	7,5	1	3	1
Digital Educational Resources (REDI)	7,5	1	3	1
Project Seminar (SPRO)	7,5	0	4	1
Electives (TWO of the following)				
Mobile Platforms (PMOVV)	7,5	1	3	1
Digital Arts (ARTD)	7,5	2	2	1
Graphics Systems (SGRA)	7,5	1	3	1
Educational Games (JOED)	7,5	1	3	1
Teaching Art (ARTE)	7,5	2	2	1
Remote Labs (LARE)	7,5	1	3	1

T-Theory; **PL**-Practice Laboratory; **OT**- Guidance Tutorial

4.2 Units Option

Gathering the number of credits/ECTS corresponding to the total required for the post-graduate, even if obtained in different academic years, you will be given the post-graduate specialization diploma and a bonus in credits/ECTS.

Each CU is made by Workshops, in principle 4, which each teacher can choose separately according to interest or availability. Each Workshop assigns credits and valid certification to teaching career progression, but it is mandatory to make the full set of UC workshops to have the CU ECTS. At your pace, you create your curricular plan making the CU according to needs, interests and availability.

As workshops and consequently the CUs are performed in blended learning (classroom + work and remote support), teachers are allowed to manage their choices.

Another strong point is the non-existence of semesters, over the year, academic or civil, because the concept gets itself confused as the workshops are always open to enrollment. As long as there are enough students, the class starts. It is an incremental process that will always work if the teachers that need of credits for the career development, are thinking on self-investment, without being stuck to academic years, semesters, annual fees and other patterns of traditional higher education. We, therefore, consider it an added value to the model.

Furthermore, being eager to continue training, progressing to the Master degree, has the possibility to integrate an associated branch of the Master Degree in Computer Engineering according to the admission rules in force.

4.3 Reached Results

These Post graduations are already in operation, we have completed 3 UCs successfully. We have obtained the results: Enough [10-12] - 11%; Good [13-15] – 44%; Very Good [16-17] – 33% and Excellent [18-20] – 12%. There was not any failure until now. The motivation behind these teachers to be students again is much stronger than any discouragement that leads to withdrawal. The Blended Learning model also is a strong motivation.

5. CONCLUSION

Given the status of the scenario of the current teaching career and the changes that are already provided for under Portuguese law, the teachers of primary and secondary schools will have to invest more in their professional training or for competitions to schools or for career advancements.

These Post-graduate specializations in technologies and computer applied to education seek to come meet these professionals, either in content or in operating mode, allowing a flexibility that most schools do not offer. Fees are paid to the workshop, registration is permanently open and with enough subscribers the module advances. There is no concept of semester or school year. All CU are open since there is interested. It is a concept of continuity and always in Blended Learning system.

As mentioned in point 4. what makes these postgraduates different?

- Each CU is an independent credited training action.
- Flexibility in CUs frequency: personal curricular plan to suit your interest, making post-graduation completion dependent from the completion of all curricular units that integrate the correspondent study plan.
- Postgraduate degree when achieving the required total credits/ECTS.
- Possibility of enrolling in a branch of IT Engineering Masters, according to the admission rules in force.

REFERENCES

ECD, 2010. ECD Portuguese legislation DL 75/2010, url: http://www.ige.min-edu.pt/cdi/imagens/ECD_com_alteracoes.pdf, view on 03 February 2016.

ESTAE, 2012. Informational site of POST-GRADUATE SPECIALIZATIONS IN TECHNOLOGIES AND COMPUTER APPLIED TO EDUCATION, url: http://www2.isep.ipp.pt/estaei/, view on 05 February 2016.

Posgraduation, 2015. What is a Postgraduate Study? url: https://askcurtin.custhelp.com/app/answers/detail/a_id/379/~/what-is-postgraduate-study%3F. View on 31 March 2016.

Posgraduation, 2016. What is a Postgraduate Degree? - url: http://www.allaboutcareers.com/careers-advice/article/what-is-a-postgraduate-degree. View on 31 March 2016.

GAMIFY AND RECOGNIZE PRIOR LEARNING: HOW TO SUCCEED IN EDUCATORS' FURTHER PROFESSIONAL TRAINING WITH OPEN BADGES

Esko Lius
Master of Arts, Helsinki, Finland

ABSTRACT

Traditional further professional training has been losing its position and importance in teacher upskilling. Traditional modes of training delivery do not work well in situations where much of the competences have been gained informally, or when teachers find it difficult to attend training days that fit poorly to their schedules or location.
This paper is a case study on how a gamified and open badge-based MOOC, namely "Learning Online" improved and recognized educators' skills related to new pedagogies and ICT in Finland. "Learning Online" consists of a 2-day boot camp, weekly online webinars and Facebook activities, and an open badge-based system for recognizing competencies. Teachers could participate in various areas of the entire system, which meant that they could visit the site oppiminenonline.com solely to apply for badges on the basis of their prior learning or also choose to join a team and participate in the game of earning the most badges.
The results of using open badges in Learning Online have been very positive. This teacher professional development program exceeded the set goals. Instead of the initially targeted 800 badges, over 4,000 were applied for and over 3,600 granted. After the initial project the system has expanded, and there are talks to make it a nation-wide system. It has also contributed strongly to the development of wider educational thinking and practices of open badges in education. Badges make it easy to create and share an ePortfolio.

KEYWORDS

Further professional training; gamification; open badges; 21st century skills; MOOC; key competences

1. INTRODUCTION

Technological revolution and digitalization affect not only societies and culture, but also education and the development of educators' competences profoundly.

> *"Taken together, these results [of OECD Skills Outlook 2013 survey] underscore the crucial importance of information-processing skills in adults' participation in the labour market, education and training, and in social and civic life. "*
> *(OECD Skills Outlook 2013, page 28, http://skills.oecd.org/documents/OECD_Skills_Outlook_2013.pdf)*

The *OECD Skills Outlook 2013* points out that Finland (along with Japan) is a top performer. Even so, the need for upskilling the 21st century skills – or digital skills, as they are defined in the EU key competences – in the rapidly changing and digitalizing world is clear.

As this McKinsey report *How the world's best-performing school systems come out on top* formulates, "The quality of an education system cannot exceed the quality of its teachers" (http://mckinseyonsociety.com/downloads/reports/Education/Worlds_School_Systems_Final.pdf)

Nowadays in Finland, much of the working-life linked education and training relies heavily on the recognition of prior learning. The TVET curriculums are competence based, and all students have personalised learning plans on primary and secondary level education. Particularly digital skills are in many cases obtained in non-formal or informal contexts.

There is a clear trend that teachers do not attend typical training days as often as they did previously. On one hand, they prefer to take care of their daily duties, on the other hand, they state that a day spent in training is not a very contemporary way of upskilling.

The learner's role has changed a lot as digitalization has changed the patterns of information retrieval and creation. From the point of life-long learning, learners must have more self-initiative and learn to share and promote their own competences. This has lead to the emergence of new kinds of training methods, e.g. MOOCs (massive open online courses) and particularly cMOOCs where peer mentoring and collaborative learning are central.

All these changes put pressure to move forward from traditional further professional training to more flexible and learner-centric methods.

2. THE NEW APPROACH TO EDUCATORS' FURTHER PROFESSIONAL TRAINING: CASE LEARNING ONLINE

Three Finnish educational institutes – Omnia, The Joint Authority of Education in Espoo Region, Oulu University of Applied Sciences / School of Vocational Teacher Education, and HAMK School of Vocational Teacher Education – have developed a gamified and open badge based MOOC to strengthen the pedagogical and digital skills of teachers and trainers in the TVET and polytechnic sectors. This project called "Learning Online" ("Oppiminen Online" in Finnish, see http://www.oppiminenonline.com/in-english), was originally a limited 1.5 year project, planned to end in December 2015. Due to its popularity, it continues today and may expand to a comprehensive national programme for teachers further professional training.

"Learning Online" consists of a 2-day boot camp, online training and an open badge based system for getting competencies recognized. In order to join a team and be included the gamification, teachers had to participate in all of these. In order just to get recognized, they could (and still can) skip the boot camp and trainings and just apply for badges. This recognition of prior learning is a central method for validating the ICT competences of teachers and trainers, since much of it has been achieved informally and non-formally.

During the boot camp, the participants got a chance to plan their own personal learning pathway on fulfilling their professional needs. Participants of the boot camps formed three teams to support social aspects of learning, like peer support, team spirit and sharing of best practices.

Apart from the bootcamps, all of the training was given online including weekly webinars in Adobe Connect, and counselling and peer mentoring in a Facebook group. All the webinars were recorded and are freely available on the project site under the Creative Commons CC BY-NC-SA (4.0) licence.

The competences that teachers were gaining during the project were based on the national "ope.fi" teacher ICT skill identification system. (See Finnish website http://opefi.wikispaces.com) The system is not a standard, but a three-level framework, offered as a nationwide guideline. It is a wide structure derived from management and working culture designed for managing online learning environments and collaborative pedagogies. For the needs of "Learning Online", four areas of expertise in which the training and the badges were defined:

- ICT Tools for Learning
- Pedagogical Models
- Networks in Projects and Development
- Enriched Learning

Under these areas, 50 limited skills/competencies were defined and badges created, eg. "Facebook in counselling" or "Pedagogy for authentic learning environments". The badges were designed so that the simply having the knowledge of tools or methods as such did not suffice. The applicants had to show how they had applied or designed to apply this knowledge in a practical setting. This means that they had to reach higher order thinking skills as defined in the Bloom's taxonomy (rev.).

The system was set up in a badge creation and management system called OpenBadgeFactory.com, where the badges were created, applications handled and where all information on the badges and achievements reside. The teachers find the badge applications on www.oppiminenonline.com site, send their application and an expert of the organizing institution reviews them. If the application is approved, the teacher gets an email containing the link to the badge. Otherwise the teacher is asked to improve the application.

The participants set up their own badge backpack. In the beginning, the Mozilla Backpack service was used, but when OpenBadgePassport.com came available, that became the standard solution, as it provided a more flexible environment. From there, the badge earners can share either badges or sets of badges directly to LinkedIn, Facebook or as hyperlinks in job applications, emails or other communication channels.

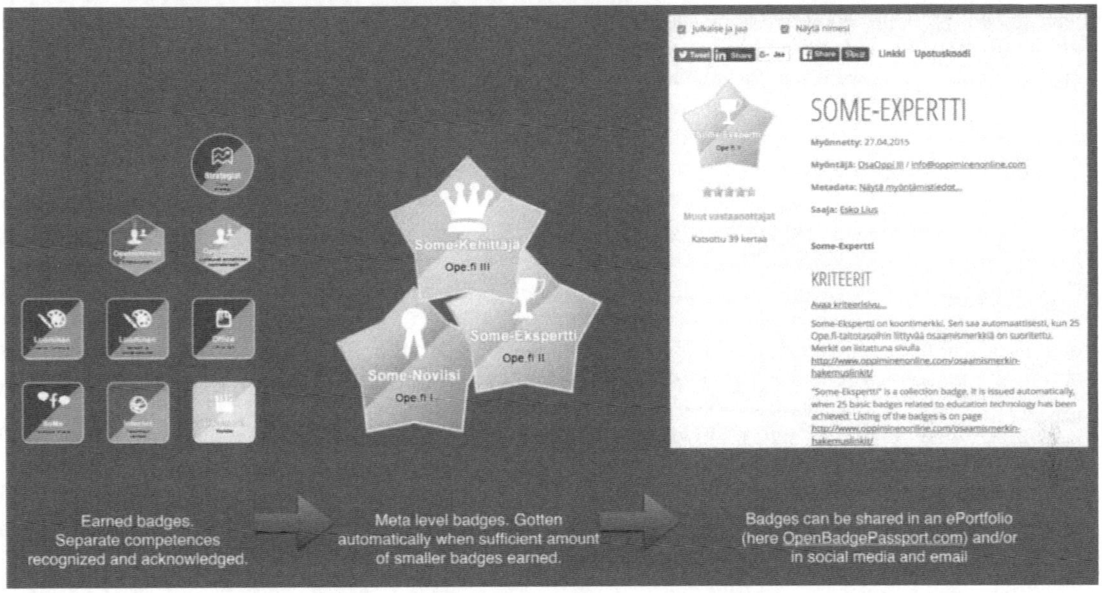

Figure 1. Process of applying and gaining open badges in Learning Online

Example on a badge application and an earned badge:

- Digital Strategies badge: application, https://openbadgefactory.com/c/earnablebadge/NE3EPMdK0Pd2/apply
- Badge in the earner's portfolio (including criteria and evidence): https://openbadgepassport.com/badges/badge_info/944/280

The major difference between an open badge and a traditional certificate is that not only the criteria, but the evidence is open and can be assessed by anyone that the badge has been shared with. In this case the badge is also a sign of a personal and practical professional skill, contrary to the traditional training certificates that indicate that a person has attended a certain kind of a training.

The boot camps were held in each city of the three organizing institutes: Espoo, Hämeenlinna, and Oulu. The camp participants formed three groups, and started competing with each other on which group would get the biggest amount of badges during the 13 months before the end of the project. Various methods were used to keep the fire burning: facilitation and competition hosting on Facebook, small prizes every month, a bigger prize for the overall winning team, etc.

The results of using open badges in further professional training have been very positive, as Learning Online exceeded the set goals. Instead of the targeted 800 badges, over 4300 were applied for by 414 applicants and over 3700 were approved. 16% of applications required further consulting by the reviewing experts.

377 Learning Online users have rated the badges' values. An average rating of all the badges is 4/5 stars. The competence criteria have been viewed approximately 42,000 times.

Considering the active use, the ratings, direct feedback and the sector media coverage, the pilot project was successful. That has lead to a decision to continue Learning Online after the initial pilot. Now there are negotiations for granting special national financing for expanding this pilot towards a common national model also for general education teachers.

For an educational organization, badges provide an effective tool to collect and analyse information on the competences of the staff. If the teachers allow, their badge data can be imported to their relevant HR systems, and the management can view and analyse the situation of the various departments. Thus, the learning analytics provided by badge statistics form a base for staff development. From the earner's point of view, the badge-based portfolio offers a tool to organize and share all imaginable areas of expertise, to be shared flexibly as relevant sets for each need or occasion.

3. CONCLUSION

The case at hand presents the advantages of designing competence development for teachers' on the basis of gamification and open badges.

Gamification proved to be one of the success factors behind the project. Showing the current amount of badges for each team encouraged the participants to gain more. It also encouraged teachers to collaborate and help their peers. The "Learning Online" Facebook group was actively utilised for raising teams' spirits. The organizers regularly gave out small prizes for notable achievers, and the winning team got a grand prize at the end of the project.

Open badges offered a tool and platform opportunity for this new kind of teacher upskilling. As the organizers defined the badges, criteria and shared the work loads together, it was easy to get the system up and running. Because of the qualitative nature of the applications – teachers had to describe their application of the competences – handling the applications has been time-consuming. The next step may be designing a crowd-sourced system of assessing applications. For example, a teacher who has already gained all badges that relate to the "Google" category might be eligible to review new applications for that category, and get a "Reviewer Badge" for completing that activity.

REFERENCES

Cort, P. & al, 2009. *PROFF – Professionalisation of VET teachers for the future*. Fetched 12.3.2016. Available http://www.cedefop.europa.eu/en/publications-and-resources/publications/5156

How the world's best-performing school systems come out on top, 2007. McKinsey & Company. Fetched 20.3.2016. http://mckinseyonsociety.com/downloads/reports/Education/Worlds_School_Systems_Final.pdf

Knight, E. & Casilli, C., 2012. Mozilla Open Badges. In *Game Changers. Education and information technologies*. EDUCAUSE, 279-284. Fetched 16.3.2016. https://net.educause.edu/ir/library/pdf/pub7203cs6.pdf

OECD Skills Outlook 2013: First Results from the Survey of Adult Skills, 2013. OECD Publishing. Fetched 20.3.2016. http://dx.doi.org/10.1787/9789264204256-en

Ope.fi eli Opetustoimen henkilöstön digiosaamisen viitekehys. Fetched 1.4.2016. Available http://opefi.wikispaces.com/

Oppiminen Online

HOW DO K-12 STUDENTS' MANAGE APPLICATIONS ON THEIR MOBILE DEVICES?

Ruthi Aladjem and Sharon Hardof
Tel Aviv University

ABSTRACT

Personal information management (PIM) is a research field that examines the activities by which users save, organize and retrieve personal information items. PIM is a one of the essential new literacies for learners in the 21st century. This paper reports results from a pilot study that explored PIM practices and strategies of k-12 students, on their mobile devices. The results reveal three practices of organizing mobile applications: Never Organize (applications are left in the default location), Organize Occasionally (applications are organized periodically) and Organize Immediately (applications are organized as soon as they are downloaded). Three main strategies for organizing the applications were found: Organization by frequency of use and relevance, Organization by themes and Organization by visual cues. Finally, it was found that when trying to allocate applications on their mobile device, most students prefer to swipe the screens, rather than use the search option, even if it means going back and forth several times. The study is a part of a larger research which examines PIM strategies on mobile devices by adults and children.

KEYWORDS

Personal Information Management, Mobile Learning, K-12.

1. INTRODUCTION

Personal information management (PIM) is a research field that examines the activities by which users save, organize and retrieve personal information items on a daily basis (Jones, 2008). PIM processes were found to be closely connected to functional, cognitive and emotional processes and therefor, are a significant part of learning processes in the digital age (Hardof-Jaffe & Nachmias, 2013). In general, PIM practices have four main objectives: information capturing and retention for later use; finding and organizing information across applications; reminders and attention management and finally, managing versions, controlling clutter, and combatting fragmentation (Jones et al., 2015). A study comparing high school students to adults, in respect to personal information management practices on a PC, concluded that there are age discrepancies in PIM practices and skills; high school students show less tendency to manage personal information, compared to older students (in college or university) and that the organizational strategies of younger students are largely driven by short-term, functional goals (Hardof-jaffe & Nachmias, 2013).

The mobile device has become an integral part of our daily lives, carried around everywhere, at all times and used for versatile needs and objectives. Mobile devices are used for a wide range of personal information related purposes, including creating documents and notes, recording audio notifications, drawing diagrams and more (Buttfield-Addison & Lueg, 2013). The interaction with the mobile device is carried through mobile applications. The mobile user may organize the applications by reordering them on the screens and also by placing them in folders. The range and availability of mobile applications is expanding rapidly and thus, the process of organizing the applications on the mobile device and the process of allocating and accessing the applications may be seen as a continuation of the "traditional" PIM tasks of organizing and accessing information items on the personal computer (PC). Mobile technologies have become a major gateway for interacting with information and effectively serve as a personal information space, yet the research on PIM and mobile is quite limited. A recent study on PIM practices of college students on their mobile devices, found four strategies for organizing mobile applications: Classification/Categorization- using folders and screens for classification and categorization of the applications, Frequency of Use- organizing the applications by frequency of use, Position- remembering the location of an application and Visual Clues –

using visual signs in order to allocate applications (Zhang & Liu, 2015). The pilot study presented in this paper, examined PIM strategies of k-12 students for organizing applications as well as strategies of allocating the applications on the personal mobile device.

2. STUDY DESCRIPTION

41 participants aged 8-18 have answered a questionnaire about their PIM practices. The questionnaire included questions regarding the size and scope of the personal mobile space (as depicted by the number of applications downloaded onto the device), the organizational practices of mobile applications, ways of allocating applications and the naming conventions of the mobile folders (for participants who used folders). Results were grouped by 3 age groups: group 1, included 7 participants aged 8-12; group 2, included 22 participants, aged 13-15 and group 3, included 12 participants, aged 16-18.

3. FINDINGS

3.1 Scope of the Personal Information Space

It was found that the average size of the personal information space (as depicted by the number of applications), was 30.6 applications and the average number of screens was 3 screens per device. 39% of the participants chose not to use folders at all for organizing the applications. The remaining 61% used 3.8 folders on average, with the largest number of folders per device being 9. It was found that the younger participants (group 1, ages 8-12), were less likely to create folders with 14.3% (representing only one participant) using one or more folders and 85.7% who did not use any folders at all.

Table 1. Scope of personal application space

Age group	Average number of screens	Average number of applications	Percentage with no folders	Average number of folders
1	3.6	26.3	85.7	1.0
2	2.6	34.8	22.7	3.9
3	3.3	26.2	41.7	3.7
Total	3	30.6	39.0	3.8

3.2 Organization and Allocation Strategies

When asked about the practices of organizing the applications, 48.8% of the participants reported that they tend to arrange the applications on their mobile device every once in a while, on an occasional basis. 26.8% of the participants reported that they organize their mobile space each time and immediately after downloading a new application, and 24.4% of the participants, stated that they do not organize their mobile space at all and leave the applications in their default location and order. When examining the variation between age groups, it was discovered that in the younger group (group 1) no one had reported organizing the applications immediately post download.

Table 2. Frequency of Organization

Age group	Organize Immediately (%)	Never Organize (%)	Organize Occasionally (%)
1	0.0	42.9	57.1
2	27.3	18.2	54.5
3	41.7	25.0	33.3
Total	26.8	24.4	48.8

Three key strategies for organizing the applications were found: Organization by Frequency and Relevance refers to organizing the applications based on the usage, with the most commonly used applications first, for example: "*the first ones are the one I use most: WhatsApp, Instagram, photos, YouTube all on the first screen".* Organization by Themes refers to categorizing the applications into meaningful groups, for example: "*I use folders according to topics such as games, photography etc.*" Organization by Design, refers to organizing the applications by visual qualities, such as the color of the icon of the application or by its shape, for example: "*I organize the screens by color (whites and blacks on one screen, green and blue on a screen and yellow, red and orange on another screen), It helps me feel better oriented on the mobile*". Several participants combine strategies. For example, one participant uses both the themes and frequency of use strategies: "*I put the applications in folders by subjects, except for the applications that I use most- I leave them out and organize them on the second screen*"

Two strategies were found for allocating the applications on the personal mobile device: Swiping refers to moving between screens and Searching refers to using the mobile search option. It was found that 85.4% of the participants use Swiping. Analyzing the allocation strategy by age group revealed that the younger group (group 1) did not use the search option at all, whereas search was used in the two older groups, though it was less popular than swiping.

Table 3. Allocation Strategies

Age group	Swipe	Search
1	100	0
2	77.3	22.7
3	91.7	8.3

3.3 Folder Naming Conventions

Two participants stated that they use the default names when creating folders (when a new folder is created, a default name is assigned automatically by the operating system), others chose to name folders based on topics (such as "Fashion" or "Social") by functionality (such as "Daily" or "Unnecessary"). One participant reported that she renames the folders using visual signs: "*I use Emoji to name the folders. For example, a camera icon (photography), music note icon (music), Earth icon (maps) etc.*"

4. DISCUSSION AND CONCLUSIONS

Personal information items are regarded as "Digital Possessions" and have become a part of the individual's identity, holding personal value and becoming an "extension of the self" (Cushing, 2013). Previous studies have found that organizing the personal information space is a key process which allows users to take ownership, as well as to reflect on their personal digital space (Hardof-Jaffe & Nachmias, 2013). The three practices that were found on our study for organizing applications (Occasional, Immediate and Never), may reflect different perceptions and mental models of the mobile as a personal information space. Specifically, the tendency to immediately organize the applications, as soon as they have been downloaded (the Immediate practice), may indicate the existence of a solid and well-structured mental model of the personal mobile information space. On the other hand, choosing to leave the applications in their default location with no organization at all may indicate a lack of classification and a less structured mental model. Further research should investigate a possible correlation between organizing the mobile space and the sense of ownership and control of the non-organizers over their mobile information space, in comparison to users who regularly organize the information items. It may also be worthwhile to compare the efficiency of allocating application between regular organizers and non-organizers.

Creating folders and assigning them with meaningful labels, essentially requires associating the newly acquired information item with existing ones. While performing this activity, users engage in cognitive processes, such as classification, sorting, grouping, naming and filtering and in knowledge construction processes (Hardof-Jaffe et al., 2009). However, this study found that 39% of the participants did not use any, which raises questions about the lever of ownership over their personal mobile space.

The majority (85.4%) of the participants in this study prefer to use swiping over search, as means for allocating applications on their mobile device. Swiping consists of moving back and forth between screens while scanning the application icons, in search of the required application. Further research is needed in order to better understand the allocation strategy. Analyzing aspects such as the number of times that users swipe back and forth, the time it takes to allocate each application and the visual clues (such as the color of the application), may lead to a deeper understanding of the allocation mechanism as well as ways of better supporting and assisting users with allocating applications in a more efficient way.

The analysis by age groups revealed that none of the participants in the younger age group (group 1, ages 8-12) organizes applications immediately after download, compared to 41.7% of the older group age (group 3, ages 16-18) that organize applications immediately after downloading. On average, it was found that the scope of the mobile information space consists of 30.6 applications, a substantial amount of items to handle, especially at a young age. The difference between age groups may stem from factors such as cognitive discrepancies (implying that the PIM competency is not yet fully developed in the younger age group) or functional aspects (such as the possibility that each group has different needs). Further research is needed on the factors underlying the differences.

Finally, it is worth noting that the mobile device often serves as the first personal digital information space for K-12 students. Hence, engaging in mobile PIM activities may be the first step in the ongoing, life long process of building a PIM literacy, which is one of the essential literacies for learners in the digital age (Mioduser et al., 2008). Although this pilot study is limited in size and scope, it provides an initial understanding of the ways in which K-12 students manage their personal mobile space. We plan to expand this study, in order to gain a deeper perspective on the ways in which users of all ages manage their personal mobile space and on strategies for supporting the process of constructing the PIM literacy.

REFERENCES

Buttfield-Addison, P., Lueg, C., & Ellis, L., 2013. iPad as PIM device: input, interrelation and indexes. *iConference 2013 Proceedings* (pp. 589-592).

Cushing, A. L., 2013. "It's stuff that speaks to me": Exploring the characteristics of digital possessions. *Journal of the American Society for Information Science and Technology,* 64(8), 1723-1734.

Hardof-Jaffe, S., Hershkovitz, A., Abu-Kishk, H., Bergman, O., & Nachmias, R., 2009. Students' organization strategies of personal information space. *Journal of Digital Information,* 10(5), 1-17.

Hardof-Jaffe, S., & Nachmias, R., 2013. Students' personal information management. In Proceedings of the World Conference on Educational Multimedia, Hypermedia and Telecommunications (pp. 820-828).

Jones, William, 2008. Keeping Found Things Found. *Morgan Kaufmann* .

Jones, W., Capra, R., Diekema, A., Teevan, J., Pérez-Quiñones, M., Dinneen, J. D., & Hemminger, B., 2015. For Telling the Present: Using the Delphi Method to Understand Personal Information Management Practices. In *Proceedings of the 33rd Annual ACM Conference on Human Factors in Computing Systems* (pp. 3513-3522). ACM.

Mioduser, D., Nachmias, R., & Forkosh-Baruch, A., 2008. New literacies for the knowledge society. *International handbook of information technology in primary and secondary education* (pp. 23-42). Springer US.

Zhang, P., & Liu, C., 2015. Personal Information Management Practices of Chinese College Students on their Smartphones. *In Proceedings of the Third International Symposium of Chinese CHI on ZZZ* (pp. 47-51). ACM.

DIGITAL STORYTELLING FOR INCLUSIVE EDUCATION: AN EXPERIENCE IN INITIAL TEACHER TRAINING

Marco Lazzari
University of Bergamo
Department of Human and Social Sciences
Piazzale Sant'Agostino 2 – I-24124 Bergamo ITALY

ABSTRACT

We present an experience of digital storytelling conducted as part of a course for initial teacher training. The students of a special education course produced a digital story as partial fulfillment of their distance learning assignment. We describe the structure of the work completed by the students and discuss the results of a questionnaire they filled out after the course, which aimed to gather their opinions about the experience. The experience was agreeable to the students, with many stating that they are likely to repeat the process in their school, either by developing stories themselves or by engaging their future pupils as designers and developers.

KEYWORDS

Digital storytelling, multimedia communication, initial teaching training, inclusion, digital competence, Universal Design for Learning

1. INTRODUCTION

The pedagogical value of storytelling is widely documented in the literature. Bettelheim (1976) suggests that classic narration of fairy tales, in addition to being entertaining, enriches children's lives, stimulates their imagination and helps them clarify their emotions, recognize their difficulties and find solutions to the problems that trouble them. Bruner (1986) highlights the cognitive, social and emotional value of storytelling for children by asserting that stories are elective tools that foster language development and build and enrich vocabulary and knowledge about the world, in accordance with the active forms of learning (Fontichiaro, 2007).

The importance of storytelling is not limited to early childhood, but crosses age barriers and reverberates across multiple fields of knowledge, from literature to philosophy and from the social sciences to physics (Nash, 1990) and mathematics (Schiro, 2004).

The growth and diffusion of digital media tools in recent years has favored the birth and popularity of digital storytelling (DST), a new kind of narrative immediately perceived as a suitable method for ensuring the interest and motivation of teachers and students (Hung et al., 2012; Robin, 2006, 2008; Sadik, 2008; Yuksel et al., 2011), for promoting narrative skills in children (Cassell and Ryokai, 2001), for encouraging positive attitudes towards working in groups (Di Blas et al., 2012) and for enhancing the experience of learning a foreign language (Casta, 2013; Nguyen et al., 2014).

Two areas for DST application that quickly attracted the attention of researchers were those of teacher education (Coutinho, 2010; Heo, 2011; Skouge and Rao, 2009; Tendero, 2006) and education of pupils with special needs (Botturi et al., 2014; Michalski et al., 2005).

Our research stands at the intersection of those two domains, offering a way to apply and discuss methods for communicating with pupils with special educational needs within a special education course offered to the students of an initial secondary school teacher training degree.

2. THE EXPERIENCE

The experience presented here took place during an initial teacher training course held at the University of Bergamo (Italy) in 2015.

It should be noted that in Italy, in order to be admitted to the public recruitment competition for secondary school teachers, after a 3+2 university career one has to complete a pre-service teaching training course (TFA) managed by a university under the supervision of the regional school office. Given that most students are already temporary substitute teachers in schools, the courses are provided in the afternoons and on weekends. This means that the same people who are students in the evening, have their own pupils in the morning.

Two groups of TFA students were exposed to our experimentation: one group of prospective teachers of literature, and one group of prospective teachers of mechanics and technical drawing.

Each of the students had to take part in a special education module comprising 30 hours of classroom teaching and 36 hours of distance learning. As partial fulfillment of the latter requirement, the students were requested to create a short sample (five minutes) of digital storytelling, to be developed by weaving together text, images, music, audio narration and possibly video. Given that the students had no experience of DST and were unfamiliar with the multimedia tools to be used, they were instructed both through short demonstrations during class time, and through documentation and examples uploaded to the e-learning platform.

The initiative had several direct and indirect educational purposes:

1) implementing a form of engaging e-learning for students who spend their mornings at work, their afternoons attending courses and their evenings studying and completing (often boring) e-learning tasks;

2) promoting digital storytelling and media composition skills suitable for TFA students to use in schools to communicate with their current or future pupils;

3) raising awareness of opportunities for involving secondary school pupils in developing original digital stories; and

4) encouraging reflective experimentation of a design methodology inspired by Universal Design for Learning (Rose and Meyer, 2002), in keeping with the content of the special education course.

The experiment was anchored to the field of research that has led to the development of the multimedia learning theory (Mayer, 2005), but also considered evidence that media production activities carried out by students are often heavily time consuming and generate ineffective products, and that the same can be said of the development of multimedia artifacts by teachers, shifting (perhaps) the emphasis from effectiveness to efficiency.

The task that was proposed to the participants was highly structured (inspired by the Coursera MOOC *Powerful Tools for Teaching and Learning: DST*, held by Bernard Robin and Sara McNeil of the University of Houston), so that between the lessons (spaced 7–10 days apart) each student had to engage in a production- and/or evaluation-phase, according to the following scheme:

Step 1: Choice of subject and purpose: the fundamental elements of DST and the essential features of a good story were introduced; the students chose a topic and defined the educational goal for their story which was to be created in the following weeks. Everyone published a summary of their storyboard on the e-learning platform, including (1) title; (2) target audience; (3) aim/strong educational idea; (4) possible use of the story in a formal, non-formal or informal educational setting; and (5) main idea to be retained by the audience.

Step 2: Setup of an effective script and creation of a storyboard: the focus was shifted to the draft of the script (screenplay), and steps for developing an effective plot were highlighted. Issues of picture selection, including size, type, quality and ownership, and the best way to create a storyboard were also addressed. The weekly task for this stage was twofold, with each student:

(1) evaluating the stories of (at least) three colleagues by posting on the forum a judgment, which consisted of a score (ranging from 0 – 3) based on six features of the story (known from the beginning of the project) and qualitative written feedback; and

(2) sketching the draft of their script, identifying the images to be used creating a storyboard with text and images and publishing this on the e-platform.

Step 3: Recording: the students learned how to use digital devices to record and edit an audio narration to be coordinated with the pictures they had chosen for their final story. The weekly task consisted of recording the audio (without publication) and evaluating the screenplays of three colleagues. The students were free to use the audio editing program of their choice; however they were shown how to use the free software, Audacity.

Step 4: Integration of multiple digital sources in a DST environment: the students were shown how to merge text, images, audio and video within a multimedia editing program. The weekly task required students to create the final movie, upload it to the Internet and share its web address on the forum. The students were free to use their favorite editing and publishing program; however they were shown how to use the free online video editing service, WeVideo, which allows both the creation and publication of digital stories (see, as examples of the final products, bit.ly/esever, bit.ly/esececi).

Step 5: Final evaluation: each student had to evaluate three movies, using rubrics similar to those in the previous steps.

After the completion of the course, we started to reflect on the experience to assess positive and negative aspects and possible implications. For reasons related to the number of course participants and to the composition of the groups, the analysis focused on students within the literary department, with a total of 41 people (F = 31, M = 10; age $\mu = 29.5$, $\sigma = 4.7$). They were asked to fill in an online questionnaire regarding their experience of DST. The questionnaire was completed by 25 subjects (response rate 61%) and consisted of 23 questions:

- Five of the questions requested an estimate of the time required (in hours) for each step of the program (e.g., How long did it take to complete Task 1, which was idea generation, identification of target audience, goal setting and preparation of the descriptive card?);
- Five of the questions asked how substantial they perceived each of the phases (conception, scripting, audio recording, video editing, and assessment) to be (using a five-point Likert scale; e.g., On a scale from *really light* to *really heavy*, how would you rate the audio recording phase?;
- Six of the questions were designed to assess students' satisfaction with the initiative and any intention to reproduce it in their school (using a five-point Likert scale, from -2 to +2; e.g., To what extent do you agree with the following sentence: 'I have acquired skills that I will use at school'?; 'For a teacher the use of DST may prove effective in communicating with pupils'; 'I think it will happen to me to ask my pupils to develop DST products');
- Seven of the questions focused on the skills of the respondents, as perceived by them (using a five-point Likert scale from -2 to +2; e.g., If at this moment I were asked to generate in Word (or Writer or similar) the table of contents of a document, I would know how to do it).

A provided space for comments was used by 10 subjects.

The questionnaire was anonymous and confidential, with a clause allowing the use of data in aggregate form for research and teaching purposes. It was decided not to include requests for personal information (sex, age and years of education) since the questionnaire had a small study sample and personal questions could have instilled suspicion of being tracked.

3. RESULTS AND DISCUSSION

Students' achievements and performances exceeded teacher expectations. The final evaluations of the stories produced by the students, based on the same quality model and the same rubrics proposed to them for their mutual evaluations, showed the experience to be more than satisfactory, as the average final score was 8.6 out of 10 ($\sigma = 1.5$). Moreover, final informal meetings following the conclusion of the course verified that the experience had fostered meaningful learning. For these reasons, we decided to activate the survey in order to collect the students' opinions, which are briefly summarized here.

The students' overall satisfaction with the type of assignment was rather high ($\mu = 1.30$, $\sigma = 0.97$), as were beliefs that they had acquired valuable skills ($\mu = 1.30$, $\sigma = 0.76$); these two opinions were fairly correlated ($\rho = 0.47$), whereas the correlation between satisfaction and initial expectations was much lower ($\rho = -0.23$). No influence of perceived expertise was detected (items with Cronbach alpha = 0.6).

The comments collected through the text field confirmed the numerical data: the experience was defined as "*exciting*", "*very useful, inspiring*", "*tough but really educational*", "*creative, and to be proposed to my pupils*", "*positive and constructive*", and as an activity that "*intrigued, amused, stimulated and fascinated*" and provided "*final gratification once the work was finished*". Two-thirds of the group said they were likely to use DST as a tool for their own classes ($\mu = 0.96$, $\sigma = 0.93$) and the same percentage plan to let their students use it ($\mu = 0.83$, $\sigma = 0.89$).

We cannot hide that the sample choice, made up of people presumably familiar with storytelling, may have introduced a significant bias; however, the opposite is also true, since they were not particularly skilled with computer programs and thus plausibly wary of educational technology. On the other hand, we attained similar results and agreement from the students excluded from the questionnaire, whose backgrounds were symmetric to those of the students being investigated.

With reference to the efficiency of the experience, the data collected regarding the time required to complete the different tasks yielded an average of 18.5 hours ($\sigma = 8.2$), which took into account the design and development phases only, and not the evaluations. This seems to be rather high, considering that the final product only runs for about five minutes (those who used tools other than WeVideo delivered longer stories), but one should take into account that almost all of the students devoted a great deal of time to learning new tools (as well as looking for pictures). Moreover, the anxiety factor for the exam certainly multiplied the number of checks and revisions performed by the novice DST authors and expanded the required times. All in all, it can be assumed that a large number of the students might eventually develop products more efficiently in the future.

4. CONCLUSIONS

We have presented an experience of using digital storytelling as a tool for effective teaching and meaningful learning. It was used during pre-service training for prospective secondary school teachers within the e-learning program of a special education course.

Despite the students' limited initial competences in DST, their final achievements satisfied the lecturer, and the students appreciated the initiative and expressed intentions to replicate it with their own pupils.

As far as future research into this area is concerned we are going to use a quality model, which takes into account multimedia communication principles, to compare the final digital storytelling products of these students with those of another group of students, who have developed PowerPoint slides for PechaKucha-style examinations. This will enable us to understand which modality is more effective and suitable for unleashing students' creativity and communication skills.

ACKNOWLEDGEMENT

I wish to thank my brilliant and patient students of TFA 2015, with my best wishes for their careers as teachers.

REFERENCES

Bettelheim, B., 1976. *The Uses of Enchantment: The Meaning and Importance of Fairy Tales*. Knopf, New York, USA.

Botturi, L. et al., 2014. Digital Storytelling for Social and International Development: From Special Education to Vulnerable Children. *International Journal of Arts and Technology*, Vol. 7, No. 1, pp. 92-111.

Bruner, J., 1986. *Actual Minds, Possible Worlds*. Harvard University Press, Cambridge, USA.

Cassell, J., & Ryokai (2001). Making Space for Voice: Technologies to Support Children's Fantasy and Storytelling. *Personal and ubiquitous computing*, Vol. 5, No. 3, pp. 169-190.

Casta, M.E., 2013. "I am Proud that I did it and it's a Piece of me": Digital Storytelling in the Foreign Language Classroom. *CALICO Journal*, Vol. 30, No. 1, pp. 44-62.

Coutinho, C., 2010. Storytelling as a Strategy for Integrating Technologies into the Curriculum: An Empirical Study with Post-Graduate Teachers. *Proceedings of the Society for Information Technology and Teacher Education International Conference 2010*. AACE, Chesapeake, USA, pp. 3795-3802.

Di Blas, N. et al., 2012. Collective Digital Storytelling at School: A Whole-Class Interaction. *International Journal of Arts and Technology*, Vol. 5, No. 2-4, pp. 271-292.

Fontichiaro, K., 2007. *Active Learning Through Drama, Podcasting, and Puppetry*. Libraries Unlimited, Westport-London, UK.

Heo, M., 2011. Improving Technology Competency and Disposition of Beginning Pre-Service Teachers with Digital Storytelling. *Journal of Educational Multimedia and Hypermedia*, Vol. 20, No. 1, pp. 61-81.

Hung, C.-M. et al., 2012. A Project-Based Digital Storytelling Approach for Improving Students' Learning Motivation, Problem-Solving Competence and Learning Achievement. *Educational Technology & Society*, Vol. 15, No. 4, pp. 368-379.

Mayer R., 2005. *The Cambridge Handbook of Multimedia Learning*. Cambridge University Press, New York, USA.

Michalski, P. et al., 2005. Digital Storytelling in the Middle Childhood Special Education Classroom: A Teacher's Story of Adaptations. *Teaching Exceptional Children Plus*, Vol. 1, No. 4, A. 3.

Nash, C., 1990. *Narrative in Culture*. Routledge, London, UK.

Nguyen, K. et al., 2014. Storytelling in Teaching Chinese as a Second/Foreign Language. *Linguistics and Literature Studies*, Vol. 2, No. 1, pp. 29-38.

Robin, B.R., 2006. The Educational Uses of Digital Storytelling. Proceedings of the Society for Information Technology and Teacher Education International Conference 2006. AACE, Chesapeake, USA, pp. 709-716.

Robin, B.R., 2008. Digital Storytelling: A Powerful Technology Tool for the 21st Century Classroom. *Theory Into Practice*, Vol. 47, No. 3, pp. 220-228.

Rose, D. and Meyer, A., 2002. *Teaching Every Student in the Digital Age: Universal Design for Learning*. Association for Supervision and Curriculum Development, Alexandria, USA.

Sadik, A., 2008. Digital Storytelling: A Meaningful Technology-Integrated Approach for Engaged Student Learning. *Educational Technology Research and Development*, Vol. 56, No. 4, pp. 487-506.

Schiro, M.S., 2004. Oral Storytelling and Teaching Mathematics: Pedagogical and Multicultural Perspectives. Sage, Thousand Oaks, USA.

Skouge, J.R. and Rao, K., 2009. Digital Storytelling in Teacher Education: Creating Transformations through Narrative. *Educational Perspectives*, Vol. 42, No. 1-2, pp. 54-60.

Tendero, A., 2006. Facing Versions of the Self: The Effects of Digital Storytelling on English Education. *Contemporary Issues in Technology and Teacher Education*, Vol. 6, No. 2, pp. 174-194.

Yuksel, P. et al., 2011. Educational Uses of Digital Storytelling all Around the World. *Proceedings of the Society for Information Technology and Teacher Education International Conference 2011*. AACE, Chesapeake, USA, pp. 1264-1271.

LEARNING FACTORY - ASSEMBLING LEARNING CONTENT WITH A FRAMEWORK

Peter Steininger
FOM – Hochschule für Oekonomie und Management gGmbH, Steubenstraße 44, 68163 Mannheim, Germany

ABSTRACT

Many of the challenges currently facing lectures are symptoms of problems with learning content creation, development and presentation. Learning Factory solves these problems by integrating critical innovations that have been proven over the last ten to twenty years in different industrial areas, but have not yet been brought or ported together in higher education. We explain that a Learning Factory Framework is a configuration of processes, templates, patterns, and tools that can be used to rapidly and cost-effectively produce an open-ended set of unique variants of a "standard product" (learning content). The new methodology promises to industrialize content creation, first by supporting the creation and development process of content, auto-mating the assembly of the content, and then by connecting these processes across organizational boundaries to form supply chains that organizes distributed teams together.

KEYWORDS

E-Learning content, production, learning factory

1. INTRODUCTION

Nobody knows about the money spend for creating, production and distribution of learning content in higher education in Germany. In any other industry, a result like this would generate a quick response aimed at restoring the bottom line. For the last years, however, everybody has looked only the other way, letting the budget absorb the cost of these production processes. In these less certain economic times, they are now calling to account for underperforming technology.

Are these problems of interest only when the economy is weak? Will they move away into the background again, as the market rebounds, or are there more pervasive and fundamental forces at work?

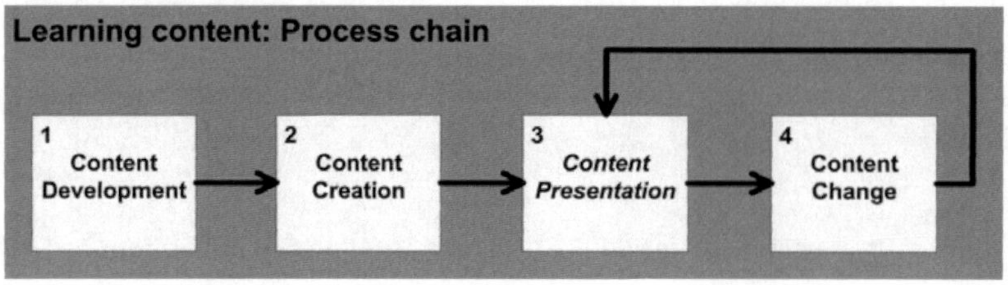

Figure 1. Process chain of learning content over their lifetime

We think the problem is that tools have not kept pace with the learning content development, creation and production. We can use the latest toolset to show video, flash movies or highly interactive content on the web or with Microsoft PowerPoint, but we still hand-stitch every content presentation. We decided to go one-step further and started a line of application to support each process and build a landscape of tools for the production process of learning content.

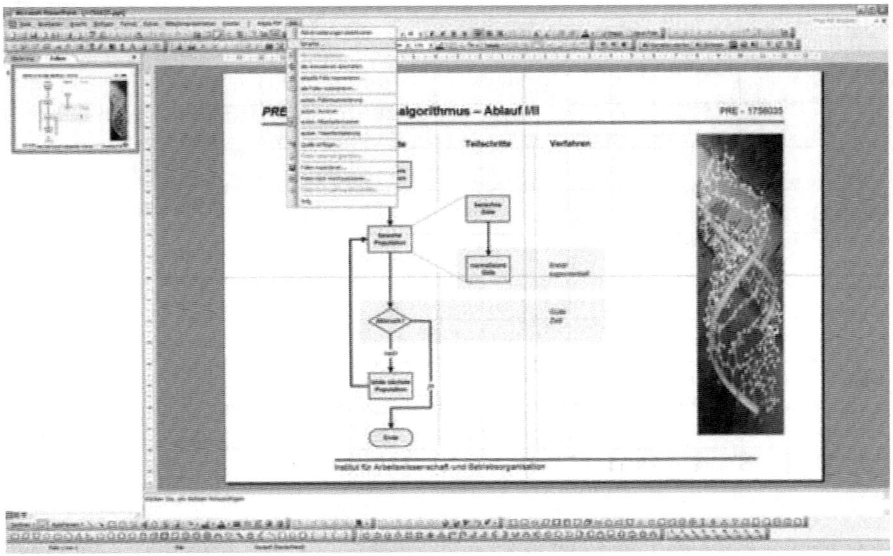

Figure 2. Microsoft PowerPoint with template and Extensions

2. THE LEARNING CONTENT LANDSCAPE

First, we explored the technology and tools, which are used to produce material for our teaching process today. To support this study, we introduce a student worker, and watched him in the process of learning content creation. We then described the architecture of the tools, processes, etc. in just enough detail to expose some of the challenges that the worker encounters using the technologies. At the end, we started to re-define the process of learning content creation with standardized, current methods, tools and best practices learned from the evaluation.

We found key elements, which are very important for our process: slides, presentations, hand out (called script), e-learning content and so on.

The most central application is Microsoft PowerPoint (see Figure 1) for producing slides, and giving presentations. Therefore, the decision to standardize this application for content creation is a vital part.

High production value, rich media content can seldom be produced outside of a team environment – this is the preserve of the professionalized organization. The same team environment produced the best learning materials using traditional media. To enlarge productivity in the team for the digital world, we have to support the team with the best tools based on the environment given as a platform for content creation. Only a minority of enthusiasts are able to operate in the production process as solo practitioners without process tools to support their work.

2.1 Presentations

Having PowerPoint addressed as the heart of our process chain for content creation, we extended it with slide templates (POTX-file) for different purposes (e.g. presenting for an audience, web presentation, etc.), different languages (e.g. German, English, and French) and different graphic (screen) resolutions. Having a slide template guaranties each slide has an identical look regarding the formal elements like parts for corporate identity of the institute, references to literature (e.g. same place, same style, etc.), and also not so well known elements like size of slide, colors used within the slide (presentation) etc.

In addition, an extension to PowerPoint itself was implemented using the *Microsoft .Net Framework* and *C#*, to support interface *IDTExtensibility2* (Microsoft 2007), which is a door to any Microsoft Office application (see Figure 2) to support and automate our specific interaction of the user with PowerPoint.

By implementing this extension, we have the ability to work with any object (elements of a slide or presentation) from PowerPoint or any other element of an Office application (e.g. document within word, chart within Excel, etc.), create, manipulate, delete and so on.

Now we had the ability to work in a full automated way with each application, specifically PowerPoint. So standardization went one step further to implement such things like:

- automated numbering of slides; giving each slide an identity of creator and a slide history,
- automated template switching; ability to convert the formal parts of a slide to supported teaching languages (German, English, French),
- automated publication to the web; convert a slide for direct integration into our e-learning system,
- standard creation of citation objects,
- etc.

All operations are assembled in one menu and are accessibly like any other menu in PowerPoint. These operations reflect locally to PowerPoint or interact with web service(s) in a service-orientated architecture.

Within a service-oriented architecture solution, services are an important component. The W3C defines service-oriented architecture as "a set of components which can be invoked and whose interface descriptions can be discovered and published" (World Wide Web Consortium 2008). This allows the services that will be consumed to be consumed by whatever business logic is calling them – thus making them platform independent. Further, services could act in isolation of one another. This makes them more resilient to updating and it makes your solutions more scalable. There are other, more complex issues to consider that are outside the scope of this paper, such as security and protocol considerations.

Integrating with PowerPoint directly, we are able to interact and extend the object model. Extending the object model gives us the ability to have not only text on a slide, but also to know if this text is a reference, slide number, graphic a specific type or theme. This means digital knowledge of slides. We have the plan of building slides.

Now it is easy to switch a slide for a German lecture to the format used for an English lecture, automating the transformation of slide template, reference style, and so on.

2.2 Handouts

Another important product for teaching is a script (handout) for students and it was very time consuming to produce one. In the old days, you have to print a slide, produce a scaled photocopy, and assemble it in a binder and so on.

This process is very time consuming and error-prone. So the decision was clear to automate that process also; after researching different products and their cost, we decided to have Microsoft Word as a production environment for handouts.

Secretaries, researches and the easiness of creating a template for handouts with different styles, languages, etc. base this decision on well-known handling of Word and of course, we have already licensed the Microsoft Office suite.

At the beginning of a handout production we have to know which slides are needed for that specific lecture. A reference list (see Figure 3) was introduced, which assigns a slide at specific place in a lecture.

Such a list is implemented inside an intranet portal as a special editor to support building and maintaining such data.

A reference list represents an ordered list of slide numbers (objects), outline text (outline and chapter information, title, etc.), explanations (text, references, etc.), and so on. All data is stored inside a relational, server-based database for later retrieval by production processes.

2.3 Searching

We also integrated a full text index of content in our content archive, which can be used to find slides, graphics, etc. very fast by issuing a query via our internal web portal (see Figure 4), or integrates with PowerPoint and Word through an implemented web service consumed by Office.

Indexing extracts the content by filtering – using filter components that understand a file's format. The format could include multi-language features such as international languages and locales. A filter component implements the filter, which supplies methods to read a file to extract text and properties. Indexing then merges the extracted information into catalogues of indexes for efficient searches. Indexing is the overall process of filtering, creating index entries, and merging them into catalogues.

The final step in the indexing process is creation of a catalogue that contains a master index (and any temporary word lists and shadow indexes) storing words and their locations within a set of indexed documents. Subsequently, searching, or querying, the catalogues for particular word combinations uses the master index as well as word lists and shadow indexes to execute queries quickly and efficiently.

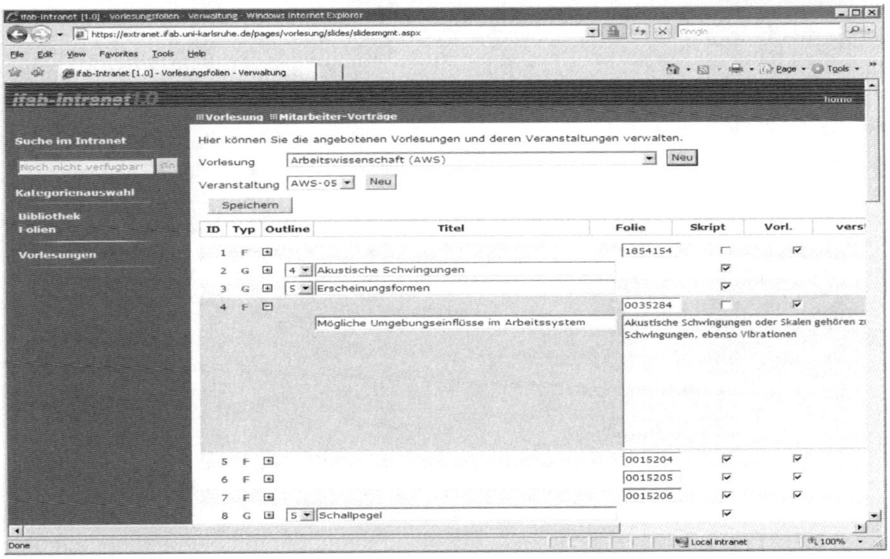

Figure 3. Intranet lecture reference editor

2.4 Benefits

The need to transform how universities produce and work with learning content points to the future, but tools to support them point to the past. It is not a modern, efficient, and flexible process, also in the timeframe of e-learning. The mission of universities is to supply the students with an up-to-date and cost-effective program that yields motivated and skilled students.

Creation processes of learning content are performed in conditions that are fairly well known and their result needs to be guaranteed because even one or few misses are considered unacceptable. This is, like other processes identically to the case of mission critical processes, assembly chain, health care processes etc. In these cases, the process is usually known with precision and the actual activities performed should strictly follow the process. We call this kind of process a hard normative process.

The activities to be performed and their order depend little or not at all on the opinions of the people running the process. This are processes which we can be supported by information technology systems to give creators more time to support student needs.

Indeed, the process is designed so that it is independent of such opinions so that the result is continuously guaranteed, regardless of the people who perform the process.

Many other processes, a lecture process for example, are somewhat different. The activities to be performed and their order are less rigidly prescribed than those in the hard normative process. Some activities may be omitted (such as not talking about a specific slide) and the order of activities can be changed.

Soft normative processes may have different versions and people driving these processes need more time to support customers (students) relying on the process.

Just what is learned is a matter of content, but helping it to happen is a matter of managing the process. In teaching and learning, as in other communicative activities, process is more basic than content. Indeed, without a minimally satisfactory process, content never gets a look in. That process, however, has to be tuned so that it helps rather than hinders learning.

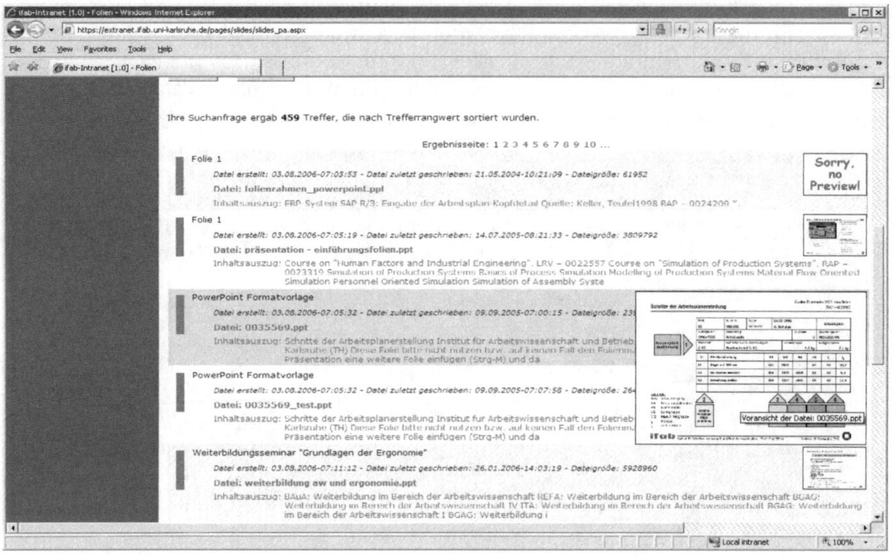

Figure 4. Intranet result of a search query against the content archive

3. CONCLUSION

We have learned many things to improve our internal processes, also we had the possibility to arrange the processes and integrate with them in a computer supported extended process.

We gain a large benefit in not concentrating in sampling slides to presentations or building handouts or lectures. Also finding a specific slide is reduced from asking colleagues, overlooking a binder archive, and so on, to issuing a query with some key words against the content archive. This is the right track and the possibilities are nearly endless, the limit is imagination. We have just built a framework (platform) for an ongoing process integration and improvement.

REFERENCES

Beck, K. and Ralph, J., 1994. Patterns Generates Architectures. *Proceedings of European Conference of Object-Oriented Programming*. Bologna, Italy, pp. 139-149.

Greenfield, Jack and Short, Keith. (2004) Software Factories, First Edition, John Wiley & Sons, Hoboken.

Microsoft Corporation. (2007) Implementing the IDTExtensibility2 Library. http://msdn2.microsoft.com/en-us/library/aa141008(office.10).aspx.

Microsoft Corporation. (2007) Research Services Developer Portal. http://msdn2.microsoft.com/en-us/office/aa905529.aspx.

World Wide Web Consortium. (2008) Web Services Glossary. http://www.w3.org/TR/ws-gloss/.

Reflection Papers

EQUALIZING EDUCATIONAL OPPORTUNITIES BY ICT

Ana María Delgado García and Blanca Torrubia Chalmeta
Universitat Oberta de Catalunya

ABSTRACT

The Open University of Catalonia (UOC) is a pioneer university in the use of technology for online learning. The virtual teaching system enables to acquire professionalizing competences and facilitates the practitioners the update of knowledge in an optimum way. That is possible, on one hand, thanks to the resources for theoretical and practical knowledge that give technical communication tools. And, on the other hand, because of the flexibility that an asynchronous learning model entails. This allows a way of learning far away from classical teaching.

KEYWORDS

Internet, higher education, e-learning, practitioner teaching

1. INTRODUCTION

Nowadays the environment of higher education is evolving and educational institutions are implementing more and more frequently in higher education the e-learning. This fact is creating new and exciting opportunities for both educational institutions and students. Initially introduced to allow individuals in remote and rural areas to gain access to higher education, distance learning has evolved significantly over time. As time goes by, more and more people gain access to the Internet, the cost of computer ownership decreases, and these trends provide educational institutions an ideal way for satisfy needs that traditional education it is not able to do it.

In this context, the Open University of Catalonia (UOC) is the first virtual University in Spain. It is an entirely online university and it follows the trail opened up by other virtual universities which appeared in other countries, in what is known as the third generation of distance learning.

The UOC was created by the Catalan Government in 1994, and from 1996, the School of Law began to develop the Degree Course in Law. Because the UOC is a distance learning institution, in which teaching takes place entirely through the "Virtual Campus" on the Internet, the development of teaching methods is a key part of its activities.

2. THE VIRTUAL EDUCATION. THE EXPERIENCE OF THE OPEN UNIVERSITY OF CATALONIA

From the very beginning, UOC University's mission was to ensure equal access to higher education and knowledge for all sectors of society using information and communications technology (ICT), making ICT an essential tool for democratising education in the knowledge society.

This university was born with a strong will to provide an adequate response to the educational needs of lifelong learning, and to make the best possible use of the great potential that the internet offers us when it comes to developing and providing education. In particular, the main distinguishing feature of the UOC, since its creation, is its educational model, which is learner-centered. This model responds to the need to provide the university with a strong identity of its own and to try to establish a methodology that can overcome the shortcomings of traditional institutions for distance learning in Spain. Moreover, the educational model also tries to suit university students' profiles, and it takes into consideration social and technological factors at the time of its creation, thus striving to guarantee non-discrimination concerning accessibility to technology. In this respect, the students are the protagonists of the training process, by managing their own time, planning their own studying pace and building their own academic itinerary.

The pillars on which this educational model was built, based on learning activities, are flexibility of time and space, personalization, interactivity and cooperation. And the values that UOC is committed to are diversity, participation, quality, innovation, and sustainability.

The university has an online community of around 60,000 students, teachers, and collaborators, spread over more than 50 countries, making it a multicultural institution focused on an international environment.

3. ADVANTAGES OF INFORMATION AND COMMUNITCATION TECHNOLOGIES IN HIGHER EDUCATION

The use of ICTs in higher education makes it possible to acquire knowledge at any time and place, depending on the availability of time and on students' educational needs.

Thus, the main advantages of ICTs are the following.

1. It is a way of adapting to students' needs, since it enables them to combine professional, personal and family commitments with their academic ones.
2. It is more flexible for students, who can study anywhere (at home, at work), and at any time (workday, weekend, holiday, daytime, night-time...). In other words, e-learning does away with inflexible timetables (asynchrony) and can overcome geographical obstacles.
3. It also saves travelling to the campus site, thus saving time (even administrative paperwork can be done via internet). This facilitates continuity in learning.
4. It also favours sustainability because it reduces transportation to the university, saving on energy and contamination by fossil fuels. Further, most of the documentation is stored and presented electronically and keeps from creating waste paper.
5. Thanks to all these factors, new possibilities open up for those who have little time or find it difficult to attend class, because of their job, a disability or another personal reason. Thus, there is a "democratization of higher education".
6. The learning process is not only more flexible, but also more personalised, attention is more individual, as students set their own pace for studying, according to their needs.

Education via the internet is a necessity, if we take into account current changes in our society. In its first years, on-line education was considered a poor alternative to classroom-based learning (Salmon, 2002). However, today the perception of this type of learning among the university community is increasingly positive. This is because on-line learning has proven to be an education model that brings students increasingly close to attaining the educational objectives of the knowledge society, given that the professional world has opted for the wholehearted incorporation of new technologies into its everyday activities. Furthermore, it is a model whereby methodologies and adequate educational resources that ensure quality learning are a key component.

The success of the model of virtual education can be seen, firstly, in the growing appearance of new virtual universities in a large number of countries; secondly, in the widespread use that all non-virtual universities are adding, more and more, of information and communication technologies in their training, so much so that nowadays they too offer exclusively virtual tuition as well as face-to-face and blended learning. Thirdly, because it is a model that, given its circumstances, has incorporated with great ease, the directives of the European Space for Higher Education.

Ensuring that students can navigate easily and confidently in virtual learning environments is no longer purely a tool that is very valuable for education, but is now an essential requirement of the new knowledge-based society in which it is necessary not only to have the sources of information available, but also to be in control of their increasingly complex management.

Distance education systems have always taken the profiles of their students into account more than classroom-based education systems. The explanation for this is that distance universities provided an alternative to classroom-based learning in the form of a system in which efforts were made to personalise the learning process as much as possible.

4. THE UOC'S LEARNING MODEL/EXAMPLE OF THE MASTER IN LAWYERING

The Master in Lawyering is in Spain a mandatory Master after the Law Degree, from 2012. It has a very clear aim: to prepare students to the future legal practice as Lawyers. This Master, according with the Spanish normative, has to be integrated by a training course of 60 ECTS and a practice course of 30 ECTS.

The virtual teaching system enables students to acquire legal professional competences and facilitates update of knowledge to legal practitioners. In fact, a lot of ours students are not only Law graduates but legal practitioners that want to update or to acquire legal competences.

Our 3D platform simulates a lawyer office, as you can see in the following picture.

Figure 1

The study system is based on the continuous assessment activities (CAA) and a work plan that includes delivery dates and solution and correction dates. The Lawyer leaves notes to students and the notes refer to each new case, advices, questions etc.

Simply by clicking on a note, the students can read its contents. For example, a note can tell the students that they have "a new client": a man convicted of domestic violence. So the Lawyer asks the students to start working on the appeal against the sentence, as there is not conclusive evidence.

To work with the case the students will find all the documents relating to it. In the same example, the Lawyer can give the students the Preliminary Ruling in the criminal proceeding and the Forensic Medical Report….

To prepare the work, the students can ask the Lawyer whatever doubt they may have. Just by clicking on the telephone, they can write and send him an e-mail.

The forum is the space where students interact with their classroom's colleagues and the Lawyer. Clicking on the cup of tea the forum appears.

And they can meet with the Lawyer for a simultaneous videoconference (webbex).

To work in groups students use others synchronous and asynchronous tools too (skype, google apps, whats app etc.).

The Lawyer can direct the students to the Youtube UOC's Channel where they can find additional information related to the case, such as specific interviews, news, statements, and trials. They go to the face to face trials with the Lawyer too.

Clicking on the books, the students can access the library where they find sentences, obtain documents and books, contract forms, access databases etc.

In the library students have access to a lot of tools that aid them to solve any legal question and they can also learn to search in an optimal way

To practice oral competences we use Present@, an online tool that allows students and teachers to record their audio and video productions and to view each other's videos

When the work is done, the students click on the tray which allows the work to be sent directly to the Lawyer.

At the RAC (Continuous Assessment Register), the Lawyer registers the marks obtained by the students in all the cases. By clicking the link the student can see the Lawyer's comment to his work.

5. CONCLUSION

Today, in a world where students are becoming the focus of the model throughout the European higher education system, it is clear that ICT are an important tool to equalize educational opportunities. So, Universities should accept this fact and work in the implementation of *on line* educational models.

Our system let all kind of students to develop the same skills and acquire the same knowledge, both with a very satisfactory quality level. This is the reason why e-learning allows to equalize education opportunities and breaking down the physical, spatial and temporal barriers of traditional education.

REFERENCES

Abras, C., Maloney-krichmar, D. and Preece, J. (2004). *User-centered design*. Sims, W. (2004*). Encyclopedia of human computer interaction*. Berkshire Publishing.

Bates, A. W. (2005). *Technology, open learning and distance education*. Routledge: London.

Biggs, J. B. and Tang, C. (2007). *Teaching for quality learning at university*. Open University Press/Mc Graw-Hill Education.

Booth, T. & Ainscow, M. (1998). *From them to us*. London: Routledge.

Kotter, J. P.: Accelerate (2015). *Building Strategic Agility for a Faster-Moving World*. Harvard Business Review.

Kramer, C. (2002). *Success in On-line Learning*. Albany, NY, USA: Delmar Thomson Learning.

Wagner, N., Hassanein, K. and Head, M. (2008). Who is responsible for E-Learning Success in Higher Education? A Stakeholders' Analysis. Journal of Educational Technology & Society. Vol. 11, No. 3.

Pelgrum, W.J. & Anderson, R.E. (2001). *ICT and the emerging paradigm for life-long learning*. Netherlands: International Association for the Evaluation of Educational Achievement.

Salmon, G. (2002). *E-activities. The key to active online learning*. London, UK: Kogan Page.

Tiffin, J. & Rajasingham, L. (2003). *The Global Virtual University*. London: RoutledgeFalmer.

THE ACCEPTABILITY OF MOOC CERTIFICATES IN THE WORKPLACE

Christina Banks and Edward Meinert
Imperial College London
Department of Primary Care and Public Health, Charing Cross Hospital, London

ABSTRACT

Massive open online courses (MOOCs) are being undertaken by hundreds of thousands of participants globally. Reasons for taking these courses vary, such as improving employment prospects, especially in the technology sector, though the impact of these certificates has not been established. Factors identified as barriers to the acceptance of these certifications include user verification issues and a lack of familiarity of MOOC content. There are positive signs in employers recommending MOOCs for training purposes and a major MOOC platform collaborating with companies to provide a work placement scheme. The discussion regarding the value of traditional and online education also applies, as employers are seeking candidates who are technically skilled and ready for work, which is not guaranteed by a traditional degree certificate. This review provides a baseline collation of current opinion and research. Independent qualitative research and further literature review should be conducted to build an evidence base regarding the use of MOOCs and their certificates.

KEYWORDS

MOOC, Employment, Online Education, Certificate

1. INTRODUCTION

Since their inception in 2008, massive open online courses (MOOCs) have proliferated to become a major feature of the online education field. A variety of MOOCs are available, from those which attract tens of thousands of participants worldwide, to courses which are built to train a specific cohort. While some individuals undertake MOOCs out of personal interest, others intend to enhance their employability through gaining certification for completed courses. Although the completion rate of MOOCs is low (generally <10%), increasing numbers are finishing and achieving completion certificates (Jordan, 2014). This raises the question of how these courses and certificates will be received by potential employers, and how they will be viewed in comparison to education obtained through more traditional methods. It is important to compare the factors standing for and against the recognition of these courses in the employment process as part of the movement towards developing standards to be used by recruiters. To date this is a subject not comprehensively addressed in the literature, and this paper sought to review information published or posted regarding the subject thus far, and describe and discuss the points arising.

2. DISCUSSION

There are multiple discussion points concerning the use of MOOCs and their certificates for employment purposes. A central issue is that of the credibility of courses and certificates, and whether or not these can be taken seriously by employers (Krumrie, 2014, Ossiannilsson, 2014). Currently, MOOC providers are developing further methods of verification to reduce the likelihood of fraud or plagiarism by participants in both coursework and assessment, a problem which hinders trust in certificates (Boeckh, 2014). The use of webcams, keystroke analysis, valid photo identification and in-person test centres is being explored by the major MOOC providers in order to definitively verify the identity of participants and confirm that they have completed the work submitted in their name (Boeckh, 2014). At present these efforts are not infallible and require refinement, though employers may choose to test prospective employees on relevant material in order to show up anyone who has falsely claimed to have completed a certain course, and it may be easy to identify these individuals during standard job interviews.

If the credibility of the MOOCs is deemed acceptable then the process of verifying the educational component of the MOOC certificate is crucial if it is to be meaningful to potential employers (Krumrie, 2014). A means of quantifying the knowledge given in courses is required so that the level of education attained is clear to those reading CVs, similar to the widely known qualifications of formal education. Moves towards awarding university credit to MOOCs began in 2013, and have continued in countries across the world. Students in many universities who complete MOOCs, (in most cases) purchase the end of course certification, and have their identity verified, can add the course to their university transcript (Haynie, 2015). This move by academia sets a positive precedent for the recognition of MOOCs in other sectors.

The notion of interpreting MOOCs on CVs is still novel and there are no established standards to aid recruiters in discerning the value of these courses or their impact on the candidate (Krumrie, 2014). Therefore, receptiveness may predominantly be a case of whether the recruiter is familiar with MOOCs and their terminology. Also, due to the novelty, companies may not have had the chance to hire or monitor employees who have previously completed MOOCs, a barrier which may potentially be solved in time. In a 2014 study of North Carolina based human resource professionals, it was found that only 31% had heard of MOOCs, consistent with the general public, though this increased to 50% for respondents from educational organisations. Interviewees who had heard of MOOCs stated they had researched these because of either management enquiries about using them to save costs within the company or through other employees who were undertaking MOOCs, rather than as part of updated recruitment guidelines (Radford et al., 2014). Coursera co-founder Daphne Koller stated in an interview in 2015 that this study showed that a significant uptake of MOOCs by employers was beginning (Koller, 2015).

While increasing numbers of businesses are looking to MOOCs and online education to reinforce or build workforce knowledge and skills, this hasn't translated into them being fully acceptable for recruiting purposes (Ng, 2016). They are seen by some as being a tool to further professional development in their workforce rather than justify the hiring of an individual (Ossiannilsson, 2014). Nevertheless, the use of MOOCs by employers is a positive step, and they are being utilised by companies recommending that employees undertake a certain MOOC available freely on online platforms, or larger institutions such as the NHS which are developing courses to target a particular element which they have identified as requiring improvement (NHS Improving Quality, 2015).

The value of traditional education when hiring is being brought into question, adding another dimension to the discussion on online education (Ma, 2015, Ng, 2016). Some employers, such as Ernst and Young, are blinding recruiters to the details of candidate's university education, and more non-graduates than ever are being hired at Google for jobs which would typically require a degree elsewhere (Andersen, 2014). It is being found that graduates are not leaving university with technical skills which are directly applicable to the working environment – meaning that employees must undergo further training before they are competent to work independently anyway. A recruiter polled by the Success Communications Group noted that a person with online certification usually uses this method as they are balancing full time work alongside their studies and may therefore have more real-world job experience which is attractive to employers, as well as demonstrating their time management skills (Larson, 2013). This being said, the traditional degree and where it was achieved are still the more valued commodities among employers in general, with the element of interpersonal and leadership skills which are developed during the course of degree programmes being as important as entry technical skill level in many settings (Larson, 2013). However, looking to the future, the recruitment environment is changing and the need for any certificates at all may diminish (Winkler, 2014).

This is particularly true in the technology sector, in which a feature of growing importance in recruitment is a practical demonstration of the candidate's abilities, rather than a piece of certification (O'Connor, 2013). The use of portfolios or coursework allows recruiters to see physical evidence of what the applicant is capable of, rather than a certificate of their expertise in a general broad subject (Belleflamme and Jacqmin, 2015, Ng, 2016, Kirsner, 2013, O'Connor, 2013). It was suggested that MOOCs could play a role in this due to the continuous collection of data from students over the duration of the course in order to build a profile of participants which may be of interest to prospective employers (Belleflamme and Jacqmin, 2015). This data and the end products of practical and projects can give a clear picture of what a participant can produce and the manner in which they go about this. However, as mentioned before the reliability of this is subject to increased measures of user verification. Also, with online platforms such as GitHub and Dribble also acting as repositories for portfolios, MOOCs must strive to offer that bit more to students (Ng, 2016). The equivalent in traditional education is the large scale final year dissertation or thesis which gives a comprehensive overview of the student's skills and standard of work; this has the additional benefit of being supervised by Professors or lecturers who can provide trusted references for job applications.

Branching out from issuing certificates to participants, an Open Education Alliance has been launched by the MOOC provider platform Udacity in cooperation with employers such as Google, AT&T, Intuit and Autodesk (Thomas, 2014). These sectors are working in partnership to equip students with the technological skills required to work for these companies, with a view to potentially hiring Udacity "graduates" (Belkin and Porter, 2013, Thomas, 2014, Ng, 2016). This is a promising avenue for MOOC providers to prove the employability of their students, and demonstrates a show of faith from industry.

It is important to consider the participant perspective on what they have gained from MOOCs in terms of employment prospects. A 2015 survey of Coursera MOOC finishers found that 72% of the 51,954 respondents reported having gained career benefits from participating, and 52% had undertaken courses with a primary aim of improving their career. Of those aiming to develop their career, a third reported a tangible benefit of partaking in MOOCs, from finding a new job or receiving a promotion as a result. An even higher percentage, 85%, stated they had received less quantifiable benefits such as enhancing their skills for a current job or improving their candidacy for a new job (Zhenghao et al., 2015). The longer time lag between tangible benefits being seen compared to more abstract benefits may mean that the number of MOOC participants achieving pay increases or new jobs could still increase over time. Although this survey was conducted by Coursera's own staff, there is a clear demonstration that many of those who complete MOOCs are able to use these qualifications or certifications to advance their career.

What is for certain is that freely choosing to partake in a MOOC demonstrates the participant's interest and passion for a subject above and beyond the norm. Courses delivered through online platforms by the likes of MIT, Harvard and Stanford are not easy to pass, and with completion rates of MOOCs generally below 10%, finishing the course and receiving the certificate shows perseverance and dedication, though this fact may not be widely known (Zheng et al., 2015). For a student to go out of their way and complete multiple courses shows them to be motivated, creative, entrepreneurial, and self-starters, traits which are key for success in the technology sector and attractive in others (Ng, 2016, Zheng et al., 2015).

3. CONCLUSION

Currently, the acceptance of MOOCs for employment purposes is warming up but is still not a mainstream phenomenon. Pushes by major MOOC providers to increase uptake of these courses by employers through work placement schemes and academic recognition are reaping benefits, and these efforts should be continued until recruiters can fully recognise their worth on a CV, though provider platforms must address issues with validity. The greater deal of flexibility in MOOC provision compared to traditional education allows providers to observe and adapt to contemporary trends. Besides the surveys published, this review relied heavily on online editorials and opinion pieces due to the lack of peer-reviewed literature. As yet, the majority of hype surrounding MOOCs is generated by those with a vested interest in the courses, so the general consensus of opinion on these courses is not immediately clear through literature and online article review and it would be useful to conduct independent interviews with companies and recruitment agencies. This paper provides a collation of current opinion and provides the baseline for future research. The long term impacts of MOOC participation on prospective employees are yet to be fully understood, however positive moves towards the acceptance and recognition of MOOC achievements are being made by industry.

REFERENCES

Andersen, E. 2014. *How Google Picks New Employees (Hint: It's Not About Your Degree)* [Online]. Forbes. Available: http://www.forbes.com/sites/erikaandersen/2014/04/07/how-google-picks-new-employees-hint-its-not-about-your-degree/#5b5734af3f27 [Accessed 9 May 2016].

Belkin, D. & Porter, C. 2013. *Job Market Embraces Massive Online Courses*. [Online] Wall Street Journal. Available: http://www.wsj.com/articles/SB10001424127887324807704579087840126695698 [Accessed 1 May 2016]

Belleflamme, P. & Jacqmin, J. 2015. An economic appraisal of MOOC platforms: business models and impacts on higher education. *CESifo Economic Studies*, p.ifv016.

Boeckh, A. 2014. *Verified Certificate MOOCs & Suggested Verified MOOCs Academic Pathways by MOOCs University* [Online]. Global Directory of MOOCs. Available: http://www.moocs.co/Credits_for_MOOCS__News.html [Accessed 27 April 2016].

Haynie, D. 2015. *Opportunity for Credit a New Hook for MOOCs* [Online]. US News. Available: http://www.usnews.com/education/online-education/articles/2015/05/27/chance-for-credit-gives-new-life-to-moocs [Accessed 10 May 2016].

Jordan, K. 2014. Initial trends in enrolment and completion of massive open online courses. *The International Review of Research in Open and Distributed Learning,* 15(1).

Kirsner, S. 2013. *Will MOOCs help you open career doors?* [Online]. Boston Globe. Available: https://www.bostonglobe.com/business/2013/10/05/will-mooc-help-you-open-career-doors/pmjHbLCghsH0lEbulWC9VL/story.html [Accessed 27 April 2016].

Koller, D. 2015. *The Hype is Dead, but MOOCs Are Marching On* [Online]. Knowledge@Wharton, University of Pennsylvania Available: http://knowledge.wharton.upenn.edu/article/moocs-making-progress-hype-died/ [Accessed April 27 2016].

Krumrie, M. 2014. *Should Employers Take Massive Open Online Courses Seriously?* [Online]. Zip Recruiter. Available: https://www.ziprecruiter.com/blog/do-employers-take-massive-open-online-courses-seriously/ [Accessed 27 April 2016].

Larson, S. 2013. *Can An Online Education Actually Land You A Job?* [Online]. readwrite. Available: http://readwrite.com/2013/12/13/mooc-online-education-jobs/ [Accessed 27 April 2016].

Ma, X. 2015. Evaluating the Implication of Open Badges in an Open Learning Environment to Higher Education. *2015 International Conference on Education Reform and Modern Management*. Atlantis Press.

Ng, T. H. 2016. *Do employers find MOOCs certificates from Coursera or edX valuable?* [Online]. Quora. Available: https://www.quora.com/Do-employers-find-MOOCs-certificates-from-Coursera-or-edX-valuable [Accessed 27 April 2016].

NHS Improving Quality. 2015. *Improvement FUNdamentals - your route to improve health and care!* [Online]. NHS. Available: http://www.nhsiq.nhs.uk/capacity-capability/improvement-fundamentals.aspx [Accessed 10 May 2016].

O'Conner, F. 2013. *Employers receptive to hiring IT job candidates with MOOC educations* [Online]. PC World. Available: http://www.pcworld.com/article/2071060/employers-receptive-to-hiring-it-job-candidates-with-mooc-educations.html [Accessed April 27 2016].

Ossiannilsson, E. 2014. Lessons learned from the European eMOOCs 2014 Stakeholders Summit. *Changing the Trajectory: Quality for Opening up Education*, 109.

Radford et al. 2014. The employer potential of MOOCs: A mixed-methods study of human resource professionals' thinking on MOOCs. *The International Review of Research in Open and Distributed Learning,* 15.

Thomas, D. 2014. *MOOC Certificates Can Satisfy Employer Needs* [Online]. Student Advisor. Available: http://blog.studentadvisor.com/mooc-certificates-can-satisfy-employer-needs/ [Accessed 27 April 2016].

Winkler, K. 2014. *Verified Certificates – MOOC'S Money Maker or Anachronism?* [Online]. EDUK West. Available: http://www.edukwest.com/verified-certificates-moocs-money-maker-anachronism/ [Accessed 27 April 2016].

Zheng, S. et al, 2015. Understanding student motivation, behaviors and perceptions in MOOCs. *Proceedings of the 18th ACM Conference on Computer Supported Cooperative Work & Social Computing*. ACM, (pp.1882-1895).

Zhenghao, C. et al, 2015. *Who's benefiting from MOOCs, and why*. [Online] Harvard Business Review. Available: https://hbr.org/2015/09/whos-benefiting-from-moocs-and-why [Accessed 27 April 2016]

ORCHESTRATION OF SOCIAL MODES IN E-LEARNING

Armin Weinberger[1] and Pantelis M. Papadopoulos[2]
[1]*Department of Educational Technology, Saarland University, 66123 Saarbrücken, Germany*
[2]*Centre for Teaching Development and Digital Media, Aarhus University, 8200 Aarhus, Denmark*

ABSTRACT

The concept of orchestration has recently emerged as a useful metaphor in technology-enhanced learning research communities, because of its explanatory power and appeal in describing how different learning activities, tools, and arrangements could be combined to promote learning. More than a buffet of tools offering possibilities to the teachers, orchestration refers to the purposeful mixture of different aspects of the learning experience, serving a particular set of learning goals. In this paper, we present the current dialogue on e-learning orchestration, identifying the questions and open issues in orchestrating different social modes and learning arrangements.

KEYWORDS

Orchestration, social modes, e-learning, learning arrangements

1. ORCHESTRATION IS MORE THAN A BUFFET OF TOOLS

Typically, e-learning arrangements and technologies either serve only one isolated purpose or juxtapose a large number of tools to interact with. There are equivalents of egg boilers in educational technology that are designed to foster understanding of one particular knowledge sub-component, e.g., an iPad app fostering proportional reasoning (Weinberger & Schmitt, 2016), as well as multi-purpose kitchen appliances that claim to support different social modes of learning with interchangeable content following any instructional approach, e.g., mash-ups of learning management systems, e-books, and social networking sites (Hori, Ono, Kobayashi, Yamaji, Kita, & Yamada, 2016). Regardless of how specific or generic an e-learning technology may be, however, there is a notion that it is not only which and how many arrangements and tools are being applied, but also how these different learning opportunities are being orchestrated. How is a specific educational technology being introduced and referred back to in an existing educational context? How are the different possibilities of a generic tool exploited and how are they interlinked? How both, egg boilers and multi-purpose kitchen appliances result in fine dining strongly depends on how these tools are part of a larger set of cooking activities, skills of the cook, and quality of the food.

1.1 Questions of Orchestration

The concept of orchestration acknowledges that learning encompasses multiple activities distributed among learners and teachers in different learning arrangements (Dillenbourg, 2013; Kollar & Fischer, 2013; Roschelle, Dimitriadis, & Hoppe, 2013). Orchestration emphasizes whether and how learning activities and arrangements are being linked. Technological tools typically serve orchestration by providing and linking different learning arrangements. Recent approaches, like the flipped classroom, are examples of orchestration that beg the question how and why re-arranging phases of presenting and practicing with the help of technology may influence learning (Prunuske, Batzli, Howell, & Miller, 2012). Moreover, orchestration also addresses the question how different devices can be used together to build a coherent learning experience, e.g., connecting learners' smartphones to smart classroom displays and interfaces (e.g., Gehlen-Baum, Weinberger, Pohl, & Bry, 2012).

1.2 Orchestration: More Than a Metaphor?

Orchestration may be a particularly useful new concept in e-learning, because of its explanatory power and appeal for the under-investigated, but crucial, aspect of combining different learning activities, tools, and arrangements. Rather than "cooking", orchestration clearly alludes to the metaphor of making music with a set of tools and people with different roles and tasks. Orchestration takes place at both design- and run-time (Kollar & Fischer, 2013). This includes setting up a technology-enhanced learning environment foreseeing different learning activities. But in actual learning situations, plans are to be commanded by learners and not the learners be commanded by the plans. Teachers and learners often adapt the plans to momentary needs. While evidence-based instructional designs can guide learners to engage in effective activities, circumstances require adaptation of original designs to realize its underlying principles – for instance, one learner may have gotten sick and groups need to be re-designed (Dillenbourg, 2015).

2. ORCHESTRATION OF DIFFERENT SOCIAL MODES OF LEARNING

Social modes of learning refer to the ways students are learning individually or in small groups or larger communities. Orchestration of social modes of learning pertains to both, structuring learning within one social mode, as well as combining different social modes in a larger learning landscape.

2.1 Orchestrating Groups of Learners

Learning together raises the questions on how the student cohort is grouped, the size of the group, the mode of peer interaction, the goal of group work, and distribution of roles and specific group tasks and sub-tasks. Each characteristic can alter the learning experience for the student and serve a different purpose. There are strong indications that defining, sequencing, and distributing learning activities with collaboration scripts substantially enhances collaborative learning (Weinberger, Stegmann, & Fischer, 2010). For example, in the case of ArguGraph (Jermann & Dillenbourg, 2002; Puhl, Tsovaltzi, & Weinberger, 2015), pairing together students that express diverging opinions on a topic could be an appropriate strategy to engage them into a meaningful dialogue and allow them to develop their argumentation skills. Larger group settings could accommodate additional roles and more complex scenarios for the students. A typical example is the jigsaw collaboration script (Aronson, Blaney, Stephan, Silkes, & Snapp, 1978) in which students are, first, organized into expert groups, each of which is focused on a different aspect of the learning activity, and next, they form mixed groups that have members from the previous expert groups. The jigsaw collaboration script is an application of the SWISH (split-when-interaction-should-happen) model (Dillenbourg & Jermann, 2010) that prescribes the intentional distribution of roles/resources amongst the group members, in order to make peer interaction a necessity for successfully completing the learning activity.

The mode of peer interaction could be face-to-face or online, written or oral, and open or blind. F2F interactions could be engaging, but also intimidating for shy or introvert students, while online communication allows for private space, but raises the risk of disengagement – particularly in MOOCs (de Barba, Kennedy, & Ainley, 2016). Oral discourse may require less effort from the students, while written interaction forces them to make their position explicit and clear (Papadopoulos, Demetriadis, & Weinberger, 2013). Finally, open interaction could provide a better context for peer interaction, while blinded-interaction could reduce biases and turn focus on what is being discussed.

The goal of groupwork could be acquisition of domain knowledge or the development of transversal skills and competences. In addition, a distinction could be made in situations where collaboration suggest transactivity (Noroozi, Teasley, Biemans, Weinberger, & Mulder, 2012) and situations where cooperation is acceptable. Collaborative learning is strongly based on the notion that students work and learn *together*, while cooperation demotes peer interaction into parallel individual processes (Weinberger, 2011). Nevertheless, both settings could appear as groupwork in a classroom setting.

2.2 Orchestrating Individual and Social Learning Arrangements

Beyond orchestration of learning within one particular social mode of learning, the second and somewhat under-investigated question is how to orchestrate different social modes. One could argue that individual learning should precede collaborative learning, so that students would acquire domain knowledge, develop their own understandings, and be able to present arguments later on. There is strong evidence that individual-collaborative orchestration can reap both, motivational and cognitive benefits. Expectancy of having to teach peers motivates individual learning and individually prepared learners can be expected to discuss learning material on higher levels (Benware & Deci, 1984). There is counter-evidence, however (Tsovaltzi, Judele, Puhl, & Weinberger, 2015), showing that in collaborative scenarios, building on argumentation of different, equally valid perspectives, individual preparation can lead to premature knowledge solidification and unwillingness to modify once taken positions. Students do not abandon their initial position easily (which they have developed while they were individually forming first arguments) and adopt a new position presented to them by a peer. In a similar vein, flipped classrooms can both fail or succeed depending on how learners expect testing of knowledge that they need to receive from individual "at-home" viewing of video explanations and how social in-classroom activities actually complement and build on the video knowledge representations (Prunuske et al., 2012).

There is not a simple answer to the orchestration question, especially not without analyzing further what goals each social mode of learning offers in a particular context. For example, if the purpose of an individual learning task is to help students get informed and get an opinion, then producing an artefact should not be encouraged, because this would solidify, in a sense, the individual understanding and make students more resilient in adopting other perspectives. And of course, in scripted collaboration, the teacher has also to take into account the expected distance between the external, i.e., collaboration guidelines, as presented to the students, and the actual script, i.e., the actual interactions that take place amongst the students (Tchounikine, 2011). The teacher needs to plan and organize the transition from one social mode of learning to the next, taking into account how each learning task will feed the next and get students closer to the overall learning goals of the course.

3. CONCLUSIONS ON ORCHESTRATION AND E-LEARNING

Technology has been a powerful agent in instructional design, necessitating and facilitating orchestration. The teacher is in the middle of a complex and elaborate technological ecosystem. Today's classroom contains a range of tools and services for teaching, assessment, management, and administration, while an additional level of complexity is added by the technology students bring into the classroom, as the bring-your-own-device model tends to be the norm. Dillenbourg (2013) underlines the need to design technology *for* orchestration, while Sharples (2013) argues that orchestration as a learning design paradigm will fail if it requires yet another level of complexity for the researchers and the teacher.

In an educational context, a technology can be deemed appropriate only according to how teachers and students perceive its e-learning affordances. Of course, not all tools offer the same. For example, there are several tools for sharing documents, while simultaneous co-authoring is offered by only a smaller set. If analysis of individual contributions to the co-produced text is desirable, then a teacher should opt for a technology that records the revision history, marking contributions made by each participant. An additional criterion or selecting a technology is whether it affords transition from one arrangement to another. In other words, how easy it is to move from an individual setting to a collaborative one and from consuming material to practice. Adaptivity and adaptability could be essential to bind seamlessly the different steps in a learning activity. Once again, literature could be the reference point for the teacher on effective/efficient uses of different technologies.

In this contribution, we summarize some exemplary empirical results of orchestration in e-learning environments and outline basic educational and technological dimensions of orchestration in e-learning environments. We are interested in exploring orchestration in an "ecology of different technologies" and we are interested in exploring how technology necessitates and facilitates orchestration. We claim that it is insufficient to look at isolated functions of learning and instruction, but that we need to comprehend learning in a concert of learning arrangements, tools, and activities.

REFERENCES

Aronson, E., Blaney, N., Stephan, G., Silkes, J., & Snapp, M. (1978). *The jigsaw classroom*. Beverly Hills, CA: Sage.

Benware, C., & Deci, E. L. (1984). Quality of learning with an active versus passive motivational set. *American Educational Research Journal*, 21, 755-765.

de Barba, P. G., Kennedy, G. E., and Ainley, M. D. (2016). The role of students' motivation and participation in predicting performance in a MOOC Motivation and participation in MOOCs. *Journal of Computer Assisted Learning*, doi: 10.1111/jcal.12130.

Dillenbourg, P. (2013). Design for classroom orchestration. *Computers & Education*, 69, 485–492.

Dillenbourg, P. (2015). *Orchestration graphs. Modeling scaleable education*. Lausanne: EPFL Press.

Dillenbourg, P., & Jermann, P. (2010). Technology for Classroom Orchestration. In S. M. Khine & M. I. Saleh (Eds.), *New Science of Learning: Cognition, Computers and Collaboration in Education* (pp. 525-552). New York, NY: Springer New York.

Gehlen-Baum, V., Weinberger, A., Pohl, A., & Bry, F. (2012). Technology Use in Lectures to Enhance Students' Attention. *In Proceedings of EC-TEL 2012, LNCS 7563* (pp. 125–137). Berlin: Springer.

Hori, M., Ono, S., Kobayashi, S., Yamaji, K., Kita, T., & Yamada, T. (2016). Fusion of E-Textbooks, Learning Management Systems, and Social Networking Sites: A Mash-Up Development. In T. T. Zin, C.-W. J. Lin, J.-S. Pan, P. Tin & M. Yokota (Eds.), *Genetic and Evolutionary Computing: Proceedings of the Ninth International Conference on Genetic and Evolutionary Computing*, August 26-28, 2015, Yangon, Myanmar - Volume II (pp. 377-386). Cham: Springer International Publishing.

Jermann, P., & Dillenbourg, P. (2002). Elaborating new arguments through a CSCL script. In J. Andriessen, M. Baker, & D. Suthers (Eds.), *Arguing to learn: Confronting cognitions in computer-supported collaborative learning environments*, 1–6. Kluwer Academic Publishers.

Kollar, I. & Fischer, F. (2013). Orchestration is nothing without conducting – But arranging ties the two together! A response to Dillenbourg (2011). *Computers & Education*, 69, 507–509.

Noroozi, O., Teasley, S., Biemans, H. A., Weinberger, A., & Mulder, M. (2012). Facilitating learning in multidisciplinary groups with transactive CSCL scripts. *International Journal of Computer-Supported Collaborative Learning*, 8(2), 189-223. doi: 10.1007/s11412-012-9162-z

Papadopoulos, P. M., Demetriadis, S. N., & Weinberger, A. (2013). “Make It Explicit!”: Improving Collaboration through Increase of Script Coercion. *Journal of Computer Assisted Learning*, 29 (4), 383 – 398, Wiley.

Prunuske, A. J., Batzli, J., Howell, E., & Miller, S. (2012). Using Online Lectures to Make Time for Active Learning. *Genetics*, 192(1), 67-72. doi: 10.1534/genetics.112.141754

Puhl, T., Tsovaltzi, D., & Weinberger, A. (2015). Blending Facebook into seminars for practicing argumentation. *Computers in Human Behavior,* 53, 605-616. doi: 10.1016/j.chb.2015.04.006.

Roschelle, J., Dimitriadis, Y., & Hoppe, U. (2013). Classroom orchestration: Synthesis. *Computers & Education*, 69, 523–526.

Sharples, M. (2013). Shared orchestration within and beyond the classroom. *Computers & Education*, 69, 504–506.

Tchounikine, P. (2011). *Computer science and educational software design – A resource for multidisciplinary work in technology enhanced learning*. Berlin: Springer.

Tsovaltzi, D., Judele, R., Puhl, T., & Weinberger, A. (2015). Scripts, individual preparation and group awareness support in the service of learning in Facebook: How does CSCL compare to social networking sites? *Computers in Human Behavior,* 53, 577-592. doi:10.1016/j.chb.2015.04.067

Weinberger, A. (2011). Principles of transactive computer-supported collaboration scripts. *Nordic Journal of Digital Literacy*, 6(3), 189-202.

Weinberger, A. & Schmitt, L. (2016). Produktive Divergenz beim kooperativen Lernen mit iPads – eine multimodale Analyse des Falls "Tarzan und Jane". Presentation at *GEBF 2016*, Berlin, Germany.

Weinberger, A., Stegmann, K., & Fischer, F. (2010). Learning to argue online: Scripted groups surpass individuals (unscripted groups do not). *Computers in Human Behavior*, 26, 506–515.

INFORMATION COMPETENCIES AND THEIR IMPLEMENTATION IN THE EDUCATIONAL PROCESS OF POLISH UNIVERSITIES EXPLORATORY STUDIES

Anna Tonakiewicz-Kołosowska, Iwona Socik and Monika Gajewska
Warsaw University of Technology Main Library, Pl. Politechniki 1, 00-661 Warszawa, Poland

ABSTRACT

The authors present the development and perspectives of improving the quality of Information Literacy programmes in Polish technical universities, considering the Bologna Process and the general conditions of the Polish higher education system. The survey conducted in selected technical and medical universities provided an overview of changes introduced recently in Polish higher education (assumptions of the Ministry of Science and Higher Education and Polish Qualifications Framework). These changes are directly related to the implementation of Information Literacy into the curriculum using different forms of teaching, including e-learning. The study comprises analysis of different teaching methods (traditional, e-learning, blended learning) in developing information competencies.

KEYWORDS

National Qualifications Framework, Information Literacy, e-learning

1. INTRODUCTION

Signing the Bologna Declaration by the Polish government introduced revolutionary changes into the Polish academic institutions. The main objective of the Bologna Process was ensuring more comparable and coherent systems of higher education in Europe. In order to achieve the goal, a plan was prepared for implementing the changes in the national educational system as well as at the European level. The project of The Polish National Qualifications Framework (NQF) is an ongoing process which started in 2006. In 2010, the efforts for preparing the National Qualifications Framework (NQF) by experts resulted in preparing document "Establishing a balance sheet of qualifications and competencies available in the labour market and developing a model of the National Qualifications Framework". According to this document, "(…) the Polish Qualification Framework shows interactions between qualifications and integrate the different national qualifications subsystems. It also describes the hierarchy of the qualification levels (…) In the Framework, each of the levels is defined by descriptors which define, in general terms, the learning outcomes required at a given level" (Chłoń-Domińczak, Dębowski, Sławiński, 2013). The Act of 18 March 2011, introduced NQF to the Polish higher educational system. New regulations were applied from 1 October 2012. Students who began their studies in the academic year 2012/2013 follow the programmes developed by taking into account the learning outcomes.

Information competencies belong to the generic skills described in the NQF and universities should give their students the possibility of gaining knowledge and developing skills of information literacy. Information competencies are described in the National Qualifications Framework as learning outcomes in terms of knowledge and skills in the area of technical, medical sciences and other sciences. The skills are divided into competencies for the university beginners and for graduate students. The basic skills include the ability of searching information through different types of resources (including printed and electronic publications). The advanced competencies additionally contain evaluation and interpretation of information.

Information Literacy competencies have also been described similarly in scientific literature. These specific skills are as a key factor in lifelong learning. They are vital in achieving educational goals (Lau, 2016). A detailed description of information competencies can be used for creating the Information Literacy programmes at universities. Libraries are natural partners for universities in building information competencies. Library's participation in teaching process can take different forms depending on the university. According to the NQF, Information Literacy programme should be implemented in two stages, the first being training for the beginners (issues related to using the library and searching resources) and the second - for more advanced issues, including search strategy and sources evaluation.

2. PURPOSE OF THE STUDY

Universities in Poland use different ways and tools for implementing information competencies. The term "Information Literacy" is used by the authors of the survey as all forms of library courses and other activities, prepared and/or supported by librarians and addressed to students, both within the curriculum and outside of it. At present, in Poland there are no standard regulations for including Information Literacy (IL) courses into the curricula. Introduction and implementation of these activities depend on each university's regulations and faculty's or library's initiatives. That is why the courses on Information Literacy can have various forms and hold various assumptions.

For this study, the authors distinguish four types of activities related to IL at universities. Firstly, the subject can take the form of a course on Information Literacy as part of the curriculum, conducted only by librarians. Secondly, the subject can be conducted by the faculty lecturer with the librarian's support. The next one is a course on Information Literacy as part of the curriculum and provided without any library support. Another type is library training courses for university beginners. Each of those courses can be implemented at different stages of university education: courses for undergraduate, graduate and PhD students.

The aim of this survey was to determine the libraries' participation in implementing information literacy courses in the curricula and to what extent is e-learning used in these courses. The other purpose of the study was to investigate the library preferences in using e-learning tools for building users' competencies in information management.

3. RESULTS

The authors prepared a questionnaire comprising 15 questions and sent it to 30 university libraries (19 technical and 11 medical). The online method was used. The universities' websites were used for collecting the libraries' emails. 83% (25 out of 30) libraries responded and filled in the questionnaire. The study conclusions are presented below.

The survey found that only 6 surveyed libraries do not conduct any type of regular courses that are part of the curricula. It means that vast majority of libraries (19 out of 25) participates in helping develop information competencies.

Most libraries provide only one type of courses. Only few of them conduct courses themselves and also give support to subjects conducted by faculty lectures. More than a half of the libraries conduct the courses on Information Literacy as part of the curriculum at each of educational stages.

The results also indicate that only few libraries conduct courses on Information Literacy in cooperation with the faculty lecturer. 36% of respondents provide this type of courses for undergraduate students, 28% for graduate students and 12% for PhD students.

The library training for beginners is the most common at the universities. All respondents indicated that their library provides such training for undergraduate students. 32% of libraries provide it for graduate students and almost 28% for PhDs. The detailed information on the course type and the university stage is shown in the table below.

Table 1. Types of Information Literacy courses and its implementation at different educational stages

	Library conducts courses on information literacy, as part of the curriculum			**The subject of Information Literacy is conducted by the faculty lecturer with the librarian' support**			**Library training for the university beginners**		
	undergrad-uate students	graduate students	PhD students	undergrad-uate students	graduate students	PhD students	undergrad-uate students	graduate students	PhD students
	Number of libraries (% of responses)								
Library does not conduct any classes	12 (48%)	11 (44%)	12 (48%)	15 (60%)	18 (72%)	22 (88%)	0 (0%)	8 (32%)	18 (72%)
Traditional courses (lecture, workshops) etc.	9 (36%)	9 (36%)	8 (32%)	8 (32%)	6 (24%)	3 (12%)	8 (33%)	8 (32%)	2 (8%)
Online courses (e-learning)	1 (4%)	3 (12%)	1 (4%)	1 (4%)	0 (0%)	0 (0%)	10 (40%)	5 (20%)	1 (4%)
Blended learning (traditional and online courses)	3 (12%)	2 (8%)	4 (16%)	1 (4%)	1 (4%)	0 (0%)	7 (28%)	4 (16%)	4 (16%)

There are various reasons for regular courses not being as popular as the library training. Firstly, library training for university beginners has a long tradition in Poland and started long before implementing National Qualification Framework. In other words, there is no need to convince faculty authorities to introduce such training at the beginning of each academic year, because it is customary at university. Usually, they are short (maximum 2 hours), so they require less effort for preparation in comparison with regular lectures or workshops that last much longer. What is more, the course content is rather general, thus easier to prepare.

Among 13 libraries that conduct courses on Information Literacy, 9 prefer traditional form of teaching for graduate and undergraduate students, 8 libraries favor it for teaching PhD students. The traditional form dominates also in courses conducted in cooperation with the faculty lecturer.

We can see that online courses are mostly used in the library training for university beginners. The vast majority of the libraries offer their users e-learning courses or blended courses. The e-learning tools are not as much popular in conducting regular subjects in the curriculum.

The libraries which offer e-learning courses usually use university e-learning platform (12 responses). 7 libraries have their own e-learning platform.

The survey also shows that librarians use various types of the materials in e-learning. There seems to be a tendency to use the text documents - 19 libraries indicated it. Such great popularity may be caused by the fact that they are easy to prepare. What is more, 12 libraries put audio and video materials on their platform. The third most frequently selected response was using interactive tools such as games, quizzes and other interactive activities. These figures can lead to the conclusion that libraries try to use as many ways and tools in e-learning as possible. They are not afraid of taking risks and are open to new teaching possibilities.

The respondents were also asked if they conduct surveys on users' preferences in teaching methods. It turned out that the majority of libraries (64%) do not conduct any surveys on this issue. The libraries that did such surveys indicate that the most preferred teaching method for users is e-learning and blended learning.

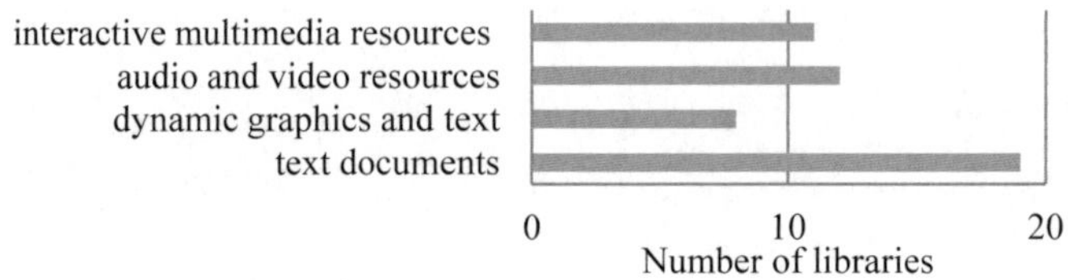

Figure 1. Types of learning materials used in e-learning

4. CONCLUSIONS

On the basis of the survey results, it may be concluded that despite the fact that National Qualification Framework has been implemented since 2010, there is still a lot to do in the area of including Information Literacy in the university curricula. The survey results also show that it is academic libraries that have taken the responsibility for including IL into curricula. Only 6 surveyed libraries do not conduct any regular courses as part of the curriculum. At 3 universities, the subject was deployed without any library support. The data analysis indicates that the medical libraries have the best achievements in this area. All of them provide courses on IL for PhDs.

The experiences of the Warsaw University of Technology Main Library show that including the courses on Information Literacy in the curriculum is a long process which encounters many considerable obstacles. The most significant one is the lack of awareness on Information Literacy importance in education. Usually, there are no general regulations at the universities that could help facilitate cooperation between faculties and the library. Faculties sometimes do not have basic knowledge on what Information Literacy really is and this is why they are reluctant to introduce it. They sometimes perceive conducting courses on Information Literacy as something which requires additional personnel and costs. This could be one of reasons why they hesitate to ask the library for help or cooperation. Another reason can be that they do not consider the library as a partner in teaching.

The vast majority of the courses were included as the result of the library and faculty initiative. The success in this process depends on the library commitment. It is also very important to keep in touch with the university authorities, participate in all possible educational meetings organized at the university and try convincing as many faculty deans as possible that developing information competencies is really important. Such proactive approach seems to be the only key to success. The worst thing that libraries can do is passive waiting for the faculty initiative.

When the library succeeds in including new courses in the curriculum it can consider using various teaching method such as e-learning, that can help them make their educational offer more attractive to users. A wide range of educational activities, flexible and tailored to the needs of specific groups, is necessary for gaining users' attention and for meeting their expectations. E-learning tools such as interactive exercises can help students get more involved in developing information competencies. We really hope that the libraries in Poland will see all possibilities in using e-learning tools in teaching and e-learning usage in regular courses will be growing.

REFERENCES

American Library Association (1989). *Presidential Committee on Information Literacy. Final Report*. Chicago: American Library Association.

American Library Association. *Information Literacy Competency Standards for Higher Education.* Available from: http://www.ala.org/acrl/standards/informationliteracycompetency#f1

Chłoń-Domińczak Agnieszka, Dębowski Horacy, Sławiński Stanisław (2013). *NQF Development in Poland.* [cited: April 14, 2016]. Available from http://www.refernet.pl/public/publikacje/_17.pdf

Lau Jesus (2006). *Guidelines on Information Literacy for Lifelong Learning.* [cited: April 14, 2016]. Available from http://www.ifla.org/files/assets/information-literacy/publications/ifla-guidelines-en.pdf

VIRTUAL & REAL FACE TO FACE TEACHING

Romeo Teneqexhi[1] and Loreta Kuneshka[2]
[1]*Director of Distance Education Center, Tirana Polytechnic University, Sheshi Nene Tereza Nr 4,Tirana, Albania*
[2]*Head of Biostatistics. Medical University of Tirana. Faculty of Medicine, Rruga e Dibres, Nr.361,Tirana, Albania*

ABSTRACT

In traditional "face to face" lessons, during the time the teacher writes on a black or white board, the students are always behind the teacher. Sometimes, this happens even in the recorded lesson in videos. Most of the time during the lesson, the teacher shows to the students his back not his face. We do not think the term "face to face" is the correct one in this case. The order in space: 1- the "knowledge" (black/white board); 2- the teacher; 3- the students, psychologically creates the idea to the student that the "knowledge" is so far away from him, beyond the teacher. We have changed this order in space to: 1- the teacher; 2- the "knowledge" (black/white board); 3- the students. So we have put the object to be studied between the teacher and the students. In this way we have set up a Real Face to Face process. Position of studied object between the teacher and the students makes the lessons much more attractive. During the time of the real lesson, it is recording in a video format using a cheap infrastructure and very simple to use by the teacher himself. The teacher is "all in one" person (screenwriter, actor, cameraman, director, audio & video editor, producer, distributor) of producing Virtual & Real Face to Face (VRFF) videos. The teacher writes on a transparent board which is between him and the students. The transparent writing board, in the same time, is an available big "transparent screen". Power point slides or different graphics can be shown on this screen with the teacher behind it. During the real lesson some of the students stay in the teacher's room the others are in classroom following the teacher via the big screen of a projector. Both category of students can see and ask the teacher any time being part of the produced video. The students can access the videos very easily via website of the university or in www.youtube.com. Technical details of this infrastructure and an experience of recording lessons generating the corresponding videos are in the presentation.

KEYWORDS

Traditional Face to Face lesson, Virtual & Real Face to Face lesson, VRFF, transparent "black board", transparent big screen, recorded lesson.

1. INTRODUCTION

Nowadays, in many environments, security cameras are used to record movements of everything even dogs and cats that pass in front of cameras. Don't you think it is a pity not to record the real lectures in classrooms? Teacher spends too much time for preparing the lectures. Students also spend time following the lesson and after the lesson ends everything the teacher said and wrote on black board has gone forever.

During the lecture students keep notes of what the teacher says and writes on the black board. This is good thing but I think it is not very effective. The student in lecture is focused to copy everything from black board and often he does not understand the essence of what the teacher is explaining. Nowadays the students often use cell phones to record the lecture. So the students need something more than the book (some time the book does not exist). Recording of real lectures carry the questions that students make during the lecture and the teacher in video is much more realistic because the real students are listening. I like this idea. In Distance Learning Education Center, Tirana Polytechnic University we are experimenting a kind of new technology of recording lessons. We have decided to denominate it Virtual & Real Face to Face (VRFF). VRFF videos are now a reality (see "Elektroteknika 1" playlist in www.youtube.com).

2. TECHNICAL DETAILS OF IMPLEMENTATION

The final result of Virtual & Real Face to Face technique is the production of videos as shown in figure 1 and figure 2.

Figure 1. Video at http://youtu.be/gDeWm9FiI6A

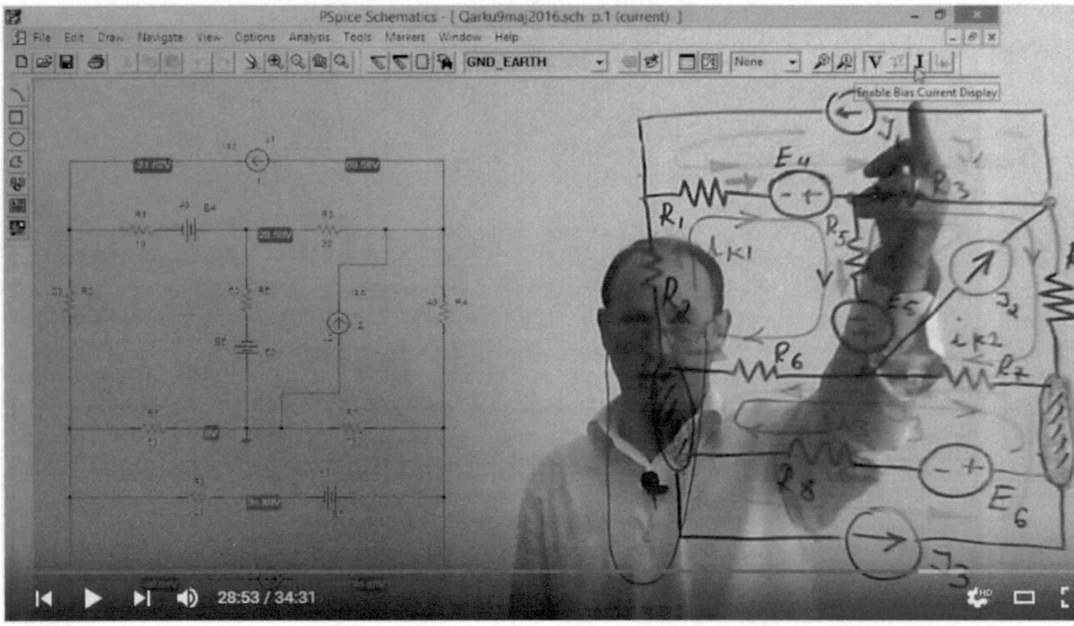

Figure 2. Video at https://youtu.be/Ba4E1PEtYek

Registration is done in real time with students who follow live lecture but through a video projector. The teacher is in a room next to the lecture hall and communicates with students through a video conference system with two cameras. The cameras have audio boxes incorporated in it and a long wired sensitive microphone. The teacher's camera has its microphone in the lecture hall and lecture hall camera has its microphone in the teacher's room. The teacher sees the students through a screen while students watch the teacher through the video projector which is set in the mirror projection mode (left site right). Teacher's camera mentioned above serves only to display the figure in the lecture hall. Recording of the video is done by a HD web camera connected to a computer which is on teacher's table. Another laptop on teacher's table is used for Power Point presentations or graphics in different simulations. A VGA monitor is connected to the laptop and it stays right behind the HD camera. On this screen teacher can display different notes, power point slides, demonstrate computer simulations etc. It is up to the teacher to show or not these notes or slides to the students. The teacher looks on the screen but on recorded video he looks like he is seeing the students (to the camera). This detail is a big advantage for generating high quality lectures even by teachers not so high qualified. As you can see the teacher has four VGA signal sources on the table: two video conferencing system cameras, computer VGA signal which is associated with HD camera and VGA signal of the laptop. These four signals enter a VGA switch which is on the teacher's table. Each channel has its own button and teacher can switch easily from one source to another, showing to the students what he wants, doing in the same time the role of video director. The final figure which students see in the classroom is displayed simultaneously on a large TV screen placed in front of teacher, shifted left. Depending on the size of the room where the teacher stays, a number of students sit facing the spine to TV. On the other side of the TV wall, there is a big mirror. The students in the teacher's room watch the transparent board (and the teacher) on TV through the mirror.

2.1 Video Editing Effects

During the real lesson two videos are produced: HD camera video (teacher with everything he writes on the transparent board) and computer screen video (Power Point or different simulations on computer). Video editing may not always be necessary. Through video editing we can create different effects (figures 3 and 4), making the recorded lesson much more attractive and understandable. The idea of large transparent screen on which the teacher writes with white marker board is created only through video editing.

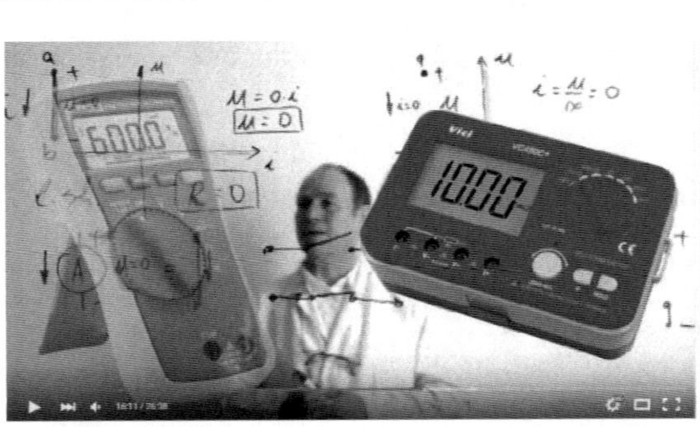

Figure 3. Video at https://youtu.be/u7H5Z9sybRQ

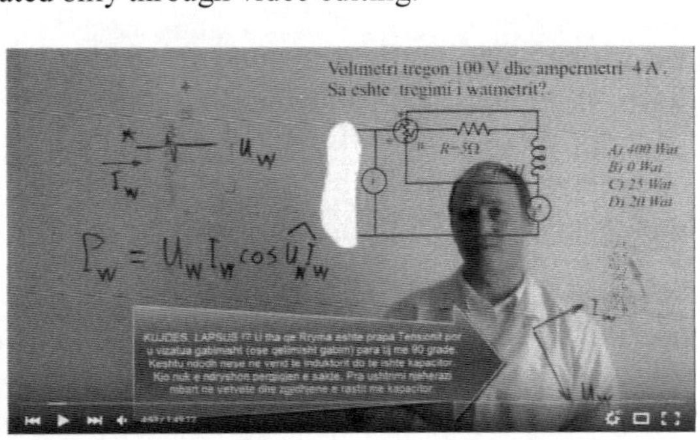

Figure 4. Video at https://youtu.be/1Z2D5BIqb4E

2.2 Accessing the Lectures via the Internet

The student can access the lessons very easily through website of university. He logins his session with the password provided and click on the YouTube icon next to the subject (figure 5). A list of all lessons recorded is on the screen. One can see videos and communicate with his teacher through the questions. YouTube provides a forum for each video. It is a fantastic opportunity for communication with your teacher.

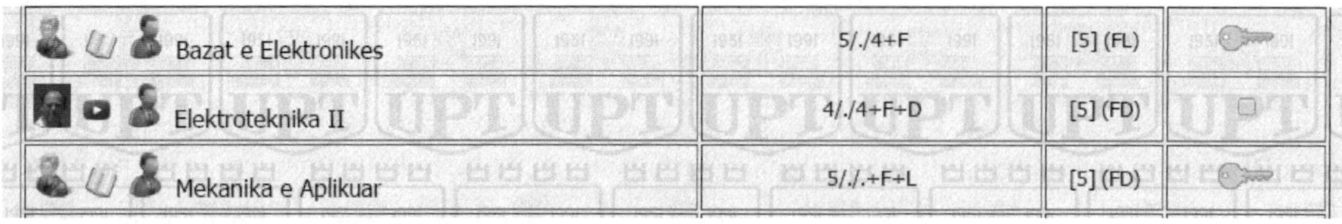

Figure 5. Accessing the lessons on internet

Long ago we asked somebody: " What did you put in your head during the study in university?". Nowadays, the time has come and we can say for sure you put everything of the university in your pocket. You have with you everywhere, everything you have learned in university. Smartphone makes it a reality. The student can "return" to the school at any time. He is only some clicks away from the university.

3. CONCLUSION

- The lesson time is spend efficiently. If in a traditional lecture the teacher repeats several times the same thing to be better understand, in VRFF lessons it is not necessary. The students can repeat listening himself till he understands what is said.
- The biggest problem of the poor results of students is continuity of studying. If for different reasons a student loses a traditional lecture he will have problems with next lessons. Recording video of real lectures exclude this factor.
- The student takes no notes during the lecture, he has no reason to do so. He is fully focused on what the teacher is explaining. This minimizes the study time at home.
- In VRFF lessons you can activate old and good professor (retired) who are not able to stand for a long time. They can sit and develop live lecture by writing on a touch screen laptop.
- Through the forum raised for each video in YouTube.com, professors constantly find reason to improve their lectures.
- If all subjects of a school have VRFF videos, it gives the colleagues the opportunity to attend lectures of each other and be updated with news of other subjects.

ACKNOWLEDGEMENT

Does VRFF method have the future? It is a fact that some teachers, in lessons, often hold pieces of paper in their hands to be sure not to make mistakes during the explanation. So sometimes some students try to do the same thing in exams. They try to copy during the exam and ... if the teacher notices this the student is punished. It is a bed taste isn't it. These teachers do not agree with this kind of recorded lessons. I tell them: "Do not be afraid of this technique. You can produce VRFF video without using pieces of paper. The computer screen placed behind the HD camera is the best ever prompter".

I would be very happy if I had today recorded lectures of my professors who are now retired or dead. A special reverence and respect for those professors we cannot see or hear anymore. Now we have the opportunity not to happen with us what happened with our teachers.

VIRTUAL SCAFFOLDING – CONSTRUCTIVISM IN ONLINE LEARNING

Lachlan MacKinnon and Liz Bacon
University of Greenwich, UK

ABSTRACT

This reflection paper considers the recent growth of online courses, in particular MOOCs, against the backdrop of growing demand for higher education, the failings of our existing higher education models, and the continued but unsuccessful attempts of new technologies to revolutionise education. The authors argue that focusing on technology alone will always be unsuccessful, as it fails to recognise that learning is a social experience, which technology can aid but not replace. They argue that online education must take on board and address the issues of social constructivism in order to be effective. They use their own experience of developing online courses, combined with a consideration of the existing research in the area, to propose a future model for online provision. They conclude by identifying the future research needed to realise this model, and highlighting research on the potential future evolution of higher education.

KEYWORDS

Online Learning, Social Constructivism, Future Models for Higher Education, Cooperative Learning in STEM

1. BACKGROUND DISCUSSION

Demand for higher education is exploding around the world and the nature of education is changing (EDUCASE, 2010). As reported by Unesco (2009), between 1970 and 2007, the number of students in higher education increased from 28.6 million to 152.5 million. INTO (2013) has analyzed OECD data, and suggests that, "Within a decade, the demand for higher education will surpass 265 million. That is greater than the population of Nigeria or Russia". However, as reported by the Wall Street Journal (WSJ, 2015) a lot more distance online education is required in future as countries simply cannot cope with the demand, to quote: "Consider India, which has 600 million people under the age of 25 and an outdated university system struggling to grow a workforce to support the third-largest economy in the world. An analysis a few years ago showed that, to address educational needs using traditional methods, India would need to build 1,500 campuses and—even more challenging—find qualified instructors to staff them".

Alongside this rapidly growing demand, there is an increasing realisation that our existing higher education models, both in terms of pedagogy and structure, are becoming less relevant to the requirements of the modern world and modern students. Critics like Sir Ken Robinson (2010) point to the need to step away from an educational system developed to meet the needs of society nearly 200 years ago, and to embrace change in providing educational opportunities designed to enhance creativity and support individual, personal development. This immediately raises the prospect, promoted by many within our community, that technology-enhanced learning, or eLearning, is the answer, and will revolutionise education! However, as ably debunked by Derek Muller (2014), the argument that a novel or ubiquitous technology will revolutionise education has been made many times before, but we still persist with the status quo. It can be argued that this is fundamentally because of inertia in the system, the massively installed base, or a lack of understanding on the part of the students of the benefits of the technology. Alternatively, we can take the view, as Muller does, that technology, in whatever form, can aid the learning process but should not be seen as a replacement for key constituents of that process. In particular, the concept that learning is a social process, and the role of the tutor is not to deliver information but to provide support and guidance for students in developing their learning skills, and their ability to learn from and with their peers. Whilst this concept has considerable support and longevity in education circles, fundamentally grounded in the *Social Constructivist* theory of education based on the work of Vygotsky (1978) and numerous others, it has been more honoured in the breach than the observance as demonstrated by a three year study by Martin Nystrand (1996) which showed very limited use of social interaction in standard classroom teaching. However, recent developments in the use of technology to aid and support classroom teaching, such as *Flipped Classrooms*, have begun to re-establish social interaction, peer discussion and groupwork as the primary medium for learning, stepping away from didactic, instructional, lecture-based information delivery (Demetry, 2010).

Social constructivism is also at the heart of the Computer-Supported Collaborative Working (CSCW) (Grudin, 1994) and Computer-Supported Co-operative Learning (CSCL) (McConnell, 2000) movements, developed in the 1990s. More recently CSCL has come to mean Computer-Supported Collaborative Learning (Stahl et al, 2006), and it remains an important area in the development of online learning tools and the promotion of online learning, particularly in STEM subjects.

One other major factor in the recent development of online learning has been the rise of the MOOC (Massively Open Online Course) and the impact this has had, in opening up and democratising access to higher education courses, in promoting the potential for new models of learning, but also in the potential negative impact on socialisation in learning and the use of groupwork. Ironically, the massive nature of MOOCs does not imply significant socialisation, and the fact that students can be in different time zones, operating to different agendas of engagement, timing, commitment, etc., makes it near impossible to engage any sort of heavyweight process of group working (Bacon et al., 2015)).

2. CURRENT THINKING

The research shows that the characteristics of the students, relative to the type of online learning and the demands it makes on them, will be a key factor in determining the success of an online course (Authors ref, anonymised). MOOCs were originally established to attract audiences of experienced, metacognitive adult learners, who could successfully manage their own learning in a heutagogic environment, but the reality is that the majority of learners in MOOCs require considerably more support than envisaged in that model (Beaven et al, 2014). In our experience, open courses attract a wide range of learners, ranging from aspirational novices to experienced students, and as a result have to tailor the collaborative elements and expectations accordingly. Clearly, online courses that offer lightweight collaborative activities, of a discursive nature, that do not require timed or timely attendance and offer participants a shared experience of learning, can be open to all. However, as the requirement changes to expect participants to take on roles within the group (Belbin, 2012), to expect regular participation at fixed times and for fixed durations, and to expect individual participants to take on responsibilities for learning and sharing with the group, the need to select and filter participants grows. Heavyweight processes, which we define as those processes that require the sharing of technical expertise and knowledge in a structured and agreed format, and require synchronous commitment and delivery, really require selection on the basis of prior experience, or selection based on known commitment and motivation.

We envisage a future mixed economy of online courses, where participants sign up to closed, selective courses to learn heavyweight processes, that they can then apply in more open courses, and a wide range of open courses using lightweight collaborative processes that are available for participant selection (Bacon & MacKinnon, 2016). In this model, we also envisage the growth of the use of social media in combination with MOOCs and similar online courses, providing the opportunities to support group activity, particularly maintenance activities, and socialisation of learning. Figure 1 shows a simple graphical representation of the relationship between student characteristics and type of online course.

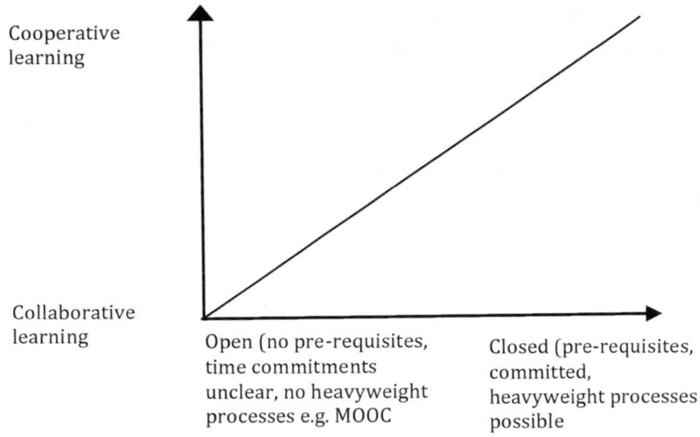

Figure 1. Graphical illustration of online course requirements

Teachonline in Canada (2016a) have published their analysis of current and future developments in online learning, and identify that "collaborative technologies and knowledge sharing will emerge as key resources for all forms of learning", as one of their key technology patterns. Whilst this may not seem a particularly surprising finding, it does once again highlight the importance of preparing our students to be effective collaborative learners.

In terms of MOOCs, the term GROOC has recently been defined, by Professor Mintzberg of McGill University (2015), to describe group-oriented MOOCs, based on one he has developed on social activism. He also argues that there is no requirement to provide additional support to address group dynamics, stating that groups should be able to handle losing a few members and still function appropriately (Poets & Quants, 2015). Whilst this might be true for collaborative learning, as discussed earlier, because no joint group output is required, i.e. it doesn't matter if all members of the group don't contribute equally or in a timely manner, or if some drop in or out, or others disappear, learning can still take place through dialogue and discussion. It probably also doesn't matter if some of the communication is not understood by all, or the composition of the group i.e. people can be randomly assigned to small groups and the particular strengths and weaknesses of individuals probably don't matter that much. However, if you are trying to achieve cooperative learning through a MOOC, which requires a group to jointly solve a problem, then the skills of the people in the group, the timeliness of their communication, their understanding of the problem etc. is critical to a successful outcome. The group may be able to sustain the loss of some members if it is large enough and those members are not assigned a critical role in the production of the joint output, but in general such losses are very damaging to cooperative learning groups. Whilst collaborative learning is important in engineering and related disciplines, cooperative learning is an absolute core requirement, and therefore the use of GROOCs or MOOCs, as currently defined, can be particularly challenging in this context (MacKinnon & Bacon, 2016).

3. CONCLUSIONS & FUTURE THINKING

In terms of group work, it has been demonstrated that collaborative work, in the sense of discussion and debate to deepen thinking and understanding, can be successful. For example Mackness et al (2010) formed groups by getting students to pro-actively put themselves forward to be placed in a group and then when there were a sufficient number to form a group, another one was started. However, for STEM courses requiring heavyweight interactive processes, the need for cooperative learning is paramount, and this requires greater selectivity in the group formation process and greater maturity and commitment by the participants.

Given the rapidly increasing global demand for higher education, and the inability of many countries to meet their local demand, it is inevitable that, due to cost, the demand for online education will increase and the mass market of MOOCs is likely to play a part in that space. STEM subjects will be part of that demand and it is therefore important the more research is undertaken to find a mechanism to develop well-formed groups in MOOCs, so that future students can benefit from a structured approach to cooperative learning using heavyweight tools and techniques. We are currently engaged in developing research on the use of social media in combination with MOOCs to determine if that can provide an appropriate level of socialisation to enhance commitment, retention and completion by participants.

The model of developing a mixed economy of online courses will also require the identification and description of the optimum types and structures of courses to be used to help guide and develop learners relative to specific skills and knowledge. For example, we might argue that a selective, closed online course (SCOC) would be best suited to help learners develop their Groupwork skills, and then develop or encourage the development of such courses for inexperienced learners. In this context, the tutor again becomes the guide and mentor for the learners, identifying the early stage, introductory courses that will enable them to develop their skills and become metacognitive, and then "fading" back to permit the learners to take control of their own learning experience. This becomes particularly important if we are to provide effective support for lifelong learning, especially in STEM subjects, that offers student-centric control, in an andragogic, or even heutagogic, environment.

Teachonline (2016b) have identified 8 key changes for Program Design, and 7 key changes for Teaching and Learning, that we can expect to see in the immediate future, as online learning impacts across the sector:

Program Design

- More flexible program designs
- More use of open educational resources
- More creative assessment processes
- More micro-credit and nano-degrees
- More co-op and experiential components within programs
- More international collaborative programs
- More transfer and international recognition agreements
- Blurring of lines between College and University

Teaching and Learning

- Learning will no longer be defined by time, place or institutional offerings
- Learners will create their own learning agendas, which reflect their own career, personal and lifelong learning goals
- Learners will secure their learning outcomes through a combination of formal, informal, self-directed, instructor-delivered, in class and online learning
- Learners will expect personalised learning services and supports for their learning agenda
- New mechanisms for meeting personal learning agendas will appear in the marketplace as the "unbundling" of learning continues
- Courses will be less important than mentoring, coaching, counselling, advising and assessment
- Diverse and new forms of credentials will appear which reflect the varied needs of learners, employers, social agencies, innovation organisations and entrepreneurs.

The vast majority of higher education institutions will be engaged with some or all of these areas, and for many of us this reflects a process that has been going on for many years. However, the argument now is simple, this is no longer a movement, or isolated instances of good practice, but rather the culmination of the movement, requiring of us significant change across every aspect of higher education. This is not about technology revolutionising education, but the evolution of a new model of education supported and enhanced by technology. Deciding how we will support the social nature of learning, and thereby enable our students to become successful collaborative learners, in online courses, is a key step forward.

REFERENCES

Bacon, L. et al., 2015. "Addressing retention and completion in MOOCs - a student-centric design approach". E-LEARN 2015 - World Conference on E-Learning, Kona, Hawaii: October 19-22, 2015.

Bacon, L. & MacKinnon, L, 2016. The Challenges of Creating Successful Collaborative Working and Learning Activities in Online Engineering Courses. Proceedings of XIV Laccei Conference, San Josė, Costa Rica, July 20 - 22, 2016.

Beaven, T. et al., 2014. MOOCs: Striking the Right Balance between Facilitation and Self-Determination, *MERLOT Journal of Online Learning and Teaching*, V. 10, N. 1, March 2014.

Belbin, R.M., 2012. *Team Roles at Work*, books.google.com

Jane E. Brindley, et al, 2009. Creating Effective Collaborative Learning Groups in an Online Environment. *The International Review of Research in Open and Distributed Learning*, Vol 10, No 3 (2009).

Demetry, C., 2010. Work in progress — An innovation merging "classroom flip" and team-based learning. *Proceedings of IEEE Frontiers in Education Conference*, Washington, 2010. doi: 10.1109/FIE.2010.5673617

EDUCASE, CAUDIT, JISC and SURF, 2010. *The Future of Higher Education: Beyond the Cam*pus.

Grudin, J., 1994. Computer-Supported Cooperative Work: History and Focus. *Computer* 27 (5): 19–26. doi:10.1109/2.291294

INTO: the global education partners, 2013. *Global Demand: The market opportunity*. http://www.into-corporate.com/higher-education/global-demand-the-market-opportunity.aspx

MacKinnon, L & Bacon, L., 2016. "How to develop a GROOC: Establishing group dynamics in MOOCs". Proceedings of the DEANZ Biennial Conference. The University of Waikato, Hamilton, New Zealand, April 17-20 2016.

Mackness, J et al, 2010. *The ideals and reality of participating in a MOOC*. Pp. 266-275.

McConnell, D., 2000. *Implementing Computing Supported Cooperative Learning*. Routledge, ISBN 9780749431358

McGill University, 2015. https://www.mcgill.ca/desautels/programs/grooc

Muller, D., 2014. *This Will Revolutionize Education*. https://www.youtube.com/watch?v=GEmuEWjHr5c

Nystrand, M., 1996. *Opening dialogue: Understanding the dynamics of language and learning in the English classroom*. New York: Teachers College Press.

Poets & Quants, (2015), *Enter the GROOC, better than a MOOC*, http://poetsandquants.com/2015/01/04/enter-the-grooc-better-than-a-mooc/

Robinson, K., 2010. RSA ANIMATE: *Changing Education Paradigms*. https://www.youtube.com/watch?v=zDZFcDGpL4U

Stahl, G. et al, 2006. Computer-supported collaborative learning: An historical perspective. In R. K. Sawyer (Ed.), *Cambridge handbook of the learning sciences* (pp. 409-426). Cambridge, UK: Cambridge University Press.

Teachonline (2016a). A 2016 Look at the Future of Online Learning - Part 1. http://www.teachonline.ca/tools-trends/exploring- future-education/2016-look-future-online-learning- part-1

Teachonline (2016b). *A 2016 Look at the Future of Online Learning - Part 2*. http://www.teachonline.ca/tools-trends/exploring- future-education/2016-look-future-online-learning- part-2

UNESCO Institute for Statistics, Global Education Digest, 2009. *Comparing Education Statistics Across the World* (Montreal:UNESCO-UIS, 2009), p. 10, http://www.uis.unesco.org/template/pdf/ged/2009/GED_2009_EN.pdf.

Vygotsky, L., 1978. *Mind in Society*. London:Harvard University Press.

WSJ, 2015. The Wall Street Journal 26th April 2015 *The Future of College: It's Online*.

Poster

ACTIVE LEARNING METHODS IN PROGRAMMING FOR NON-IT STUDENTS

Olga Mironova, Irina Amitan, Jüri Vilipõld and Merike Saar
Faculty of Information Technology, Department of Informatics,
Chair of Software Engineering, Tallinn University of Technology
Akadeemia tee St. 15A, Tallinn 12618, Estonia

ABSTRACT

The purpose of this study is to demonstrate a teaching approach and some teaching strategies in an Informatics course for the first-year non-IT students at the Department of Informatics of Tallinn University of Technology, Estonia. The authors suggest some solutions for making the course, which is usually complicated, more dynamic and attractive, thereby raising students' interest and motivation with the aim of achieving the set learning outcomes.

KEYWORDS

Programming basics, non-IT.

1. INTRODUCTION

In recent years information technology is rapidly developing and playing a great role in contemporary life. This role is equally important at work or study and at home. Consequently, students have to grasp different computing skills to feel confident and be ready for the future work and able to participate effectively in the IT-world. Therefore, the main objective of modern computer education for the non-IT students today is to teach them to be always well-informed in technical fundamentals and be able to find a common ground with IT-specialists at their future workplace.

In the current work the authors try to find answers to questions about how to achieve better results in the teaching of programming basics for the non-IT students who are beginners in this field.

2. PROGRAMMING BASICS

2.1 The Informatics Course

Computer education basics have been included into all the curricula at Tallinn University of Technology (TTÜ, 2016) and have been consolidated for all non-IT specialities into a course named "Informatics". The named course lasts for two semesters and students have two academic hours weekly at computer classes. Usually the students' group size is approximately 25 students; this number annually depends on the total number of the matriculated students.

During the course lecturers apply modern and classic face-to-face classroom methods, pair or group work and provide students with independent learning in the Moodle e-environment (Moodle, 2016).

The first Informatics module is informational work such as text processing, presentations and spreadsheets handling. The work tools here are MS Word, MS PowerPoint and MS Excel. In addition, we use Google tools as an alternative to the Microsoft products.

The programming basics part of the Informatics course lasts for one semester and it starts with Scratch (Scratch, 2016). Scratch is a graphical programming environment, which is very intuitive and greatly helps learners to take on board the main concepts and terms of modelling and programming such as the data, process, branching or iteration. Such visual programming lasts for 5 or 6 weeks, depending on the students' level in each group.

The next course module is dedicated to Visual Basic for Applications (VBA) (Sissejuhatus VBAsse, 2016) or Python (Python Software Foundation, 2016), (Tutvumine Pythoniga, 2016). VBA choice is reinforced by the already familiar environment MS Excel – it is one of the Informatics first module topics in the Informatics course. In addition, it is comfortable for beginners to keep their data in the same fail with the programme. Python does not require any declaration of simple variables, which makes working with it easier for the beginners.

The main learning outcomes of the Informatics course are introduced below (Õppeinfosüsteem, 2016). A student who completes the course:

- acquires the foundations of problem analysis and system modelling.
- analyses relations between objects and provides rationale for the algorithms and methods applied.
- is familiar with the nature of data and objects and can specify them and use them in programs.
- is familiar with and describes, using VBA/Python and UML activity diagrams, the main activities occurring in programs and algorithms.
- is familiar with the nature and main concepts of object-oriented programming.
- composes programs consisting of multiple procedures and organizes the data flow between them.

The course aims at reaching the results in two different but tightly linked ways: learning to understand the object-oriented approach and getting the necessary skills in building algorithms. Both skills have to be implemented in simple applications.

It should be mentioned that the programming part of the Informatics course seems to be rather complicated for most of the non-IT students. The course authors and teachers face some problems. The biggest of them is lack of preparation and lack of prior knowledge in programming among the first-year non-IT students. As a result, learners immediately lose their motivation at the beginning of the programming part of the course. This deplorable fact, in its turn, leads to poor knowledge and poor academic results. Consequently, the authors of the course try to improve the program and content from year to year with the aim of finding the best solutions to achieve the goals and fully get the outcomes (Robins et al, 2003), (Kak, 2014).

2.2 Modelling and Algorithmization

In the programming module of the Informatics course we try to focus mostly on the models and algorithms. Our aim here is to teach students how to build a model and an algorithm of the problem and describe it using both familiar and new tools.

For these programming tasks, teachers and students together try to build UML (Unified Modelling Language) activity diagrams to describe the algorithms. It is the first step in any task solution. In addition, a verbal description and a pseudo code are typically used.

As was mentioned above, we start the programming practice with Scratch. At this stage students have to understand the problem and be able to describe it. Syntax errors are impossible in Scratch and this fact gives students an opportunity not to think about mistakes but concentrate only on the model and the algorithm. Moreover, Scratch graphical blocks give a holistic and lively picture of the created model.

After creating the Scratch projects as an introduction to programming, the course instructors can also use its scripts to visualize, formulate and describe the problem. Thus, we get one more opportunity to introduce to our students a problem to be solved – providing them with a Scratch script.

It should be mentioned that the course teachers do not give students volume tasks for solving. Our main idea is to explain through small tasks why and how it works.

2.3 Active Teaching and Learning

To raise and keep students' motivation in the learning process it is necessary to make the routine learning process more attractive and dynamic for them. In the current section of the paper the authors suggest some ways for making programming more engaging for non-IT learners with the aim of raising their interest.

2.3.1 E-learning

As was mentioned above, during the semester all students work in the Moodle e-environment. This independent work mostly consists of grasping the new material, taking self-tests and other learning tasks.

For better understanding, the theoretical material should be presented to non-IT students in simple and clear forms. A multitude of books and any other materials provided for them does not mean that they are useful for the students; moreover, this can be intimidating for the beginners.

During the Informatics course development and evolution its authors have been trying to adapt theoretical teaching materials for the e-environment and deliver it to students in most suitable forms. Our conclusions here are to provide students with small portions of the learning material and maximally visualize them. In this context, a small portion does not mean that students will lack some knowledge – it means that they are provided with well-filtered materials, which are adapted to non-IT beginners. A great role here is played by short teaching videos that explain the main programming concepts and usage cases. The same principles have been used in the Khan Academy (Khan Academy, 2016).

After each new topic students have to fulfil corresponding tests. Modern testing systems provide us with a variety of test types and, using them the course authors have worked out a test system which uses tasks similar to the pre-prepared program tasks. As experience shows, the most effective type of the test, which greatly helps non-IT students, is "fill in the gaps" type. Students get the problem description and the corresponding program text with some gaps and their task is to fill in gaps and check their results afterwards. Doing this, students learn the syntax and learn to understand the algorithm. In addition, tests where students have to make the program text out of sentences and arrange them in the correct order, teach students to see and understand a model of the proposed tasks.

It is very useful for the students to check and correct their classmates' programmes. This activity develops such an important skill as the ability to read and understand a code written by another person. The Moodle environment provides us with this opportunity and we periodically use it in the course.

It should be mentioned that students' independent work in Moodle is divided into stages, which are ordered and a transition to the next stage is possible only after finishing the previous one. Such course construction helps the course teachers to monitor the current situation in students' knowledge. Moreover, such a system brings a competitive note into the learning process and makes it more attractive.

2.3.2 Face-to-face lessons

It should not be expected from non-IT students and especially from the beginners that they immediately start to write a program code after the first explanations. The best option here is a simple copying task from the teacher's screen projected on the board. During this copying students do not think about why it is so, their interests are limited to the fact that they need to copy some text on time and afterwards check whether the program works. It is great if they are able to do it on their own, however, usually students are not able to check and correct it due to incomprehension of the solution. To make the situation more positive, our group of teachers have worked out some strategies that can help to involve students in the coding process during face-to-face lessons.

Firstly, it should be mentioned that during the programming module of the course, the majority of the created applications are small games that students can play. Using Scratch, students make games and within the process, learn to understand their algorithms (Rakenduste loomine Scratchiga, 2016). Scratch gives an opportunity to test and, if necessary, correct the algorithm immediately without thinking about the syntax. Afterwards, when an algorithm is already clear, it is simple to translate it to VBA or Python, concurrently learning the syntax. Thus, a teaching tool like Scratch already adds an element of attractiveness to the course.

Secondly, as a group-work assignment during a face-to-face lesson it is possible to offer students a possibility to play a game: they have the algorithm of a program and each student in the class should write one line in the code. The named method is quite controversial, but it is useful at the beginning of coding, when students just learn the basics. Afterwards, when each student has his/her own programming style, it is not so useful. However, it teaches to understand others' manners and proves and demonstrates why one solution can be better and more logical than another. It should be noted that this is important knowledge in any subject, not only in programming. In addition, this game greatly helps teachers to maintain a high level of students' attention during the lesson.

The next assignment for students, which we successfully apply, especially before practical tests, is correction of mistakes in a programme text. As usual, the students have their task descriptions and a ready program, which does not work at all or does not work properly. The number of mistakes is also known. The mistakes are different: from simple misprints to syntax or logical errors. As our experience shows, such assignments are useful if offered as pair work. Here we also develop group work skills among our students and teach them to understand the programme code. Besides, in such a way students learn the syntax by discussing it.

In addition, compared to the previous learning task, the new system works effectively. This is a bonus. During the semester students can collect the bonus points and, if necessary, use them at the final exam. Students can get these points, for example, for solving some additional tasks in the lesson, at home or in the Moodle environment. Usually the bonus system is determined at the beginning of the semester and sometimes it is an additional reason for students to attend the lesson.

When new theoretical material is explained, the course teachers often use ready-made programmes to introduce some topics to learners. In such a case, it is advisable to prepare, in advance, some mistakes in the code and within the discussion, correct them together with the students. This way, new concepts are assimilated much better and students learn to respond to different types of errors and afterwards are not afraid of them.

The teaching strategies mentioned above are the main types that we apply in the Informatics course and they are aimed at raising students' interest in the programming subject by better engaging them into the learning process. As students' feedback shows, these methods work and bring positive results. It is necessary to apply different strategies in teaching, not only in programming, with the aim of varying students' learning and educators teaching experience and style.

3. CONCLUSION

Based on the above said, it should be concluded that the authors of the Informatics course for the first-year non-IT students focus mostly on the model, algorithm and also their visualization, rather than teaching syntax and coding techniques (Vilipõld et al, 2013). The course authors consider that active learning greatly helps not only students to grasp new knowledge and achieve better results but it helps teachers to develop, improve and raise their pedagogical skills to a new level.

In the future development of the Informatics course, the authors try to keep up with times and main trends in pedagogy and computer education (George Lucas Educational Foundation, 2014), (George Lucas Educational Foundation, 2014).

REFERENCES

George Lucas Educational Foundation, 2014. Coding in the Classroom. http://www.edutopia.org/topic/coding-classroom

George Lucas Educational Foundation, 2014. Project-Based Learning. http://www.edutopia.org/project-based-learning

Kak, A., 2014. Teaching Programming. https://engineering.purdue.edu/kak/TeachingProgramming.pdf

Khan Academy, 2016. http://www.khanacademy.org

MIT Media Lab, 2016. Scratch. http://scratch.mit.edu/

Moodle – Open-source learning platform, 2016. https://moodle.org/

Õppeinfosüsteem, 2016. http://ois.ttu.ee

Python Software Foundation, 2016. https://www.python.org/

Rakenduste loomine Scratchiga, 2016. http://rlpa.ttu.ee/scratch/Rakenduste_loomine_Scratchiga.pdf

Robins, A., Rountree, J. & Rountree, N., 2003. Learning and Teaching Programming: A Review and Discussion. *Computer Science Education*, 13(2), pp. 137-172.

Sissejuhatus VBAsse, 2016. http://rlpa.ttu.ee/vba/VBA.pdf

Tallinn University of Technology, 2016. http://www.ttu.ee/

Tutvumine Pythoniga, 2016. http://rlpa.ttu.ee/python/Python.pdf

Vilipõld, J., Antoi, K., Amitan, I., 2013. Rakenduste loomine ja programmeerimise alused. Valikkursus gümnaasiumitele. http://rlpa.ttu.ee/RLPA_opik.pdf

AUTHOR INDEX

International Association for Development of the Information Society (IADIS)
Rua Sao Sebastiao Da Pedreira
No. 100, 30, 1050-209
Lisbon, Portugal

ISBN 978-1-5108-6525-9
9 781510 865259

CURRAN ASSOCIATES INC.
proceedings.com